GW01418270

HENRY
COYLE

HENRY
COYLE

A Forgotten Freedom Fighter

By Gerry Coyle

©Copyright 2022 Gerry Coyle and James Laffey

All rights reserved. No part of this publication may be reproduced, distributed or transmitted in any form or by any means, or stored in a database or retrieval system, without the prior written permission of the copyright owners. Every possible effort has been made to ensure the contents of this book are accurate, based on the information currently available. The author regrets any omissions or oversights and will endeavour to correct them in any future edition.
Printed by ReproWest, Toneybane, Ballina, Co Mayo

ISBN: 978-1-9998911-4-5

Contents

Dedication

This book is dedicated to my wonderful parents,
the late Henry and Mary (Molly) Coyle,
Doolough, Geesala, Co Mayo

A hero inside and outside our home

THIS book is about my father, IRA Commandant Henry Coyle, and although written about him, I also wish to remember all of Ireland's forgotten freedom fighters, some of whom are mentioned in these pages. There are, however, many more men and women who fought for the cause of Irish freedom and whose names sadly are not recorded in the history books.

As I researched the story of my father, I was shocked at the amount of men and women whose sterling contribution to Ireland's journey towards political independence is largely forgotten. I hope I can do justice to some of them and encourage others to do more research to give them all the recognition and respect they so richly deserve. It is my intention to set up a website and a Facebook page in their memory and to have their names listed there.

It is not my intention to cast judgement on people or their reasons for involvement in the violent struggle for Irish freedom or, indeed, to cause hurt to their families or to my own relatives or friends. We should never judge from afar because we cannot put ourselves in the shoes of those who lived through such violent and volatile times. The father I knew – and, indeed, the man my older siblings knew – was unrecognisable to the younger Henry Coyle who drove across Scotland and England with carloads of gelignite and delivered defiant, headline-making speeches.

Later in the book, I will try to give some insight into how someone who had been involved in dangerous and deadly activities in his youth could, in later years, become an amazing and very caring father to his children and a wonderful husband to his wife. This has taught me that people can change and become very responsible citizens and be great contributors to society.

It is possible to leave the past behind. But it helps when you have a great woman at your side.

My parents, Henry and Molly Coyle, as I remember them in their later years.

HENRY AND MOLLY – AN UNBEATABLE TEAM

Where to start is difficult as my memories of growing up in a wonderful household in Geesala in County Mayo are far removed from what was my father's turbulent and tragic past. If you were to pick a family or place in which to grow up, then you could not pick a better place than the townland of Doolough beside the village of Geesala on the west coast of Ireland. You were not just looked after and reared at home but you were also looked after and reared by the wonderful people of the village and townland.

To give a true and accurate account, I must first pay tribute to my wonderful mother, Mary (Molly) Ginty, who came from Dooriel in Ballycroy in northwest Mayo. Her contribution to the Coyle household in Geesala can never be underestimated and she certainly made us the people we are today.

Her easy-going, hardworking and jovial manner gave us a great start in life. Her wisdom of the world far outweighed the simple national school learning she had received before leaving her native Ballycroy. Her positive attitude and approach to both life and work, and her will to overcome every obstacle helped to make me the person I am today.

I was the youngest of a family of ten, one of whom died at birth, and due to emigration my mother had already said goodbye to her eldest when I was four or five. In fact, I was six years old before I realised I had two older brothers!

At a young age, I quickly realised that money was very scarce but we always had plenty to eat as the small bit of land provided the vegetables and our few hens, ducks and geese provided the eggs, which was all we needed for a tasty meal. My mother always made sure we had plenty to eat, and however she managed to do that, I will never know but all meals went down a treat.

My mother worked 12 or 14 hours a day inside the home and outside on the land. She loved working with the few cows and calves we had on our three acres and they too would get the best of care from her. She would also pick cockles and mussels on the shore next to our home and make very tasty meals from them.

I never questioned why she thought she had to work so hard but often she would say that her biggest fear in life was that she would end up in the County Home. I wonder what it was that she encountered in her younger days that instilled such fear in her of that institution? Had she ever visited it or had someone close to her or someone she knew ended up there and given her the dread of the place? Did it stem from the fact that she and my father did not own their own home for the first 15 years of marriage and moved from one rented cottage to another?

It was obvious that she had some knowledge of what was going on in the County Home. I very much regret that I never asked her what it was that gave her such fears. But whatever it was, it had a big influence on our upbringing, as it made me more determined to make money so I could reassure her that such an episode would never befall her. I realised that all of her children had the same view and that all those who had left home were also making contributions to keep the bills paid, so that the dread of the County Home could be forever allayed. She certainly didn't deserve any worries after the way she took care of everyone with her strong work ethic.

My mother also had a great faith in her God and went to church every Sunday and Holy Day. We were washed and scrubbed and sent off to Mass, and no matter what happened in life, she would put it down as God's will, quietly telling us that 'God is good'. I suppose it was her great faith that helped and sustained her during her toughest days.

Although things were tough and times were hard, there was also great fun and laughter in our home where freedom of speech, expression and questioning of all issues within and outside the home were encouraged. Money might have been scarce but care, kindness and attention were plentiful. When I read horror stories of the way some children were abused and neglected both

With my siblings outside the family home in Doolough at a family reunion in 1983, from left to right: Henry Joe, Pat, Agnes, Willie, Mary, John, Ann, Noel, Margaret and Gerry.

at home and in care homes during that era it gives me a greater appreciation of the way we were looked after and cared for. My parents weren't just heroes outside the home but inside it as well.

MY FATHER'S PAST

While there was a big age difference between my father and mother, they were very happy and whatever decisions were made seemed to be made jointly. They were a kind and caring couple and were always there to help us and others who found themselves in a traumatic or difficult situation.

My father was almost 63 years old when I was born; my mother was 21 years younger. I never thought anything about it as they were always available when needed. I only ever remember my father walking with a limp and a walking stick. I was told later that he fell off a ladder when he was building the house in which we lived, but as I researched this book I learned that some of his ailments could be attributed to his activities during the War of Independence and Civil War. He carried these injuries with him all his life but it never seemed to prevent him in whatever work he undertook. In later years, his walk and movement was greatly restricted. For approximately a year and half before his death, he was mostly confined to a wheelchair but through most of this time his mind remained crystal clear.

As I got older, I would hear the whispers and stories of olden times and many people called to the house to see my father and many stories would be recalled about his exploits overseas in the fight for Irish freedom. Others called

I am pictured with my sister Mary Conway and oldest brother Henry Joe in the GPO Museum in Dublin in July 2022. We are standing in front of the teapot presented to my father on the day of his wedding in Glasgow in June 1922.

to him to have official forms filled out and to write letters to different government departments for them. I would hear the stories about the War of Independence, the Civil War and his escapades in England and Scotland, as well as his friendship with Michael Collins, and that he helped to carry the coffin of General Collins. Every time he spoke of Collins, his eyes welled up as he recalled the terrible tragedy that befell the country on August 22, 1922.

I began to realise that my father had a fascinating story to tell so I started to record his reminiscences on an old tape recorder. He gave a very precise account – in writing and on tape – of his activities in Scotland during the War of Independence, and I have drawn on those handwritten notes for some of the material in this book.

I also visited and taped other people in the locality who he mentioned as been involved in 'The Struggle'. One man, in particular, Michael Cafferkey from the neighbouring village of Coolaba proved very helpful. Michael told me how he and my father fought on different sides in the Civil War but had since become best friends. He often said: "Your father was always a peacemaker. He would bring sworn enemies together and some would become great friends afterwards."

Whenever my father spoke about the Civil War his voice would quiver with sadness and regret. The untimely deaths of many of his close former comrades and friends must have had a huge impact on him because he would get emotional talking about them some 50 years later.

I am pictured in Cork for the Michael Collins centenary commemoration with TD Paul Keogh who as Minister for Defence helped to bring the Sliabh na mBan armoured car to Geesala for the annual festival in 2018.

As well as his exploits in the fight for Irish freedom, my father was also elected a Teachta Dála (TD) for Mayo North in 1923, and has the dubious distinction of being the only TD ever debarred from the Dáil after he was jailed over a controversial incident involving a cheque to the value of £450. What I have tried to establish is why a TD, just elected to the Dáil from one of the most impoverished constituencies in the country, was handling a cheque for an amount that that was the equivalent of €28,965.00 in today's money. It is one of the mysteries I will try to shed some light on in this book.

As with every story, there are many different tellings, but what doesn't change is the fact that he paid an enormous price for that episode, and is still paying the price today, some 43 years after his death. If you Google the name 'Henry Coyle TD', the incident involving the cheque will immediately crop up, but there was so much more to my father's life than that single episode in 1924, an incident his own solicitor described as 'strange'.

This book is about setting the record straight in relation to Henry Coyle but it is not about settling old scores or upsetting people. That is not who I am and it is not how I or my siblings were reared, but I was certainly taught from a young age to call out injustice when I see it.

The incident with the cheque is just one of the more perplexing aspects in the turbulent and sometimes chaotic life of a man who grew up on a small farm in a quiet rural village in the west coast of Ireland, far away from the bravery, glamour and sorrow of gun-running and politics. I have spent the past

I was privileged to be at Béal na Bláth in Cork on Sunday, August 21, 2022 to watch history in the making as Fianna Fáil leader and Taoiseach Micheál Martin and Fine Gael leader and Tánaiste Leo Varadkar jointly commemorated the centenary of Michael Collins' death.

25 years piecing together Henry Coyle's extraordinary early life. What emerges is a sad story of turbulence, sorrow, regret, betrayal, disillusionment and humiliation, but it is also a story of resilience and defiance in the face of adversity. This is a man who told a judge in Edinburgh that he was prepared to step upon the gallows or face the firing squad for Irish political freedom.

He and his comrades succeeded in winning independence for the 26 counties we now call the Republic of Ireland, but instead of enjoying the fruits of victory, he was totally abandoned by the state he fought so hard to establish. He was not alone. Many of those who fought alongside him in Scotland and England were abandoned too, and that is why I believe the story of Henry Coyle needs to be told. My father was one of the lucky ones because he eventually met my wonderful mother who brought great happiness and stability into his life, but many of those who served with him were not so fortunate and died in poverty and loneliness, as you will see when the story unfolds.

We all learned in our history books about the great Irish people who died for Ireland but we forgot about the great Irish people who lived for Ireland and whose contribution gave us the freedom we have today. What happened to those people when the fighting was over and they had to get back to ordinary living? Who fought for them when they were no longer able to fight for themselves?

This book is about one of those great Irish people, my brave, kind and brilliant father Henry Peter Coyle.

Photo by Evita Coyle

'My story, if all told, would
be a very long one.'

Henry Coyle, June 1964

Henry Coyle's service medals from the War of Independence alongside a medal commemorating his hero and friend Michael Collins.

CHAPTER 1

The making of a rebel

WHAT is it that makes men and women get involved in a fight for freedom? What have they encountered in their lives that makes them want to become part of an organisation that is willing to go to any lengths to achieve its aims, putting their own lives at risk and ending the lives of others who try to prevent them?

I have often wondered why my father became so involved in the Irish republican struggle. I know how he started and the beating he took from members of the RIC after trying to prevent the eviction of a widow whose three children and husband had died some years earlier. Was this enough to drive him on to become one of the most daring and important freedom fighters in Scotland or Ireland in the autumn of 1920, a man who sourced and supplied many of the explosives and weapons used in the War of Independence, a man who was willing to kill or be killed for the cause of Irish freedom? Why did he think his opinion was right and did he realise the consequences of his actions on other members of his family at home in Ireland or the wider public?

What thoughts went through his mother's mind when her son was in Peterhead Prison in faraway Scotland on Christmas Night 1921? Did she support his actions or did she at any time try to dissuade him and maybe tell him he was wrong in trying to force his opinion on others? Did other members of his family agree or disagree with him? I also wonder what kind of man would he have become had he followed some other path in life such as emigrating to the United States like some of his brothers.

I do not have answers to most of these questions – and I never will. I can, however, give an accurate account of most of my father's activities in Scotland and England during the War of Independence, his involvement in the Civil War and his election to the 4th Dáil in 1923.

I have obtained records from the English courts and newspaper archives, as well as copies of sworn statements from the Bureau of Military History and

My father was born in one of the most picturesque parts of Ireland but he learned from a young age that a great view doesn't put bread on the table. Picture: Evita Coyle

the Irish Military Service Pensions Collection. Having viewed all of the material over a period of many years now, I can simply conclude that Henry Peter Coyle was a man of many parts. He was a terrorist to some, a freedom fighter to others and a father to me.

The first trace of my father in an official state document is in the 1901 Census of Ireland when he was six years old. At that time, he was living with his parents, Patrick and Mary, and three siblings in a thatched cottage in Muingdoran, Dooyork, a little coastal townland west of Geesala village and

within a short stroll of the broad Atlantic. The children listed in the Coyle household in 1901 were Patrick (10), Henry (6), Martin (4), and Mary (1). A fourth brother, William, had already left the family home and would eventually settle in the United States.

The Coyle homestead had two rooms, one window and no outhouses. Initially, I was surprised to discover there was no place to house animals because the cow, in particular, was such an important resource for every family in rural Ireland in those days. My 91-year-old cousin Pap, who lived next door to my father's birthplace up to his death earlier this year, put me in the picture.

My cousin Pap Coyle, who passed away in January 2022 at the age of 91, was a great help when I was researching this book.

"The cows were housed with the people," he explained. "That was the custom back then because people couldn't afford to build outhouses and anyway the cow was so valuable she had to get the best accommodation."

Pap's explanation makes sense. Landlords also charged higher rents to tenants with additional buildings, and the Erris 'ranchers' were notorious for trying to squeeze every last drop from their struggling leaseholders, so an outhouse was an unnecessary luxury. There were 47 homes in my father's native village, but just 12 boasted outbuildings and the majority of these were 'barns'. In fact, there was only one stable, one cow-house and one piggery between the 47 houses.

There were 266 people living in those 47 dwellings, which were all ranked as third or fourth class, meaning the occupants were experiencing conditions that were as bad as one might expect to find in Ireland at the turn of the 20th century. In one cottage, there was a family of ten, ranging in age from 13 and 60, and a family of seven lived in another one-room building. My father's family – with their two rooms and six occupants – actually had it better than many of their neighbours, but the truth is that everyone in Dooyork was struggling to eke out a daily existence.

By the time the next census of Ireland was held a decade later, my father's childhood was already behind him, but little had changed in his family's circumstances. They still shared the same third-class thatched cottage with their livestock, and the only real change was the number of mouths to feed, three more children having been born in the intervening years. John (8), Edward (5) and Peter (1) were the new arrivals since the previous census while the other siblings were all at home despite Pat (Sonny) having reached the age of 18.

If the circumstances of the Coyle family hadn't improved much in the first decade of the new century, the same could be said for their neighbours. There were now 53 houses in the village and all were still ranked as third or fourth class, while the number of outhouses had increased marginally to 19.

This is the house in Dooyork where my father was born and raised.   Picture: Evita Coyle

I can only imagine the hardship my father experienced in those ten years between the ages of six and 16 when he journeyed from the innocence of childhood to the responsibilities of young adulthood. By 1911, he was already travelling to Scotland each summer with his father and older brother to work in the potato fields (or 'tatie' fields as they were known), so the days of carefree youth – if he ever knew such a thing – were already long past.

It is impossible to know whether Henry Peter Coyle had already become radicalised by his mid-teens, but there are pieces of the jigsaw of my father's early life that fit together very easily, and I think his experience of growing up amid the utter deprivation of early-20th century Erris was crucial to his subsequent decision to join Ireland's fight for political independence.

I have no doubt my father was greatly influenced by the Erris of his youth, a place where the inequities of seven centuries of British rule were there for all to see, but I believe there were other important factors influencing my father's formative years too. Key amongst them had to have been his mother Mary Kerrigan, a formidable woman with a passion for education, who possessed a skill-set many women of her generation were sadly lacking: she could read and write.

In 1901, just 42 of the 141 residents over the age of 16 in my father's village were able to read and write. Mary Kerrigan was among the select few,

	CENSUS OF
	Two Examples of the mode of filling
	FO

RETURN of the MEMBERS of this FAMILY and their VISITORS, BOARDERS, SERVAN

Number.	NAME AND SURNAME.		RELATION to Head of Family.	RELIGIOUS PROFESSION.	EDUCATION.	AGE (last Birthd and SEX.	
	No Persons ABSENT on the Night of Sunday, April 2nd, to be entered here; EXCEPT those (not enumerated elsewhere) who may be out at WORK or TRAVELLING, &c., during that Night, and who RETURN HOME on MONDAY, APRIL 3RD. — Subject to the above instruction, the Name of the Head of the Family should be written first; then the names of his Wife, Children, and other Relatives; then those of Visitors, Boarders, Servants, &c.		State whether "Head of Family," or "Wife," "Son," "Daughter," or other Relative; "Visitor," "Boarder," "Servant," &c.	State here the particular Religion, or Religious Denomination, to which each person belongs. [Members of Protestant Denominations are requested not to describe themselves by the vague term "Protestant," but to enter the name of the Particular Church, Denomination, or Body to which they belong.]	State here whether he or she can "Read and Write," can "Read" only, or "Cannot Read."	Insert Age oppos each name:—the of Males in colum and the Ages o Females in colum For Infants under year state the ag months, as "und month," "1 mon "2 months," &	
	Christian Name.	Surname.				Ages of Males.	Ag o Fema
	1.	2.	3.	4.	5.	6.	7
1	Patrick	Coyle	Ha of Family	Roman Catholic	Cannot read	54	
2	Mary	Coyle	Wife	Roman Catholic	Read & write		4
3	Patrick	Coyle	Son	Roman Catholic	Read & write	20	
4	Henry	Coyle	Son	Roman Catholic	Read & write	18	
5	Martin	Coyle	Son	Roman Catholic	Read & write	16	
6	Mary	Coyle	daughter	Roman Catholic	Read & write		
7	John	Coyle	son	Roman Catholic	Read	8	
8	Edward	Coyle	Son	Roman Catholic	Read	5	
9	Peter	Coyle	Son	Roman Catholic	—	1	
10							
11							
12							
13							
14							
15							

I hereby certify, as required by the Act 10 Edw. VII., and 1 Geo. V., cap. 11, that the foregoing Return is correct, according to the best of my knowledge and belief.

Francis Mara, Const. Signature of Enumerator.

The census return for the Coyle household in 1911. My father's age is given as 18 but I believe he was only 17, having been born in October 1894.

ELAND, 1911.

ble are given on the other side.

.A.

who slept or abode in this House on the night of SUNDAY, the 2nd of APRIL, 1911.

NK, PROFESSION, OR OCCUPATION.	PARTICULARS AS TO MARRIAGE.				WHERE BORN.	IRISH LANGUAGE.	If Deaf and Dumb; Dumb only; Blind; Imbecile or Idiot; or Lunatic.
particular Rank, Profession, or other Employment of each Children or young persons ng a School, or receiving instruction at home, should rned as *Scholars*. y should be made in the case s, daughters, or other female s solely engaged in domestic at home.] ling this column you are re- to read the instructions on er side.	Whether "Married," "Widower," "Widow," or "Single."	Completed years the present Marriage has lasted. If less than one year, write "under one."	State for each Married Woman entered on this Schedule the number of:— Children born alive to present Marriage. If no children born alive, write "None" in column 11.		If in Ireland, state in what County or City; if elsewhere, state the name of the Country.	Write the word "IRISH" in this column opposite the name of each person who speaks IRISH *only,* and the words "IRISH & ENGLISH" opposite the names of those who can speak both languages. In other cases no entry should be made in this column.	Write the respec- tive infirmities opposite the name of the afflicted person.
			Total Children born alive.	Children still living.			
8.	9.	10.	11.	12.	13.	14.	15.
armer	Married				Co Mayo	Irish & English	
	Married	21	9	8	Co Mayo	Irish & English	
armer's Son	Single				Co Mayo	Irish & English	
armer's Son	Single				Co Mayo	Irish & English	
cholar	Single				Co Mayo	Irish & English	
cholar	Single				Co Mayo	Irish & English	
holar	Single				Co Mayo	Irish & English	
cholar	Single				Co Mayo	Irish & English	
	Single				Co Mayo	—	

I believe the foregoing to be a true Return.

his
Patrick ⨯ oyle _____ Signature of Head of Family.
mark
Witness F. Mara

and presumably she filled in the census form for the Coyle household in 1901 and again in 1911.

Today, it's hard to understand how almost two-thirds of a townland could be unable to read and write but Dooyork didn't have its own schoolhouse, and in an age long before free school transport, it was difficult for parents to send their children to Geesala, several miles away. My grandmother, who was from the nearby village of Shraigh, seems to have completed the full primary cycle, or at least she was there long enough to master the art of reading and writing.

Mary Kerrigan was clearly a woman who placed a lot of store in education because many years later, when her own children were raised, she became involved in a battle with the parish priest of Geesala to have a school opened in Dooyork. Pap recalled how my grandmother wrote to the Department of Education after she became tired of the priest's procrastination whenever the prospect of a school at Dooyork was mentioned.

"She was very brave," he told me, "because this was a time when people didn't challenge the authority of priests or teachers. She collected names on a petition and wrote to the Department demanding a school for Dooyork."

While most women in those days were confined to working at home, my grandmother provided midwifery services in the area. She wasn't a trained midwife but she clearly had sufficient knowledge and expertise to tend to women who were giving birth in primitive conditions where loss of life – of the mother or child or sometimes both – was sadly a none-too-rare occurrence.

My father initially attended Shraigh National School in his mother's home village before transferring to Geesala where he must have greatly benefitted from the very high standards of teaching. As an adult, he bore the hallmarks of someone who had a really good formative education, and his standard of writing was more akin to a man who went to second-level instead of leaving primary school at about 13.

My father was greatly influenced by his mother and always spoke of her with great reverence. Indeed, I firmly believe he would never have become a freedom fighter without his mother's encouragement and approval.

Like so many parts of Ireland, Geesala was enjoying a cultural reawakening in the early 1900s and a branch of the Gaelic League was established in 1902. A concert was held in the schoolroom in January 1903 at which several local people performed Irish songs, dance and stories. The *Western People* reported that the venue was 'packed to overcrowding, and many had to content themselves by listening outside'.

A key man in the revival of the Gaelic culture was local priest Fr Anthony Timlin and the *Western People* gave a fascinating insight into his motivation for starting a branch of the Gaelic League in Geesala.

"[Fr Timlin] is untiring in his efforts to have the old Irish games, customs and amusements revived," wrote the *Western*, "and to keep down those ungodly and profane words and songs which too often find their way across from England and Scotland by those who are forced to go there for the harvesting season."

Henry Coyle would soon join that seasonal exodus to Scotland, accompanying his father for the first time when he was just 14 to work on the potato fields.

It was a tough apprenticeship.

I believe my father's first summer in Scotland was 1910 when he was aged 14 and had finished primary school. He travelled over with his father who had been going across to Glasgow each summer since he was a teenager. While some Irish migrants provided general labour for British farmers, most of the men and women from Erris were involved in harvesting the potato crop, which was often a full-time job in itself.

My father never talked in much detail about his teenage summers in Scotland but I have a fair idea of the hardship he experienced from my conversations with older people around Erris who were also migratory labourers, including my late mother-in-law, the wonderful Celia Lally. Indeed, there was a time when almost every house in the barony had someone across the Irish Sea, either on a permanent or temporary basis.

Members of the older generation were not ones to complain and they often tended to downplay any hardship they might have endured in their younger years. That was especially true of many of the migratory labourers from Erris, and it is only while researching this book that I have come to fully appreciate the adversity they had to overcome in Scotland to earn a few pound for the folks back home.

In 1918, a public meeting was held on Achill Island as part of a campaign by the United Irish League (UIL) to organise a Migratory Labourers' Union. The UIL organiser told the meeting that the farm labourers were 'very badly paid' and 'barbarously treated in regard to boarding and sleeping accommodation'.

"[The migrants] had to work for a ten-hour day at 4s each, and for overtime they were paid at the same rate as within the ordinary hours," a report in the *Western People* said. "When there was a rush on the potato market, they were often called out to work at three or four o'clock in the morning, and whether the weather was good or bad they were kept in the fields until the required consignment of potatoes was made up for dispatch.

"But their greatest hardship, and the most shameful aspect of the question, was the manner in which they were housed by the Scottish farmers. In many cases, they had to sleep on pallets of straw on an earthen floor in sheds that were occupied by cattle and horses during the winter, and with coarse blankets that were no better than horse-rugs to cover them, and frequently five or six of them were crammed into compartments which, bad and squalid as they were otherwise, were only large enough for two occupants, while sometimes both sexes had to sleep in one room. In short, they were treated as if they were cattle."

Treated as if they were cattle… those are hard words to read yet this was the bleak, brutal reality of the apprenticeship my father served from the age of 14 to 20. His last summer in Scotland was in 1916 and he returned home that autumn to find Ireland still reeling from the dramatic events in Dublin the previous Easter. A new era of armed insurrection was about to commence and Henry Peter Coyle would soon be at the heart of it.

CHAPTER 2

Pikeheads and spears

UNLIKE other parts of Co Mayo, the Irish Volunteer movement was not especially prominent in Erris prior to 1916, but there was a small company formed in Belmullet in 1914-'15.

The Irish Volunteer Force was a military body founded in Dublin in November 1913 to reinforce the demand for Home Rule and to act as a counterbalance to the Ulster Volunteer Force, which was also established that year and had a mandate to resist Home Rule. The new movement proved a runaway success and was soon attracting young men from all over Ireland. Dick Walsh, a Balla shopkeeper, who was an organiser for the Irish Volunteers in Mayo from 1916 to 1918, later recalled that 'no national movement [in the history of Ireland] got such a spontaneous and enthusiastic welcome'.

"Companies sprang up like mushrooms all over the country. It was a common sight, if cycling along a country road of an evening, to see groups of young men forming fours at every crossroads. Older ex-British Army men living in nearby towns and villages were induced into the Volunteers to act as drill instructors. In fact, the movement grew so rapidly and displayed such strength and vigour that the then dominant political party, the Irish Parliamentary Party or the Redmondite Party, as it was commonly called, became alarmed."

The Irish Volunteers split in September 1914 after John Redmond appealed for its 160,000 members to enlist in the British Army and fight the 'Great War' against the Kaiser. The vast majority took Redmond's side and broke away to form the National Volunteers, leaving fewer than 3,000 militant nationalists in the original organisation.

The Volunteers in Belmullet were among those persuaded by Redmond's rhetoric that Home Rule would be delivered if Ireland stood shoulder to shoulder with Britain in the fight to protect the 'small nations' of Europe. Recruitment rallies were held in many towns throughout Mayo and proved very successful with thousands from the county joining regiments like the Connaught Rangers. Indeed, by early 1916, Ballina had sent an estimated 700 young men to the battlefields of Europe – more than any other provincial town in Ireland – and it was claimed that the town's rate of recruitment per head of population was bettered only by Belfast.

It is estimated that as many as 40,000 National Volunteers enlisted in the British Army, but as the body count mounted in the trenches, enthusiasm waned and fears of conscription began to rise. In fact, migratory labourers stopped travelling to England and Scotland because they were worried they might be forced to enlist in the British Army. Dick Walsh later claimed that a 'considerable number' of Irish migrants, including many from the West of Ireland, were conscripted while working on farms in England and Scotland.

Even as early as 1915, the *Irish Independent* was reporting that fewer than 13,000 migrants had travelled to England and Scotland, a reduction of almost 50 per cent in a decade. I suspect my father's decision to cease his annual summer trips to Scotland after 1916 may have had as much to do with a desire to avoid conscription as any political activities at home. In truth, there wasn't much happening on the revolutionary front in the West of Ireland in the spring of 1917 as the Irish Volunteers sought to rebuild their local network in the wake of the Easter Rising. In Mayo, Dick Walsh initially feared that 'all enthusiasm was knocked out of the national movement' after the failed rebellion, but signs of a renaissance came earlier than expected.

"About September 1916, things were again stirring and everywhere groups of young men assembled," Walsh recalled. "The whole talk was about the Rising and what happened in it. Songs like 'Easter Week', 'The Soldier's Song', 'Wrap The Green Flag Around Me', and others of a similar nature, were heard everywhere. The young people were thinking about the chances of having a further round with Britain."

Into this politically charged atmosphere came 22-year-old Henry Coyle. He'd just spent another backbreaking summer in the potato fields of Scotland and now faced the reality that he'd have to stay in Ireland for the foreseeable future to avoid conscription. The life of a migratory worker might be grim, gruelling and often degrading but at least it provided a steady income that was simply unavailable in Erris. Some migratory workers could earn as much as £20 during the summer, which was then used to keep the home fires burning through winter. Now even *that* door had been shut in my father's face.

It's easy to become a revolutionary when you have nothing to lose, and Henry Coyle was a man with very few options in 1917. He couldn't make a living at home, and if he took his usual summer trip to Scotland, he ran the risk of being packed off to the battlefields of France where he'd inevitably become fodder for the German cannons. It seems my father made up his mind in the summer of 1917 that if he were going to die in a war he'd prefer to do it under the flag of his native land than some distant colonial power that had foisted nothing but hardship and misery on him and his people for as long as anyone could remember.

The die had been cast. The next decade in Henry Peter Coyle's life would be as turbulent as the independent nation he helped to found.

óglaiġ na héireann
IRISH VOLUNTEERS
ARMS & AMMUNITION
A COLLECTION
IN AID OF THE
DEFENCE OF IRELAND FUND
WILL BE HELD IN THIS DISTRICT COMMENCING
On SATURDAY, 2ND OCTOBER
AND CONCLUDING
On SUNDAY, 10TH OCTOBER

The Proceeds of the Collection will be applied to the Arming and Military Training of the Irish Volunteers of the District in which the money is subscribed.
By Order.
Central Executive Irish Volunteers,
BULMER HOBSON, Hon. Secretary.

Printed by P. Mahon, 3 Yarnhall St., Dublin.

The Irish Volunteers were desperate to get their hands on weapons in 1915 and held a collection in October of that year to raise money to purchase guns and ammunition.

In his first application for an IRA pension, my father said he joined the Shraigh Volunteers in November 1917. Among the other members of that company was my granduncle, John Kerrigan, then in his early forties and a little long in the tooth to be waging war against the Empire. But the Kerrigans were dyed-in-the-wool republicans and I believe my father was very influenced by his maternal grandparents and uncle, as well as his mother. The Kerrigan home was a place of learning and my great-grandparents could read and write, which was quite extraordinary for two people born in 1839 and 1843 respectively. How they got an education in post-Famine Erris is beyond me but they clearly passed on their twin passions for learning and Irish nationalism to their grandson who lived with them for a short period while attending the local national school.

Henry Coyle was among many young men in their teens and twenties who joined the companies of Irish Volunteers that were springing up in Shraigh, Belmullet, Bangor Erris, Binghamstown and Carratigue in 1917. A new Irish army was being established but it lacked the necessary weaponry with which to wage war against the most powerful empire in the world. Earlier in 1917, Dick Walsh attended a convention in Fleming's Hotel in Dublin at which senior figures in the Volunteer movement, men like Cathal Brugha, Richard Mulcahy, Liam Lynch and Alec MacCabe, bemoaned the dearth of arms in Ireland.

"It was found after discussion that practically all arms in the country pre-1916 had been handed over to the British," Walsh recalled. "The re-arming

BARRACK STREET.

Belmullet, _19/ 10 ____ 193_6_.

M _____

_To_ **Charles Cawley**, _Es_

BLACKSMITH.

NEW PLOUGHS, SCUFFLERS AND IRON GATES
MADE TO ORDER.

To all whom it may concern

This is to certify that
Michael Henry, Shrogh
Belmullet, Ballina arranged
for the making of pikeheads
+ spears with me about
1st week november 1917 from
that date until april 1918 I
forged about 200 pikeheads
+ 150 spear III fixing tools
change + delivered same
to different unit These pikeheads
were made within 300 yds of
R I Co Barrack I had two
sentry at door Henry helped
at the making and sentry
+ delivered same

signed
Charles Cawley
Belmullet

The Shraigh Volunteers, of which my father was a member, found it impossible to get their hands on guns and instead paid a Belmullet blacksmith, Charles Cawley, to manufacture pikes. This receipt from the 1930s, which I found in the Irish Military Service Pensions' Collection, refers to the manufacture of the pikes in the winter of 1917-'18.

of the Volunteers was a big problem that had to be faced, but was never practically accomplished. All sorts of suggestions [for] arms supplies were put forward, some most fantastic."

In faraway Erris, the members of the newly-formed Shraigh Company decided the best way to arm themselves was to draw inspiration from the 'Men of the West', the men of 1798. In November 1917, they approached a local blacksmith in Belmullet, Charles Cawley, and asked him to hand-forge 200 pikeheads and 150 spears for the burgeoning company of Volunteers. However, there was one problem: Cawley's forge on Barrack Street was located just 300 yards from the RIC station.

The blacksmith later recalled that two sentries stood at the door of the forge while he worked through the winter and spring of 1917-'18, eventually completing the arsenal of old-fashioned weaponry on March 31. The pikeheads and spears were used in close-order drills throughout the summer of 1918.

Even the most ardent, sentimental nationalist had to concede that a war waged with weaponry of a bygone era would be a spectacular failure. My father must have looked on in despair at the impossible predicament faced by the company he had joined. Pikeheads and spears might have been sufficient to scatter the Redcoats in Castlebar in 1798, but they wouldn't make much of an impression on the heavy artillery that the British Army was capable of unleashing on Ireland's rebels in 1917.

I believe my father's early experiences in the Shraigh Company inspired some of his later, more daring escapades as a prolific IRA arms smuggler in Britain. He knew what it was like to stand sentry at the door of a forge as a blacksmith made weapons more than a century past their sell-by date and he was determined that if his friends and comrades in Erris, Mayo and Ireland were to go down fighting, they'd do so with the best weapons he could find for them.

It wasn't long before Henry Coyle had graduated from pikeheads, spears and dummy guns to rifles, grenades and gelignite, but first he had to serve a little time at His Majesty's pleasure before he could embark on his new 'career' as a gunrunner.

———————

The overhaul of Erris' archaic landlord system may have been slow to happen but it wasn't from want of trying by the local tenants who were vociferously agitating for better conditions throughout my father's childhood. In fact, there was simmering tension in the salty Atlantic air and it often erupted into outright conflict when process servers attempted to issue eviction notices on poor families. In April 1905, one such process server told Ballina Quarter Sessions that he was unable to serve a raft of processes because he was too afraid, although he had six policemen for protection.

Amid such tension between landlord and tenant, it's no surprise the United Irish League (UIL) rapidly expanded across the barony, with a branch formed in Geesala a few months after those court proceedings in Ballina.

Launched by William O'Brien in 1898, the UIL was a nationalist political party whose motto, 'The Land for the People', strongly resonated in places like Erris where sprawling grazier farms existed cheek by jowl with the uneconomic three-acre holdings of families like the Coyles and the Kerrigans. At its first meeting on Saturday, April 22, 1905, the newly-founded Geesala UIL demanded the abolition of the so-called 'Erris ranches' and, in particular, the ending of the 11-month grazing system whereby farmers from other parts of Mayo could send their cattle to the vast grazier farms on the Mullet peninsula, as well as in Dooyork and Doolough.

"Those people [who send the cattle] are the chief mainstay of the owners of those lands who cannot stock their lands themselves," a report of the meeting stated. "It is hoped they will have sense enough to keep their cattle at home or sell them, and so give a chance to those poor peasants who reside on miserable patches on the outskirts of those grazing lands to have their holdings enlarged, as the owners of the grazing lands must give them up if they don't get cattle to graze them."

A small number of landlords owned vast grazing ranches in Erris in the early 1900s, leading to tensions with the local smallholders who were often trying to survive on less than three acres.   Picture: Evita Coyle

But the owners of the grazier farms were not about to give up that easily and the next decade would see a constant friction between the 'ranchers' and the 'rebels'. The ranchers employed locals as 'herdsmen' for their large estates and one such man was Patrick McHugh, who lived in Doolough with his family. McHugh and his wife Ellen suffered terrible tragedy with the deaths of three of their children and then Patrick passed away, leaving his teenage son James as the new herdsman. The McHughs were very popular and carried out their work in a fair and decent manner.

A talented musician, James became a member of the Irish Volunteers and this may have been the reason why the local landlord tried to evict him and

his mother from their home in 1919. According to a report in the *Western People*, my father and other members of the Irish Volunteers prevented the eviction by forcibly resisting the RIC who had come to carry out the order.

Henry Coyle was not arrested at the scene, but some days later, the RIC came to his house and another violent struggle ensued, ending with his arrest and detention in the RIC barracks in Belmullet. He was brought before a midnight court in the town on a charge of illegal assembly. The Resident Magistrate for Mayo, John Charles Milling, sentenced my father and three other protestors, John Barrett, Ned Mangan and Paddy Keane to two months in Sligo Jail after they refused to recognise the court or post bail. Interestingly,

I am pictured with my brother Henry Joe and his daughter Mary Coyle-Sullivan outside the old McHugh homestead in Doolough, which was the scene of an attempted eviction in 1919. The fourth person in the photograph is Professor Michael Heneghan, grandson of James HcHugh, who was to have been evicted along with his widowed mother. Michael is a renowned medical consultant at King's College Hospital in London.

there was never another attempt to evict the Widow McHugh and she continued to live at the house in Doolough up to her death.

I have no knowledge of the people my father encountered in Sligo Jail or whether he was further radicalised during those two months behind bars in the spring of 1919. All I know is that by the time Henry Coyle emerged from prison, he was more committed than ever to the cause of Irish freedom and was willing to sacrifice his young life in pursuit of that ideal.

The Henry Coyle who left for Scotland in the spring of 1919 was a very different man to the one who went there picking potatoes just a few years earlier. The making of a rebel was now complete.

CHAPTER 3

Irish rebels in exile

I T IS one of the peculiarities of Irish history that it took the execution of a Scotsman to ultimately turn the tide of public opinion in favour of the 1916 rebels. Irish people, many of whom had been skeptical or downright opposed to the Easter Rising, were appalled to learn that the badly wounded James Connolly was sent out to face the firing squad strapped to a chair. His death, coming at the end of a week of executions, became a watershed for so many of the young Irish men and women who later took part in the War of Independence.

When Connolly marched into the GPO on Easter Monday 1916, he was upholding a proud tradition of Scottish involvement in the fight for Irish independence that went all the way back to the Young Ireland rebellion of 1848. Scotland had a very large Irish immigrant population – proportionately higher than England – so it was inevitable that many of these displaced Irish men and women would sympathise with the fight for Irish freedom. Parnell, for example, had a lot of support in Scotland, as did the Fenian movement in the late 19th century. The secretive Irish Republican Brotherhood (IRB) had circles (branches) in several Scottish cities and towns in the early 1900s, and lots of its members hailed from Ulster where they had learned many a harsh lesson about the injustices and inequities of life as an Irish Catholic under imperial rule. They were determined to do whatever they could to aid the struggle back home.

Derry man Daniel Kelly attended an IRB meeting in Glasgow in 1908 where there was a discussion about the practical assistance that could be given to colleagues in Ireland.

"At this meeting a discussion was held as to ways and means of obtaining arms," Kelly told the Bureau of Military History. "The question of getting control of quantities of explosives from the coalmines was also discussed."

Westport-born Major John Mac-Bride visited Glasgow in the years before the Easter Rising and exhorted IRB members in the city to prepare for an armed rebellion in Ireland.

Leitrim native Seán Mac-Diarmada visited Scotland on several occasions in the 1910s and was a very popular figure among Irish nationalists in places like Glasgow.

A few years later, Kelly attended a rally at Port Glasgow Co-operative Hall at which leading Irish republicans Seán MacDiarmada and Major John MacBride – future leaders of the 1916 Rising – were the guest speakers. A private meeting of IRB members was held afterwards.

"[MacDiarmada and MacBride] stressed the importance of making preparations for striking a blow for Irish freedom and dealt with the various ways in which work could be done in preparation for a rising, such as organising, drilling and training," recalled Kelly.

The Irish nationalist tradition was also strong among the sons and daughters of the immigrants. Seamus Reader, who went on to become one of the leading Irish republicans in Glasgow, was born into a home where pictures of Robert Emmet hung on the wall. At a young age, Reader learned the words of 'The Wearing of the Green' and 'Who Fears to Speak of '98', songs my father was singing in faraway Erris. Reader's parents, and many more like them, might have been exiled from their native land, but they were not about to turn their back on Ireland.

The Ancient Order of Hibernians had a very strong presence in Scotland and their musical bands attracted the interest of many young boys of Irish descent, including Reader. There were Scottish branches of other Irish nationalist organisations too, including the Gaelic League and the Young Irelanders, while the boy scouts movement, Na Fianna Éireann, had a strong presence in Glasgow. Reader joined Na Fianna in 1911 and even embarked on a camping expedition to Ireland, which was a novel thing to do in an era when many people never got the chance to travel overseas unless it was to emigrate.

But it wasn't all plain sailing amongst the Irish nationalists in Scotland. The Ancient Order of Hibernians, which was very widely organised, strongly opposed the establishment of the more militant Sinn Féin.

"Our efforts to organise Sinn Féin openly in Scotland met with strenuous attempts to intimidate and suppress us, sometimes leading to fisticuffs," recalled Daniel Kelly. "On one occasion, Andrew Devlin was walking along the street reading a Sinn Féin paper when a navvy, who was working in the vicinity, passed some sarcastic remarks. Words passed between them and finally they came to blows.

"The navvy knocked Devlin to the ground with a blow on the head. Devlin got up and there was a severe struggle between them, which resulted in the navvy being put to flight.

"Devlin was informed afterwards that he had beaten a man named Docherty, light heavyweight champion of West Scotland."

The last thing Irish nationalists needed to be doing was fighting amongst each other because they had more than enough enemies as it was. Some of the staunchest supporters of the British Empire resided in Glasgow and the Orange Order had a very strong presence in the city. The Ancient Order of Hibernians and other pacifist Irish groups were tolerated, but there would be little forbearance for men like Reader and Kelly who believed in a more radical form of Irish nationalism. Both men became members of the Irish Volunteers and stayed loyal after the split. In 1914, Reader brought a shipment of detonators to Dublin, having joined the IRB earlier that year. It was the first of numerous smuggling trips the Glaswegian would make across the Irish Sea in the years ahead.

The Irish Volunteers in Scotland were tremendously proud of the role played by Edinburgh-born James Connolly in the 1916 Rising, and many young men and women were inspired to join Volunteer branches in Scotland in the aftermath of Connolly's execution.

Glasgow-born Seamus Reader was one of the leading republicans in Scotland.

With so many Irishmen employed in the Scottish coalmining districts, it was inevitable that raids on colliery armouries would become a favoured *modus operandi* for the Irish Volunteers in Glasgow and elsewhere. Reader was one of a number of Volunteers who raided the magazine store at Uddingston Colliery in 1915, but subtler methods were employed too in the quest to obtain explosives for the armed insurrection that MacBride and MacDiarmada had promised was coming. Sometimes, a sympathetic colliery engineer was persuaded to overestimate the amount of explosives needed for a contract, and the surplus would be quietly passed on to the Irish Volunteers.

Quite a few of the Volunteers in Scotland had family ties to Mayo. Patrick Mills left Belmullet in 1907 to seek work in Motherwell where his uncle, John Mills, was a member of the local IRB circle. Young Mills soon became involved with the IRB and was present when Seán MacDiarmada visited Motherwell prior to the 1916 insurrection.

There was a desire among some of the Motherwell men to travel to Dublin for the Easter Rising, but senior figures in the Scottish IRB ordered them to stay put. Michael Burke, a native of Keady in Co Armagh, was one of those forced to sit out Easter Week.

"I was in the engineering section of the Scottish Volunteers from 1915," Burke recalled. "I was trained in the use of different explosives. I collected explosives prior to 1916. Owing to the mobilisation order arriving too late, I was deprived from taking part in Easter Week 1916."

Eamonn Leo Mooney emigrated to Glasgow with his parents at the age of eight and later became a member of Na Fianna Éireann before transferring to the Maryhill Company of the Irish Volunteers in 1915. Mooney was involved in the procurement of weapons for the Easter Rising, as were dozens of other Scottish-based Volunteers, but the rebellion itself proved an anti-climax for the exiles.

James Connolly's execution may have served to unite Irish people behind the rebels, but in his native Scotland, the Easter Rising was the catalyst for serious divisions in the Irish Volunteers. The expected mobilisation order never happened, resulting in a blame game that caused a lot of acrimony and ultimately split the republican movement in Scotland for a period.

It took one of Michael Collins' most trusted lieutenants, a man named Joe Vize, to heal the wounds and put the Scottish-based Volunteers back on a path where they could once again provide invaluable practical assistance to their colleagues in Ireland. My father would be at Joe Vize's side for much of the critical period from 1918-'21.

My father's decision to depart for Glasgow after his release from Sligo Jail was not especially surprising. He knew there was a guarantee of steady work in Scotland, which was more than could be said for the fate that awaited him back home in Geesala. His commanding officer in the Erris Volunteers, Ned Mangan, told the Army Pensions Board that my father emigrated in the spring of 1919 for economic reasons.

"The poor circumstances (financially) of his parents left him no choice but emigration in order to help them. However, while in Glasgow he devoted his time solely to the IRA and his connection with the supply of arms to HQ are well-known facts."

Economic factors certainly influenced my father's decision to leave Erris, but there were political motives too. In a poem composed in 1921, he describes the harassment he suffered at the hands of the RIC in Erris:

The Peelers watched me night and day, they tracked me high and low,
So I bade farewell to all my friends in the county of Mayo.

Perhaps the 24-year-old Henry Coyle felt he could best serve the republican cause by becoming a Glasgow-based gunrunner, especially as he was familiar with Scotland and its extensive network of Irish communities, having undertaken seasonal work there since his early teens.

Seamus Reader is on record as stating that my father's original purpose in going to Glasgow was to acquire guns for the IRA brigades in Mayo and Sligo, but such a mission would have required permission from GHQ in Dublin. Seán Healy, who worked closely with my father in Scotland, had to receive 'the necessary permission from GHQ' before travelling to Glasgow to procure arms for the Cork IRA in 1919. Henry O'Hagan, a member of the Meath Volunteers, received authorisation from the most senior military man in the county, General Seán Boylan, to procure weapons in Manchester, but later ran into problems because GHQ had not approved the mission.

"I had about £20 saved and was very anxious to procure arms for the Trim Company," O'Hagan told the Bureau of Military History. "I went to Manchester and I met Seamus Barrett (an IRA sympathiser) in his second-hand shop in Liverpool Road, but I could not get arms. He told me Boylan's credentials were no good to him; he wanted Collins' authority."

Many of the Scottish-based Volunteers later described my father as being 'attached to GHQ' and that was certainly the case for much, if not all, of his time in Scotland, but I have been unable to definitively establish the precise date when the initial link was made with Michael Collins and GHQ. However, there is a lot of evidence to suggest that GHQ was aware of my father not long after his arrival in Glasgow and he was operating at a fairly senior level by the summer of 1919.

Dubliner Denis Fitzpatrick, who was a veteran of the Easter Rising, moved to Denny, Stirlingshire, in March 1919 where he established a company of the Irish Republican Army (IRA), the name given to the Volunteers after 1919. Fitzpatrick recalled getting in touch with my father some time in 1919 and later collaborating with him on various gunrunning expeditions.

"Coyle was well-known," Fitzpatrick told the Army Pensions Board. "He became a TD afterwards. He was a very good man."

Henry O'Hagan accompanied Fitzpatrick to Scotland and established a company of the IRA in the town of Falkirk, a few miles from Denny.

"Henry Coyle came from GHQ, got in touch with me and came down with Seamus O'Keeffe [a prominent member of Sinn Féin in Scotland] and swore the company into the IRA," O'Hagan told the Bureau of Military History.

James McHugh arrived in Glasgow in July 1919, having completed a two-month term in Castlebar Jail for illegal assembly at Doolough on St Patrick's Day. In his application to the Army Pensions Board, McHugh said he started 'working for Henry Coyle' upon arrival in Scotland – a claim my father corroborated in a letter to the Board dated December 28, 1937:

> *From the end of July 1919, [James McHugh] done most valuable work for me in the collection of war material until my arrest on December 4, 1920. During the whole of that period he was one of my most reliable men.*

Although my father wasn't on the full-time payroll of GHQ until August 1920, he seems to have devoted most, if not all, of his time to the acquisition of 'war material'. Upon arrival in Glasgow, he became a member of 'B' Company in the Scottish No 1 IRA Battalion, and was known to many of his colleagues as 'Harry' Coyle. 'B' Coy was based in Bridgerton in east Glasgow and boasted about 200 members at full strength, including James McHugh and my father's younger brother Martin.

There were 33 companies and five battalions of the Scottish IRA Brigade, comprising an estimated 2,500 men, and they were spread throughout most of the country. The 1st Battalion in Glasgow boasted nine companies, while the 2nd Battalion, with eight companies, was based in the industrial coalmining district of Lanarkshire, including large towns like Motherwell and Hamilton.

The 3rd Battalion, with eight companies, had Edinburgh as its centre; the 4th Battalion, consisting of four companies, was based around Dundee and Fife, while the 5th Battalion covered towns like Greenock, Port Glasgow, Paisley and Kilmarnock. There were also 14 branches of Cumann na mBan across Scotland, so there was a very good structure in place, but it needed a man with the organisational skills of Joe Vize to realise the full potential of this small army of Irish nationalists.

Wexford-born Vize, a gentle giant of a man, had trained as an engineer before devoting himself fully to the cause of Irish freedom. He took part in the Easter Rising and formed a particularly close bond with Collins when the two were interned in Frongoch in Wales.

Dooyork.
Geesala.
Co. Mayo.
28-12-37.

To whom it may concern.

This is to certify that I knew the bearer Mr. James McHugh as an active member of the Volunteers in this district from March 1917 to April 1919. He was sentenced on the 14th of May 1919 in Castlebar for an illegal assembly.

I afterwards knew him in Glasgow from the end of July 1919 where he done most valuable work for me in the collection of war material until my arrest on the 4th of December 1920. During the whole of that period he was one of my most reliable men.

He was always prepared to make any sacrifice in the cause of National Independence.

Henry P. Coyle.

DEPT. OF DEFENCE
RECEIVED
30 DEC 1937
PENSIONS BRANCH

A reference my father gave for fellow Geesala man James McHugh in 1937 when McHugh was applying for an IRA pension. The RIC had attempted to evict McHugh and his widowed mother in 1919.

The son of a bank manager, Vize first came to live in Scotland in 1912 to work with the Clan shipping firm as a marine engineer. In December 1915, his ship was torpedoed near Malta *en route* to England from Australia. According to Joe's obituary, published in 1959, the Wexford man showed real

Joe Vize was sent to Scotland by Michael Collins in 1918 to organise a system of arms smuggling to Ireland. My father worked closely with Vize in 1919-'20.

coolness amid the pandemonium on board the stricken vessel.

As the ship was sinking beneath feet and the crew clambered aboard the small lifeboats, one man was remarked upon – Joe Vize – who stood calmly awaiting his turn and smoking his inevitable pipe.

Later, when an account of the sinking was published, an officer of the ship specially mentioned his courage and calm behaviour in the face of such danger. They were six hours in the small boats, and having reached the Algerian shore safely, they were all brought back to England and thence to home.

Within months, Joe had joined the Dublin brigade of the Irish Volunteers and was fighting in Jacob's Mills on Easter Week, as well as helping to reinforce St Stephen's Green with troops under the command of Countess Markievicz. His friendship with Michael Collins blossomed in Frongoch and the two remained incredibly close for the rest of Collins' short life.

Loyalty was one of Joe Vize's finest traits – as my father would discover when he faced dark days in the mid-1920s – and there were few men Michael Collins trusted more. The name of Joe Vize may not feature prominently in modern accounts of the War of Independence but he was a real hero of that momentous period in Irish history. Like so many of the men and women who will feature in the pages of this book, he is one of Ireland's forgotten freedom fighters.

CHAPTER 4

Golfing for Ireland

ONE evening in 1975, my father and I were watching the RTÉ television news when the newscaster Charles Mitchel announced in his distinctive voice that six Irish men had been found guilty of the infamous IRA pub bombings in Birmingham in which 21 innocent people were killed. The Birmingham Six case had been closely watched in the Coyle household because my older brothers Pat and Willie lived in Birmingham and I spent some time there too in my teens. Birmingham was such a welcoming city to so many Irish emigrants and my family were appalled at the bombings. On that particular evening, my father and I sat in silence as video footage showed the men being led from the courthouse and into the waiting prison vans to begin their long sentences. The reporter explained how the six men were 'members of a deadly IRA cell' and were arrested while trying to take a ferry to Belfast hours after the pub bombings. Henry Coyle wasn't buying the story, however.

"Those are all innocent men," he emphatically declared when the report ended.

"What are you on about?" I asked.

"Those men were caught at the boat. If they did the bombings, the last place they'd have been that night would be at the boat, or on a plane or train for that matter. The people who did that were at their normal jobs the next day."

"How do you know this?" I responded.

"Sure even in our day we'd have known not to go to the boat. We'd have been tired after being out all night on a job but we'd be at work the next day. We always made sure of that."

My father turned 80 the year the Birmingham Six were jailed. He had slowed down to the point where he didn't leave the house too often, but his mind was lucid and he still sat at his usual berth at the kitchen table with stacks of newspapers in front of him.

Unusually for a teenager, I had a healthy interest in Irish history and my father's cryptic comments about the Birmingham pub bombings piqued my curiosity. I got a tape recorder and sat down with him in the evenings to record our occasional conversations about his time in Scotland between 1919 and 1921. The age of the Internet was still a long way off, which meant I couldn't search old newspapers to corroborate my father's stories or find out additional information with which to probe him. I was totally dependent on what he recalled and didn't have the background knowledge to ask the searching questions that might have garnered more information, but we still got through a lot of work, and much of the material from that series of interviews is included in this book.

Incredibly, the newspaper reports I have since sourced, both in the Irish and British archives, as well as statements from the Bureau of Military History and Military Service Pensions Collection, have confirmed virtually everything my father told me almost 50 years ago. In particular, there is one lengthy document I persuaded him to write that contains a wealth of astonishing details about the IRA campaign in Britain in 1919-'20, information that has never been published before.

Sometimes our interviews happened accidentally. I recall coming into the house one afternoon to find my father seated at the fire chatting to a relative named Pat Calvey. They were talking about golf, of all things, and my father spoke authoritatively about eagles and birdies and nine-irons and four-irons. I was absolutely astounded because it was far from golf we were reared! To me, golf was a posh man's sport and I couldn't fathom how a man who grew up in a two-room cottage in Dooyork, with cows for company, knew so much about this sport of the gentry (as it was in his day).

"What's the story with the golf?" I asked him after Pat left. "You never told me you played."

"I never played a game in my life," he replied.

"So how do you know about it?"

"I had to learn every bit of it when I was over in Scotland running guns for Michael Collins."

My father went on to explain that one of his duties was to collect guns in various parts of Scotland and bring them by train to 39 Bishop Street in Glasgow, which was owned by a coal merchant named James Chambers from Derry. A lot of the guns were long-barrelled service rifles owned by Scottish veterans of World War I, who sold them for cash or handed them over out of sympathy for the Irish independence struggle. Getting the rifles was one thing but transporting them by train was another matter entirely because they weren't going to fit into a conventional suitcase.

"I found a golf bag very useful in conveying rifles in numbers of four or less," my father recalled. "This was done by screwing off the butts, which were carried in an attaché case, while the barrels were carried in the golf bag with the heads of four clubs cut short and pared to a pencil-point sticking up."

My father used the 'golfing' disguise on many rail trips in 1919 and 1920 and was – in his own words – 'never detected'. Thirty years later, IRA Volunteer Joseph Booker still marvelled at the ingenuity and audacity of this simple ruse.

"Henry Coyle had a rather original method of bringing rifles to Bishop Street," Booker told the Bureau of Military History in 1952. "He took the butts off the rifles, placed the rifles in a golf bag and screwed golf club heads into the barrels of the rifles. With the golf bag slung over his shoulder, and another person with him carrying the butts in a suitcase, he gave the impression of a man going off for a game of golf, and a person carrying his suitcase to the station."

The man carrying the suitcase was, more often than not, 'wee' Charlie Strickland, who became my father's shadow during this period. A native of the Falls Road in Belfast, the diminutive Charlie moved to Glasgow in 1915 to live with an aunt. When he joined the Irish Volunteers, Charlie changed his surname to his mother's maiden name of 'McGinn', partly to protect his Catholic family in Belfast, but also because he was getting a fierce ribbing from the Mayo-born members of 'B' Coy, who kept asking if he was related to Charles Strickland, the 19th-century local agent for Lord Dillon in Mayo and the founder of Charlestown!

Charlie and my father came from very different backgrounds – one was a born and bred city kid and the other was a farmer's son – but they formed a wonderful friendship that endured long into old age.

"He was 19 at the time but he only looked like a boy of 12 or 13," my father recalled. "He was very small for his age. He was the smallest assistant I had, but he was certainly the best. On several occasions he passed unnoticed when a full grown man would be suspected."

My father made every effort to ensure that his golfing disguise held up under interrogation.

"I had to know all about golf in case someone struck up a conversation with me on the train. I learned all of the terminology even though I never struck a ball in my life," he told me.

Henry Coyle only had a basic education but he was a man who never stopped learning and could speak authoritatively on numerous subjects. He

Michael Collins radicalised a whole generation of Irishmen and women, including my father, with nothing other than a pen and paper and a bicycle. He was a truly amazing man and my father remained in awe of him long into old age.

was an intelligent, resourceful man and I think that was why he was eventually appointed as the IRA's Director of Purchasing in Scotland in place of Joe Vize. Just a few years earlier, my father had been picking potatoes on a Lanarkshire farm; now he was being elevated to a very senior role in the Irish Volunteers.

Joe Vize and Michael Collins clearly saw something in my father that prompted them to thrust responsibility onto his young shoulders. He would repay their faith by dramatically increasing the amount of 'war material' coming from Scotland. Joe Vize later claimed that two-thirds of all arms used by the IRA during the War of Independence originated in Scotland and I have no doubt that a large proportion of these weapons passed through my father's hands in 1919-'20.

There were 33 companies of Irish Volunteers in Scotland but 'B' Coy of the Glasgow-based 1st Battalion was the most active in the smuggling of arms to Ireland. Many of the men who became key allies of my father were members of 'B' Coy and they worked very hard to acquire weapons from every available source.

There was a great sense of camaraderie among the Scottish Volunteers and that comes across very strongly in their statements to the Bureau of Military History and the Army Pensions Board. The Volunteers came from all sorts of backgrounds and professions. In Dundee, for example, a Galway-born priest, Fr John Fahy, was involved in gun smuggling, while in Edinburgh, a businessman and World War I veteran named Frank Gordon gave practical assistance and financial aid.

Joe Vize was already well on the way to re-organising the Irish Volunteers in Scotland by the time my father arrived in Glasgow in April 1919. Indeed, Glasgow was where Vize concentrated most of his early efforts, establishing a new company of Volunteers in Govan that soon had 50 members. In Motherwell, Patrick Mills was appointed lieutenant of another company that consisted of about 40 men.

"At the beginning, membership of the Company was confined to IRB members, but later non-IRB men who were considered to be reliable were taken in," he explained. "The strength of the Company then increased to about 70. The officers were selected from members of the IRB."

Mills' comments are noteworthy because Collins and Vize were keen to use members of the IRB for gun-running activities. I do not know when my father was sworn into the IRB, but his membership of this secretive organisation would be key to his eventual role as GHQ's principal arms smuggler in Scotland. He states in his pension application in 1925 that he was a member of the IRB but does not give the date when he joined.

In his pension application, Charlie Strickland said Joe Vize swore him into the IRB in April 1919, so perhaps my father was sworn in on the same day.

Vize set about recruiting men who were cut from the same cloth as himself, i.e. completely loyal to Michael Collins. The historian Mairtín Ó Cathain makes the following observation about 'Collins' Scottish wire-pullers', as he called them: "It was their Irish Republican Brotherhood oath as well as their friendship with Collins on which their fealty rested."

A coal merchants on Bishop Street in Glasgow was one of the locations used by the IRA as an arms dump during the War of Independence.

That was certainly the case with my father who was proud to be one of Michael Collins' 'Glasgow boys', as Joe Vize liked to call them.

In Henry Coyle, Michael Collins found a Volunteer whose allegiance was absolute, a man who idolised the 'Big Fella' so much he was willing to sacrifice his young life for the cause of Irish freedom.

While researching this book, I visited Michael Collins' birthplace in Clonakilty in rural Co Cork, and as I stood there in that little cottage, I marvelled at how a young man from such humble beginnings could radicalise a whole generation of Irishmen. What was it about Collins that made him such a charismatic leader? Could anyone other than Michael Collins have persuaded Henry Coyle to carry out the dangerous, daring IRA missions for which he was later convicted before a Scottish court? I don't think so.

I have no idea when my father first met Collins but he often described the 'Big Fella' as a personal friend. Indeed, I strongly suspect that Henry Coyle might never have become involved at such a senior level in the IRA were it not for his utter devotion to Michael Collins. He was a Collins' loyalist through and through, and I think it was his absolute fidelity to a man who came from the same rural background as himself that influenced most of the key decisions my father made in the early 1920s.

Henry Coyle would have happily followed Michael Collins to hell and back, and sometimes I think he did. My father's involvement in the fight for Irish freedom would bring him to some very dark and lonely places in the years ahead.

CHAPTER 5

Gelignite in a wellington

THE Volunteers in Scotland left no stone unturned in their quest to procure as many armaments as possible for the war in Ireland. Matthew Tipping, who was IRA quartermaster for the Govan district in Glasgow, said weapons were purchased from 'anyone we got word had them'. It was the same in Liverpool where a young Offaly Volunteer named Paddy Daly was sourcing armaments from all over the north of England.

"The extensive Irish population, even the unorganised members associated with Irish communities or even those of Irish dance halls, somehow always knew what to do with a gun or a weapon if they managed to acquire one," recalled Daly. "Of course, members of Sinn Féin clubs and especially members of the IRA and IRB were always on the lookout for weapons that might be of use. The type of weapon and its lethal value varied considerably, some being very inadequate such as pin-fire revolvers and old rusty grenades from the previous world war. Revolvers, even of the more modern pattern, varied much in their calibre. I think the .44 revolver was of a Canadian pattern. There were even Peter-the-Painters. The latter were modern at the time."

Manufactured by the German firm Mauser in 1896, the Peter-the-Painter, as it was commonly known during the War of Independence, was a clip-fed semi-automatic gun that held ten rounds. It could be equipped with a shoulder stock to make it more accurate and was used to deadly effect in close-quarter fighting during the Easter Rising.

Peter-the-Painters were far from ideal for guerilla warfare but were better than some of the weapons falling into the Volunteers' hands in England and Scotland.

"On one occasion, some German machine-guns were sent from Newcastle [to Liverpool] complete with the sleighs belonging to them," recalled Daly. "They had, apparently, been in use on the eastern front of the world war. Unfortunately, the sleighs were kept in a backyard [of] one of our dumps, and

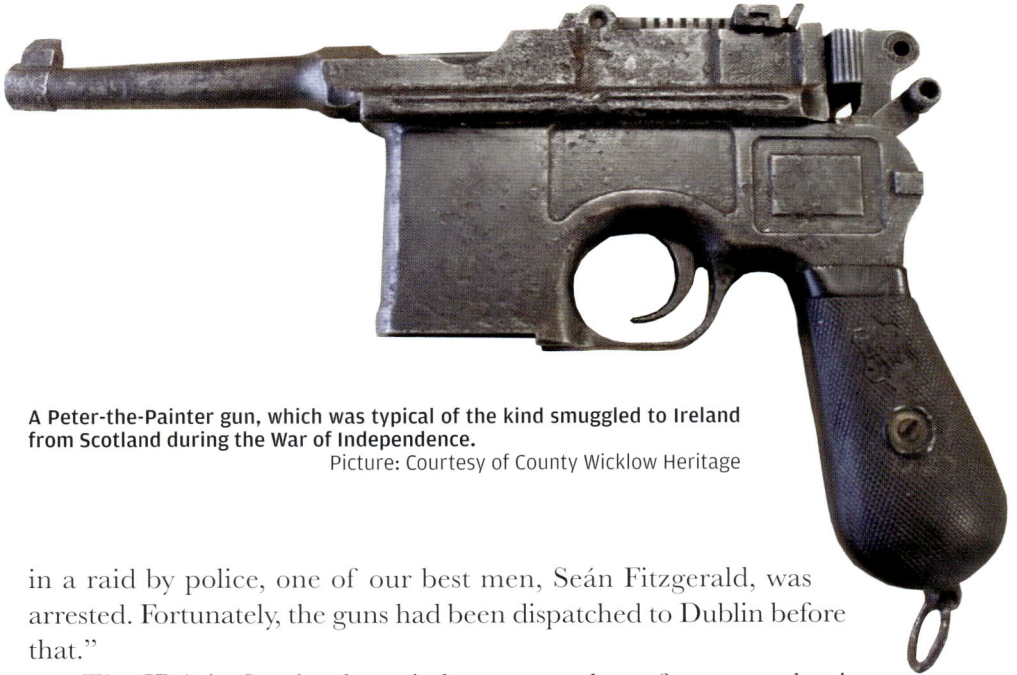

A Peter-the-Painter gun, which was typical of the kind smuggled to Ireland from Scotland during the War of Independence.
Picture: Courtesy of County Wicklow Heritage

in a raid by police, one of our best men, Seán Fitzgerald, was arrested. Fortunately, the guns had been dispatched to Dublin before that."

The IRA in Scotland carried out a number of very productive raids on military barracks in 1919 and 1920, but Vize's preferred method for acquiring guns was to offer financial inducements to soldiers to smuggle weapons and ammunition from their barracks. Soldiers or civilian staff could also be persuaded to facilitate an IRA raid on a magazine store in the dead of night. A letter from Vize to Collins in February 1920 gives an insight into the number of IRA operations ongoing in Scotland at that time:

> In Maryhill, we are in direct contact with the sergeant in the machine gun stores… He is only waiting now to get his right man on sentry for to start working for us… We are getting rifles from Hamilton [Barracks], this place is just developing, up to now we have ten out of it, expecting many more, Houston & Sterling is giving us some Webleys (new), the latter place is newly opened up to us, anticipate a good many more from there, we are also waiting for the wire to lift two machine guns from Dumfermline, another new opening.

In May 1919, the IRA in Glasgow had a stock of just four revolvers and two rifles, but the arsenal had increased to 80 revolvers and 20 rifles by February 1920. Of course, Collins did not want a build-up of weapons in the Scottish arms dumps because he needed every gun he could get, especially as the situation in Ireland worsened throughout 1920. Initially, the Scottish IRA smuggled 'war material' from Ardrossan into the ports of Belfast and Larne, but the chances of being detected in the Ulster ports were high. In November

1917, two Scottish members of Na Fianna Éireann were arrested in Belfast with 230 two-ounce sticks of gelignite and a substantial amount of blasting powder. Belfast and Larne also presented an added complication of having to transport the contraband onto Dublin, which further increased the chances of detection.

By the summer of 1919, the Scottish IRA were going to enormous lengths – and taking considerable risks – to provide a steady flow of guns and explosives into Ireland, but their work would be totally pointless if the weapons were seized as soon as they crossed the Irish Sea. Vize decided to change the point of departure to Liverpool Port, where there were a lot of dockworkers who were sympathetic to the Irish cause.

The new arrangement meant he needed someone to drive cargoes of deadly weapons from Glasgow to Liverpool, a treacherous 300-mile trip across enemy terrain. My father was appointed to the position of transport officer for the Scottish Brigade while also being promoted to Vize's purchasing committee, a key group of IRB men in charge of the acquisition of 'war material'. He now had access to every arms dump in Glasgow, and was privy to very sensitive intelligence about the IRA's operations throughout Scotland and the north of England.

Vize was putting a lot of trust in a man whom he had met just a few months earlier, but Henry Coyle would not disappoint his genial commanding officer. He revelled in the additional responsibilities and was soon devoting every waking hour to the republican cause as more and more weapons were acquired for dispatch to Ireland.

It was clear Joe Vize intended to keep his new transport officer busy, and Henry Coyle was only too happy to oblige, especially when the prize was something he had dreamed of since boyhood: Irish independence.

———————

While researching this book, I encountered some wonderful people through my Facebook page, 'Ireland's Forgotten Freedom Fighters', and one of them is the historian Stephen Coyle (no relation) from Glasgow. Stephen is among the foremost authorities on the IRA in Scotland and I have drawn heavily on his research for the second part of this chapter. In a lecture in 2020, Stephen gave a fascinating insight into the workings of the Scottish IRA Brigade around the time my father was serving on the purchasing committee.

"Every battalion had purchasing staff, medical orderlies and a chaplain," explains Stephen, "and each Company had an OC, Quartermaster and a First and Second Lieutenant.

In July 1919, the mining village of Glenboig in Lanarkshire was the scene of the first major raid by the Scottish IRA Brigade.

"The Volunteers paid weekly dues and attended drill. The Brigade had its own ordnance unit based in Glasgow, which carried out repairs, as they were anxious that no defective weapons should be sent to Ireland.

"The Scottish Brigade, which was two-and-a-half times larger than the IRA in England, largely avoided taking part in offensive action. Attacks were to be confined to England, based on an understanding that the Scots and the Welsh were fellow Celtic victims of English oppression. This understanding dated back to the 1790s when the United Irishmen, which had two lodges in Glasgow, worked in close co-operation with the Society of United Scotsmen who stood for an independent Scottish Republic… The Fenians in Scotland adopted the same position."

Stephen cites a letter from Joe Vize to Michael Collins on May 10, 1919, in which he stated: *There is now passing into our hands 500 revolvers and 200,000 rounds of .303 [ammunition], don't think I have made a mistake in the figures, it is right.*

Vize's letter must have been music to Collins' ears, but it wasn't all good news from Scotland. On another occasion, Vize reported that he had accumulated about 100 detonators on a visit to coalmines in Motherwell, but had to get them 'in ones and twos, the watch is so keen'.

The coalmining districts of Lanarkshire were the most fertile ground for Vize and his men, who could rely on plenty of support among local miners, especially those with family ties to Ireland. Glasgow-based Andrew (Andy)

Fagan was brigade quartermaster for the IRA in Scotland in 1919-'20 while simultaneously serving as the chief organiser for the local miners' union.

"His area extended over the whole of Lanarkshire and, in fact, covered the entire Scottish coalfields," a summary of Fagan's application for an IRA military service pension stated. "He used his position as such to a considerable extent in recruiting agents for the purpose of obtaining explosives and war material."

In one Scottish mining village, near Blantyre, a company of Irish Volunteers consisted entirely of miners.

"In nearly every house where a Volunteer lived, at the end of the week they collected one, two, three or four sticks of gelignite and detonators per man and handed it over," recalled Eamonn Mooney. "They would not be paid for the gelignite or detonators. The only munitions they would be paid for would be where somebody had a rifle or machine gun to sell."

Stirlingshire and Fife were other coalmining districts where the Irish Volunteers had plenty of sympathisers, while the local steelworks in Motherwell also delivered its share of 'war material'. Vize even managed to secure the services of a mining contractor, William Corbett, from Co Clare, who had easy access to large quantities of explosives. Parkhead-based Corbett trained a number of Glasgow IRA members, including my father, in the use of explosives. It was hoped the knowledge would prove very useful to the Volunteers if they returned to Ireland to join a flying column.

Mooney claimed that dozens of Scottish coalminers got into trouble with the authorities – and some even received prison sentences – for illegally removing gelignite and detonators from the collieries where they were employed. However, most of the miners were never caught because they were removing small quantities from the large stockpiles of explosives and detonators in these vast coalfields. The miners often brought up tiny amounts of gelignite in their wellington boots. The IRA in Glasgow occasionally received 'inside' information about recent deliveries of explosives to coalfields and quarries, and several nighttime raids were organised.

On July 26, 1919, three carts of gelignite and 100 detonators were taken from Greenfoot quarry in Glenboig, Lanarkshire, in the first major raid carried out under Vize's command. Although it was merely a village, Glenboig was the leading manufacturer of firebricks in the world, its bricks having been used to build the furnaces that fuelled the Industrial Revolution. Rich deposits of fireclay, found between the seams of coal, produced first-class bricks that could withstand extremely high temperatures in industrial furnaces. With better fireclay than anywhere else in Britain, Glenboig became an industrial powerhouse in the 19th century, and its quarries were inevitable targets for Irish Volunteers who were desperate to get their hands on explosives.

One of the most daring operations involving members of the Scottish IRA occurred on April 24, 1920, when over 100 Volunteers were mobilised for a raid on Robroyston Colliery on the outskirts of Glasgow. My father was among the participants, along with two other North Mayo men, Patrick McDonnell and Michael Naughton, who were both from Belderrig.

"It was a dangerous thing because we had to creep on our hands and knees in order to approach it unseen and without making noise," Naughton later recalled.

The Volunteers made off with 101.25kg of gelignite, 4.05kg of gunpowder, 550 detonators and 13.5kg of fuse.

Stephen Coyle cites police records that logged 29 raids on collieries in Scotland from July 1919 to the signing of the Anglo-Irish Treaty. Interestingly, he also quotes Christine Keeley, a member of Cumann na mBan in Glasgow, who said women joined the raiding parties and helped to carry away the 'war material'.

McDonnell and Naughton also accompanied my father on a raid at Darnley Glen coalmine on the south side of Glasgow in November 1920. The large party of Volunteers also included Eamonn Mooney:

"Darnley was outside Glasgow, about seven or eight miles, and we went out to this place – it was a colliery – and we were prepared for a lot of stuff that night judging by the number of men there," Mooney explained. "It was gelignite and detonators we were to get from the colliery, but I believe the stuff was buried down in the bottom of the pit and the job was called off."

The interviewing panel from the Army Pensions Board asked Mooney if the Volunteers got anything at all during the raid in Darnley Glen.

"Personally, I got nothing only a cold!" the Glaswegian memorably replied.

Mooney said my father and John Carney (Vize's successor as OC of the Scottish brigade) called off the raid, but the trip to Darley Glen wasn't a total waste of time. My father noticed a rifle range nearby and returned a week later to successfully raid it, obtaining a number of miniature rifles. The collection of small rifles was a poor second prize to a large haul of gelignite but at least Henry Coyle was leaving Darnley Glen with something other than a cold.

CHAPTER 6

'In the enemy's country'

NOT long after arriving in Scotland, Joe Vize warned his main IRA personnel to avoid attending Sinn Féin meetings or other public events that might connect them to the struggle for Irish independence. Indeed, a veil of secrecy was thrown over the work of key operatives like my father, and it took many years before I was able to trace his activities in those critical years.

"During this period, 1919 and 1920, the collection and dispatch of munitions was, to a great extent, confined to a very few people," Paddy Daly remarked. "All the members of the IRB circles were aware of this, I think, but only a small percentage of them was asked to take part."

Once the War of Independence was over, a view formed in Ireland that the efforts of the IRA in Scotland were peripheral to the rebellion at home, but Joe Vize had a very different perspective and came to regard the Scottish Volunteers as the unsung heroes of that turbulent period.

"They were working in the enemy's country, and under far more difficult circumstances than some of our own men at home," he remarked in 1925. "Every day they were watched, not only by the detectives and police, but by members of the civilian population also, and during my time in Scotland they were always on the go, purchasing, transporting, supplying information, and carrying arms and explosives all over the country."

A month after the successful raid in Glenboig, Vize's men carried out an equally audacious mission when a large caché of guns was taken from the military barracks in the town of Hamilton. Volunteers from companies in Glasgow, Motherwell and Blantyre took part in this operation, which yielded a total of 75 rifles and 50 bayonets, a huge arsenal for men who were more used to acquiring weapons in ones and twos. The IRA's contact in the barracks was a shoemaker who repaired boots and saddles for the military.

In August 1919, my father participated in an IRA raid on Hamilton Military Barracks that yielded 75 rifles and 50 bayonets, which was one of the biggest arms hauls of the entire War of Independence.

"He supplied full particulars of where the rifles were stored and succeeded in procuring a key that would give the raiding party access to the stores concerned," explains Stephen Coyle. "On the night of the raid, six Volunteers succeeded in getting over the wall of the military barracks and entered the stores, with the key in their possession."

Several members of the Motherwell Company took part in the raid, including Patrick Mills and Michael Burke.

"I was in charge of the carrying party," Burke recalled. "I took the gate. Harry McMahon and Pat Duffy crossed the gate and handed through the bars of the gate to me 75 rifles and 50 bayonets, which I gave to the carriers…"

The weapons were loaded onto a waiting lorry for dispatch to Liverpool. In fact, the lorry was back in Glasgow before the military authorities discovered their loss.

A second raid on Hamilton Barracks took place in June 1920 when 40 German rifles and bayonets were seized. Once again, Joe Vize was the commanding officer and my father took charge of the transport.

A lot of planning went into the operation as can be seen from the evidence of Andy Fagan to the Army Pensions Board. Fagan knew a soldier in the barracks, and 'worked' on this man over an extended period by purchasing 'war material' from him. The man eventually put Fagan in touch with a colleague who was in charge of the quartermaster's storeroom where the weapons were kept. The storeman had little interest in Irish independence but was persuaded (Fagan used the phrase 'oiled') to cooperate with the rebels.

"I had to get in touch with the quartermaster's storeman and win him to smuggle the material from the stores to a little hut, a tin place, that was convenient to the outside wall," Fagan recalled. "It took some time to get the required quantity of material transferred from the stores to the hut."

Once a sufficient quantity of weapons was in place, Fagan told the storeman the IRA planned to raid the barracks at midnight on a June evening.

"Vize was on that raid personally so that we could have motor transport and men available at the shortest possible time," Fagan explained.

In his account of the raid, Michael Burke said: 'Henry Coyle arrived with a taxi and took away the consignment.' It is hard to believe my father managed to persuade a taxi driver to transport an arsenal of 'war material' from Hamilton to Glasgow, a journey of ten miles, so I presume the car was hired or borrowed. Another member of the raiding party, James Rodgers from Blantyre Company, said the car had to be 'pushed' down the road such was the weight of its deadly cargo. Somehow my father managed to make his escape and deliver the weapons to one of the arms dumps in Glasgow where they were stored, possibly for several weeks, before dispatch to Liverpool and then Dublin.

In the winter of 1919-'20, Volunteers were continuing to use trains to transport armaments from Scotland to England, a *modus operandi* that carried enormous risk. On one occasion, Paddy Daly and a colleague, Tom Kerr, whose family was central to the IRA operations in Liverpool, travelled to Motherwell to collect weapons from Joe Vize.

"We went on the night train," Daly told the Bureau of Military History in 1953. "It was most uncomfortable travelling all night. We arrived in Motherwell in the early hours of the morning and went to the house of [Michael] Burke where Joe Vize was staying.

"As far as I can recollect, we had two suitcases each. These were loaded up for us with all kinds of material like gelignite and revolvers – anything in the nature of a lethal weapon. I still remember the weight of these suitcases.

"We walked into the railway station later on in the day; some of my companions never thought of taking a taxi in those days. However, we got back to Liverpool safely the next day."

Patrick Mills also transported 'war material' from Scotland to Liverpool.

My father made his home in Parkhead in Glasgow, but spent much of his time travelling around Scotland and the north of England for the IRA.

"The arms and ammunition were put in suitcases and two men or, if the consignment was large, three men took them to Liverpool. We usually left Glasgow by the 10.10am train for Liverpool and got off at either Bootle or Aintree stations."

My father purchased a motorbike and sidecar and used it to convey small quantities of armaments to central dumps in Glasgow. Charlie Strickland and Joe Booker were given a handcart to carry weapons around the city, much to the surprise of Seán Healy.

"I thought this highly dangerous but Joe [Vize] pointed out to me that there was little out of the ordinary to see a lad pushing a handcart – so long as the stuff was well covered, of course – along the street, and young Joe [Booker] wore working clothes. I saw his point. Nothing ever happened while this cart was being used."

The handcart proved very useful when Strickland had to move arms at short notice after receiving a tip-off that the police were about to raid one of the IRA's central dumps. The Belfast teenager wheeled the handcart, laden with guns and explosives, through the 'principal streets of Glasgow' before safely depositing his illegal cargo in another central dump.

The Volunteers were incredibly inventive when it came to transporting armaments, using all manner of subterfuge to cover their illegal activities.

"One very safe method I had of taking stuff from place to place was in a violin case – for small quantities, of course," recalled Seán Healy. "As well as playing the pipes I did a little on the violin as well and took that instrument to Glasgow with me. You would be surprised how much that case would hold when packed carefully with either revolvers or explosives."

The success of Joe Vize's arms smuggling operation can be seen from the amount of money sent to Scotland in 1919-'20. Collins sent £2,150 to Vize between June 11, 1919 and June 23, 1920, which was a greater sum than went to Liverpool or London in the same period. On one occasion, Vize spent £800 acquiring 37 rifles, 111 revolvers, 258Ib of explosives, 1,700 rounds of ammunition, 4,100 detonators, field glasses and batteries.

Some in GHQ would later allege that the money sent to Scotland was not spent wisely – and the issue became a source of tension between Michael Collins and Cathal Brugha – but conditions on the ground were very difficult, and men like my father and Joe Vize often had to do business with all sorts of dubious characters. It's worth remembering that many in Glasgow were fiercely loyal to the Crown and wouldn't have hesitated in contacting the authorities if some Irish rebels approached them about the illegal purchase of guns or explosives. The Volunteers had to be extraordinarily careful when dealing with weapons' suppliers and were vulnerable to being conned by people who knew only too well that an arms smuggler couldn't go to the police if he was done out of money.

GHQ sent thousands of pounds to Scotland from 1919 to 1921, but plenty of money crossed the Irish Sea too. According to Stephen Coyle's research, membership subscriptions for the 65 Sinn Féin clubs in Scotland in 1921 amounted to £4,045, so it is quite possible that over £10,000 was sent to Dublin during the course of the War of Independence. Therefore, I don't think anyone could possibly claim that the Scots-Irish did not play their part in the fight for Irish freedom.

———————

By early 1920, my father was living in the home of Thomas and Kate Lee at 7 Todd Street, Parkhead, and masquerading as an insurance agent, which provided a useful cover for his constant travel and frequent meetings with other IRA volunteers. Thomas Lee was employed at Parkhead Forge where munitions were manufactured during World War I, while his Sligo-born wife was a member of Cumann na mBan. The following summary of Kate Lee's evidence to the Army Pensions Board provides a fascinating insight into the activities of the IRA in Glasgow in 1919-'20.

Henry Coyle stopped in her house for about 12 months. He was a prominent member of the IRA and was responsible for securing quantities of rifles, revolvers and ammunition and also all kinds of explosives. A large quantity of these were brought to applicant's house where they were kept for a time and packed for dispatch.

She herself bought arms (revolvers) from young Irishmen who were in sympathy with the movement. She believes they were obtained by breaking into gunsmiths' shops, etc. She got instruction from Coyle during his absence to take in these guns and to pay for them. He supplied the cash. She believes she got a couple of dozen in this way.

Men came from the outskirts of Glasgow who worked in the mines. They brought explosives. They generally stopped for a few hours and she gave them dinner and tea.

She kept explosives in the coal cellar mixed up with coal in sacks. She took out these explosives, put them in a suitcase and gave them to Coyle who brought the stuff to the boat. The rifles and revolvers were generally hidden in the house. The house was raided on one occasion but they had got rid of the stuff beforehand. Nothing was taken except a Volunteer uniform…

She helped to remove revolvers and ammunition, also explosives, from one house to another in Glasgow dozens of times. She carried gelignite in egg boxes from which the sections had been removed.

She brought rifles in parts rolled up in linoleum and also revolvers in a basket, with the assistance of another girl named Mary Ann Ward, a member of Cumann na mBan.

Another Glasgow woman who was instrumental to my father's gunrunning activities was Jean Quinn, just 20 years of age and the manager of her family's furniture store at 49 Kent Street. Inspired by the 1916 Rising, Jean joined Sinn Féin's James Connolly Cumann in Glasgow in September 1916 and quickly became involved in storing weapons.

"I remember a number of young men bringing a quantity of explosives into the hall," Jean recalled. "Certain members of the Cumann, who professed to be opposed to physical force, objected and I offered to keep it as I had a store quite near. After that, it became quite a common thing for stuff to be sent to me. This could be done without attracting any special attention as I possessed a good furniture business and there was nothing unusual about goods continually coming in and being dispatched. I had numerous opportunities of buying rifles and revolvers. I also made good use of my trade with furniture dealers in Ireland."

As early as 1917, Jean Quinn was sending weapons to Ireland and even managed to procure six rifles and six revolvers – a fairly sizeable haul – from Maryhill Barracks in Glasgow after a former British Army soldier put her in contact with some colleagues there. During 1919 and 1920, my father and

Charlie Strickland regularly visited Jean's shop, which became a dispatch centre, as well as a central dump, for the IRA in Scotland.

"Her business premises in the Bridgerton area was constantly used by the purchasing and transport officers," recalled Charlie Strickland. "She was responsible for procuring supplies of arms and ammunition, which brigade transport officer Henry Coyle and myself collected in motor cars, etc, from time to time. The arms and ammunition were packed in trunks, suitcases, golf bags, etc, which were conveyed for shipment to Ireland."

Charlie Strickland, Jean Quinn and my father also concealed weapons in cases of furniture for dispatch across the Irish Sea, usually to Belfast but on two occasions to Dublin where they were 'lifted by the IRA at the Quays'. Jean also carried weapons through the streets of Glasgow and 'left them at clubs and indicated addresses'.

GHQ representatives like my father and Joe Vize wouldn't have been able to successfully operate in Glasgow without the co-operation of people like Jean Quinn and Kate Lee who owned properties in the city and could, therefore, store the ammunition that was being collected throughout Lanarkshire and as far away as Dundee. Eamonn Mooney also kept an arms dump at his house in Glasgow.

"On account of my long residence in Scotland, I was better suited than men coming over from Ireland, who in strange surroundings would not be in a position to keep an arms dump in a lodging house or hotel and would also find it difficult to pick up connections," Mooney explained. "About every six weeks or so the Coy O/C with the Battalion QM would order (after inspection) these arms to be taken to a clearing dump for transport to Ireland, sometimes via England. Once or twice I accompanied these shipments to distant parts of Scotland with Comdt Henry Coyle and Charlie Strickland. On each occasion, there would be 60 to 80 assorted small arms and two to three thousand rounds of ammunition shipped. At times I had to take charge of five or six dumps in different parts of Glasgow and my own home was continually used as a clearing-house. A great deal of time was occupied in cleaning and keeping arms in good condition and guarding the dumps.

"Besides looking after the dumps, a special fund was in my charge. This fund was provided by members' subscriptions, concerts, plays and other social functions, and the purchase of arms was generally done in company with O/C, QM, Battalion QM and myself. This fund had no connection with Dublin GHQ. All loss of employment, travelling expenditure, etc., was provided for out of our own monies."

My father also devoted all of his time to the republican cause but was only put on the payroll of GHQ in August 1920 when he was granted a weekly salary of £4-4s after being placed in charge of weapons' purchasing following Joe Vize's return to Ireland. He was also appointed brigade adjutant (assistant) to the new commanding officer John Carney, a native of Glasgow.

"Joe Vize asked to be recalled as there was fierce fighting taking place all over Ireland and Joe wanted to be in on it," recalled Seán Healy. "GHQ granted his request and sent over another Wexford man, Joe Furlong, to appoint somebody in his place. Furlong appointed a west of Ireland man, Henry Coyle, a very hard worker. He chucked whatever job he had to take over the responsibility of purchasing munitions in Scotland."

By the end of August, my father was the most senior GHQ representative on the ground in Scotland, and quickly began to make a name for himself by dramatically increasing the amount of 'war material' for dispatch to Ireland. The weapons were badly needed because the War of Independence was entering its deadliest phase and my father knew the struggle for Irish freedom would fail if men like him did not step up to the mark. Henry Coyle would not be found wanting in Ireland's darkest hour.

CHAPTER 7

The Big Man's idol

O N September 3, 1920, my father set off for Liverpool with a lorry containing one of the largest consignments of arms the IRA in Scotland had assembled up to that point. It included 50 service rifles, a Hotchkiss machine gun and thousands of rounds of ammunition.

The deadly cargo was to be stored in the basement of Moran's Men's Outfitters at 93 Scotland Road, Liverpool, one of the central dumps used by Neill Kerr, the Armagh-born Volunteer who was so vital to Michael Collins' gunrunning operations in England and Scotland.

Born in 1862, Kerr spent most of his adult life working on ships that sailed the transatlantic routes from Liverpool to North and South America, but his life's devotion was really to Ireland and there are few men who did more – or sacrificed more – in that long struggle for independence.

"Neill Kerr was the guiding light in Liverpool," my father recalled. "He was 60 years of age at that time and was working for the cause of Irish freedom long before I was born."

A veteran of the Fenian movement of the late 19th-century, Kerr first moved to Liverpool in 1892 and became deeply involved in a wide variety of Irish organisations. He was one of the founding fathers of the local company of Irish Volunteers and his home at 6 Florida Street in Bootle became the movement's unofficial headquarters.

Kerr smuggled arms to Ireland in the months before the Easter Rising and his three adult sons, John, Thomas and Neill Jnr, took part in the fighting – Neil Jnr in Jacob's Biscuit Factory (where he fought alongside Joe Vize) and John in the GPO. The boys' mother had died some years earlier and their father started a new family with his second wife, Elizabeth (née McNally) with whom he had a son and a daughter.

Twenty years younger than her husband, Elizabeth was as committed to the cause of Irish nationalism as Neill and even travelled across to Dublin on

Most of the weapons smuggled to Ireland during the War of Independence came via Liverpool Docks.

Good Friday 1916 with supplies for the Irish Volunteers. When the fighting broke out on Easter Monday, she took up duties as a nurse at 11 Emerald Street, off Seville Place, and treated some of the first men wounded in those early skirmishes. Upon her return to Liverpool, Elizabeth and her husband visited the interned Irish Volunteers in various prisons in Wales and the north of England, bringing them food, clothing and other essentials.

"When one mentions Neill Kerr, you mention Ireland," Michael (Mick) O'Leary, a leading Irish Volunteer in Liverpool wrote in the 1930s. "For to my mind he was the second O'Donovan Rossa; and what he was, Mrs Kerr also was, for she was Neill Kerr and Neill Kerr was she as far as Ireland and the Irish [nationalist] movement was concerned."

This remarkable couple turned their home into a boarding house so they could provide a safe refuge for on-the-run Volunteers who were using Liverpool as a departure point for the United States and other destinations. During World War I, the Kerrs also housed Irish men seeking to escape conscription, and Neill used his many contacts in Liverpool Docks to obtain a safe passage for countless men who were wanted by the British authorities, including Captain Robert Monteith, the accomplice of Roger Casement on his doomed gunrunning mission to Ireland in 1916.

When Michael Collins and Harry Boland travelled to England in January 1919 to spring Éamon de Valera from Lincoln Jail, they stayed with the Kerrs, and Neill later organised de Valera's escape to America. Kerr was especially close to Michael Collins and even gave up his £10-per-week job as a foreman with the famous Cunard Shipping Company to become a full-time organiser for the Irish Volunteers at £5 per week.

"Neill was the Big Man's idol," Joe Vize wrote in 1925. "He had charge of the purchasing of arms, ammunition, and all war material, in Liverpool, Manchester, Birmingham, etc.

"He had charge of all war material purchased in, or landed in England, from all over the world. He was responsible for getting it all over to Ireland, practically every weapon used against the enemy, every round of ammunition, every ounce of other war material, passed through Neill's hands.

"It was always a great relief to me as Director of Purchasing to know that the big consignments that we were often anxiously waiting for had got into Neill's hands because then I could always count on hearing of same being smuggled into Ireland inside 24 hours. In fact, so perfect was Neill's organisation on the ships that in his whole career of handling hundreds of tons of supplies, he only lost seven rifles, and that was through a bit of hard luck."

The young Offaly Volunteer, Paddy Daly, arrived in Liverpool in 1918 with the intention of becoming a priest, having spent the preceding year studying medicine at Trinity College Dublin. The 20-year-old had been a member of the Irish Volunteers in his native Ferbane and wondered if the movement even existed in Liverpool. He made inquiries and was put in touch with Thomas Kerr who introduced Daly to his father. The Offaly man came to know Neill Kerr very well.

"He was of medium build, his hair was prematurely grey and he had a very pale complexion, which was accentuated by a black hat, which he habitually wore. He always affected a military bearing, which was negated by a slight stoop.

"He had a very high standard of intelligence and was much thought of by Michael Collins. He had the capacity to get things done and to inspire people to do them effectively."

Kerr's three adult sons also worked at the Liverpool Docks and were adept at finding sympathetic seamen to do their bidding, men like Jeremiah Hurley and William Verner who regularly called to 6 Florida Street to collect and deliver dispatches or weapons.

"In connection with seaports like New York, Hamburg and Antwerp, there were Irish sailors on board British vessels plying between these ports and Liverpool," explained Paddy Daly. "They were organised to bring back munitions on their return journeys.

"Apart from the purchase of munitions, Liverpool was the most important port for communications between Dublin and America, and the continent.

The liners plying between Liverpool and New York, especially the White Star and Cunard boats, had Irishmen aboard who were employed to take dispatches from Liverpool for New York and vice versa. These sailors also engaged in the stowing away of leaders who wished to avoid arrest. The mode of procedure was for such a person or persons to go aboard several hours before the liner was due to leave the dock for a landing stage and to be hidden away in the bowels of the ship."

Éamon de Valera, Harry Boland and Liam Mellows were among the leaders of the Irish republican movement who travelled to America in this manner, and they all stayed in the home of Neill and Elizabeth Kerr prior to their departure.

"The Kerrs were a great family," Seán Healy recalled. "Mr Kerr and either two or three of his sons were all seamen working on the Dublin-Liverpool ships, and goodness only knows the amount of stuff taken over by them. They would take a cannon over if necessary.

"The bulk of all munitions procured in Scotland found its way to Dublin via Liverpool. We didn't seem to have men on the Scottish-Irish boats that could be relied on. Small quantities may have been shifted by individuals for Northern [Ireland] brigades, but the bulk of GHQ stuff went by Liverpool."

My father and Charlie Strickland made many trips to Liverpool in 1920 and came to know Neill and Elizabeth Kerr very well. The rifles they smuggled from Scotland were packed into seamen's haversacks and taken to the docks by men like Paddy Daly.

"The Liverpool Docks extended about seven miles along the Merseyside, covering hundreds of acres," Daly recalled. "The dockland was separated from the city by a high wall [and] entrance to the dock was by a gateway or a doorway at which a policeman was always on guard.

"To carry arms into a boat it was necessary to put them into a sailor's packing bag with old clothes, if possible. The bag was carried on one's shoulder, giving the impression that the person carrying it was a sailor about to join his ship."

The Volunteers also received vital assistance from Cork-born Stephen Lanigan, a custom and excise officer at Liverpool Port who, like Kerr, was a leading member of the IRB in Liverpool. Lanigan and his wife Mary were 'two great workers in the Irish cause', according to Seán Healy, who stayed with them on one of his gunrunning trips to Liverpool. The Lanigans were also among the few people in Liverpool who had full knowledge of my father's activities – and for good reason. Members of the Royal Irish Constabulary were known to have travelled across to England and Scotland to assist in investigating the activities of the Irish Volunteers. Consequently, there was a

Members of the Liverpool Company of the Irish Volunteers after their release from Dartmoor Prison on February 14, 1922. Included are Seamus McCaughey (Tyrone), Bartley Keane (Ballymote, Co Sligo), Matthew Fowler (Co Meath), Charley O'Gorman (Co Antrim), Sean McPhillips (Ballaghaderreen), Sean O'Byrne (Co Waterford), Barney Meehan (Cliffoney, Co Sligo), Ernie Hayes (Broadford, Co Clare), Paddy Lowe (Dublin, Seamus O'Malley (Oughterard, Co Galway) and Sean Pinkman (Sligo and Leitrim).

lot of suspicion in the ranks of the Volunteers in Britain and every new recruit or casual contact was viewed with suspicion.

"Our security arrangements were so tight at that time – 1920-'21 – that we trusted no one arriving from Ireland. He might be anything, a defector, an absconder (deserter), or even a spy," noted John P. McPhillips, a native of Ballaghaderreen who was a member of the Liverpool Volunteers. "We had a double check on everybody, so that if someone tried to infiltrate, even though one may have known him to be alright in Ireland, nevertheless, he did not get into the circle until he was cleared of suspicion. Everyone had to 'go through the mill'. This precaution enabled the whole scheme of operations in Liverpool to go through successfully without any hitch or tip-off to the police or other agencies operating against the IRA. Not one operation was known to the police beforehand."

I have seen my father described as an 'intelligence officer' for the IRA in Scotland, and I am fairly sure his role extended beyond the acquisition of arms to include the vetting of new recruits, as well as gathering information on potential targets for any future military campaign in Britain. Collins liked to

The Gladstone Dock at Bootle was within walking distance of Neill Kerr's home at Florida Street.

maintain a bit of distance between his key operatives and my father would have been advised to keep a low profile whenever he ventured south to England. He may have been widely known among Irish nationalists in Glasgow, Motherwell and other parts of Scotland, but in Liverpool men like McPhillips did not even know of Henry Coyle.

"There were only five people outside the Kerr family in Liverpool who knew me or anything about me," my father recalled. "Those were Stephen and Mrs [Mary] Lanigan, Paddy Daly, Seamus McCaughey and Mick O'Leary."

As was often the case with the IRA gunrunning expeditions, my father was delayed for a considerable period *en route* from Glasgow on September 3, 1920, and the men waiting for him in the basement of Moran's Men's Outfitters became increasingly nervous. The party consisted of Neill Kerr Snr, Tom and Neill Kerr Jnr, Paddy Daly and Seamus McCaughey.

"The arms did not arrive at the scheduled hour," according to a report in the Military Service Pensions Collection. "The tension of waiting kept increasing. After a couple of hours of this tense waiting, one of the Volunteer party accidentally discharged his revolver."

The incident could hardly have been more tragic. Tom Kerr was toying with his brother's revolver when it went off and the bullet struck Neill Jnr in the head, killing him instantly.

"When the accident happened a doctor was called immediately and, of course, through him the police, and I was due to arrive at any minute," recalled my father. "The next move was to send out scouts to stop me driving right into the place… Then it was necessary to get another place of storage without delay."

Neill Kerr Snr instructed Paddy Daly and Seamus McCaughey to go out onto the Scotland Road to intercept my father's lorry, while he and his son remained with Neill Jnr's body. Daly and McCaughey succeeded in flagging down my father and a decision was taken to seek the assistance of Stephen Lanigan who agreed to store the arsenal in his private residence. It was an enormous risk for anyone to take, let alone an employee of the British civil service. Lanigan's wife, Mary, even assisted in unloading the weapons.

When the work was done, my father set off to Bootle to offer his condolences to Neill Kerr Snr and to discuss what should be done with the gun used in the accidental shooting of his son.

"I suggested to him that it might be better to hand up the revolver to the police as by doing so it would throw off suspicion," my father explained. "[Neill] walked up and down the floor and didn't answer me for at least five minutes, and then he turned towards me and these were his words: *Henry, if Neill lived they would never get his revolver and they'll never get it from me. He is gone, but if the three of them were gone the work must go ahead.*"

It was an extraordinary statement for any father to make, let alone one who had just lost his son, and it underlined Kerr's unshakeable commitment to the cause of Irish independence. The police were duly told that Neill Kerr Jnr had died from a self-inflicted gunshot wound and his body was immediately sent back to Dublin for burial with full military honours, the Irish Volunteers providing an impressive guard of honour when the remains arrived at Dublin Port. The revolver that killed him was later sent back to Ireland to be used in the War of Independence.

Even in old age, my father still marvelled at the bravery and sacrifice of old Neill Kerr.

"The spirit and determination of that man I shall never forget," he remarked in an article in 1964. "It was Neill Kerr and men like him in their day who laid the foundation that the fight for freedom was afterwards built on."

No wonder Neill Kerr was the Big Man's idol.

CHAPTER 8

Red-hot rebels

G LASGOW was the command centre of the IRA's gunrunning operations in Scotland, but there were very active cells in other parts of the country too. In Edinburgh, businessman Frank Gordon and his wife offered a safe house to my father, Joe Vize and the many other Volunteers who travelled from Glasgow and other parts of Scotland to either collect or deliver weapons. Like Jean Quinn, Gordon owned a second-hand furniture shop, which provided a useful cover for the IRA's activities.

"Mrs Gordon was a great worker for the movement," recalled Seán Healy. "She was either Irish-born or of Irish descent and intensely patriotic, and would keep any 'stuff' when needed to.

"Her husband was an ex-soldier, having served in the First World War and was invaluable for getting reliable contacts, even among serving soldiers who would hand rifles or anything that they could lay their hands on over the wall for money for drink."

Vize made good use of his old colleagues in the shipping industry and paid members of boat crews sailing out of the port of Leith to smuggle weapons back from Hamburg. One of the IRA's most important contacts was the captain of a German ship, which docked at Leith once every fortnight.

"The captain would bring 12 to 15 Parabellums or 'Peter-the-Painters' and ammunition [on] each trip," recalled Joseph Booker. "He would contact a barber [who] in turn contacted Mr Gordon, who although not a Volunteer was very friendly and used to buy guns for us whenever he got a chance.

"Mr Gordon would send us a telegram when the ship had arrived. We were never allowed to have any direct contact with the captain or go near the ship. The arms were delivered by members of the crew to the barber's shop and collected by Mr Gordon.

"At Gordon's house, we oiled and greased the guns and packed them in suitcases ready for dispatch to Liverpool."

The IRA paid sailors to smuggle weapons from Hamburg to the Port of Leith, Edinburgh.

Frank Gordon's assistance was critical because IRA sympathisers were thin on the ground in Edinburgh, as Seán Healy discovered.

"Early in 1920, the Edinburgh branch of Sinn Féin decided to hold a monster meeting in the Usher Hall, the largest in that city, and invited Arthur Griffith, Eoin MacNeill and Liam Sears to speak at it.

"I'm afraid it wasn't a great success. Compared to Glasgow and other cities, there wasn't a very big Irish population in Edinburgh. Neither were they very patriotic, with the result that the hall was only half-filled. I've seen lots more enthusiastic meetings in my time despite the fact that the then Bishop of Edinburgh presided."

Joe Vize formed the Scottish IRA's 3rd Battalion in Edinburgh in early 1920 and its membership was drawn from a wide area, including Falkirk and Denny. Henry O'Hagan said the Volunteers were happy to accept assistance from people with no historic ties to Ireland, including two Italian brothers who owned a café in Falkirk.

In his statement to the Bureau of Military History, O'Hagan also listed eight members of the Falkirk branch of Cumann na mBan who were all born in Scotland, proving that many native Scots were willing to play their part in the fight for Irish freedom.

The Bishop of Edinburgh's presence at the Sinn Féin rally shows there was support from the Catholic Church in Scotland. Indeed, several priests were involved in the gun-smuggling expeditions, including Galway native Fr John Fahy who was – in the words of Seán Healy – 'a red-hot rebel' and 'game for anything'.

Fr Fahy was a curate in Dundee where the IRA's commanding officer was Sean O'Doherty, who lived with his widowed mother and provided a safe house to the visiting Glasgow Volunteers, including my father with whom he became very good friends. O'Doherty was assisted by Lena McDonald, a member of Cumann na mBan and a tireless advocate for the republican cause.

"Lena lived over an antique shop with her widowed mother and sister Cathy," recalled Seán Healy, "and their house was the unofficial HQ of the Dundee lads…

"The antique shop was run by the mother and Cathy, and right across the road was a grocery and confectionery business run by Lena. It was in the back of the grocery shop that munitions bought by the lads were hidden."

Dozens of rifles and revolvers passed through Lena's hands between 1918 and 1921 and she took two trips to Glasgow every week to deliver the weapons to Jean Quinn. Lena told the Army Pensions Board that her mother often provided the financial resources to pay for the weapons, which were acquired through pawnbrokers and soldiers in Dundee's military barracks. Among Lena's most trusted confidants was Fr Fahy, who regularly attended at the family shop where he helped to package the weapons for dispatch to Glasgow.

Another priest, Fr Robert Scott, was heavily involved with the Falkirk IRA Company, which had about 100 members by 1920.

"The [Volunteers] were very useful for procuring gelignite," recalled Henry O'Hagan. "I do not think it cost the IRA more than £5 for the stuff. These men procured it themselves as the majority were miners."

In the town of Paisley, near Glasgow, Mary Brannick and her husband William Gore worked tirelessly for the republican cause and gave invaluable assistance to my father. William Gore and his wife were members of the IRB and Cumann na mBan respectively and were trusted to store weapons when necessary.

"Mary Brannick's home was in constant use as a dump and was ever at the disposal of army officers," noted Joseph Booker.

Charlie Strickland recalled visiting the Gores' house on many occasions in the company of my father to collect weapons for transfer to Liverpool. The Gores, like so many others, were taking a huge risk because the police were becoming increasingly vigilant by the summer of 1920 and were starting to identify some of Joe Vize's key men. Joe Booker came under scrutiny while staying with the merchant James Chambers at Bishop Street in Glasgow.

"While I was staying with Mr Chambers, I was raided frequently and always on a Sunday morning, but no arms or ammunition were ever discovered," he recalled. "Chief Detective Noble knew very well I was dealing with arms but could not get any evidence and he could not directly associate me with the IRA as I did not attend parades and made sure not to have any arms in place for any length of time."

Chambers' coal merchants' yard at Dorset Street was another of the central dumps for the IRA and proved a very secure location.

"Chambers evidently wasn't suspected as he was never questioned about his own activities, nor were there any raids on his business premises," recalled Booker. "Although Chambers was not in the Volunteers, he helped the movement in many ways. He often removed arms from his private house in 39 Bishop Street to the dump. For a while, I occupied the upper part of his private house where I used to bring some of the arms I had collected. The short arms I collected were usually brought to the dump in paper parcels and shopping bags. The rifles were dismantled and generally carried in sacks."

One of the first decisions my father made after becoming the IRA's Director of Purchasing in Scotland was to seek authorisation from GHQ for the purchase of a lorry that could be used to transport the ever-increasing volumes of 'war material' to Liverpool.

"The quantities increased so rapidly that the old method of transport by rail became obsolete and I had to ask Headquarters in Dublin to supply me with motor transport," he recalled. "On receipt of my application, this request was granted without delay."

In September 1920, Joe Furlong was dispatched from GHQ with £1,000 to fund the acquisition of a lorry and to buy more weapons. Robert McErlane, an IRA sympathiser in Glasgow, purchased the lorry on behalf of my father and it was registered in the name of Bernard McCabe, a Cavan-born shopkeeper who owned four stores in Glasgow, including two at Duke Street in the heart of Parkhead on the city's east side.

McCabe was an intriguing character because he was a successful, self-made businessman who had a lot to lose by becoming involved in the struggle for Irish independence. Aged 35, the Cavan native enjoyed a prosperous World War I by importing large quantities of eggs and butter from Ireland, and was often the only provision merchant in Glasgow to have these scarce products during the war years. At one stage, he had 7,000 rationed customers in a single shop and was doing so well he spent several hundred pounds on the purchase of war bonds, an act of patriotism that really put him beyond the suspicion of the authorities. Indeed, the only time the shopkeeper came to adverse attention was when he sold margarine as butter!

The city of Glasgow as my father would have known it in the early 1920s.

On September 23, 1920, my father asked Robert McErlane to purchase a high-sided 20 horse-power Fiat lorry from the Glasgow firm, Ross & Christie. My father paid for the vehicle in cash, and unusually for a gunrunner, insisted on getting a receipt, which was duly sent back to GHQ in Dublin.

There are, of course, good reasons for not keeping receipts when smuggling deadly weapons and that little piece of paper would come back to haunt Henry Coyle.

Bernard McCabe also gave my father permission to use another vehicle – an old and notoriously unreliable Austin that became affectionately known among the IRA Volunteers in Scotland and England as 'The Sinn Féin Motorcar'. I am not sure whether McCabe acquired the vehicle solely for my father's gunrunning activities, but if he did he must have had a good sense of humour because the Austin was green in colour, just perfect for an Irish rebel!

The Sinn Féin Motorcar (registration number SN 1385) traversed the highways and byways of Scotland in the autumn of 1920 with my father at the wheel and young Charlie Strickland in the passenger seat. One day they might be with the Gordons in Edinburgh and the next they'd be at Seán O'Doherty's in Dundee or Mary Brannick's in Paisley.

Access to a motorcar changed the way the IRA moved weapons because they could now retain large quantities at central dumps for dispatch in bulk to

Liverpool. Denis Fitzpatrick and Henry O'Hagan brought small arms, explosives and detonators to Seán McGovern's house at Larne Street in Edinburgh 'on numerous occasions' where the material would be stored until my father and Charlie arrived. McGovern, a cousin of 1916 leader Seán MacDiarmada, operated the main weapons dump for the IRA in Edinburgh.

"It was arranged that the stuff I collected in the mining district should be brought to Edinburgh," Fitzpatrick told the Army Pensions Board. "I brought the stuff to Edinburgh and dumped it with McGovern. The stuff was collected by car by Henry Coyle who brought it to Glasgow."

Patrick (Paddy) Thompson, who was the quartermaster of the IRA 3rd Battalion, told the Army Pensions Board that he met my father in Edinburgh 'on many occasions' and gave him guns and explosives. The green Austin also made numerous trips to the home of Michael Burke at No 2, Scott Street, Motherwell, which was the IRA's 'principal dump in Lanarkshire', according to GHQ representative P.J. Clinton.

"Most of the munitions sent from Scotland to Ireland via Liverpool were sorted out and packed by Burke, his wife and his elderly father-in-law," recalled Clinton in 1927.

Patrick Mills said there could be four or five men arriving at Burke's house every day. Indeed, when applying for an IRA pension, Burke recalled an incident that perfectly illustrated the risks involved.

"Two men arrived from Liverpool to take away two bags of rifles. I had only one bag packed and it was in Blantyre. I took one man to Blantyre and left him with the bag. I came back to Motherwell and packed a handbag of explosives and other material for the second man.

"When we went to catch the train, the Orange procession was in Mary Street, so I had to break through the procession with the material, which I did. Vize was standing looking on."

Little did the marching Orangemen think that an Irish rebel was walking through their ranks carrying a bag of explosives! Mick Burke was a member of an IRA committee that took responsibility for the acquisition of weapons in Motherwell.

"The purpose was to provide money for the purchase of arms by any member of the Volunteers who was in a position to do so," recalled Patrick Mills, who was also on the committee, "and to co-ordinate the purchase and dispatch of arms and ammunition through the proper channels. This led to much better organisation. The members of the purchasing committee had the funds and authority to purchase arms. £3-10 was the price fixed for a revolver and £4-10 for an automatic."

GHQ provided the money for the purchase of arms and several thousand pounds passed through my father's hands in the autumn of 1920. Joe Furlong brought money from Dublin in September and Charlie Strickland was sent across to collect more cash in October as the amount of 'war material' going to Ireland increased dramatically. The availability of a car and a lorry meant it was now a lot easier to move weapons in the dead of night when there were fewer prying eyes.

It was only when I started researching this book that I came to realise the vast network of Volunteers – brave men and women – who assisted my father in Scotland during that critical period. It would be impossible to list them all but I have tried to include as many names as I can because these people went unrecorded in Irish history. We know all about the brave men who *fired* the guns during the War of Independence but what about the equally courageous men and women who *acquired* those weapons in Scotland and England, often at huge personal cost to them and their families. Some of the Scottish Volunteers paid for these weapons out of their own meagre resources, others gave up their jobs to focus solely on gunrunning and all of them put their liberty at risk by engaging in such illegal activities. When things started to go wrong in Scotland, many of those who assisted my father ended up in jail or lost their jobs.

They are Ireland's forgotten heroes and it is about time we started remembering and honouring them.

CHAPTER 9

The Sinn Féin Motorcar

ONE evening in late October 1920, Paddy Daly found himself seated beside a fire in a small flat in Glasgow with a large sack of gelignite at his feet. Neill Kerr had instructed the young Offaly man to guide a lorry of 'war material' from Glasgow to a particular address in Liverpool.

The lorry was, of course, the high-backed Fiat purchased a month earlier and the person behind the wheel was my father – a man who Daly later described as 'not a very expert motor driver'.

I think Paddy Daly was being generous. My father's driving skills – such as they were – had been acquired 'on the job' because there weren't too many cars where he came from. In fact, there weren't too many cars around Geesala when I was growing up, let alone in the early 1900s.

One of the main sources of weapons for the IRA were the Scottish Territorial (Reserve) Army's network of drill halls, which were located in almost every town and village.

"I was on several raids with the Glasgow lads," noted Seán Healy. "They specialised in raiding Territorial halls where Lee Metford rifles were often stored for drilling purposes…"

There was minimal security at these halls – usually just a caretaker – so it was easy to enter them late at night, unlike military barracks where the risk of an armed confrontation was much greater. But success was not always guaranteed.

"I felt terribly sorry for Henry [Coyle] on one occasion," recalled Seán Healy. "He got what he thought was most reliable information that there were at least 50 or 60 rifles in a Territorial Hall in Broxburn, about ten miles outside Edinburgh, which was only looked after by a caretaker and his wife.

"He called to me one morning to tell me about it and to ask me if I would care to come along. I immediately said I would. There were six other lads there, making eight in all. He thought that should be sufficient for the job.

"That night we arrived at the Territorial Hall about 1am. It was a short distance outside the village and there was nobody around at that time. Coyle took three men with him and left me in charge of the other three. They got in without much trouble and without disturbing the caretaker. But a quarter of an hour later they came out empty-handed. Not a single solitary rifle did they find and they went over the place thoroughly.

"Coyle was terribly disappointed as GHQ had arranged for a lorry from Liverpool to meet him at Newcastle to take the stuff.

"It was coming up for dawn when we got back to Glasgow, where we left Henry who had to carry on to Newcastle anyway and tell his tale of woe to the Liverpool man. Luckily, that sort of thing didn't often happen."

My father participated in several successful raids on Territorial halls, especially after purchasing the motor lorry, which made it a lot easier to remove large cachés of weapons.

"It was a big improvement on the handcart anyway!" noted Seán Healy. "It also came in handy for taking the lads on raids if they had to go any distance."

On October 27, my father took charge of a large group of Volunteers during a raid on the Territorial drill hall in Bothwell, a village about ten miles south-east of Glasgow and three miles from Motherwell. Michael Burke and the other members of the IRA Coy in Motherwell were centrally involved in planning the elaborate operation, which was expected to yield a significant quantity of weapons.

"I was in charge of 50 men as the carrying party," Burke recalled. "The arrangement was that when the lorry was half-loaded, I was to place a man in charge of the carrying party. I was to proceed to Overtown with the half-loaded lorry where I had about 20 men lying there with a large consignment of revolvers, explosives, ammunition and other war material."

My father planned to drive the fully-laden lorry back to Glasgow where he would collect Paddy Daly, who was to accompany him on the long journey to Liverpool and direct him to a storage unit, which was located in a 'respectable residential area' in the city. The level of meticulous preparation suggests this was going to be one of the largest consignments of 'war material' the IRA had smuggled out of Scotland. One of the raiding party, Patrick Mills, told the Bureau of Military History that the raid itself was cleverly planned and perfectly executed.

"Two Volunteers, one with a Scottish accent, were dressed up in Lanarkshire Constabulary uniforms [newspaper reports said the uniforms were belonging to the RIC]," he explained. "These two men knocked on the door and when the caretaker asked who was there, they replied 'Constabulary on duty'. When he opened the door a little and saw the uniforms, he was taken off guard and admitted them.

"The party then seized the caretaker, tied him up and carried off 38 rifles and bayonets, which were put into a small lorry and driven away by Henry Coyle. The lorry was just been driven away when I heard a shot."

Mills rushed to a nearby field where several Volunteers were on lookout.

"They pointed the position where the shot was fired. I rushed to the place, which was a gateway where two other men were on guard and saw a policeman lying on the ground with a man standing over him and about to fire another shot."

Andy Fagan was one of the Volunteers to exchange shots with the police officer, a man named Alex McKay who had arrived on the scene with a colleague after receiving a most unlikely tip-off. McKay was seriously injured in the incident but made a full recovery.

"It was an unforeseen accident [that] happened, something we had not taken into account," explained Fagan. "There was an unofficial miners' strike on at the time and it was becoming pretty ugly, and there was a Masonic meeting held [in Bothwell]. This meeting was called at a time in which it would raise no suspicion with a view to breaking up this affair. That same night we had the raid on the Territorial Hall.

"This Masonic meeting was just dispersing as we collected for the raid at various points and they saw one or two of the chaps and were suspicious of them. I don't mean that they knew it was a raid but Motherwell is a very aristocratic place and it might have been a burglary, so two of them went back and informed the police and the police came and attempted to arrest some of our fellows."

On hearing the gunshots, my father headed straight for Glasgow, leaving the other half of his intended cargo ten miles away in Overtown where Michael Burke had instructed his party of Volunteers to wait until the lorry arrived. In fact, Burke wasn't able get to Overtown either.

"I got home about 3am," he recalled. "I was not fit to walk to Overtown to give instructions to the men I had there all night. The men put the material in a place of safety for the day."

Mills instructed the Volunteers to 'scatter', warning them to keep to the fields and avoid the roads at all costs.

"The warning was not heeded by two men who were caught walking along the open road, armed with revolvers," he recalled.

Another four men were arrested in follow-up searches of the area. Their capture was a setback to the IRA's operations in Scotland but the key personnel – my father, Mills, Burke and Fagan – all made their escape and the authorities

The village of Bothwell in Lanarkshire was the scene of a dramatic shooting in October 1920 when a party of IRA volunteers, including my father, raided the local Territorial Hall.

were unable to trace them to the 'Bothwell incident', as it became known in the Scottish press. However, the shooting – and serious wounding – of a police officer put the IRA's activities under the sort of intense scrutiny that made it increasingly difficult to acquire and transport cachés of guns, ammunition and explosives.

Not surprisingly, my father abandoned his original plan to drive straight to Liverpool after the raid in Bothwell. Instead, he emptied the rifles at one of the central dumps in Glasgow, returned the vehicle to Robert McErlane's garage, where it was usually stored, and decided to let the dust settle for a few days. Paddy Daly was ordered to remain in the small flat and await further instructions. Later that week, Daly was told to prepare for a nighttime journey to Liverpool, but this time there would be no lorry involved. Instead, Daly was to take a ride in the now famous 'Sinn Féin Motorcar'.

"On the night of our departure for Liverpool I awaited [Coyle's] arrival in a small flat sitting on a couch beside a coal fire with a large sack of gelignite beside me," he recalled. "Eventually the car arrived and we loaded up. It was an old Austin with a hood."

As usual, my father was in the company of his trusted lieutenant Charlie Strickland, but the duo was ill-prepared for another passenger, having tightly packed the car with 'war material'.

"The back of the car was packed up to the level of the top of the front seat," recalled Daly. "One of us was forced to recline on the top of this load at the back and it was a most uncomfortable position, but we changed around as we proceeded on the journey."

It was a voyage like no other. The Austin broke down about 20 miles outside Glasgow and the three men were forced to spend the night at the roadside until a mechanic could be procured at daylight.

"While we stood on the roadside, he did whatever was necessary and drove the car up and down the road but apparently didn't look under the rug behind him where our cargo was concealed," Daly recalled. "We were all armed with guns."

THE BOTHWELL OUTRAGE.

R.I.C. Overcoats Discovered.

Six men have been arrested in connection with the shooting of a policeman at Bothwell in the early hours of Thursday morning, and it is probable the others will be taken into custody. The Lanarkshire police authorities are satisfied that Constable Mackey, who was wounded, and his comrade, Constable Gray, were the means of frustrating a raid by Sinn Feiners on the Territorial Drill Hall in the hope of obtaining arms, although it is now stated that there were no arms on the premises, the armoury not having been replenished since the war. It is believed that the raiders reached Bothwell in a motor char-a-banc, which the police are endeavouring to trace.

In the course of their search, yesterday the police discovered a number of R.I.C. overcoats believed to have been stolen in Ireland.

VICTIM OF SINN FEIN.

The incident in Bothwell made headlines on both sides of the Irish Sea. This report appeared in the *Belfast Telegraph* on October 29, 1920.

The intrepid trio resumed their journey but suffered another setback when the Austin's gearbox began to emit smoke while passing through Carlisle. Fortunately, they were able to locate a mechanic and the problem was quickly resolved, but the car's reliability was not the only concern. Paddy Daly was also beginning to have grave reservations about the motoring skills of the man behind the wheel.

"Passing through Cumberland Mountains, Coyle managed to get into a rut on the mountain road. The car wobbled very much. I became so alarmed that I made a grab at the wheel but fortunately we didn't go off the road."

By now, the men had been travelling for over 20 hours, and tempers (and nerves) were frayed, so I can only imagine the reaction when the Sinn Féin Motorcar conked out for a third time.

"Our next spot of bother occurred in Preston when the lighting system failed. This included the horn," recalled Daly. "Luckily, the shops weren't all closed so we purchased a policeman's whistle for the driver and two bicycle lamps. The man seated in front beside the driver held out a bicycle lamp as well as he could and the man on the top of the load at the back of the car was able to hold one out at the rear as a further protection. This lighting system worked very effectively. As we travelled through Liverpool a policeman whistled

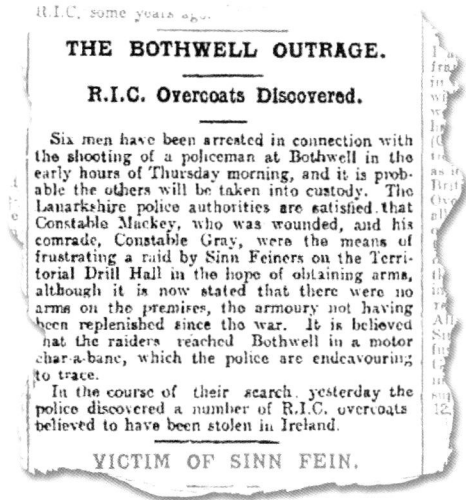

us up but we didn't stop and we arrived safely at our destination approximately 24 hours from the time we had set out from Glasgow."

When I first encountered Paddy Daly's colourful description of his journey from Glasgow to Liverpool with my father I could hardly believe it. The man I knew – a quiet and sensible father – is unrecognisable from the desperado portrayed in Paddy Daly's evocative account of that audacious journey across 'enemy country' at the height of the War of Independence.

So what was it that made a man from a little village in Mayo drive from Glasgow to Liverpool in a car laden to the roof with a deadly cargo of guns and gelignite? My only explanation is that Henry Coyle, like so many young Irish men and women of that era, had a fierce, unwavering determination to win independence for their country and was willing to go to extraordinary lengths to achieve that aim. By late October 1920, the Black and Tans were engaging in arson attacks in towns and villages across Ireland, so men like my father didn't need much motivation to do what they were doing. If Henry Coyle was a desperado it was because he lived in desperate times, and we should all be grateful we have never had to make the kind of choices he was forced to make as a young man.

The only pity is that he didn't have a more reliable car because that old green Austin caused all manner of trouble; indeed, the fabled Sinn Féin Motorcar seemed as rebellious as the freedom fighter steering it, so perhaps they were well suited to each other!

CHAPTER 10

Mamie and the eggs

W HILE my father was acquiring large quantities of weapons in Glasgow, it was a very different story back home in Mayo where his old colleagues in the Erris Volunteers were desperate to get their hands on some guns.

The need for proper weapons became very apparent in the late summer of 1920 when the notorious Black and Tans made their first appearance in Mayo. Up to then, the county had been relatively quiet, but the shooting of a popular RIC sergeant, Thomas Robert Armstrong, on the streets of Ballina in mid-July caused considerable shock, as did the killing of an RIC Constable Pierce Doogue during an altercation at the fair in Belmullet in June. The Irish Volunteers in Mayo also suffered their first casualty that summer when John Joe Kellaghan sustained fatal burns in an attack on the temporary RIC barracks in Shrule in the south of the county.

With armed struggle now inevitable, IRA units all over the country were doing whatever they could to get their hands on weapons. Volunteers in Erris carried out raids on British military huts at Binghamstown, Elly Bay and Tarmon during June and July, but only managed to seize four revolvers.

In August, members of the Bangor Erris IRA Coy raided Bangor Lodge, a shooting lodge with historic ties to the Bingham family, the notorious landlord dynasty in Mayo.

"The two occupants, who held high rank in the British Army, refused to give up their arms," recalled James Kilroy in a submission to the Bureau of Military History. "Anthony Barrett, who was O/C of the Bangor Coy, ordered his men to open fire. After shots were exchanged, the two men surrendered. There were two revolvers and one shotgun captured."

On August 29, a party of Barhauve Volunteers attacked the Coastguard Station in Ballyglass for the dual purpose of seizing weapons and destroying the building.

Bangor Lodge was the scene of an IRA raid during the War of Independence.

"The Company under the command of Capt James Dixon was divided into four sections," explained James Kilroy. "A section of six men were placed on outpost duty. Two sections comprising 15 men under arms were placed in positions to attack the station from front and rear, and another section commandeered in the neighbourhood tins of paraffin for setting fire to the station.

"The sections at the front and rear got within close range. They fired through the windows and demanded surrender. After an exchange of shots, the occupants surrendered and handed up their arms, which consisted of three revolvers, a box of ammunition and a field glass.

"The three occupants were then taken out and placed under guard and the whole building searched but nothing of any military value was found."

It was a disappointing yield for such a dangerous mission, and to make matters worse, the Volunteers were ambushed on their way home.

"About 500 yards from the station shots rang out," recalled Kilroy. "We found ourselves attacked by a strong force of RIC and auxiliaries who kept up an intensive fire from several points. The armed men took cover and returned the fire to cover off the retreat. All the ammunition we had was used to hold up the enemy while covering off the retreat. In retreat, two of our men were captured."

Kilroy's detailed description of the attack on Ballyglass Coastguard Station is indicative of the challenges faced by companies of brave Volunteers the length and breadth of Ireland. In this instance, the Barhauve Company had lost two men and exhausted its supply of ammunition – and all for the sake of three revolvers.

The raid on the coastguard station was an example of the Erris Volunteers' desperation to get their hands on the guns that would allow them to properly take the fight to the British. Nothing was too risky for them, as the founder of the Shraigh Volunteers, Michael Henry, later explained to the Bureau of Military History when describing another incident during the War of Independence.

"The lorries of Tommies came from Castlebar, including a machine-gun section. Paddy Keane, John Heston and I raised the swing-bridge at Belmullet after the lorries crossed, with a view to their isolation. The parish priest came forward and compelled us leave. I suppose our act was foolhardy, but we were desperate for arms."

The Shraigh Volunteers had been trying to source weapons from Scotland before my father's departure in 1919. Michael Henry's father was based in Glasgow and worked as an agent for the Scottish farmers that employed seasonal labourers from Erris each summer.

"Some of us were getting impatient for arms, and following a Company staff meeting it was decided that I go to Scotland and procure some," Michael Henry recalled. "There was no fund, but I was hoping my father would help us out. Through him I contacted two men in the Edinburgh area… I collected four revolvers, some gelignite and detonators."

Henry packed the revolvers and gelignite into 'a good second-hand suitcase' and put the detonators in his waistcoat pockets.

"I didn't know as much of the danger of these [detonators] then as I did know in later years," he told the Bureau, with a fair degree of understatement. He was, in fact, a ticking timebomb as he set off for Erris, travelling via Belfast where he was accosted by a policemen at the docks in the early morning.

"How far are you going?" the constable asked.

"Enniskillen."

"You wouldn't be going to Belmullet?"

"Not tonight," replied Henry, trying to appear relaxed.

"My hair stood on end," he recalled, "but [the constable] passed on. He must have known me, but didn't connect me with carrying contraband."

Men like Michael Henry and James Kilroy were well aware of my father's gunrunning activities for GHQ, so it was no surprise they sought his assistance that autumn.

"On or about October 20, 1920, the Shraigh Coy collected about £200 for purchase of arms," noted Kilroy. "Arms were later imported from Glasgow through Henry Coyle."

It was some achievement in 1920 to collect £200 (about €13,000 in today's money) in a poor area like Erris. In the Military Archives, the men who

collected the money are listed as Michael and James Henry, Shraigh, Bunnahowen; Patrick and Michael Leneghan, Muingmore, Geesala; John Donohoe, Lakefield, Bunnahowen; Peter Barrett, Shraigh, Bunnahowen; and John Gaughan, Bunnawilliam, Geesala. I believe it is important to list those names because so many of these ordinary footsoldiers of the War of Independence have been forgotten. What sacrifices did these men have to make to gather £200 at a time when there was so much deprivation in Erris?

It wasn't the first time they had collected money either. Michael Henry said the Erris Volunteers were asked to make a contribution to an arms fund established by the Mayo IRA brigade in the autumn of 1920. They collected

My aunt Mamie walked across Doolough Strand with a basket containing the revolvers my father had brought back to Ireland for the Shraigh Volunteers. Picture: Evita Coyle

£288 and gave it to brigade headquarters in West Mayo, which pooled the money with other contributions from the three other IRA brigades around the county to fund a gunrunning expedition to England. Dick Walsh, one of the most senior Volunteers in Mayo, was selected to purchase the weapons. Walsh, a most honourable man, acquired a lot of guns and had them shipped back to Dublin, but they never made it as far as Mayo because GHQ seized them for use in Munster where the fighting was at its most intense.

The debacle involving Dick Walsh's shipment of arms may have been the reason why my father decided to embark on a most dangerous mission in early November 1920 when he personally delivered a small consignment of revolvers and ammunition to his old comrades in Erris. GHQ must have sanctioned the trip, and while I have no documentary evidence of a meeting between my father and Michael Collins, it seems highly probable their paths crossed that November.

By then, GHQ was considering a major military campaign in England involving high-profile assassinations, arson attacks and bombings. In his statement to the Army Pensions Board, Eamonn Mooney says my father told him there were plans to establish an 'active service unit' in Scotland. The conversation with Mooney occurred only weeks after my father's return from Ireland, which suggests he had discussed the plans with GHQ.

The British authorities were not aware of the full extent of my father's gun-smuggling activities, but evidence produced in a court in Liverpool in 1921 makes it clear he was a marked man during that visit to Ireland. The RIC in Erris were certainly suspicious of him and I can only imagine how tense and terrifying that period must have been for his parents and siblings, especially when the Black and Tans embarked on a sinister campaign of reprisals against the families of known IRA operatives.

My grandparents were very supportive of my father's involvement in the independence struggle, so it was no surprise that he brought the caché of revolvers to the family home in Dooyork. The next morning the revolvers were wrapped in cloth, placed in the bottom of a wicker basket and carefully covered over with freshly laid eggs. The intention was to deliver the weapons to the Kerrigan home in Shraigh, and my aunt Mary (better known as 'Mamie'), then just 20 years of age, was given the task of carrying the basket. She set off alone, walking at a brisk pace, but stopping every now and then to switch the heavy load from one arm to the other. Shortly into her journey, Mamie heard the unmistakable clip-clop of horseshoes, and looking over her shoulder, saw the local RIC sergeant approaching. With heart thumping in her chest, she stepped aside to let the horse and trap pass, but instead the sergeant pulled up.

"Are you going into the village, Ms Coyle?" he asked.

"I am sergeant."

"Would you like a lift?"

How was Mamie supposed to answer a question like that? If she refused, the sergeant's suspicions would be immediately aroused, but if she agreed he would surely offer to assist her as she climbed onto the trap… and if he picked up that basket then the game was up because not even the finest hen in Erris could lay eggs as heavy as the ones in Mamie's wicker basket! My aunt had to think – and think fast.

"Thank you sergeant, a lift would be great," she said, trying to remain as nonchalant as possible.

"Here, let me help you with the basket," said the sergeant, leaning down from the trap.

"No, no," Mamie replied firmly. "You might break the eggs and I'll get into fierce bother with my mother if those eggs are broken."

And with that, the bould Mamie clambered onto the trap, basket of eggs and all, and coolly sat down beside the unsuspecting sergeant. When they reached the turn-off for the strand, Mamie again insisted on taking the basket down from the trap and set off as quickly as she could for the beach where the tide was out, which meant she could walk across to Shraigh, free from any further nerve-wracking encounters with helpful RIC sergeants.

The revolvers were duly delivered to the Kerrigans and a relieved Mamie set off for Belmullet to meet her older brother and tell him the good news. Later that day, the sergeant learned that Henry Coyle was home from Scotland and had been spotted in Belmullet with his sister.

"I should have looked in that bloody basket," the sergeant told an RIC colleague. "There were more than eggs in it, that's for sure!"

Some 50 years later, Mamie could still recall every tiny detail of that November morning in 1920 when an RIC sergeant became the unwitting participant in an IRA gunrunning expedition. She also recounted a conversation with my father in which he poignantly revealed that he had desperately wanted to return to Ireland to see his mother. Perhaps my father knew the net was closing in on him and this visit might be the last opportunity he would get to spend time with his parents. As it turned out, that gunrunning expedition was indeed my father's final trip to Ireland for a considerable period. The next time Henry Coyle would set foot on Erris soil, Ireland had won its freedom – and he was being hailed as one of the local heroes of the valiant fight for national independence.

CHAPTER 11

Love in a time of war

UPON his return to Scotland, my father resumed where he left off. In early November, he and five other Volunteers, including Eamonn Mooney, raided a military drill hall at the Rutherglen Road in Glasgow.

"When [the] premises were raided and searched, no rifles or arms were found," recalled Mooney. "The raiding party then destroyed documents and records of a military nature."

The Volunteers also had their eye on an Orange Hall in the Cowcaddens district, near the centre of Glasgow, where it was suspected the Orange Order had some rifles stored. My father and John Carney were keen to get their hands on the guns but were also acutely aware that the hall was located across the road from a police station. Eamonn Mooney was one of the men instructed to raid the hall late on a November evening.

"I was ordered out with other men from 'B' Company – about 30 men – and when we got up there, Comdt Coyle and Comdt Carney were there and other officers. They went into the place and examined it, and found it would be very difficult to tackle the job with so many men around, and the police watching us. Whatever the reason was, they thought it better to leave it alone for a while."

Ten day later, my father returned to Cowcaddens with Charlie Strickland and three others, including Mooney.

"I was after coming back from an ordinary parade of 'B' Company and I found a message from my brother [Seán] and a man named Charlie Strickland to go down [to Cowcaddens] immediately and be armed," recalled Mooney. "When I got down there I found Coyle and Strickland, my brother and another man, and we went into the place."

Seán Mooney and Strickland stood guard while my father, Eamonn Mooney and a man named Duggan entered the hall.

"After searching around the place, we discovered rifles and boxes of ammunition under the stage or platform…" recalled Mooney "We had to break open the boxes, packing boxes where they kept their Orange sashes."

The men took away about half a dozen rifles and ammunition, and scrawled the words 'Commandeered by the Irish Republican Army' across a wall. Needless to say, the sashes were left in their boxes!

"We discovered that the [rifles] had been there from the time of Carson's Army, and they intended to use them for what purpose I do not know," Mooney remarked.

My father's cautious approach in raiding the Orange Hall in Cowcaddens may have been influenced by the Bothwell debacle, which had placed the IRA in Scotland under intense police scrutiny. About a week after the shooting of Constable McKay, Michael Burke's home in Motherwell was raided for the first time.

"The detectives told me to hand them 18 revolvers and five bayonets," Burke recalled. "I told them that was a rather tall order."

In fact, Burke had 18 revolvers and five bayonets buried in a tin trunk in the garden of an Irish Volunteer named Peter Quigley at Waterloo, Wishaw. These were the weapons my father had intended to collect in Overton on the night of the Bothwell raid.

"[The detectives] told me I was at Bothwell Drill Hall," Burke recalled. "I denied it. They told me I was the ringleader. I said someone was bluffing them. They asked me if I was a Sinn Féiner. I said 'yes and one of the best'!"

Burke held up under questioning but the detectives were clearly well informed and intended to keep him under surveillance, which meant his house was now out of bounds for my father.

"About two or three weeks after the Bothwell stunt," recalled Burke, "I received instructions from Michael Collins for me to be very careful when any raids were carried out and to have my house cleared because the authorities were going to jump on me first, no matter what was done in Scotland."

My father was in the advantageous position of having no fixed place of residence, even if he had been boarding with Kate and Thomas Lee in Glasgow since the start of 1920. He continued to masquerade as an insurance agent and even found time for a little romance. His girlfriend was a woman named Margaret Maxwell Ferrie, who lived at 34 Hillfoot Street, Dennistoun, just around the corner from the Lees' home at Todd Street. I have no idea how they met or whether Margaret was aware of my father's activities as an IRA gunrunner, but they quickly fell in love and she remained utterly loyal to him throughout the best and worst of times, and sadly, there would be more bad times than good in the years to come.

Margaret Maxwell Ferrie pictured in the spring of 1921, about a year after she met my father.

Margaret, or 'Madge' as she was better known, came from a respectable Glasgow family. Her late father had been a salesman for a spirits company and her older brother Daniel joined the Gordon Highlanders regiment of the British Army during World War I, meeting his death in France in March 1918.

The Ferries were a Catholic family and Madge's mother was originally Murphy, so there was obviously Irish ancestry in the blood, but whether they were sympathetic to the cause of Irish independence I do not know. They certainly were not implicated in any of my father's activities and I have no reason to believe they knew anything about his work, so it must have come as a huge shock when he was eventually arrested.

My father's constant travels throughout Scotland and the north of England meant his early courtship with Madge was much interrupted. He visited Liverpool at least once a week and also brought weapons to Manchester, accompanied by a brother of Manchester IRA Volunteer John McGallogly, who acted as a guide. These arms were possibly from the Bothwell raid.

"My brother was sent to Glasgow to escort to Manchester a lorry load of arms and ammunition on the track of which the police in Glasgow had been rather active," McGallogly told the Bureau of Military History. "The load of stuff came to Manchester and caused consternation in several houses where it was stored, until finally we hired a garage attached to a maternity home into which we dumped it without the knowledge of the proprietors."

Patrick O'Donoghue, who was the commanding officer of the Volunteers in the Manchester area, told the Bureau of Military History that the Glasgow IRA used the garage in Manchester 'from time to time'. My father also recalled travelling as far south as London to collect weapons, and I suspect he'd have happily gone the whole way to the cliffs of Dover if he thought there might be a few rifles to be got, although I am not sure the Sinn Féin Motorcar would have made it that far!

Prior to the autumn of 1920, the principal role of the Irish Volunteers in England and Scotland was the acquisition of weapons, and they were urged to be cautious and to avoid engaging in activities that might attract too much public attention. But that strategy was abandoned once the Black and Tans began its campaign of reprisals in Ireland.

"Following the deliberate burnings by the Auxiliaries, the Army Executive decided that the Volunteers in the English cities should adopt retaliatory measures in their areas," explained Patrick O'Donoghue. "I was summoned to a meeting in Dublin at which Michael Collins was present. A general discussion took place on the question of activities to be carried out in Manchester and other cities in England where Volunteer units existed. It was felt that the people in England should be made conscious of what the people in Ireland were suffering as regards depredations carried out by the Crown Forces. And it was definitely understood that any burnings the IRA might carry out… would not be solely for the purpose of reprisals but merely to bring home to the British people the sufferings and conditions to which the Irish people were being subjected by their police and soldiers."

The Volunteers in Manchester identified two key targets – the city's electrical power station and the waterworks – and began to lay the groundwork for their planned attacks.

"I returned [from Dublin] accompanied by Mr Cripps, a chemist who understood electrical construction and the power house system," explained O'Donoghue. "We succeeded in getting him to go through the electrical power house as a visitor. He reported that it was possible to put this plant out of action by the use of a certain amount of explosive material."

O'Donoghue and John McGallogly also inspected the Manchester Ship Canal locks with a view to blowing them up, but 'Dublin did not favour the project', according to McGallogly. GHQ sent Rory O'Connor, the IRA's Director of Engineering, to Manchester to oversee plans for a series of major attacks in England, while my father, as the IRA's Director of Purchasing, was instructed to play a key role in sourcing the materials necessary for the proposed campaign.

O'Connor visited Liverpool where he met with the Kerrs and drew up an elaborate plan to blow up the city's dock gates.

"There were four main entrances into the Liverpool Docks," explained Hugh Early, a member of the Irish Volunteers in Liverpool who was familiar with the plans. "The water was kept at the necessary level in the Docks by large gates. At low water in the river, there would be a difference of 25 feet between the level of the water in the river and that of the docks. One gate might serve three or four docks.

"All the transocean-going vessels berthed in these docks. If the dock gates were blown out by explosives, it would mean a sudden drop of 25 feet or so in the water level of the docks, resulting in the grounding of the ships and the

A raid on the lodgings of IRA Chief of Staff Richard Mulcahy uncovered several documents linking my father to GHQ.

general entanglement of the vessels on breaking their moorings."

It was such an audacious and potentially calamitous act that the members of the IRA in Liverpool were not really sure of the consequences.

"It is hard to visualise really what would have happened," noted Early. "Some of [the ships] might even turn over on their side. At least it would have caused great confusion and damage and upset sailings and communications for a considerable time."

The plans for the attacks in Liverpool and Manchester were sent to Dublin where the IRA's Chief of Staff Richard Mulcahy was struggling to stay one step ahead of the British authorities. In the early morning of November 10, Mulcahy was lodging in the home of Professor Michael Hayes at South Circular Road when members of the British intelligence service burst through the front door. Still in his night attire, Mulcahy scrambled through a skylight and escaped, but the Chief of Staff left a treasure trove of documents in his wake, including the plans for the IRA campaign in Britain.

"Among the documents found was our plan for the destruction of the dock gates [in Liverpool]," recalled Hugh Early. "During the next few days, these plans were published in all the leading English newspapers, including the Liverpool papers. The British now placed a very strong guard on the Docks and that was the end of our proposition."

The dossier seized in Professor Hayes' house also included a receipt for the purchase of a motor lorry in Glasgow on September 23, 1920, and another receipt, signed by someone called 'H.P. Coyle' for £500 in cash that had been received from Major Joseph Furlong. There was now a very definite paper trail from Henry Coyle to GHQ, and those documents would prove crucial in any future criminal prosecution against my father.

The raid in Dublin marked the beginning of a hectic, tumultuous period in my father's life. The authorities now had 'H.P. Coyle' in their sights, but this Mayo freedom fighter was not going down without an almighty struggle. Henry Coyle still had a few powerful punches left to throw, and he and the many other brave Volunteers in Scotland and England intended to strike the British Empire where it hurt the most.

CHAPTER 12

'God send you luck in all of your adventures'

FIVE days after the raid on Richard Mulcahy's house, my father visited Liverpool to prepare for a new IRA operation in the city: the burning of cotton warehouses and timber yards adjacent to the docks.

"The cotton warehouses extended along the whole dockside convenient to the docks and separated from them by the dock wall," explained Paddy Daly. "They ran almost parallel to the docks [and] were tall buildings with narrow floors and had iron doors. And since Liverpool was, I think, then headquarters distribution centre of raw cotton, the warehouses were always fairly well stocked."

Entry to the warehouses could only be achieved by severing the sturdy locks on the wrought-iron doors, and one of my father's first tasks was to acquire 15 pairs of bolt-cutters. These were heavy tools measuring three feet in length that would also be used to cut the steel bands on the bales of cotton. In addition, my father needed to source a large quantity of paraffin oil, but was conscious that to do so on his own might attract suspicion, so he turned to the members of Cumann na mBan in Liverpool for assistance.

"Kathleen and Sheila Browne were sisters and natives of Cork," he recalled. "Kathleen was a member of the office staff of Hughes' Provision Stores [in Liverpool], and Sheila was a teacher. They bought almost all the paraffin that was used in burning the warehouses."

My father described the Browne siblings as two of the bravest women that Ireland ever produced, and they certainly performed their duties diligently in the days leading up to the burning of the warehouses. He drove them around Liverpool in the Sinn Féin Motorcar, stopping off at various provision stores to purchase cans of paraffin.

Inevitably, the car broke down and had to be repaired in a local garage. My father gave his name as 'John Daly' – a pseudonym he had used before –

On November 27, 1920, the IRA targeted more than a dozen six-storey cotton warehouses in the Liverpool docklands. My father played an important role in the daring operation.

and handed the receipt for the car repairs and another receipt for the purchase of 15 pairs of bolt-cutters to Neill Kerr, who retained both documents at 6 Florida Street, presumably with the intention of sending them to GHQ in Dublin. Once again, my father's desire to account for every penny of the IRA's money meant he was leaving an incriminating paper trail in his wake.

In a detailed account of the warehouse fires, Mick O'Leary says GHQ sent Rory O'Connor to Liverpool to oversee the operation, which was to be in retaliation for the recent burning of towns in Ireland. In O'Leary's native Sligo, the Black and Tans had rampaged through the town of Tubbercurry in late October, destroying several local businesses, including two co-operative creameries.

"Wholesale burnings were then taking place in Ireland," said O'Leary, "so that I am sure reprisals in England of a similar nature at this time would be considered very appropriate, as we believed 'an eye for an eye'."

O'Leary was introduced to O'Connor at a meeting of the Liverpool Volunteers in the basement of Moran's Men's Outfitters some days before the fires, which were scheduled to take place on Saturday night, November 27.

"[O'Connor] was very pleased to see that the Company had responded to a man and were ready to carry out the assignments given to them. From him we understood that similar operations were to take place in London and Manchester. He said he was going to Manchester and would be back to see us again before the fires."

Of course, Bloody Sunday occurred in Dublin on Sunday, November 21, so the timing of the fires a week later was very deliberate, although I think the Liverpool attack would have gone ahead regardless. However, the shooting dead of 14 innocent civilians at a GAA match in Croke Park only strengthened the resolve of men like Mick O'Leary and my father.

The targeting of 20 cotton warehouses and timber yards was a massive undertaking for the Liverpool Volunteers and involved dozens of men. Paddy Daly says the Volunteers were divided into groups of four or five men and were given the location of a warehouse in either Liverpool or Bootle.

"I cannot say how each party received detailed instructions regarding the job they were told to take, but in my case I was told to take a party of four or five men to a warehouse in Bootle. I was instructed to force an entrance by cutting the lock on the main door and then start the fire with the aid of paraffin oil. I should say the paraffin oil was collected by the Cumann na mBan some days previously and stored in their houses from which it was collected by the different groups."

Mick O'Leary recalled a meeting the night before the fires that was attended by many of the Volunteers who were due to take part, as well as Rory O'Connor.

"I asked him [O'Connor] what would be our position after the fires or how were we to act," recalled O'Leary. "He replied: 'Keep quiet for a fortnight and repeat similar operations.'

"I pointed out that some of us were well known to the police authorities and that I did not think we would be available in a fortnight's time, as perhaps the majority of us there that night would be under lock and key."

O'Leary suggested that the men start a second wave of fires on the same night because they might not get the opportunity to strike again.

"I thought we should start a second line of fires after the first line had got going… our object would be the big shops in the principal thoroughfares of the city and afterwards the outskirts. Then we should form a flying squad, continue our activities until arrest or perhaps laid to rest. To this, however, Rory would not agree."

O'Leary had mixed feelings about the attacks and wondered if they would be counterproductive.

"I knew that after the fires some of us would be arrested and that those arrests might do great harm, if not destroy, the [gun-running] work we were engaged in."

GHQ obviously felt the risk was worth the reward, and the warehouse fires went ahead as planned at 9pm on the following night.

"I cannot say why Saturday night was selected but I believe there was some very good reason for it," noted Paddy Daly. "Perhaps the strength of the police force might be reduced for weekends and that people in general would be relaxing on this night. There would be a little more drinking taking place on Saturday night."

There was also an Irish dance taking place at St Joseph's Hall on the Scotland Road and many of the Volunteers went there afterwards with the intention of using the céilí as an alibi when questioned by the police.

All of the leading personalities in the Liverpool Volunteers were involved in the fires, including Hugh Early who was instructed to set fire to a cotton warehouse at Effingham Street.

"I was accompanied by two other men, one of whom stayed at the door and the other man took up position at the corner of the street. We were armed with revolvers. We had bottles of paraffin, which were held for us by sympathisers in places nearby.

"I went upstairs to the top of the warehouse and set a couple of bales alight. I then came down and set five or six bales on the ground floor alight. I had to cut the bands on the bales with the bolt-cutters. Having set the bales alight, I made my escape."

Some 16 cotton warehouses and two timber yards were set alight along a seven-mile stretch of the Liverpool Docks from Seaforth to Gaston. It was a highly professional operation and the men left nothing to chance, setting fire to the six-storey buildings from the top down.

"The cotton was scattered as much as possible and saturated with paraffin oil," explained Paddy Daly. "This was done on several floors. It started from the top floor and each bale of scattered cotton was set alight. Our task was accomplished by the time we were leaving the place. And we got safely away before my particular warehouse was well alight."

Not everyone got on as well as Daly. Mick O'Leary and two other Volunteers, both from Mayo, had been tasked with setting fire to a cotton warehouse at Bank Hall, a cul-de-sac near a police station. One of the men, Tommy Moran, was attempting to gain entry to the building when two detectives accosted him at gunpoint. O'Leary exchanged gunshots with the detectives and the three Volunteers escaped, their night's work incomplete.

A far greater tragedy unfolded at Parliament Street where locals alerted the police after seeing a number of men using bolt-cutters to force open the doors of a cotton warehouse. The police quickly arrived on the scene and exchanged shots as the men attempted to flee. One of the bullets struck Daniel William Ward, a local teenager, who died instantly. It was the only life lost on that dramatic Saturday night in November 1920 when Ireland's War of

Independence came to Liverpool, but it was one life too many.

When I started to research this book more than 20 years ago, I went to Liverpool Library where I found a copy of *The Daily Mirror*, dated Tuesday, November 30, 1920, with a picture of a fresh-faced Daniel William Ward on the front page. Later that day, I visited his grave and said a prayer for the eternal repose of his soul. He was an innocent victim of a political conflict that had nothing to do with him and of which I am sure he knew nothing about. He came from a poor part of Liverpool and was just a working class boy with his whole life in front of him. Indeed, he was not unlike my father, and if circumstances were different on

Liverpool teenager Daniel William Ward lost his life on the night of the warehouse fires in November 1920. He was the innocent victim of a conflict not of his making. This picture appeared on the front page of *The Daily Mirror* two days after the fires.

that night, or many other nights in 1920, it could easily have been Henry Coyle lying in a lonely grave in Liverpool or Glasgow.

Irish independence came at a terrible price for some families and I believe it is just as important to remember an innocent victim like Daniel William Ward alongside the likes of the remarkable Browne sisters, forgotten heroines of that daring strike at the heart of the British empire.

"The work done by Irish men across the water was no small factor in bringing the members of the British government to their senses and it proved to them that the people in England and Scotland would have to bear the brunt of it," my father wrote in the early 1960s. "When I mentioned the work done by Irishmen over there, I should have included Irish women too, for they certainly done their part as well as the men."

I am sure my father was thinking of the Browne sisters when he wrote those lines, as well as women like Elizabeth Kerr, Kate Lee, Jean Gillespie, Mary Brannick, Lena McDonald, Mrs Gordon in Edinburgh and the many other members of Cumann na mBan who assisted in the IRA's activities in 1919-'20. My father grew up in an age when women weren't even trusted to vote, yet he had a great belief in equality and, in particular, education for women. He believed a woman could do a job as good as a man and his desire to see the members of Cumann na mBan receive due credit for their role in the Liverpool fires was typical of his way of thinking. He was very much ahead

of his time when it came to issues around gender equality and I think a lot of that had to do with his mother who was such a positive force in his life. As I mentioned earlier, she was an educated woman in an era when many of her contemporaries could not read or write.

On the week of the Liverpool fires, my father received a letter from his parents in which they expressed delight that their son was 'still at large' following his visit to Ireland. The letter, extracts from which were later produced as evidence against him, bore his father's name, but I have no doubt it was the work of his mother.

"We were very uneasy about you…"the letter stated. "If you are coming to Ireland be careful. God send you luck in all of your adventures."

That letter opened my eyes because I had often wondered whether my grandparents, whom I never knew, were even aware of the extent of my father's activities during the War of Independence. Not only were they aware, they fully approved of everything he was doing and were wishing him 'luck' in his 'adventures'. Now that was an Irish mother's blessing, if ever there was one, and my father certainly needed it in the days after the warehouse fires because one by one his IRA colleagues were being arrested and their homes searched. He could have been forgiven for lying low for a few weeks, but instead he decided to embark on another daring arms smuggling mission from Scotland – or 'adventure' as his mother might have called it!

The Sinn Féin Motorcar and its rebel driver were about to set off on one last eventful voyage for 'dear old Ireland'.

CHAPTER 13

'The police sent out the hue and cry'

IT didn't take long for the police in Liverpool to identify the perpetrators of the city's most devastating arson attack in living memory. The flames were still roaring into the night sky in Bootle when 16 detectives descended on Neill Kerr's home.

"Great destruction [was] done," recalled Elizabeth Kerr. "The floors were pulled up, beds torn, backs torn off pictures and chairs, sofas cut open, the cellar and yard were dug up in search of arms and other war material. Letters and papers that never could be replaced were taken…"

Among the items seized were a receipt for £4 from a garage in Liverpool for repairs to a green five-seat Austin car on November 15 and a second receipt for the purchase of 15 bolt-cutters. Crucially, however, a book containing a list of names that would have proved very useful to the police went undiscovered. Elizabeth gave it to IRA member Francis Hearty after the detectives left her home. The events of that dramatic evening remained etched in her memory years later.

"While [the] work of destruction was being done, I was held up by a detective with revolver cocked. When they finished their awful work, I was left with two young children and a wrecked home. My husband was one of the men arrested and taken away."

Seamus McCaughey was also arrested in Kerr's home, and among the others picked up later that night were Steve Lanigan and Tom Kerr, while Mick O'Leary, his brother Denis and several other Volunteers were arrested the following evening. By then, the inferno across seven miles of Liverpool's docklands had been brought under control, but not without significant destruction to several warehouses. Some 16 warehouses and two timber yards had been set alight and the damage to buildings and contents was estimated at over £1m, although it was later revised down to about half that figure. In its edition of Monday, November 29, the *Irish Independent* provided a vivid portrait of Liverpool's night of terror.

Rapid repetition of fire alarms was heard at the brigade headquarters from 8.30 onwards. By 9 o'clock, the whole of the staff and fire engines were in attendance at outbreaks…

At 2am, the huge buildings were burning fiercely, forming a spectacle visible from all parts of Liverpool, as well as from the Mersey in Cheshire… The police commandeered all the telephone wires, and every step possible was taken to prevent further outbreaks by concentrating police along the line of docks.

The Daily Mirror in England carried several photographs of the destruction in its edition of Tuesday, November 30, as well as a mugshot of Matthew Fowler, an IRA Volunteer from Co Meath who had just been charged with the murder of Daniel William Ward following his capture at the scene of the shooting. Despite receiving severe beatings at Parliament Street and in custody, Fowler refused to give his name to the police and became known in the press as 'No 87'.

I was not surprised to learn that the fires in Liverpool made headlines in Britain and Ireland, but what amazed me was that the incident also made *The New York Times*. Its front page of Monday, November 29, led with the headline, *18 Warehouses Fired In Liverpool, Sinn Féin Accused*, and there was extensive coverage of the incident. The reported stated:

The line of docks extends for seven miles, and fires, which broke out simultaneously about 9 o'clock, were spread over almost the whole of the area. The premises were set alight by means of rags soaked in paraffin, entrance having been secured to the various warehouses by the use of clippers on iron locks securing doors.

To each building marked out for destruction were allotted four or five men, all young and athletic, well coached for the task.

Interestingly, *The New York Times* also reported that an attempt had been made to set fire to a timber yard in Finsbury in London, but the plot was foiled when 'an alert constable' challenged six men who promptly fled the scene.

"After the incident, detectives found a number of revolvers and also several oil cans and other material, which it is alleged the men dropped as they ran away," the newspaper stated.

The extensive coverage on the front page of *The New York Times* shows that the fires in Liverpool were a significant event in the War of Independence, just as significant, in my view, as the Kilmichael Ambush in Co Cork, which occurred on the same weekend. Indeed, one can only imagine the fate that awaited poor Matthew Fowler in a police cell in Liverpool when word came through that more than a dozen British military personnel had just been killed in Ireland in a battle with Fowler's IRA comrades. In the photograph on the

THE DAILY MIRROR, Tuesday, November 30, 1920.

15 POLICEMEN KILLED IN AMBUSH IN IRELAND

The Daily Mirror

CERTIFIED CIRCULATION LARGER THAN THAT OF ANY OTHER DAILY PICTURE PAPER

No. 5,332.   Registered at the G.P.O. as a Newspaper.   TUESDAY, NOVEMBER 30, 1920   [20 PAGES]   One Penny.

CHARGE OF MURDER AGAINST MAN KNOWN AS 'No. 87.

STARTLING FIRES IN LIVERPOOL.

LARGE NUMBER OF OUTBREAKS.

YOUTH SHOT DEAD

TWO BIG WAREHOUSES BURNED OUT.

FOUR MEN UNDER ARREST

whose conduct made him suspicious in the doorway of a warehouse.

BOY SHOT DEAD.

He informed the police on duty. The latter tackled the men, who replied by firing 2 revolver shots, which missed their mark, but another man who had witnessed what took place fired with a revolver at Ward, killing him on the spot. The man who fired got away, but two of the four men were arrested. Later two other men were detained on suspicion. At every one of the fires traces of paraffin used for the purposes of ignition were found. It is impossible to estimate the damage, but a rough computation puts it

SEVENTEEN FIRES

Mysterious Outbreak in Liverpool Causes Enormous Loss of Property

DAMAGE ESTIMATED AT £1,000,000

Exciting Street Scene During Which Young Man is Shot Through the Heart

The Liverpool warehouse fires made headlines all over the world. Pictured here are reports from *The Daily Mirror* (UK), *Irish Independent* and *Freeman's Journal* (Ireland). *The Daily Mirror* headline refers to a charge of murder against 'Man No 87', which was IRA Volunteer Matthew Fowler who had refused to give his name to the police. *The New York Times* also published the story on its front page.

front of *The Daily Mirror*, the Meath man looks battered and bruised, and I have no doubt he was the victim of repeated beatings. With emotions running high, it was not a good time to be an Irish Volunteer in the custody of the British police.

Two days later, *The Daily Mirror* reported that there was a lot of activity in both London and Liverpool as police upped their efforts to identify and arrest 'Sinn Féin plotters in England'.

An energetic campaign has been begun by the police to track down Sinn Féin conspirators in England. Numerous raids were made yesterday in London and Liverpool. Two men were detained in the metropolis and a large number of documents seized at the Merseyside headquarters of the Irish Self-Determination League.

The newspaper coverage reflected the sense of panic in Britain in the wake of the Liverpool attacks. In fact, barriers were even erected around Downing Street to thwart any possible attack by the IRA.

While most of the media focus remained fixed on England, the public in Scotland were also becoming more aware of the IRA campaign in Britain and began to keep a lookout for any suspicious activity. Fighting a war in enemy terrain had been a dangerous business from the outset – as Joe Vize correctly pointed out – but it became quite treacherous following the Liverpool fires and the discovery of planned IRA attacks on several other English cities.

Henry Coyle, however, seems to have been utterly oblivious to the dangers he now faced. He continued with his gun-smuggling work, travelling from Glasgow to Edinburgh days after the fires to collect 'war material' from Patrick Thompson.

"I gave him 1,000Ib of explosives, revolver ammunition and 11 Peter-the-Painter revolvers," Thompson told the Army Pensions Board.

Another man who intended to carry on the IRA's work in Britain, regardless of the consequences, was Paddy Daly, now one of the few senior IRA men in Liverpool still at large. Indeed, of the half-dozen people in Liverpool who knew my father, he was the only one not arrested in the days after the fires.

"There was no one left to direct operations," Daly recalled. "So I came over to Dublin some days afterwards when matters had quieted down somewhat."

Daly met Michael Collins who told him to 'carry on in the place of Neill Kerr and the other leaders who had been arrested'.

"My talk with Collins filled me with enthusiasm to carry on with any work that was to be done or any work that he wished to have done…," remarked Daly. "I returned to Liverpool by the Holyhead boat, making plans to take up the threads of the organisation where Neill Kerr left off, particularly in connection with communications and munitions. The organisation of seamen on board the boats working for us was intact, as they had taken no part in the burnings."

The seamen were crucial to my father's gun-smuggling activities and he intended to make good use of them in the weeks ahead. On Saturday, December 4, he and Charlie Strickland set off in the Sinn Féin Motorcar for Cowdenbeath, a town about 50 miles north-east of Glasgow. It wasn't the most obvious place to go in search of 'war material', but there was a company of Irish Volunteers in Cowdenbeath and they clearly had done a good job in acquiring gelignite from the mines in Fifeshire. My father was to collect the goods at Lochgelly, a small town a few miles to the north of Cowdenbeath.

Later that evening, my father left Lochgelly with 2,980 cartridges of gelignite, 10 cartridges of samsonite, 248.5 feet of fuse, 404 detonators, two rifles, three pistols, ammunition and two swords. It was quite some haul, though what my father and his trusty lieutenant Charlie intended to do with those swords I am not so sure!

The Sinn Féin Motorcar limped out of Cowdenbeath, creaking and groaning under its mammoth load. The gelignite and samsonite weighed

300Ibs alone and the rest of the cargo must have pushed the total weight beyond 500Ibs. The poor old Austin was going to struggle to manage a five-mile trip, let alone the 50-mile journey to Glasgow, but my father and Charlie hadn't even finished for the night: they intended to call into Denis Fitzpatrick in Bannockburn to collect more 'stuff' before continuing on to Glasgow.

Not surprisingly, the Austin packed it in before it had even reached Dunfermline, a distance of just six miles. The headlights began to flicker and fade until it got to the point where my father was struggling to see the road ahead. Driving a car on a dark, unfamiliar road is a nerve-wracking business at the best of times, but when you happen to have headlights that don't work and 2,980 cartridges of gelignite in the back seat, then it is definitely not a job for the faint-hearted!

However, Henry Coyle was certainly not faint of heart and I will leave it to the *Scottish Daily Record and Mail* to take up the story.

About nine o'clock on Saturday evening, an open car, with the hood up, and containing two men, drew up in a side street in Dunfermline, alongside two constables on duty.

The motorists asked the policemen to direct them to the nearest garage, as there was something wrong with their headlights, and they had no desire to infringe any of the laws of the road. The officers readily complied with their request.

When I first came across that newspaper report I was dumfounded. The Henry Coyle I knew as my father would have been the last person I could have imagined behaving in such an audacious and even reckless manner. It is one thing to drive a car loaded with gelignite and guns across Scotland, but to stop and ask the police for assistance along the way? Well, all I can say is he must have had nerves of steel.

Remarkably, the policemen took no notice of these two Irishmen driving a car with a suspicious-looking load in the rear and instead directed them to the nearest garage. It may seem like my father was driving the most unreliable car in the whole of Scotland, so I feel I should say something in defence of the Sinn Féin Motorcar. While I can't offer much expertise on gelignite, revolvers or even swords, I do know a thing or two about motor engines, and I have great sympathy for that poor old Austin, which was being set a near impossible task with the weight on board. This was the era before alternators, when cars were powered by dynamo-charged batteries, and in the case of my father's Austin, all of the available power would have been needed just to keep the engine rotating, meaning there was nothing left for the headlights. Of course, my father and Charlie wouldn't have known this, and even if they did I suspect they'd have taken a chance anyway because they were determined to move as much 'war material' to Liverpool as they could, especially as the situation was now worsening in Ireland.

Having said their farewells to the two Dunfermline constables, the intrepid duo set off for the local garage where they explained their dilemma to the mechanics, who promptly set to work on repairing the car. Once again, I will let the *Daily Record* and *Mail* take up the story:

At the garage, the behaviour of the men while the lights were being repaired excited the suspicions of the mechanics. The cushions from the driver's seat were lifted and transferred to the rear, obviously with the purpose of covering something in the body of the car.

The garage hands could not make out the nature of the car's contents, but knowing the strict watch being observed by the police authorities for possible Sinn Féin gun-runners, they communicated their suspicions to the police.

Alarmed at the intentions of the mechanics, however, the motorists made a speedy exit from the garage, and the officers arrived just in time to see the car disappear along the street in a westerly direction.

Assured now that their suspicions were well grounded, the police sent out the hue and cry over the whole district, and bands of constables patrolled the main roads in order to intercept the car should it travel in their direction.

Henry Coyle had absolutely no intention of surrendering peacefully. As police sirens rang out across Dunfermline, he pressed down on the accelerator as hard as he could and the Sinn Féin Motorcar lurched from side to side before vanishing into the inky blackness of a lonely December night in the peaceful Scottish countryside.

The chase was on.

CHAPTER 14

'Why wait 'til dawn?
You are as well to shoot me now.'

SGT JAMES Denholm was on duty in Alloa that Saturday night when he received a 'phone call from colleagues in Dunfermline who instructed him to set up a checkpoint for the purpose of detaining the occupants of a green-coloured Austin car believed to be travelling towards his town.

Alloa was a fairly small town in 1920, with a population of about 12,500, so Sgt Denholm is unlikely to have had too much experience of dealing with major criminal investigations. It was an era when very few people possessed motorcars, and policemen like Sgt Denholm wouldn't have had cause to set up many checkpoints of this kind. He and two constables immediately left the station on foot and set off in search of this mysterious Austin. A short time later, they saw a car matching its description emerging at speed from the Clackmannan Road.

"I stepped into the middle of the road," recalled Sgt Denholm, "and signalled to the occupants to stop. They did not do so, but drove on. I just got clear of the car in time."

Having managed to travel the 15 miles from Dunfermline to Alloa without the Austin breaking down, my father and Charlie were becoming increasingly hopeful of making it back to Glasgow, but they needed to lighten the load to have any chance of avoiding arrest. Once they passed through Alloa and were on the way to Stirling, they pulled into the side of the road and began to dump some of the precious 'war material', which was packed into jutebags. Meanwhile, Sgt Denholm and his colleagues had commandeered a private car and were hot on the heels of the Sinn Féin Motorcar.

"When we came within sight of it, it was standing on the left side of the road and two men took something from the car and threw it over the hedge," Denholm recalled.

It was in the town of Dunfermline that my father and Charlie Strickland first encountered the police on the night of December 4, 1920, but they managed to escape to Alloa where they were confronted by another police patrol.

On seeing the police, my father and Charlie leapt into the Austin and took off again at speed. The Scottish-based *Weekly Record* described the ensuing chase as 'suggestive of a cinema drama' as the two cars raced along the dark, country road from Alloa to Stirling.

"The quarry had headed for Stirling, and they were soon sighted by the pursuers, who, after an exciting race, forged ahead of the fugitive car and drew up across the road," reported the *Daily Record and Mail*. "This time the hunted men were trapped. They jammed on the brakes, but not quickly enough to avoid a collision with the blockading vehicle. The constables rushed at their men…An exciting struggle ensued. The fugitives produced revolvers, but before they could use them they were seized and disarmed.

"They fought wildly, but the police numbers told in the end, and the men were overpowered."

My father received a severe beating on the roadside in Alloa as the police desperately tried to get him to talk. However, he refused to co-operate – to the point where he would not even give them his name – and attempted as best he could to avoid incriminating anyone else. Charlie Strickland adopted a similar strategy and even claimed he was a hitchhiker who had met my father for the first time in a restaurant earlier that day and knew nothing about the Austin's deadly cargo or the purpose of the trip to Cowdenbeath.

WEEKLY · RECORD

GUARANTEED LARGEST SALE IN SCOTLAND OF ANY WEEKLY NEWSPAPER.

No. 3068. Registered at the G.P.O. as a Newspaper. SATURDAY, DECEMBER 11, 1920. 16 PAGES

GLASGOW'S SINN FEIN PLOT UNMASKED.
CITY'S ESCAPE FROM DISASTER.
CONSPIRATORS' SIGNIFICANT MOVE TO WRECK CLYDE DOCKS.

BY 'WEEKLY RECORD'S' SPECIAL INVESTIGATOR.

My father, meanwhile, accepted full responsibility for the car's contents but repeatedly told the police he had been acting alone, having heard there were explosives to be got in Cowdenbeath. When told he would be shot at dawn if he did not start naming names, he replied: "Why wait 'til dawn? You are as well to shoot me now."

At one stage, a constable placed a gun against my father's head and threatened to pull the trigger if he did not co-operate.

"I thought of my poor mother," my father later told me. "I thought of her hearing the news of my death and it broke my heart but I would not give them the information they were looking for."

One of the things I found remarkable when I began to research this book is that every story my father told me over the years proved correct in almost all details, and I have found documentary evidence to support so much of what he recounted in our taped conversations in the 1970s. For example, the beating he took on the roadside in Alloa is referenced in the *Weekly Record's* account of his appearance before the local court days later.

One of the men arrested in the motorcar had his head swathed turban-wise in a large white bandage, a result of the exciting struggle with the police on the Stirling Road in the midnight darkness of Saturday.

I think the wounds to my father's head had more to do with the beating he took in police custody than any 'exciting struggle' on the roadside. Despite his best efforts to thwart the police investigation, he could not hide several incriminating documents in his jacket pocket, including a driver's licence in the name of Edmond Magner, an IRA sympathiser in Glasgow. There was also a document addressed to him as 'Brigade Adjutant H.P. Coyle', as well as the letter from his parents in which they expressed delight that he was 'still at large' and £190 in cash.

In Charlie Strickland's possession, there was a letter addressed to two persons in Port Glasgow, which contained the passage: *The bearer of this note is alright. Treat him so. Take stock of goods and prices before giving them up.*

The police were also able to trace the ownership of the Austin to Bernard McCabe, who was arrested the following morning, along with Magner and another IRA sympathiser James Devine. As the police began to put the various pieces of evidence to my father, he again tried to take full responsibility by claiming that McCabe loaned him the car without any knowledge of the purpose of his journey to Cowdenbeath and that he and Magner had accidently mixed up their driver's licenses. The latter story was stretching credulity to breaking point but my father didn't care; he was willing to shoulder all of the blame if it meant his colleagues could continue their important work for Irish freedom. He eventually admitted to Chief Constable Tom Johnston of Alloa that the weapons in the car would 'probably find their way to Ireland'.

The Scottish media, however, wrongly assumed that the explosives were to be used in Scotland and there were several sensational and misleading headlines in the newspapers that week. *Glasgow's Sinn Féin Plot Unmasked* blared the headline on the front of the *Weekly Record* on the Saturday after my father's arrest. The newspaper said the capture of the car in Alloa had saved the city 'from disaster' by preventing the 'conspirators' significant move to wreck Clyde docks'.

"Examination of the car revealed the awful fact that 3cwts of gelignite and samsonite were stowed in it," the newspaper remarked. "Three hundred weights of gelignite! This is a greater charge than is used to fire a big naval 15-inch gun, which sends a ton 25 miles.

"This explosive would have flung 5,000 tons of material 20 feet into the air. It would have wrecked a whole street in a city."

The newspaper claimed the explosives were to be used to destroy the docks in Glasgow and spared no effort in conjuring up a doomsday scenario for its readers.

The 3cwts of gelignite were to have been exploded in the docks area, where shipping is moored, and tremendous damage would have ensued to the wharves, stores or ships, and all

THE PAPER WHICH GETS THINGS DONE.

Daily Mail Keco

The All-Scotland Newspaper. Sale Three Times That of Any Other Mor

ESTAB. 1847—No. 23,057. GLASGOW, MONDAY, DECEMBER 6, 1920.

THREE CITY MEN IN SINN FEIN CONSP

GLASGOW SINN FEIN COUP. SQUANDE VOT

CAR CAPTURED WITH 3 CWTS. EXPLOSIVES.

2 ARRESTS NEAR ALLOA.

CONSPIRACY CHARGE AGAINST GLASGOW CAR OWNER.

Dramatic Arrest.—After a thrilling midnight motor chase, two men have been arrested by the Alloa police. They are supposed to be associated with the Sinn Fein terror gang. Both were armed, and a desperate struggle ensued before they were taken into custody.

It is stated that in the motor car, which is believed to belong to a Glasgow merchant, were found 3 cwts. of gelignite and samsonite, 300 detonators, and revolvers, rifles, and swords.

Three arrests in co... ... with the ...

GOVERNMEN BY LABOUR

WATCH YO

Rev. Michael O'Fla... Who has sent a telegram to the Premier inviting him to make a move towards peace with Sinn Fein.

their speed, and they soon left the patrol far behind.

The officers at once procured another motor and started off in pursuit, and about a mile and a half along the Alloa-Stirling road they ... ...ry, ...hunted

The bad time which maniacs had in the House Friday night, might ... much worse, if they ha to rush up their tame su to avert defeat.

But, at anyrate, thos preferred to be loyal to their constituents and instead of glossing ove po icy of the Master-spe ced in giving effect to C Wilson's outspoken and r to "give the Government up in the interests of eco

A NARROW

Only by the v votes in a d ...nia

Glasgow would have wakened to the roar of the explosion, which would have been heard for 20 miles around the city.

There was, of course, no truth in the story but reports such as these created a huge amount of fear and anger in Glasgow, which played perfectly into the hands of the police who wanted the public to report any suspicions they might have about IRA sympathisers. The same newspaper reported that two men had been arrested in Clydebank on suspicion of procuring rifles for 'the Sinn Féin organisation'.

Early in the forenoon a strong party of the local police carried out a raid on a tenement house at Gordon Street, Clydebank, and effected the arrest of two brothers alleged to have attempted to purchase rifles from local members of the Territorial Force for Sinn Féin use. No rifles were found in the house, and later in the day one of the men was liberated.

Another man was also taken into custody under suspicion of having endeavoured to induce local Territorials to sell their rifles to an agent of Sinn Féin.

Two further arrests have been made by the police late at night in the Clydebank district. It is stated that the two men taken into custody are suspected of acting on behalf of the Sinn Féin organisation. All four have been committed to Duke Street Prison, Glasgow, from which they will be taken to the Sheriff Court at Dumbarton.

MOTOR CAR CHASE OF SINN FEIN SUSPECTS.

Firearms and 8-cwt. of Explosives Seized.

FIGHT IN SCOTLAND.

Supposed I.R.A. "General" and Comrade Arrested.

An exciting midnight motor chase in Fife and Cowdenbeath ended yesterday in the arrest of two men suspected of being active Sinn Feiners, and of whom is believed to hold rank of brigadier-gen...

The fallout from my father's arrest reverberated through the ranks of the Irish Volunteers in Glasgow and numerous raids and arrests were carried out in the weeks leading up to Christmas 1920. The Volunteers refused to be deterred, however, and continued with their work as best they could. Indeed, one of the amazing details I learned when researching this book was a plot to rescue my father and Charlie from the police station in Alloa. Meath man Henry O'Hagan was one of those who gathered in the home of Johnny Sweeney in Falkirk on the night after my father's arrest.

"Joe McCauley came in and told me that Henry Coyle and [Charlie] McGinn were arrested in Alloa and we would have to try and release them. He sent a messenger to John Sweeney to send some men and equipment right away. About 7 o'clock, six or seven men arrived from Glasgow. Two of them I knew – Mick O'Carroll and Sean Flood. Denis Fitzpatrick, Felix O'Hanlon, George Coyle, Paddy Smith and John Murphy, all from Denny, were there also and Johnny Sweeney, the son of the man of the house.

"Sweeney's [at] Kerse Lane was our dump and headquarters. Sweeney's daughter made masks for all of us. Mick O'Carroll from Glasgow and myself went by train to Alloa where the prisoners were and the others went by car. We got there all right and met at our allotted places but the prisoners had been moved before we arrived. We had to walk back. It took us all night. It must be 30 miles the way we came back."

The Glasgow contingent, which included Matthew Tipping, the quartermaster of the Irish Volunteers in Govan, and Seán Coyne had even further to walk and some of them missed work the next day. Coyne told the Army Pensions Board that the failed mission to Alloa cost him his job.

My father, Charlie Strickland, Edmond Magner, Bernard McCabe and James Devine were all charged under the Explosives Act 1883 at a sitting of Alloa Burgh Court on Tuesday, December 7, 1920.

"Keen interest was taken in the proceedings at Alloa Burgh Court today when the five men concerned in Saturday night's motorcar Sinn Féin affair were brought before Bailie Grant," wrote one newspaper. "The courtroom was

UESDAY, DECEMBER

MEN IMPLICATED IN DASH

Of Motor Car Through Fife

Remitted at Alloa Court To-Day.

Keen interest was taken in the proceedings at Alloa Burgh Court to-day when the five men concerned in the Saturday nigh

filled, and a large crowd waited outside in the hope of getting a glimpse of the accused."

The proceedings lasted just a few minutes and all five were remanded in custody to prison in Glasgow.

That court appearance in Alloa was the first for my father since the midnight sitting in Belmullet almost three years earlier. That had ended in a relatively short jail sentence of three months, but the sanction he now faced would be much more severe. As the prison van left Alloa on that December evening, my father resigned himself to the fact that he was now facing a long stretch in a Scottish jail. What he didn't realise was that the police in Liverpool were already taking a very keen interest in events in Scotland and had plans of their own for IRA Brigade Adjutant H.P. Coyle.

CHAPTER 15

A first Christmas behind bars

E VEN before my father's arrest, the police in Liverpool were on the trail of the Sinn Féin Motorcar. They had the garage receipt made out to 'John Daly' and also had several sightings of the car in Liverpool in the days leading up to the warehouse fires. Crucially, the police learned that the green Austin was spotted carrying two well-dressed women to various stores in Liverpool and Bootle in the week before the fires. At each store, the women purchased gallons of paraffin, as well as empty gallon tins, and police were able to deduce that a total of twelve and a half gallons of paraffin and 19 gallon tins were purchased in this manner. Several identical gallon tins were found in the burnt-out warehouses.

My father's diligence in retaining documents also came back to haunt him when police in Alloa found in his possession a receipt for breakfast for two people at a hotel in Liverpool. The date on the receipt was November 15 – the same date as the receipt found in Neill Kerr's home for the repairs to the motorcar.

By now, the police in Liverpool were in contact with colleagues in Dublin who had shared some of the documents seized in the raid on Richard Mulcahy's lodgings. The name 'H.P. Coyle' appeared on a receipt for £500 and there were other references to my father that convinced the police in Liverpool he had played a key role in the fires. Investigating officers were also working on the assumption that a car was needed to transport some of the IRA teams to their targets and believed the green Austin must have been used that night.

Sheila and Kathleen Browne were soon identified as the two women who purchased the paraffin and were taken into custody. They were fearless young women who refused to wilt under questioning and gave nothing of evidential value to their interrogators. By refusing to co-operate with the police, the

Duke Street Prison in Glasgow, where my father was held on remand after his arrest in Alloa in December 1920.

Browne sisters made it much more difficult for the Crown to obtain convictions against the men who were involved in the fires.

Having been remanded to Duke Street prison in Glasgow, my father expected to stay there for several months pending his trial, but got a surprise on the weekend after his arrest when a senior police officer, Inspector Thompson, arrived from Liverpool. Thompson put some of the evidence to my father and told him he was to be transported to Liverpool to face trial for the warehouse fires. When charged at Liverpool Bridewell, my father replied: "The only thing I have to say is that there is no truth whatever in the statement. I was in Glasgow."

Charlie Strickland, who was also taken to Liverpool and charged, replied: "I was in Glasgow too."

On Monday, December 13, my father and Charlie were brought before Liverpool Police Court and charged with having 'conspired together with other persons unknown to set fire to warehouses, storehouses and other buildings in Liverpool on November 27 and other dates'. They pleaded not guilty and were remanded in custody to Walton Prison where Neill Kerr and the other arrested Volunteers were being held. Elizabeth Kerr worked tirelessly to ensure the prisoners got everything they needed.

"I went twice a day to Walton Prison at 12 o'clock with their dinner and 4 o'clock with their tea," she recalled. "Henry Coyle and many others were brought to Liverpool in the meantime and I catered for them all."

Far from being deterred by the arrest of her husband and stepson, Elizabeth became more involved than ever in the work of the Irish Volunteers. William Vernon, a close associate of Neill Kerr, saw at first hand the remarkable work of this brave mother of two young children.

"I was constantly employed on the Dublin boats between Liverpool and was one of the chief carriers of arms, dispatches, ammunition, as well as conveying important personages to Liverpool and vice versa," Vernon recalled. "I had occasion to call at every landing at Neill Kerr for orders.

"When Neill Kerr was arrested, I continued there as usual, that was two or three times weekly, and received my orders from Mrs Kerr. She, in fact, took up the running and responsibility after her husband's arrest.

"It will be understood that [Paddy] Daly was in charge of supplies, dispatches, etc, but No 6 Florida St was still headquarters, and if Dr Daly was not present when I called, Mrs Kerr always gave me the necessary instructions.

"It would be impossible for any person to do justice to the work carried out by Mrs Kerr during, before and after Neill Kerr's arrest," Vernon added.

When I think of Elizabeth Kerr bringing dinners to my father and the other IRA prisoners, it saddens me that such a remarkable woman, like the Browne sisters, was written out of the story of the War of Independence. In publishing this book, I wanted to tell my father's story, but equally I wanted to give due credit to people like Elizabeth Kerr and the many others who were so crucial to the work of the Irish Volunteers in England and Scotland during those eventful years. They made incredible sacrifices and we should never forget their bravery and selflessness.

In the case of Elizabeth Kerr, she knew her children would be effectively orphaned if she were also jailed for IRA activities, yet she carried on regardless and, in fact, took on greater responsibilities once her husband was imprisoned. Her brave deeds and those of the Browne sisters and so many others should be told to every student in Ireland because these ordinary people are the forgotten heroes of Ireland's fight for freedom.

Elizabeth Kerr also played a crucial role in the return to Ireland of Éamon de Valera, who had been in America since October 1919.

"Before [Neill] Kerr had been arrested," recalled Paddy Daly, "he had been informed that Mr de Valera was returning from the United States and that it had been arranged for him to travel as a stowaway on The Celtic.

"Kerr had kept this information very secret and when he was arrested he realised there was nobody left to make plans for the arrival of Mr de Valera in Liverpool. Kerr was confined to the local gaol where his wife was allowed to visit him occasionally. During her visits, he managed to convey this information to her. So Mrs Kerr informed me of the facts.

"My second Christian name is Gabriel but I was known to all in Liverpool as Paddy. Neill Kerr knew that in my home I was called Gabriel. So when speaking to his wife in the presence of warders he referred to me as 'Sister Gabriel' and Mrs Kerr was quick enough to understand who he meant while the warder, no doubt, was under the impression that Neill was speaking of a nun."

Organising the safe passage of the president of the Irish Republic was an onerous responsibility to place on the shoulders of a young man but Paddy Daly had served a good apprenticeship. Indeed, any man who survived a cross-country escapade in the Sinn Féin Motorcar with its rebel driver was more than capable of smuggling Éamon de Valera back to Ireland!

THE LIVERPOOL FIRES.

MEN OF THE GREEN CAR BEFORE THE BENCH.

(From our Correspondent.)

LIVERPOOL, MONDAY.

Henry Peter Coyle (24), described as belonging to County Mayo, and Charles McGinn, or Strickland (19), who gave an address in Glasgow—the two men who were arrested by the Scottish police—appeared at the Liverpool Police Court to-day charged with having conspired together with other persons unknown to set fire to warehouses, storehouses, and other buildings in Liverpool on November 27 and other dates.

Mr. Howard Roberts, prosecuting for the police, asked, in both cases on behalf of the Director of Public Prosecutions, for a remand until Thursday. The two men had been arrested by the Scottish police in Alloa. They were in a motor-car, which contained 300 pounds of gelignite and various arms and ammunition, proceeding in the direction of Glasgow from Dunfermline late on the night of the 4th instant.

On Coyle was found a receipt showing that ...ons had had breakfast in ...November 1...

Daly met the president off the boat and brought him to the house of an Englishman, Billy Humphreys, who worked on The Celtic and had looked after de Valera during the voyage.

"Humphreys brought de Valera ashore and took him home to his house," recalled Daly. "He kept him there for the night. But before retiring they smeared butter on the bolts of the back door so that they could be opened noiselessly if the house was raided during the night."

The next day, Daly collected de Valera from Humphreys' house and brought him to the docks to catch a B&I boat to North Wall in Dublin.

"In conveying Mr de Valera to the boat, we were accompanied by an old member of the IRB called John Fitzgerald. We travelled by tram and bus across the city," recalled Daly. "When going down to the boat, I asked Mr Fitzgerald to accompany the Chief. I did this as a tribute to Fitzgerald, giving him this honour, because he had been an older worker in the movement. I walked a few paces behind them and I remember Mr de Valera wearing a rather short raincoat. He looked anything but a sailor and he could not be disguised very effectively as a sailor. We delivered him on board anyway without any misadventure and I left him in the safe keeping of the mate, Mr Hackett."

Had he been captured, de Valera would have probably ended up in Walton Prison with my father, Neill Kerr and the many other Irish Volunteers now on remand there.

My father was transferred to Liverpool to face trial for the warehouse fires. He and several other IRA Volunteers were remanded in custody to Walton Prison (pictured). A number of other IRA men, including Mick O'Leary and Tom Kerr, were shipped back to Ireland and imprisoned in Mountjoy.

I know very little about my father's time in Walton Prison during December 1920 and January 1921. If he wrote letters to his parents – and I am sure he did – they never survived, and he did not speak too much about his experiences there. However, another Mayo man who was in Walton Prison just weeks before my father was Patrick Hegarty from Addergoole, near Crossmolina, a member of Mayo Co Council and a leading Irish Volunteer who was captured in July 1920.

"I was courtmartialled in Victoria Barracks [Belfast], given two years' hard labour and deported on a destroyer to Walton Jail," Hegarty told the Bureau of Military History. "We were treated as human beings while there. The governor was a gentleman; the chaplain, a Canon Sigerson, a lovable character, said if he could let us go he would."

Hegarty was one of more than a dozen Irish Volunteers in Walton to be transported to Lincoln Jail on the night of the warehouse fires.

"A rumour got around that a rescue was planned after the 'Ruddy Warehouse fires' in Liverpool (as they called them) so, at about 2.30am, we were ordered to get ready. Fourteen of us were handcuffed separately and then a chain contraption linked us all together so when one moved all moved. In Manchester, as we were having a stop, a gang – presumably Irish – noticed us and shouted 'Up the Republic'."

My father missed Paddy Hegarty by a matter of weeks but there were other Mayo men in Walton Prison, including Seán 'Mór' Lynchehaun from Polranny on Achill Island who participated in the warehouse fires.

"I knew Seán Lynchehaun as a member of the Volunteers before I left home," my father recalled. "I didn't meet him in Liverpool until I saw him in the Bridewell after he was arrested. I had just been brought from Scotland to stand my trial."

Another Mayo man in Walton Prison at that time was Michael Brennan, a native of Kiltimagh, who was also charged with the fires. He actually had no involvement in them at all.

The only written record I possess of my father's spell in Walton is a poem he penned entitled 'The Sinn Féin Motorcar' in which he recounts his adventures in the famous green Austin with his great friend Charlie. The poem is reprinted in full on the next page and I think it reveals a lot about my father's frame of mind as he awaited trial in Liverpool. Far from being downhearted, the poem possesses a cheerful, buoyant and defiant tone, and it is certainly not the work of a man who has any regrets about the predicament in which he now finds himself.

That first Christmas behind bars cannot have been easy – and my father must have realised he was facing into a long sentence if convicted – but the poem sounds as carefree as if it had been written at home in Dooyork instead of a prison in faraway Liverpool.

I don't know when my father started writing poems and songs (or 'ditties' as they would have been known back then) but I am very fortunate to have several of the pieces he penned while in prison in England and Scotland. As I mentioned before, he was clearly an educated man – even if he had left school at a young age to go working on the farms in Scotland – and he was someone who possessed a keen interest in reading and writing. It is wonderful to have these poems and songs because they are his words – not mine – and I think they will give you, the reader, a better understanding of Henry Peter Coyle. He was no ordinary freedom fighter, that's for sure. On the one hand, he possessed a fierce determination to rid Ireland of colonial rule, so fierce he drove carloads of gelignite across Scotland. Yet weeks later, we find him writing poetry in a prison cell in Liverpool. It is a contradiction I struggle to understand and the more I delve into his past the more I am amazed at the life he led in his early 20s.

My father's wonderful way with words was to serve him well in the months ahead as he faced high-profile trials in Liverpool and Scotland. Henry Peter Coyle's name was unknown to the public before December 1920, but by the following spring he was making headlines on both sides of the Irish Sea.

The Sinn Féin Motorcar

It was on the fourth of December, a motoring I did go,
I steered my course through Fifeshire, I'll have you all to know.
To help my faithful comrades, who were fighting in the war,
And to strike a blow for Ireland with a Sinn Féin Motorcar

I said unto our Volunteers, 'This day I am going to see
What I can do for my country and to set old Ireland free,
To drive out the Tans and tyrants who are making on this war,
And to fight for dear old Ireland with a Sinn Féin Motorcar.'

I had a faithful comrade, young Charles Strickland.
Our firm determination was to free our native land.
But coming back that very night, we did receive a scar,
While working for old Ireland with a Sinn Féin Motorcar.

The police in Alloa and the car they did surround,
And told us we would never more set foot on Irish ground.
Through threatened with execution,
Battered, bruised and bleeding on that country road,
We refused to tell the secrets as to where we got our load.
Early next morning, we were charged before the bar,
For breaking the law in Scotland with our Sinn Féin Motorcar.

One day in Glasgow Prison, a stranger there I spied.
The Governor said you must come out to be identified.
Said he, 'I am an English chief constable and I have travelled very far,
To see this dangerous rebel and his Sinn Féin Motorcar.'

He said, 'Coyle you have conspired with people we do now know,
You have tried to ruin our country and our government to overthrow,
You brought explosives to Liverpool and paraffin in a jar,
And you tried to burn our cities with your Sinn Féin Motorcar.'

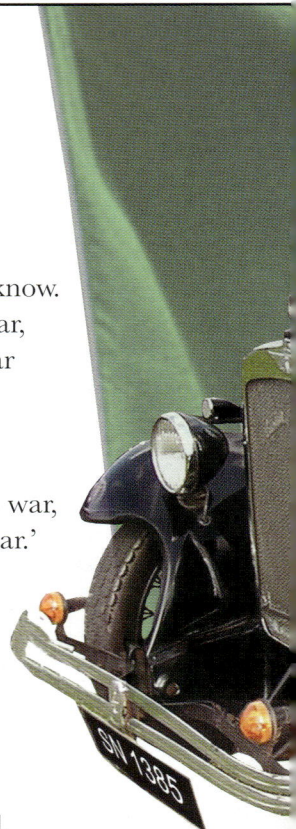

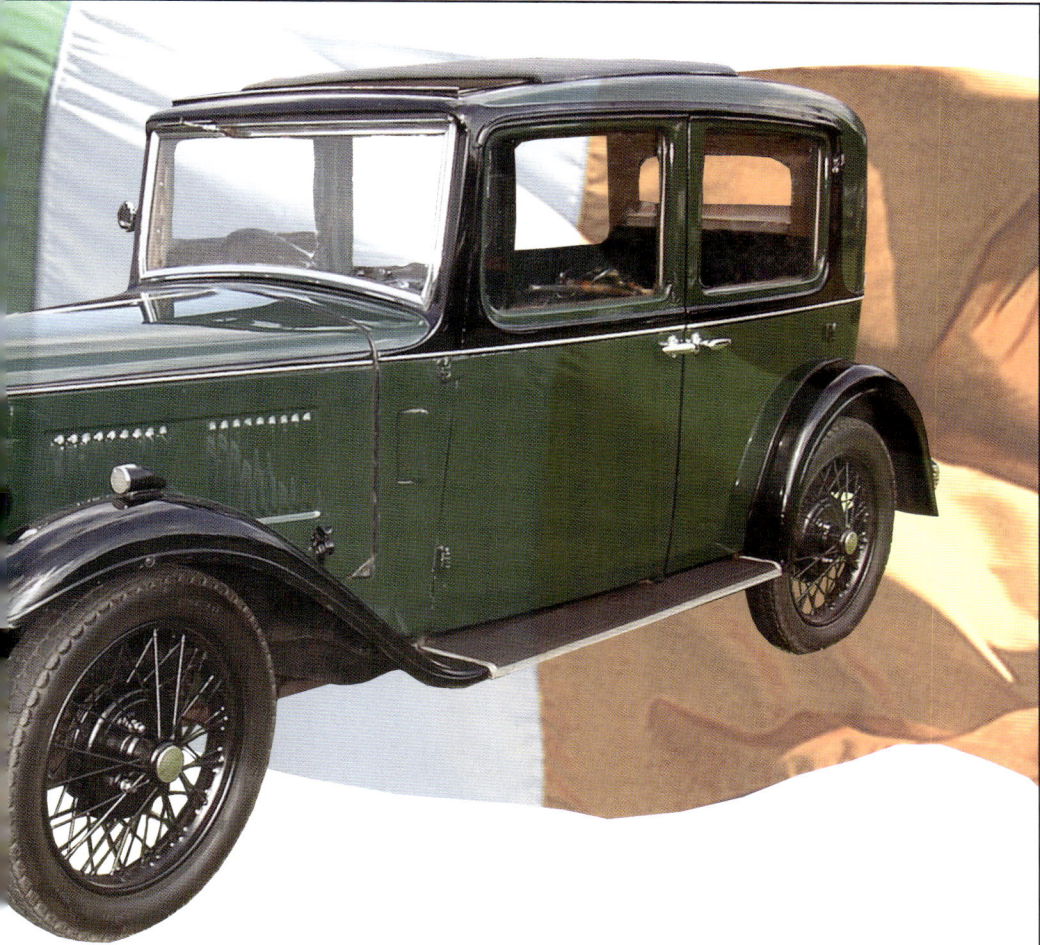

They drove me off to England, my trial there to stand,
For being an Irish rebel from dear old Ireland.
And now I am in a prison cell, a prisoner of war
for possessing high explosives and a Sinn Féin Motorcar.

But God will grant my liberty, for that I always pray.
I hope to meet the tyrants upon some future day.
Although they got me this time, I feel not wound or scar,
And I will fight again for Ireland with a Sinn Féin Motorcar.

**Composed by Henry Coyle
in Walton Prison, Liverpool, December 1920**

CHAPTER 16

'Where is the evidence?'

THE British government wasted no time in prosecuting the alleged perpetrators of the Liverpool warehouse fires. On December 29, 1920, six men and two women were brought before a special court in the city for a preliminary hearing of the evidence against them. The prisoners in the dock were Neill Kerr (57), Henry Peter Coyle (24), Sheila Browne (30), Kathleen Browne (24), Matthew Fowler (28), Michael Brennan (39), Seamus McCaughey (32) and Francis Patrick McPartlin (19). All eight were charged with conspiracy to murder, to commit arson, to set fire to goods and to commit damage upon property. Fowler and McPartlin were also charged with the murder of Daniel William Ward, while McCaughey was charged with the attempted murder of a police constable.

Dublin native McPartlin had been arrested just days earlier in a raid on Leahy's public house on the Scotland Road, which was a favoured haunt of the Irish Volunteers in Liverpool. Like Brennan, he had no involvement in the fires but was put on trial nonetheless and even charged with Ward's murder. The haste with which the case was brought before the courts meant there was little opportunity for the police to obtain compelling evidence against my father or the other accused, and much of what was presented at that preliminary hearing was circumstantial.

The public prosecutor, F.J. Sims, told stipendiary magistrate Stuart Deacon that 'evidence would be called to show that each one of the prisoners was an ardent supporter of the Sinn Féin movement'.

Sims' opening remarks were heavily biased against Sinn Féin and there was no acknowledgement whatsoever of the party's comprehensive victory in Ireland in the general election of 1918.

"Sinn Féin has for its object the separation of Ireland from England by the use of arms, the destruction of property and, if necessary, the taking of life or by the adoption of any violent means which would be likely to compel the people of this country to acquiesce to the demands of Sinn Féin," the prosecutor explained.

At that time, Sinn Féin and the IRA had a policy of instructing their members to refuse to recognise English courts but my father and his co-accused participated fully in the judicial process in Liverpool.

"Had we been on trial in Ireland at the time we would not have recognised the courts," my father later explained, "but if we denied the right of the British government to try us in our country, we didn't deny their right to try us in theirs, and furthermore, headquarters in Dublin wanted the publicity of the trials."

GHQ certainly got the publicity it was seeking. The subsequent trial at Liverpool Assizes garnered a lot of coverage in the English and Irish press in the early weeks of 1921. It commenced in late January and continued until February 14. The stipendiary magistrate found there was insufficient evidence to pursue a case against Brennan but the other seven defendants were sent forward for trial before a judge and jury.

The seriousness with which the British government viewed the case is reflected in the fact that the attorney general Sir Gordon Hewart was asked to lead the Crown prosecution team.

"The trial in Liverpool was the first big Sinn Féin case in England," my father recalled. "Sir Gordon Hewart was one of the British representatives who signed the Treaty afterwards along with Lloyd George, Winston Churchill and Lord Birkenhead. It was little he thought during the course of that trial early in 1921 that he would be signing a peace treaty with the hated rebels before the end of that same year."

Hewart certainly pulled no punches in his two-hour opening address, describing Sinn Féin's 'activities' as 'organised terror intended to intimidate the public into taking a course they otherwise would not take'.

"All of these prisoners are closely identified with the Sinn Féin movement, and the essence of the charge is that these prisoners, associated as they are with the criminal side of that organisation, were united with other persons to set fire to a large number of warehouses, and were prepared, if they should be frustrated in their efforts, to resist arrest to the uttermost degree."

The depiction of Sinn Féin as a ruthless and dangerous terrorist organisation was one of the characteristics of the trial, and it wasn't just Hewart who was making such claims. The presiding judge Sir Alfred Aspinall Tobin even went so far as to warn the press not to identify an army officer called to give evidence against my father. The officer had led the raid on Richard Mulcahy's lodgings in Dublin.

"I absolutely forbid anyone to take photographs in this court and anybody who takes them will be seriously dealt with," instructed Tobin. "We cannot have this officer photographed."

The unnamed officer gave evidence of finding in Mulcahy's papers a receipt for £500 signed by Henry Coyle and then given to Joe Furlong. There was other circumstantial evidence against my father too, including the receipt dated November 15 for the repairs to the green Austin and another receipt on the same date for breakfast for two in a Liverpool hotel, an undated receipt

THE LIVERPOOL OUTRAGES

Prisoners in Court.

COUNSEL AND THE SINN FEIN CONSPIRACY.

At Liverpool yesterday there was a sequel to the Sinn Fein outrages of 27th November, when Matthew Fowler, aged 28; Neil Kerr, aged 57; Sheila Brown, aged 30; Kathleen Brown, aged 24; Henry Peter Coyle, aged 24; Michael Brennan, aged 39; James M'Caughey, aged 32; and Francis Patrick M'Partlin, aged 19, were charged with having conspired with others unknown to set fire to premises in Liverpool. Against M'Partlin and Fowler there was an additional charge of the wilful murder of the youth William Joseph Ward, who, it will be remembered, was shot dead on the occasion in question; while M'Caughey was charged with the attempted murder of Police-Constable Sloane.

Mr. J. F. Sims, who appeared for the Public Prosecutor, recounted the story of the fires and subsequent discoveries of tins and bottles, some containing paraffin, and cloth gas masks and bolt cutters. The damage done, he said, over an area of nine miles was in excess of £1,000,000. A considerable number of persons must have been employed in the outrages, and motor cars used. The evidence to be forthcoming went to show that the prisoners were actively engaged in the policy of terrorising the Government and people of this to concede the demands of

The trial of my father and seven others in Liverpool in February 1921 made headlines on both sides of the Irish Sea.

from the North-Western Hotel in Liverpool for apartments, as well as the letter referring to him as an IRA Brigade Adjutant and the letter from his parents expressing delight he was 'still at large'.

Sir Gordon Hewart tried his very best to connect my father to the fires, claiming he made 'some mysterious journeys' in the green Austin (indeed, he did!) and transported revolvers from Glasgow to Liverpool.

"Just before November 27, a raid was made upon the premises in Dublin of a man named Richard Mulcahy, who was no small part of the brains of the criminal organisation of Sinn Féin," Hewart told the jury. "In his possession were a considerable number of letters and receipts, one of which, dated September 27, was for £500, given by Coyle to a man named J. Furlong. I ask you, the jury, to believe that Coyle was the man with the motor car and the arms and ammunition and that he was instrumental in the purchase of the bolt-cutters."

The manager of the garage where the Austin was repaired took the stand and identified my father as the man who brought the car for repair. But that incident occurred on November 15, almost two weeks before the fires, and try as they might, the prosecution could not place my father in Liverpool on November 27.

"It is suggested by the Crown that the prisoner Coyle came to Liverpool with revolvers in his motor car. Where is the evidence of that?" asked defence counsel Edward Hemmerde.

LIVERPOOL OUTRAGES.

SIX MEN AND TWO WOMEN CHARGED.

CROWN COUNSEL'S OPENING STATEMENT.

DAMAGE PUT AT OVER ONE MILLION POUNDS.

The Sinn Fein outrages in Liverpool on November 27th, when warehouses and timber yards were set ablaze and when a youth named William Joseph Ward was shot dead, were investigated by the Stipendary magistrate at the Liverpool Police Court, to-day. Six men and two women made their appearance in the dock in connection with the affair, viz., Neil Kerr (57), Sheila Brown (30), Kathleen Brown (24), Henry Peter Coyle (24), Matthew Fowler (28), Michael Brennan (39), James McCoughney (32), and Francis Park McPartlin (19).

Mr. F. J. Sims and Mr. Howard Roberts were for the prosecution. Mr. Madden appeared for Fowler, McCoughney, and Kerr

SINN FEIN WAR ON ENGLAND.

GRAVE CHARGES AT LIVERPOOL.

Eight in Dock.

ALLEGED MURDER, ARSON AND CONSPIRACY.

When reading the various reports of the trial, I was surprised at the excellent legal representation afforded to my father and the other defendants. In opting to defend the case, Sinn Féin adopted a clever strategy by employing two legal teams – one for Kerr, Fowler and McCaughey and the other for the Browne sisters and my father (McPartlin was found not guilty at an early stage). There was far more evidence against Kerr, Fowler and McCaughey than there was against my father and the Browne sisters, so it made sense to put as much distance as possible between them. The prosecution had hoped to prove that Sheila and Kathleen Browne purchased large quantities of paraffin oil during the week of the fires, but they could find few witnesses to positively identify them.

"None of the prisoners could be identified in regard to these purchases," noted one newspaper report, "but a witness said one of the women customers wore a scarf similar to the one found in the house where the female prisoners lodged, and her hair was of a bright colour like that of the two women."

The Crown prosecution described the Browne sisters as 'ardent Sinn Féiners' who were found in possession of various incriminating documents.

"When their house in Litherland was searched, a large quantity of Sinn Féin literature, membership cards, and a list of names were found," the court was told. "The police also found a sealed envelope [addressed to 'Flo'] which they opened. This contained a document which stated, among other things, *'Stuff left behind. Sending 23 rounds of ammunition, 26 automatic detonators at 3d, 50 at 2d, other stuff secured gratis; also 14 rounds of revolver ammunition.'* There was also a balance sheet showing transactions amounting to £50."

No.	NAME, AGE AND TRADE.	Court and date of committal for trial.	Date of first rece... prison and whe... admitted to l...
1	2	3	4
20	**Clifford Ralph Worthy**, 19, Wireless Operator ... ... Adjourned *sine die*, and handed to escort, Highgate, 9th July, 1919 (stealing £4, etc., naval deserter). 14 days, Manchester, 19th January, 1920 (unlawful possession of discharge certificate). Bound over, Clerkenwell, 3rd March, 1920 (stealing jewellery).	Liverpool City... 14th January, 1921.	22nd December,
21	**Neil Kerr**, 57, Labourer	Ditto	9th December,
22	**Henry Peter Coyle**, 25, Farmer	Ditto	31st December,
23	**Matthew Fowler**, 28, Labourer	Ditto	9th December,
24	**James McCaughey**, 32, Labourer	Ditto	Ditto ...
25	**Francis Patrick McPartlin**, 19, Plasterer ... ... 6 weeks and £5 Bail or 14 days, Dublin, 23rd July, 1918 (illegal drilling), Francis McPartlan.	Ditto	31st December
26	**Sheila Brown**, 30, School Teacher	Ditto	10th December
27	**Kathleen Brown**, 24, Clerk	Ditto	Ditto ...

The charge sheet from Liverpool City Assizes in January 1921 when my father and seven others went on trial for the warehouse burnings in November 1920.

OFFENCE.	Before whom tried and date.	Verdict (or Pleaded Guilty).	Previous convictions charged in Indictment and proved in Court.	Sentence or Order of the Court.
	6	7	8	9
...oting with intent to murder, and larceny.	*Acton J* ~~The Hon. Sir Edward Acton, Knight,~~ 25th January, 1921. ~~His Honour Judge~~ Sir A. A. Tobin, K.C., Knight, 28th Jan., 1921.	Not Guilty of shooting with intent. Pleaded Guilty of larceny.	... ...	...18 Calendar Months Division 2.
...onspiracy to murder, to commit arson, to ...t fire to goods and to commit damage upon ...operty. ...KERR, COYLE, FOWLER, McCAUGHEY and ...cPARTLIN : Arson. ...FOWLER and McPARTLIN : Murder. ...FOWLER and McPARTLIN : Shooting with ...ent to murder. ...McCAUGHEY : Shooting with intent to ...rder.	*Tobin SC* ~~His Honour Judge~~ Sir A. A. Tobin, K.C., Knight, 7th, 8th, 9th, 10th, 11th, 12th, 14th Feb., 1921.	*Not Guilty Conspiracy C Murder* Guilty (1) *Not Guilty of Conspiracy in remaining indicts* (2) Not tried.	...	~~10 Years Penal~~ ~~Servitude and 2~~ ~~Years Imprisonment~~ ~~(concurrently).~~ *(altered by C.C.A)*
	Tobin SC ~~His Honour Judge~~ Sir A. A. Tobin, K.C., Knight, 7th, 8th, 9th, 10th 11th Feb., 1921.	Not Guilty (1 & 2)	... ...	...To be discharged.
	Tobin SC ~~His Honour Judge~~ Sir A. A. Tobin, K.C., Knight, 2nd, 3rd, 7th, 8th 9th, 10th, 11th, 12th and 14th February, 1921.	Not Guilty (3), Guilty (1) of conspiracy to commit arson, (2, 4 Not tried)	... ...	...2 Years Imprisonment.
	Tobin SC ~~His Honour Judge~~ Sir A. A. Tobin, K.C., Knight, 4th, 7th, 8th, 9th 10th, 11th, 12th, 14th Feb., 1921.	Guilty (5) Guilty (1), (2) Not tried.	... ...	...10 Years Penal Servitude, 10 Years Penal Servitude & 2 Years Imprisonment (concurrently).
	Tobin SC ~~His Honour Judge~~ Sir A. A. Tobin, K.C., Knight, 2nd, 3rd and 4th February, 1921.	Not Guilty (3) Not Guilty (1, 2 and 4).	... ...	...To be discharged.
	Tobin SC ~~His Honour Judge~~ Sir A. A. Tobin, K.C., Knight, 7th, 8th, 9th, 10th, 11th, 12th February, 1921.	Not Guilty	... ...	...To be discharged.
	Ditto ..	...Not Guilty	... ...	...To be discharged.

A man named Clarke also told the court that Sheila Browne purchased a number of paraffin cans in his shop, a claim she strenuously denied.

"Although I am a Sinn Féiner," she said. "I knew nothing of any proposal to burn warehouses or goods in Liverpool or Bootle. I have never bought oil for any such purpose.

"On Saturday, the 27th of November, I was at a whist drive in the Foresters Hall, Seaforth, and my sister was there, and many people saw us there. The document, which was found in the envelope addressed to 'Flo', I had not seen before the police took it from the drawer in the kitchen."

The prosecution also queried why the Browne sisters were buying paraffin oil when their lodgings were connected to the local gasworks. It was a question that might have flummoxed lesser witnesses, but the siblings were educated, confident young women who more than capable of holding their own in the intimidating atmosphere of this high-profile trial, which lasted for over two weeks. Interestingly, there were four women on the jury, and my father later said it was the first time female jurors participated in a major criminal case in England, having only received the right to vote three years earlier.

The case against Neill Kerr was almost as circumstantial as that of my father and the Brownes. Several documents had been found in his home that connected him to Sinn Féin, including Irish republican bonds and an Irish Volunteers uniform, but the only item of any real significance was the receipt for the bolt-cutters. The prosecution threw everything into the mix – from anti-English poems found in McCaughey's possession to a letter in Kerr's home in which Éamon de Valera sent his best wishes.

McCaughey was questioned by Hewart who asked him whether he was 'one of the more peaceful sort of Sinn Féiners'.

"I should say I am peaceful enough," replied McCaughey.

Hewart then quoted from some verses found in the defendant's possession:

Let every man be ready, then, to strike a fatal blow,
For England's been our enemy from years long, long ago.

McCaughey said he agreed with the verse but that was 'a different thing to burning and shooting'.

"Are you in favour of rebellion," asked Hewart

"Yes, if we are forced to it," replied McCaughey.

Neill Kerr also took the stand and explained how he came to Liverpool over 30 years earlier and always sympathised with the idea of establishing an Irish republic by constitutional means. He knew nothing of any conspiracy, he said, and had nothing to do with the fires. Kerr claimed he and McCaughey were at the Irish dance in St Joseph's Hall that night and several female witnesses corroborated his evidence, prompting an unimpressed Hewart to describe the Irish dance as 'an alibi factory'. He wasn't wrong. In fact, the Browne sisters organised the dance for the specific purpose of providing the members of the IRA arson teams with alibis.

Kerr was also questioned about a letter found in his house that included the following passage: *The President wishes specially to be remembered to you and sends his very best regards.*

Initially, the Armagh man claimed he could not tell who the president in question might be, but under cross-examination agreed it was de Valera and said they had been introduced to each other in Dublin some years earlier.

"Witness [said he] had done nothing for de Valera to entitle him to special remembrance," the court reporter noted.

Of course, de Valera had every reason to be grateful to Kerr, who had ensured the president's safe passage through Liverpool, not once but twice.

The most incriminating piece of evidence against the Armagh man was the receipt for the bolt-cutters, which he claimed to have found while walking along Stanley Road in Bootle. It was an implausible explanation but it was the best Kerr could muster.

The jurors never got to make up their minds about my father's innocence or guilt. The trial had entered its third week when Sir Alfred Aspinall Tobin instructed the jury to deliver a verdict of not guilty in the case of Henry Peter Coyle, but the judge made it clear he was under no illusions about my father's involvement in the warehouse fires and other IRA 'activities' in England.

"Though I firmly believe that Coyle is a dangerous criminal, I must ask the jury to return a verdict of not guilty as there is not sufficient evidence to convict him," Tobin said. "But, of course, he will be handed over to the Scottish authorities to be tried in Scotland for the crimes committed there."

The *Liverpool Echo* described the moment the verdict was delivered:
Coyle left the dock after shaking hands warmly with two of the other prisoners.

My father had managed to escape conviction in Liverpool, but the weight of evidence against him in Scotland was considerably greater. As the handcuffs were placed on him inside the courtroom, he must have known that even Houdini would struggle to evade the lengthy jail term awaiting him up north. Instead, he intended to use the upcoming trial to advance the cause of Irish independence by making people in Scotland and England aware of the reasons why young Irishmen like himself were willing to sacrifice their freedom and even their lives for the Sinn Féin cause.

Edinburgh Courthouse in March 1921 would be the setting for one of Henry Coyle's most important contributions to the fight for Irish freedom.

CHAPTER 17

'The law of Scotland will sternly deal with them'

THE trial in Liverpool continued for several more days after my father's acquittal. The Crown opted not to proceed with the charge of conspiracy to murder against the Browne sisters and they were acquitted on that indictment. However, Sir Alfred Aspinall Tobin directed that the second charge – conspiring to set fire to the warehouses – be put to the jury, along with the conspiracy charges against Neill Kerr, Seamus McCaughey and Matthew Fowler. The murder charge against Fowler was withdrawn due to a lack of evidence.

In mounting a robust defence of Neill Kerr, Edward Hemmerde said the only evidence against him, apart from the fact that he was a Sinn Féiner, was a receipt for bolt-cutters found in his possession.

"The case for the Crown apparently was that he had something to do with something that happened on November 27th," counsel remarked sarcastically. "The jury is entitled, apparently, to infer that the prisoner had something to do with anything. Why limit it to a charge of conspiracy? Why not throw in any other criminal offences?"

Hemmerde described the prosecution's attempts to use documents and poems, such as 'A Rebel's Greeting', to support its case as 'a travesty of English justice', adding 'it would be unfortunate if one were to be convicted for the sentiments of the poet whose books were on one's bookshelves'.

"Many an Irishman, even in Ulster, has during the last century been proud to call himself a rebel, and my clients are not only Sinn Féiners but they glory in it. A son of Neill Kerr was an officer in the Irish Republican Army and he is not ashamed of the fact. He denies, however, having taken any part whatsoever in the events of November 27."

Referring to a membership card for the Irish Volunteers found in McCaughey's possession, Hemmerde said his client had 'as much right to belong to the Irish Volunteers as distinguished lawyers had to be members of the Ulster Volunteers', which was a pointed reference to Sir Edward Carson.

Despite Hemmerde's best efforts, Kerr and McCaughey were convicted of conspiracy to murder and Fowler was found guilty of conspiring to set fire to the warehouses. The Browne sisters were acquitted.

Imposing ten-year jail terms on Kerr and McCaughey, as well as a maximum two-year sentence on Fowler, Sir Alfred Tobin said they had 'hoped by their acts to strike terror in the hearts of the citizens of Liverpool'.

Former Conservative MP and leading judge Sir Alfred Aspinall Tobin presided over the trial in Liverpool involving my father and the other Sinn Féin members charged with the arson attacks in November 1920.

"Your hopes were in vain," he said. "The British people will not be terrorised by such means."

Tobin, a former Tory MP and the son of a wealthy Liverpool merchant, took a dim view of the campaign for Irish independence.

"I'm sure he would be delighted in sentencing us all to death if he could," my father later remarked.

Neill Kerr successfully appealed the conspiracy to murder conviction, and his ten-year term was overturned, but a concurrent two-year sentence for conspiring to burn the warehouses was upheld. He served his sentence in the notorious Wormwood Scrubs in London and Michael Collins actually got approval from UK Prime Minister Lloyd George to visit Kerr during the Treaty negotiations later that year. It shows how highly Collins regarded Kerr.

The Browne sisters were unable to return to their lodgings at Laburnum Grove in Seaforth in the immediate aftermath of the trial. The reason? There were still 17 rifles hidden in the coal cellar!

Incredibly, the detectives who raided the rented property failed to find the rifles, but I can only imagine the pressure those two women must have been under for the three months they were in custody, fully aware that this secret stash of weapons might be uncovered at any moment.

It wasn't the first time these two remarkable women hid weapons for the IRA. In fact, they once participated in a raid for arms in Everton, joining the Irish Volunteers in the early hours of the morning after attending a céilí. Some 20 rifles were seized that night and the Browne sisters carried one each under their coats for a distance of five miles to Seaforth.

The two sisters came from a well-to-do farming family in North Cork and had joined Cumann na mBan in Liverpool after the 1916 Rising. One of their first tasks was to visit some of the Irish prisoners in Knutsford Jail and to make parcels for them. They also organised bazaars and dances to raise funds for Sinn Féin's general election campaign in 1918 and for the purchase of weapons. Sheila Browne, who was the elder of the sisters, brought money to Ireland on several occasions and also carried dispatches between Liverpool and Dublin.

When Terence MacSwiney died on hunger strike in Brixton Prison, the Brownes were among a party of Sinn Féin members in England who travelled to Cork for the funeral, using the trip to smuggle some munitions.

Apart from regularly storing war material in their lodgings, the sisters also opened their door to any IRA man who was on the run or needed accommodation at short notice. Their arrest was inevitable because the police had long suspected them of being active in Irish nationalist circles in Liverpool. The detention of two professional women on such serious charges prompted a lot of interest in the media and the *Liverpool Echo* published a report about their unsuccessful application to secure bail in the run-up to Christmas. The newspaper stated:

Mr Justin Lynskey, for the prisoners, said his clients had previously borne very good characters, the elder girl being a schoolteacher under the Bootle education authority, while her sister was employed as a clerk in a Liverpool establishment.

They had been brought up in considerable comfort, if not luxury, and for girls of that type to be kept in prison was a heavy ordeal, and, at this time of the year, was particularly unpleasant… If ultimately they were found not guilty, he was sure that even the prosecution would not desire that these girls should go through life with the bitter memory of a Christmas spent in gaol.

When the sisters finally got their freedom two months later, they struggled to resume their old lives. They returned to Laburnum Grove after the IRA managed to remove the rifles from the coal cellar in the dead of night, but a police detective tracked the siblings everywhere, forcing them to reluctantly sever their links with Cumann na mBan.

Sheila and Kathleen Browne must have been a great loss to the IRA in Liverpool because they were – in the words of my father – 'two of the bravest girls that ever went across [from Ireland]'. It is a privilege to be able to recount their heroic deeds and I know it is something my father would have wanted.

Although he was initially charged with the Liverpool fires, Charlie Strickland never stood trial due to a lack of evidence. Instead, he was sent back to Scotland to face charges arising out of the IRA raid in Bothwell on October 28, 1920. Charlie was one of seven men to appear before a special sitting of the High Court in Glasgow on February 8, 1921, to face charges of rioting and the attempted murder of a police officer. The other defendants were Robert McErlane, James Rodgers, Patrick Clark, Patrick Martin, Patrick Moan and William Doherty.

SHOOTINGS IN BOTHWELL

Seven Men Charged at Glasgow High Court

MOB AND THE LORRY

Witnesses and Question of Identification

A special sitting of the High Court of Justiciary was held in Glasgow yesterday to inquire into charges against seven men who are alleged to be involved in the shooting of a constable named Alexander McKay, at Bothwell, near Glasgow, on October 28th. [...]med are:—Charles McG[...]

My father's friend Charlie Strickland was returned to Glasgow where he faced trial in relation to the shooting of two police constables in Bothwell in October 1920.

"It is alleged that they formed part of a riotous mob, armed with revolvers, pistols, and other firearms, and with bayonet sticks [and] that they attempted to murder two constables, one being seriously wounded," reported the *Freeman's Journal.*

Several members of the local Masonic lodge gave evidence of attending a meeting that night and seeing men acting in a suspicious manner near the police station. There was a suggestion that the motor lorry the men were using had broken down (which is entirely possible!) and this caused a crowd to gather, resulting in the eventual altercation in which Constable McKay was shot and wounded.

Charlie Strickland, who was still using the pseudonym McGinn, took the stand to vehemently protest his innocence.

"McGinn, who looks much younger than the 19 years he gave to the court, said he went to Dublin three weeks before the Bothwell outrage to get work," the *Freeman's Journal* reported. "On the 29th October, he crossed from Dublin to Birkenhead on a cattle boat. He well remembered the night of the crossing because a man lost money, and there was trouble (laughter)."

Charlie knew a thing or two about keeping a close eye on money while travelling across the Irish Sea because he brought large amounts of cash to my father from GHQ on a number of occasions. His youthful looks were the cause of much mirth in the courtroom when counsel suggested he was 'in charge of the men in the dock'.

"Have you ever seen them before?" asked counsel.

"No," replied Charlie.

"Is it true you gave orders to fire?"

"No."

"Or that you shot Constable McKay?"

"No."

Despite the vehement protestations of innocence and his boyish appearance, Charlie was convicted and sentenced to a harsh ten-year term as 'the leader' of the 'Bothwell outrage', as it was called in the press. Rodgers, Martin and Moan were jailed for eight years, while the cases against McErlane, Clark and Doherty were deemed 'not proven'. In delivering his verdict, the judge Lord Anderson was unsparing in his condemnation of the Sinn Féin campaign in Scotland.

"There is no use winking at the fact that there is congregated in Scotland an alien populace, without a drop of Scottish blood, who care nothing at all for Scottish national feelings," he said. "They have, unfortunately, succeeded in capturing a considerable following, although the vast majority of Scottish workmen are impervious to their doctrines.

"These people should take warning because if they attempt their revolutionary or criminal methods to propagate their doctrines – social, economic or political – the law of Scotland will sternly deal with them."

Lord Anderson's comments reflected a mounting anti-Irish sentiment in Scotland, especially in Glasgow where some people still believed that the huge haul of gelignite found in Alloa was to be used to blow up the city's docks. Jean Gillespie was taken into custody on Christmas Eve 1920 after Glasgow police raided her shop and found some 'incriminating' documents. Mary Brannick took over the running of the business while Jean awaited trial.

"Public feeling was very high against those who took part in the struggle for Irish liberty," she recalled.

By the time my father returned from Liverpool, there were 15 others facing trial arising out of the IRA operations in Scotland. The arrest of so many key members of my father's gun smuggling team was already being felt back in Ireland where the lack of munitions was causing concern at GHQ.

"In February 1921, Michael Collins complained that the quantity [of munitions] being procured by the Clydeside men was declining," wrote historian Gerard Noonan in his book *The IRA in Britain, 1919-1923*. "[Collins] reflected wistfully on what the situation had been 12 months previously when gunrunning was going 'well' and 'the stuff was coming inn [sic] at a fine rate'.

Now 'nothing' was being received. He blamed the deterioration on the fallout from the Bothwell incident and the arrest of Henry Coyle."

Collins had good reason to feel concerned. The commanding officer of the Scottish IRA Brigade, John Carney, was struggling to replace the arrested men, while D.P. Walsh, who was dispatched from GHQ following my father's arrest, had found it difficult to obtain 'war material'. The capture of Joe Vize in Dublin in October 1920 compounded the problems because he would have been the best person to rebuild the Scottish gunrunning operation. In my father's application for an IRA pension, Vize gives an insight into how successful they had been in 1920 when, as Collins stated, 'war material' was arriving from Scotland 'at a fine rate'.

"During his time with me," stated Vize, "[Henry Coyle] worked very hard in the purchase department getting a good amount of stuff for us. It was only when I was arrested and Scotland got disorganised that he was arrested also.

"Four different men were sent out from Dublin to take charge there at different times. The result was disorganisation of all my work and wholesale arrests."

The disintegration of the Scottish gun-running operation could not have come at a worse time for Michael Collins who needed every weapon he could get to deal with the worsening situation in Ireland. In my father's case, the War of Independence was now being fought in courtrooms, and he intended to mount a defiant defence of Ireland's right to self-governance when he appeared in the dock in Edinburgh for one of the most high-profile trials in recent Scottish history.

CHAPTER 18

A mother's anguish

HOURS before my father appeared in the dock at the High Court of Justiciary in Edinburgh on Monday, March 14, 1921, an event occurred at Mountjoy Prison in Dublin that shocked Irish people all over the world. Commencing at dawn, six republican prisoners were hanged – two each at intervals of one hour – on charges of murder and high treason. Not since the immediate aftermath of the 1916 Rising had so many Volunteers being executed on a single morning.

"Scenes of the utmost solemnity were witnessed outside the prison while the grim tragedy was being enacted within its walls," wrote the *Freeman's Journal*. "It was a bitter cold and dreary morning, but this did not deter people from coming out as soon as the lifting of curfew would permit, and shortly after five o'clock thousands from all parts of the city were wending their way to Mountjoy."

The six men who gave their lives for Ireland on that dismal spring morning were Thomas Whelan (22), Patrick Moran (33), Thomas Bryan (24), Patrick Doyle (29), Frank Flood (20) and Bernard Ryan (20). Whelan and Moran were West of Ireland men – Whelan from Clifden in Co Galway and Moran from Ardcarne in Co Roscommon – while the other four were Dubliners. Some 20,000 people gathered outside Mountjoy Prison on the morning of their executions.

"Many bore lighted candles, and on the high wall, close to the gate, were statues of the Sacred Heart and Our Blessed Lady, surrounded by lights," wrote the *Freeman's Journal*. "Here the heroic mother of Thomas Whelan, clad in her Western clothing, took her place to join in the chorus of prayer for her dying boy. The scene at this juncture was so touching that even the soldiers in an armoured car stationed some yards away leant over in silent awe and wonder, and seemed to forget, for the moment, the grim occupation in which they were

and ❧ rost

MOST WIDELY CIRCULATED EVENING PAPER IN SCOTLAND OUT OF EDIN

DUNDEE, MONDAY, MARCH 14, 1921

SIX IRISH REBELS HANGED IN DUBLIN.

DOUBLE EXECUTIONS AT HOURLY INTERVALS.

Sensational Sinn Fein Trial Opens To-Day in Edinburgh.

Six Irish rebels, two of whom had been found guilty of murder, were hanged in Montjoy Prison, Dublin, to-day.

The executions began as early as six o'clock the morning, and the men were

My father went on trial in Edinburgh on Monday, March 14, 1921, just hours after six men were hanged at Mountjoy Jail for their involvement in the IRA campaign in Ireland. Had my father been tried in Ireland, he would have almost certainly faced the death penalty.

the participants. As the fatal hour approached, the crowds grew in immensity, and the Rosary continued to be recited up to the very last moment."

Had my father been captured in Ireland with the quantity of explosives and weapons found in his car in Alloa, he too would surely have been making that long, lonely walk to the gallows in Mountjoy. As it was, the trial in Edinburgh bore all the hallmarks of a major murder case with the police imposing strict security measures around the courthouse and in the chamber itself.

The 16 prisoners were taken under a heavy guard from Carlton Prison in Glasgow to Edinburgh, a distance of about 50 miles.

"Great interest was taken in the trial," reported the *Scottish Evening Telegraph and Post*, "and special precautions were taken by the authorities, a large force of police being stationed outside and inside the Court Buildings in Parliament Square.

"The accused were taken from Carlton Prison to the High Court manacled together in batches of three. Special tickets were issued to the public and press for admission to the High Court."

Joining my father in the dock were Bernard McCabe, Charles McGinn (Strickland), Edmond Magner, James Devine, Robert McErlane, Henry McErlane, Ambrose McErlane, Peter Quinn, Michael Gallagher, Jean Quinn, Thomas Gillespie, Patrick Carrigan, James Fagan, Robert O'Donnell and Hugh Traynor. They were all charged with conspiring to endanger life and property in the United Kingdom, while my father and Charlie Strickland were also charged with contravening the Explosive Substances Act and the Firearms Act.

If my father and his co-defendants were worried about what lay ahead, they certainly did not show it on that first morning.

"The prisoners were nearly all young men, and were, in most cases, well dressed," reported the *Scottish Evening Telegraph and Post*. "On entering the dock, they smiled quite cheerfully to one another.

"The woman prisoner appeared to be 20 years of age, is good looking, and has red hair."

Another of Scotland's popular newspapers, *The Daily Record and Mail*, gave a fascinating insight into the intense security surrounding the trial.

Elaborate police arrangements were made, and in addition to a considerable force being held in reserve, an exceptionally large number were on duty inside and in the precincts of the High Court.

The dock was not big enough to hold all the accused, some of whom had to be accommodated in a seat behind, formerly reserved for the Press.

In addition to officers being in attendance on the accused in the dock and in the seat behind, a third seat immediately behind these again was also occupied by stalwart policemen, who sat with drawn batons in their right hands.

The jurymen, of whom 200 were summoned, had to show their citations before admission…

Unlike the trial in Liverpool, the Crown had assembled a wealth of evidence that it intended to put before the jury, including 250 exhibits and statements from 79 witnesses. The Sinn Féin Motorcar and the lorry my father used on several occasions to transport weapons from Glasgow to Liverpool stood at the door of the courthouse, while the long list of exhibits included cartridges of gelignite, coils of fuse, rifles and bayonets.

"The detonators and the high explosives were on account of the safety of the public stored outside the court," reported *The Daily Record and Mail*.

During my research, I found a remarkable document in the pension application of Kate Lee, who was summoned to the trial because my father lodged at her home up to the time of his arrest. Kate retained a copy of the charge sheet and submitted it to the Army Pensions Board two decades later as part of her application for an IRA pension. By then, the pages were frayed around the edges, but the type is still perfectly legible, as readers can see from the accompanying images in Appendix II at the end of the book.

I could not believe it when I stumbled across this fascinating snapshot of Irish history, and it is a privilege to be able to publish it a century later and to remember and honour the brave woman who retained it as a keepsake from a momentous period in her life. Kate is another of those forgotten heroines of the era. She carried dinner into my father and the other prisoners while they were in Carlton Prison awaiting trial and she organised a fundraiser to assist the prisoners and their families.

The significance of the Sinn Féin trial is reflected in the fact that it was presided over by the most senior judge in Scotland, Lord Justice General James Avon Clyde. A Unionist member of parliament for Edinburgh West from 1909 to 1920, Clyde had just assumed the Lord Justice General role having worked for four years as Lord Advocate, the name given to the British government's chief legal officer in Scotland.

In fact, there was no shortage of 'lords' in the courtroom.

"The case was taken up by the Lord Justice General, Lord Clyde, instead of the Lord Justice Clerk, Lord Scott Dickson," wrote the *Freeman's Journal*. "The Lord Advocate, with Mr D.P. Fleming and Lord Kinross, appeared for the Crown, and Mr Morton, K.C., and Mr Morrice MacKay, K.C., were among the counsel for the defence."

The newspaper also noted there were quite a number of women in the public gallery, so my father and his colleagues were going to be in the company of lords and ladies for the trial, which was scheduled to last a full week.

Although there was a wealth of evidence inside and outside the courtroom, the prosecution favoured a general charge of conspiracy against the 16 defendants who pleaded not guilty to all matters. It might seem surprising that my father would deny his involvement in the Sinn Fén plot in Scotland, given that he had been caught red-handed with 2,980 cartridges of gelignite and an assortment of other 'war material', but he had to plead not guilty if there was to be any chance of gaining acquittals for his co-defendants. It was better to deny everything and let the prosecution try to piece together a case that might or might not convince the jury of the defendants' guilt.

Much of the morning was taken up with empanelling the jury. Each prisoner was allowed to object to four jurors so there was a possibility that 64 of the 200 potential jurors could be rejected. An early application by the defence counsel to have the charge of conspiracy dismissed on the grounds that it was too vague was refused, with the Lord Justice General ruling that 'conspiracy to commit a crime was, in itself, a crime'.

Thomas Whelan (right) and Patrick Moran photographed shortly before their executions at Mountjoy Jail in March 1921.

Most of the evidence on that opening day concerned the Christmas Eve raid on the home of Jean Quinn, who was described as 'the treasurer of the Jim Connolly Sinn Féin Club'.

"The police found a quantity of literature relating to the Sinn Féin organisation, " wrote the *Daily Record and Mail.* "There was also a quantity of receipts and balance sheets of the Jim Connolly Sinn Féin Club.

"Telegrams bearing to be dispatched from Belfast, membership cards with the name of Jean Quinn on one of them, were also found."

The trial was told that Jean's home at 19 Kent Street and her mother's shop at 47 Kent Street were searched. An attaché case containing a Sam Browne belt and a water bottle, two Sinn Féin flags, an Irish Volunteers uniform and a handbag containing 11 rounds of ammunition were among the items found. The accused initially denied all knowledge of these items, but when the police threatened to arrest her mother, she immediately stated: "I alone am responsible."

Jean's boyfriend, Thomas Gillespie, was also among the defendants, and letters between the two were produced as evidence, including one in which Jean said she 'could not go to sleep at night for dreaming of the police'.

Evidence was also produced against Gillespie, who had a bandolier and six rounds of ammunition in his residence, while a third defendant Peter Quinn was found to be in possession of a revolver, Sinn Féin membership card, a Sinn Féin buttonhole badge, Morse code cards and a flash lamp.

Many of the exhibits produced on that opening day were not, of themselves, proof of conspiracy to commit a crime, but the prosecution hoped that by linking the accused to my father they would convince the jury that all 16 had been 'acting in concert' as part of a wider conspiracy 'to endanger life and property in the United Kingdom'. The evidence against my father, which was scheduled for the second day of the trial, would prove crucial to the Crown's broader aim of securing convictions against the other 15 defendants.

The trial became front-page news from day one and was immediately linked to the events in Dublin earlier that morning. *The Evening Telegraph and Post* of March 14 carried the banner headline *'Six Irish Rebels Hanged in Dublin' and a sub-heading 'Sensational Sinn Féin trial opens today in Edinburgh'.*

I have no doubt my father, who was an avid newspaper reader from a young age, would have been fully aware of the coverage and may even have read the front-page of the March 14 edition of the *Evening Telegraph and Post*, which I have reproduced earlier in this chapter. If he did so, he would have learned of a poignant visit by poor Mrs Whelan from Clifden to her young son on the eve of his execution.

Thomas Whelan was entirely innocent of the crime for which he was condemned and it must have been a desperate ordeal for his mother to have to kneel in prayer outside the walls of Mountjoy while her beloved boy was walking to the gallows.

I am sure my father thought of his own mother on many occasions before and during the trial in Edinburgh. He knew a lengthy term of imprisonment awaited him if he was found guilty and, in truth, there was never any doubt the jury would convict him on all charges. As I mentioned earlier, had the case been in Ireland he would have been joining Thomas Whelan and the other five men who that morning gave their young lives for the same cause my father and so many other young Irish men and women were fighting for.

During my research, I found another report in the *Derry Journal* about the hangings in Dublin, and it would bring tears to your eyes. The report states that at 8.30am that morning, a notice was affixed to the entrance of Mountjoy

This remarkable image was taken outside Mountjoy Jail on the morning of March 14, 1921, when six brave Irishmen were executed.

Jail, stating: *The sentences of the law passed upon Thomas Whelan and Patrick Moran, found guilty of murder, and Francis Flood, Thomas Bryan, Patrick Doyle and Bernard Ryan, found guilty of high treason by levying war, were carried into execution this morning. By order.*

The newspaper describes in heartbreaking detail what happened next:

At this point, a number of relatives of the condemned young men for the first time gave way to a sudden convulsion of grief…

Mrs Whelan, the poor old mother, still dressed in her striking Connemara attire, who occupied a chair beside the gate, gave way to heartrending sobs, and insisted on the notice being taken down so that she might kiss the name of her dear son. The wish was complied with.

That newspaper report deeply affected me because it could so easily have been my grandmother, Mary Coyle, who had to make that long journey from the West to hold vigil outside Mountjoy as her son went to the gallows. When we commemorate the struggle for Irish freedom, we rightly honour the dead but we sometimes forget the living, the ones who shouldered an unbearable burden for the rest of their days; I think, in particular, of Mrs Whelan and all the other brave mothers and fathers who lost sons or daughters as a result of those terrible times. They, too, are heroes of the struggle for Irish independence and we should never forget them and the sufferings they endured for the freedom we enjoy today.

CHAPTER 19

'We were dealing with a very dangerous situation'

THE *Daily Record and Mail* was the biggest-selling morning newspaper in Scotland in 1921, with a circulation three times its' nearest rival. On Wednesday, March 16, the trial in Edinburgh dominated its front page. *Sensational Stories in Scots Conspiracy Trial* declared the banner headline above a series of sub-headings that included 'Money From Ireland' and 'Alloa Motor Car Chase'. The newspaper noted there had been 'no diminution of public interest in the trial'.

Among the prosecution witnesses on the second day was the unnamed military officer – described only as a 'lieutenant of the South Lancashire Regiment' – who carried out the raid on Richard Mulcahy's lodgings on November 16, 1920.

"There he found a number of papers," reported *The Scotsman* newspaper. "One of these documents referred to the distribution of £3,600, and it included among other items: - '15th August, M.G., £500; 9th September, Coyle, £1,000'. Another paper, found on the same occasion, contained an item with the name 'Henry Coyle' and 'four guineas a week'.

"There was also found a receipt from a Glasgow motor firm to 'Robert McErlane' for £565 [and] items referring to arms and explosives."

The lieutenant told the court that the documents seized were also found to contain references to some of the other accused, including Bernard McCabe.

"Have you any evidence that any of these documents were ever seen by any of the accused?" asked defense counsel Mr Mackay.

"None at all," replied the witness.

A military sergeant from Dublin corroborated the lieutenant's evidence, but conceded in cross-examination there was nothing in the documents to

The High Court of Justiciary in Edinburgh where my father and 15 others faced trial in March 1921.

connect them to Glasgow, apart from the receipt for the motor lorry. He also agreed that Coyle was a very common Irish name.

The trial also heard from Rev Michael Herrington from the town of Barrhead, which is located about 13 kilometres southwest of Glasgow, who advertised a motorcycle for sale in 1920. The purchaser's name was Duffy or Daly, he said.

"Have you lost your memory about this?" asked the Lord Advocate.

"Pretty well," replied the priest. "Once the transaction was over I paid no more heed to it."

Fr Herrington said the price of the motorcycle was £70 and the purchaser handed him a £100 note. He gave him back £30 in change.

"Did it not strike you as odd that he should pay with a £100 note?" asked the Lord Advocate.

"No," replied Fr Herrington.

One of the most interesting aspects of the trial was the evidence from Sgt Denholm and the other policemen who arrested my father on the night of December 4, 1920. The court was told of a 'prolonged, fierce and very vicious fight on the roadside as Coyle fought desperately to evade capture'.

"A number of the constabulary and the prisoner Coyle were injured before they were finally able to bring the situation under control," the court heard. "Officers with batons eventually managed to disarm and subdue Coyle and take him into custody."

Detectives produced one of the revolvers, a .22 automatic, knocked from my father's hands during the violent struggle. Two fully-loaded revolvers were found in the car.

The jury was left in no doubt that my father received a severe beating that night but the police claimed all of his injuries were sustained on the roadside and not in the station in Alloa. Evidence was given that a doctor had to be called to the police station to treat the 'severe bleeding and arm wounds sustained by Coyle'.

Under cross-examination, one of the policemen admitted my father was 'very unresponsive for a period of time' after he was taken to the police station, and the doctor had to clean and stitch his wounds.

Chief Constable Tom Johnston told the court that all of my father's injuries were sustained prior to arriving at Alloa Police Station.

"How long did the doctor spend treating my client's wounds?" asked Mr Mackay.

"I cannot be sure," replied Johnston, adding that my father received 'quite a number of stitches' to his face, head and arms.

Mr Mackay: "So you didn't see the prisoner Coyle being threatened or abused in any way while in custody."

"No, nothing like that," came the reply.

When Mackay raised several questions about my father's detention and, in particular, the amount of time that elapsed before he was formally charged, Chief Constable Johnston had this to say:

"We were dealing with a very dangerous situation and with daring and dangerous individuals on the night. We also had to call for reinforcements to arrive to keep guard on the prisoners in case there was any attempt by others to break them out and that was the reason why Coyle and his companion were moved to more secure detention centres."

Despite the evidence of the Chief Constable, I have no doubt my father was severely beaten while in police custody. Indeed, he said as much in his application for an IRA pension and in interviews I conducted with him in the 1970s. The police beat him on the roadside and again at the station because they could not get any information from him. In fact, Chief Constable Johnston admitted at the trial that my father 'would not even divulge his address' and claimed he was staying at a Glasgow hotel.

"Investigations were going on through the night to try and establish where he was staying and it took several days to finally establish that he had a rented room [with Kate Lee] at 7 Todd Street, Dennistoun, Glasgow."

My father's stubborn refusal to reveal anything about himself ensured that people like Kate Lee had time to remove incriminating material from their homes before the police came knocking. Kate's next-door neighbour, a lady named Agnes Leith, told the court that 'a good number of people came by the house when Coyle was there', including the defendants Bernard McCabe and Hugh Traynor.

"[Mrs Leith] gave further evidence of seeing Coyle coming and going on a motorcycle," wrote the *Daily Record and Mail*, "and sometime later there was a sidecar attached to the motorcycle and she would see Coyle taking golf bags from the sidecar into the house.

DENOUNCED AS SPY AT SINN FEIN CLUB.

DETECTIVE'S STORY AT EDINBURGH CONSPIRACY TRIAL.

Alleged Concerted Move to Endanger Life and Property.

"When asked did it seem odd to her that so many people came to the house, she said that she was told that Coyle was in the insurance business and she thought the callers were customers of his."

Under cross-examination, Mrs Leith said police first called to her house on December 11 and asked her to go to the police station to identify some men in custody. She identified McCabe and Traynor as visitors to 7 Todd Street, but was 'unsure of Coyle's identity as his head was heavily bandaged and his face and eyes were swollen'.

I think Mrs Leith's evidence is very revealing because she saw my father a full week after his arrest in Alloa, so he must have taken a ferocious beating if he was still unrecognisable seven days later. It is to his credit that he didn't divulge any information that might have implicated those who were assisting him. In fact, he tried to create the impression that he had recently arrived from Ireland, was staying in a hotel in Glasgow and had borrowed the car from Bernard McCabe without telling him what he intended to do with it. My father also pretended that Charlie Strickland (McGinn) was innocent of any wrongdoing.

"One of the first things Coyle said was that McGinn had nothing to do with the stuff in the car, and knew nothing about it," said Chief Constable Johnston. "McGinn did not know for what purpose they went to Cowdenbeath."

But my father could not easily explain away the documents found in his possession, in particular the driver's licence in the name of Edmond Magner.

SENSATIONAL STORIES
MONEY FROM IRELAND.

ESTAR. 1847—No. 23,112.

STARTLING EVIDENCE IN CONSPIRACY TRIAL.

ALLOA MOTOR CAR CHASE.

DRAMATIC HAND TO HAND FIGHT IN DUBLIN.

Capture of Explosives.—Sensational captures of explosives, ammunition, and arms in houses in Glasgow were detailed by police officers in the High Court in Edinburgh yesterday during the trial of the fifteen men and one woman who are charged with being concerned in an alleged Sinn Fein conspiracy in Scotland.

Motor Car as Arsenal.—Evidence was also given regarding the exciting chase after a motor car at Alloa, which was found to contain about 3 cwts. of explosives. A detective inspector related how, on visiting a Sinn Fein club in Glasgow, he was challenged as a spy

Money from Dublin.—A military officer from Dublin stated that during a search in Dublin receipts were found for money totalling £2000, and three of the receipts were in the names of Bernard M'Cabe, Robert M'Elwane, and "Coyle."

CONSPIRACY TRIAL. | **DUBLIN MELEE.**

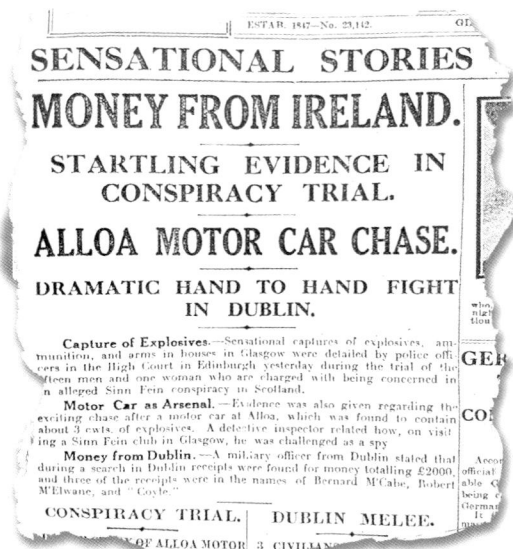

The trial heard that police in Glasgow searched the home of the Cork native later that night but found no incriminating material. When asked for his driving licence, Magner claimed he gave it to a man named 'Charlie' who he met at church in order to help him get a job. It was a fairly lame excuse and Magner made his situation worse by telling the police: "I am a rebel, but not here. If I was at home I would be like the rest."

Detective Constable John Wiseman gave evidence of the search of Hugh Traynor's home at 11 East John Street in Glasgow where police found a trunk containing two bayonets, two live rounds and two blank rounds of rifle ammunition and five dummy cartridges for musketry practice. They also found a considerable quantity of Sinn Féin and Irish Republican Army literature, including a copy of the constitution of Sinn Féin, nomination forms of members and several subscription sheets for the Prisoners' Defence Fund.

"Mixed with other documents was found a card of authority to the prisoner Henry Peter Coyle to attend as delegate the Central Committee meeting of the Comhairle Ceanntair on November 1, 1919," wrote the *Daily Record and Mail*. "Another letter dated May 5, 1920, from Sinn Féin headquarters acknowledging receipt of a large sum of money addressed to the prisoner Coyle was also found among Traynor's papers. There was also an Irish Volunteers membership card in the name of Hugh Traynor and a pencil note showing the election of Henry Coyle as chairman and Hugh Traynor as secretary."

The Sinn Féin branch of which my father was chairman was the Major John MacBride Club, based in Parkhead. I am not sure whether my father was a founding member of the club, but the Mayo link is certainly evident in its name. Interestingly, the trial heard that Traynor resigned from the club when he joined the priesthood in the summer of 1920.

My father did his best to distance himself from his co-defendants but the police had carried out a thorough investigation and it was clear from the evidence they had been keeping a keen eye on Sinn Féin's activities in Glasgow long before the Alloa incident. Detective Inspector John Wylie told the court he was aware of two Sinn Féin clubs in the city – the Pearse Club and the Alderman MacCurtain Club – and attended the latter's inaugural meeting. However, he was forced to hastily leave when a man accused him of spying.

Wylie admitted that the police had their eyes on two of the defendants – Quinn and Gallagher – for some time, so it was inevitable their homes would be raided in the wake of my father's arrest. The search of Quinn's residence yielded little by way of 'war material' other than a pistol with a missing pin, but Gallagher was found to be in possession of six parcels containing six and a half pounds of samsonite, 214 feet of fuse, 16 detonators, rifle cartridges, 60 revolver cartridges, a revolver and 'various books and papers relating to Sinn Féin'.

"There was a balance sheet showing in pencil an entry of £13 spent on arms, and an apparently later entry in ink showing the same sum spent on 'goods'," wrote *The Scotsman*. "There was also an undated minute of a branch which stated that business of national importance was discussed, and time and place were fixed for examination of military report. There were lists of names, one being that of Henry Coyle, with a Glasgow address and 'County Mayo' beside it…

"There was a handbook for Irish Volunteers and there was a document giving particulars of explosives and containing references to bridges, iron girders, removing rails, water tanks and rifles. There were copies of the official organ of the Irish Volunteers, and training instructions for the same organisation."

The police put forward ample evidence to connect my father to the Irish Volunteers in Glasgow. A motor engineer and garage proprietor both gave evidence that my father called to their premises and asked for garage room to store a motorcycle and sidecar. He gave his name as John Daly and said he was a sales traveller. Another motor engineer from Liverpool gave evidence of travelling to Glasgow where he identified a green Austin motorcar as the one he repaired in Liverpool on November 15. He also identified my father in a police lineout as the man who brought the car to the garage and had given his name as John Daly.

Many of the 260 exhibits in the trial related to my father, including the huge haul of explosives and guns found in Alloa – both in the green Austin and inside a hedge adjoining the roadside where my father and Charlie dumped two kit bags and two jute bags filled with gelignite. Police told the court that the amount of explosives, ammunition, detonators and guns was 'the single largest consignment ever uncovered being transported by any person or persons on the British mainland'.

An explosives expert said he had examined the cargo and found some of the explosives to be 'in a very dangerous condition and could have very easily ignited and exploded in the car causing the immediate death of the occupants and anyone in the vicinity'. In particular, he said the samsonite was 'very volatile and could explode if the temperature it was stored in dropped below freezing'. It was a good thing there was no Big Freeze in Scotland in early December 1920!

The expert told the court that the explosives were the type used in collieries and quarries for blasting purposes. Handwritten instructions and maps were also produced to the court that showed how to use the explosives for blowing up bridges, buildings, railway tracks, water tanks and 'fuel stacks'. The expert witness said these notes were the work of 'someone who had an intimate knowledge and training in the use of explosives and detonators'.

Investigating detectives told the jury that my father was 'sent over specially from Ireland to organise, recruit and liaise with others in a conspiracy to transport guns, ammunition and explosives to Ireland for the sole use of the Irish Republican Army in their deadly war there'.

"They also claimed that by apprehending Coyle and his very lethal cargo they have prevented much loss of life and damage to key infrastructure in Ireland and the British mainland," one newspaper wrote.

In a week when the Scottish newspapers were carrying stories about shootings and 'riots' on the streets of Dublin, and ambushes on policemen in other parts of Ireland, the Crown was prepared to do whatever it took to put Henry Coyle behind bars for a very long time. The Lord Advocate described my father as being in the pay of the 'extremely militant wing of the Irish Republican Army whose sole aim [was] to break the rule of the British government and His Majesty's forces in Ireland'. He wanted the jury and the media to believe that Henry Peter Coyle was a terrorist and a mercenary who inveigled the other defendants to become involved in a sinister and deadly campaign against King and country.

My father, however, had other ideas and was determined to put his side of the story across before the trial ended. The journalists in the *Daily Record and Mail* would have a few more 'sensational' headlines before the week was through.

CHAPTER 20

'Since last Sunday, I have been arrested every night'

BERNARD McCabe covered his tracks well. When five police officers raided his house at Cumbernauld Road and the two shops at Duke Street, they found not a solitary piece of incriminating evidence. There were no documents relating to the Sinn Féin movement, Irish nationalism or any political organisation, and McCabe hadn't purchased any Dáil loan bonds or supported Irish prisoner defence funds. To all intents and purposes, Bernard McCabe was the model Scottish citizen, a law-abiding, hard-working businessman who seemed utterly indifferent to the political turmoil engulfing his native land.

"His own staff and several businessmen in the East End affirmed that he appeared to be immersed only in the business," wrote the *Scottish Sunday Mail.* "As a most loyal and patriotic citizen, they said, he purchased considerable war stock."

Mary Poane, who worked for McCabe for three years, told the trial that she 'never heard him talk about the Sinn Féin movement'.

In the end, McCabe was convicted on a single piece of paper found in the files of Richard Mulcahy. It was a receipt for £809-7s-6d issued in McCabe's name on September 18, 1920. There was now a paper trail linking the Cavan native to IRA headquarters in Dublin, and much of the prosecution case against McCabe rested on that document. Of course, the shopkeeper also had the problem of explaining his ownership of two vehicles – the Fiat lorry and the Austin car – for which there was no record of payment on his accounts. Detective Inspector John Montgomery told the trial that he seized McCabe's business books shortly after my father's arrest.

"The business books contained no reference as to the purchase of motor cars or for petrol or for garage charges," noted the inspector.

A Glasgow solicitor who acted for McCabe told the trial his client admitted to having a motor lorry and 'a touring car – an Austin'. The latter was 'a source of trouble to him from the beginning' and Robert McErlane, another of the accused, had been doing repairs on it.

John George Ross, of Ross & Christie, 28 Bothwell Street, Glasgow, gave evidence of selling a 20-horsepower Fiat chassis, fitted with lorry body and high sides, to Robert McErlane for £566 on September 23, 1920. Payment was made in five £100 bills and the rest in smaller notes. The receipt from Ross & Christie was, of course, later found in Mulcahy's papers.

In his summing up, the Lord Advocate devoted a considerable amount of time to the involvement of McCabe in the purchase of the lorry and car.

"McCabe lent his name to the purchase of [these vehicles]," reported the *Daily Record and Mail* in a synopsis of the Lord Advocate's case, "and according to his business books not a penny piece had been shown as the purchase price in them. They were got, the Lord Advocate declared, by money supplied by Coyle, and they [the jury] knew where that came from."

The case against McCabe was far from conclusive but there was even less evidence to support the prosecution of the three McErlane brothers, two of whom had seen service in the British Army during World War I. When Henry McErlane was arrested at his home in Springburn, Glasgow, he declared: "I am not in the Sinn Féin movement. I have been in the Army. I have repaired a lot of cars in Petershill Road. I have not taken part in buying or repairing cars for Sinn Féin."

Henry's brothers, Robert and Ambrose, also protested their innocence and said they had merely been repairing the lorry and car for Bernard McCabe and knew nothing about an arms smuggling plot. The only evidence the prosecution could put forward by way of exhibits were a couple of tents and a soldier's kitbag, seized from Ambrose McErlane's house, and a Sinn Féin Rebellion Handbook, dated 1916, found in Henry McErlane's home. The court was told that when Ambrose was charged with 'unlawful possession' of the tents, he responded: "This is a joke. I have had these tents for a long time. I camped with them last summer."

Defence counsel Morrice Mackay wasted no time in dismantling the case against Ambrose McErlane.

"Do you know that McErlane served in the British forces," he asked Detective Inspector John Wyllie.

"Yes, that is so," replied the witness.

"There is nothing suspicious in finding his old army kitbag along with a bell tent in his house?"

"No," conceded Wyllie.

Bernard McCabe (centre), Edmond Magner (left) and James Devine stood trial with my father in the High Court of Justiciary in Edinburgh in March 1921.

A police constable who undertook a regular beat near the garage at Petershill Road, where the McErlane brothers worked, gave evidence of seeing the Fiat lorry enter and leave the premises on several occasions late at night. However, he was unable to say whether any of the other defendants were with the McErlanes on these occasions.

It took three days for the prosecution to present all of the evidence against the 16 defendants, who got the chance to rebut the Crown case on Thursday morning, March 17. All of the main Scottish newspapers faithfully reported everything that went on in the courtroom throughout the week and the *Daily Record and Mail* made the case its front-page story on each of the five days.

"The High Court of Justiciary in Edinburgh was again the theatre of absorbing interest yesterday," wrote the *Daily Record* on March 17. "The story of the alleged [Sinn Féin conspiracy] has flitted from Glasgow to Kirkintilloch, to Cowdenbeath, Dumfermline to Alloa, where the sensational 'hold-up' by the police was made of a motor lorry containing upwards of three cwts of high explosives."

It was only fitting that the defence should open its case on St Patrick's Day, but quite a number of the defendants did not take the stand, including my father, Charlie Strickland and Bernard McCabe.

Robert McErlane, however, put forward a very stout protestation of his and his brothers' innocence. He said it was not unusual for people to ask him to inspect motor vehicles prior to purchase and that was what had happened in this case. He had no idea how his name ended up on the receipt from Ross & Christie and believed it was a forgery. Nor did he know the purpose for which Henry Coyle intended to use the lorry.

McErlane, of course, knew full well what my father wanted the lorry for but had little choice other than to lie under oath. He was the father of three young children and it would have been a disaster for him to end up in prison.

"Can you give any explanation as to how your name should have been mixed up in this matter?" asked the Lord Advocate.

"No," replied McErlane, "I was horrified when I was arrested."

"You say you have really been made a victim of in this matter?"

"Undoubtedly," McErlane firmly replied.

The McErlane brothers claimed their only connection with McCabe was via a Kirkintilloch man named John Devine, another of the defendants, who was described throughout the trial as McCabe's 'chauffeur'.

"Had Devine a car?" Ambrose McErlane was asked.

"Yes, but it was a dud," came the blunt reply.

The cases against James Fagan and Robert O'Donnell arose out of an incident in early December when they tried to purchase arms from a non-commissioned officer at Maryhill Barracks in Glasgow. The officer told the court the two men promised to pay him £1,000 if he helped to remove machine guns, rifles and ammunition from the barracks. A meeting took place in a nearby shop on December 2 at which Fagan said he was willing to purchase 500 rifles.

"The rifles and ammunition were to be taken out of the barracks on a motor lorry," the court was told. "Arrangements were completed as to the taking out of the rifles and ammunition. A rough sketch was drawn showing the route to be followed…"

This incident occurred prior to my father's arrest so I presume he was going to be involved in the operation and would probably have driven the lorry. However, unbeknownst to Fagan and O'Donnell, the officer had already contacted the police and two detectives were ready to pounce. They burst into the shop, seized the sketch and arrested both men. The charges against them were not directly linked to my father's arrest but the prosecution saw fit to lump all of the cases together with the aim of convincing the jury of a widespread and insidious Sinn Féin 'conspiracy' in Scotland.

Several family members of the defendants gave evidence on their behalf, including a sister of the McErlanes and the wife of Peter Quinn. The trial also heard that when Patrick Carrigan was arrested for possessing Sinn Féin literature, he remarked: "That doesn't bother me, Charlie died for it."

Carrigan was referring to his older brother Charles who was one of a 20-man contingent from Glasgow that travelled across to Dublin to participate in the 1916 Rising. The 34-year-old was killed during the evacuation of the GPO.

Elizabeth Carrigan, sister of Charles and Patrick, told the trial that Countess Markievicz once visited their home and they had other visitors too who were involved in the Irish independence movement.

Jean Quinn's mother, Mary Ann, also took the stand to protest her daughter's innocence, and said her views about Sinn Féin 'were always of the peaceable type'. The Lord Advocate then quoted from one of Jean's letters to Thomas Gillespie in which she stated: "I have become very restless. I never go to sleep now without dreaming about police. Is that not strange? Since last Sunday, I have been arrested every night. I wonder what crime I have committed."

The Lord Advocate continued with his probing:

"Did you know your daughter was a 'lieutenant' and signed herself so?" he asked Mrs Quinn.

M'CABE'S DUAL LIFE.

SUBTLE PRODUCE MERCHANT.

HOW HE PROFITED BY SINN FEIN.

FAMOUS GREEN CAR.

There was a lot of media interest during the trial in Cavan-born merchant Bernard McCabe who was accused of conspiring with my father.

"She never did it in the shop!" replied the redoubtable Mary Ann, prompting the courtroom to erupt into laughter.

Jean Quinn, in her evidence, denied having anything to do with 'matters of a military or artillery interest', but refused to disavow the Sinn Féin movement, of which she was a proud member.

"Are you ashamed of your connection with your organisation?" asked defense counsel Mr Mackay.

"No," the 22-year-old replied.

"If your connection with this organisation is sufficient to run you in [to prison], you are prepared to be run in?"

"Yes."

Like the Browne sisters in Liverpool, Jean Quinn is another of those brave young women who richly deserves her place in the annals of Ireland's independence struggle. There are not many people today who would be willing to go before a court and risk imprisonment for their principles. Jean Quinn was barely into adulthood yet she demonstrated an unshakeable courage on that St Patrick's Day in 1921 as she defended her right to be involved in the struggle for Irish independence. As a young businesswoman who was engaged-to-be-married, Jean had so much to lose, but she refused to sell out on her principles. It is wonderful to be able to acknowledge her unwavering commitment to Irish independence, and that of the 14 others who stood trial

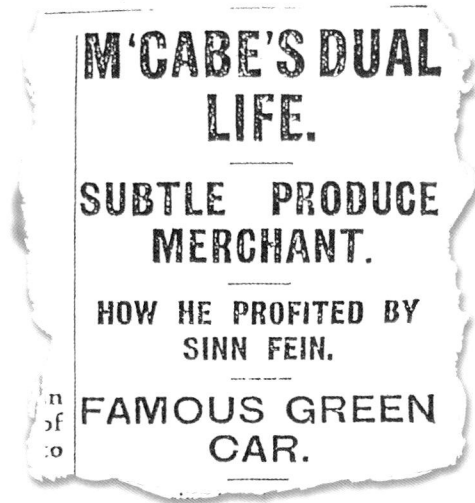

SINN FEIN PLOT ?

Alleged Conspiracy in Scotland.

STARTLING EVIDENCE.

Sensational details regarding the inner workings of Sinn Fein in Scotland have come to light as the result of the trial in the High Court in Edinburgh of fifteen men and one woman on a conspiracy charge. Not only were explosives, ammunition, and arms captured in Glasgow houses, but it was stated that the alleged conspiracy was assisted financially from Ireland.

...extraordinary public inter...

alongside my father in Edinburgh Courthouse during St Patrick's Week in 1921.

In his final address to the jury, the Lord Advocate said he did not need to emphasise 'the gravity of the case [and] the importance of the case to the public'.

"A conspiracy has been entered into, which is unprecedented in its scope, which is, as far as I know, unparalled in its nefarious design, and which is unexampled in the terrible consequences and sufferings it might have brought upon innocent people. It may have been loose in its set-up but deadly in its purpose."

The Lord Advocate explained to the jury that it was 'the right' of the citizens of Ireland to argue for any change in the laws they desired by 'constitutional means', but not by violence.

"There is no doubt in my mind that the whole deadly affair was financed and collaborated in Dublin by Mr Richard Mulcahy, who calls himself the chief of staff of the illegal Irish Republican Army, and that Coyle was a willing agent and mercenary working on their behalf and financed by them as part of a vicious plan to collect and send guns, ammunition and explosives to Ireland to unlawfully wage war and overthrow the legal authority of the British government and His Majesty's forces there."

The Lord Advocate and Morrice Mackay did not find much common ground during the week-long hearing but the one point they both emphasised in their final addresses to the jury was the singularity of the case. Mackay believed it was 'the most remarkable case ever submitted in this court to a jury'.

"There is no evidence of secret meetings between any two or more of the accused, no evidence of intercepted writings which would establish guilt of conspiracy…

"What the police did was to search Glasgow for all the people connected with the Sinn Féin organisation to find if they could get anything in the nature of firearms or cartridges, and when they found it, they swept all the people into the net."

Mr Mackay said the Lord Advocate had referenced the 'illegal' Irish Republican Army, but there was 'no more than one of the 16 accused who was ever connected with the Irish Republican Army'. The 'one' to whom he referred was, of course, my father, who Mackay acknowledged was in 'a serious position' as regards the evidence.

Unusually, the court continued into Saturday when the Lord Justice General delivered his directions to the members of the jury who took just 95 minutes to reach their decision. Verdicts of guilty were delivered in the cases of my father, Charles Strickland, Bernard McCabe, James Devine, Michael Gallagher, Jean Quinn, Thomas Gillespie, James Fagan and Robert O'Donnell. Five of the defendants – the three McErlane brothers, Peter Quinn and Patrick Carrigan – were found not guilty, while the cases against the remaining two defendants, Edmond Magner and Hugh Traynor, were deemed 'not proven'.

Notwithstanding the huge crowd in the packed courtroom, the verdict was delivered in 'absolute silence', according to the *Sunday Mail*, which described what happened after Mr Mackay and the other defence counsel completed their pleas for mitigation.

There was a dramatic interlude when Henry Peter Coyle, one of those found guilty, also addressed the court…

Just a few years earlier, my father had been picking potatoes on Scottish farms, a migratory labourer forced to leave school before he had even reached his teens. Yet here he was now, aged just 26, in a courtroom filled with some of the greatest legal minds in Scotland and he was prepared to do battle once more for the Irish Republic he so passionately believed in. The odds might be stacked against him but Henry Coyle had no intention of retreating meekly to the prison cell that surely awaited him. Rising to his feet, he stared defiantly around the courtroom at the men on the press bench, the ladies in the public gallery, the Lord Advocate and finally at the bemused Lord Justice General seated regally on his bench, and then he began to speak…

CHAPTER 21

'My only regret is that I could not do more'

WHEN I was in school in the 1960s, I learned all about Robert Emmet and his famous speech from the dock in Green Street Courthouse in Dublin when he declared that his epitaph should not be written until Ireland had taken her place among the nations of the world. Little did I think that the quiet, placid man sitting opposite me at the breakfast table each morning had also delivered a rebellious speech from the dock many years earlier, a speech that made headlines all over Scotland.

As I have mentioned on several occasions, my father rarely spoke about his involvement in the War of Independence, and even his written account of that period makes only passing reference to the events in the High Court of Justiciary in Edinburgh on March 19, 1921. Indeed, were it not for the various Scottish newspapers that reported on the trial, I would have no record of the remarkable speech my father delivered that day. Each of the newspapers carried their own particular account of the speech – some included more of it than others – but I have been able to piece together the various accounts so I can reproduce the speech in full, or as close to the complete version as possible. Several newspapers also described the scene in the courtroom and my father's general appearance as he stood to address the Lord Justice General.

There was perfect silence as the prisoner Coyle stood defiantly in the dock to speak. His demeanour didn't look like a man that would be a member of Sinn Féin and a leader within the militant Irish Republican Army. Or indeed that he had just been found guilty of the most serious charges of conspiracy and the illegal acquisition, use and transportation of a large amount of explosives and firearms with intent to endanger life or cause death and serious harm to others.

He displayed no sign of worry, stress, emotion or concern about his predicament and conviction, and of course the long term of imprisonment about to be imposed on him.

I am pictured on a visit to the High Court of Justiciary at Parliament Hall in Edinburgh where my father made a remarkable speech from the dock on March 19, 1921.

Coyle, who is a tall, sturdy and standout character, addressed the judge and the court politely without reference to any written script. He delivered his dramatic and defiant speech calmly and passionately in a strong and characteristic Hibernian accent.

The following is my father's speech at the High Court of Justiciary in Edinburgh on March 19, 1921:

"My Lord, the statement I have to make is one I intended to make in the witness box, but having acted on the advice of my counsel, I didn't take that opportunity.

"I don't want to deny anything I have done. If I have any regrets, it's not for what I have done but for being deprived of the opportunity of doing more.

"Neither do I want to deny my membership of the Irish Republican Army. I am a soldier of that army and I pride myself on that.

"Of course, it has been said during the course of this trial that the Irish Republican Army is an illegal organisation, but in my opinion it is not. Ireland is as much entitled to an army as any other country, and I and everyone else are entitled to our beliefs.

DRAMATIC SCENES AT SINN FEIN TRIAL.

COYLE, IN APPEAL TO JUDGE, SHOULDERS ALL THE BLAME.

SWEETHEARTS' EMBRACE IN THE DOCK.

Sentences ranging from five years' penal servitude to twelve months imprisonment were passed on nine of the sixteen accused in the Sinn Fein conspiracy trial, which concluded at Edinburgh yesterday.

My father's speech from the dock made headlines in newspapers across Scotland in March 1921.

"Even the learned Lord Advocate in his address to the jury yesterday said that the citizens of any country are entitled to choose any form of government they want by constitutional means. Now, I ask what more than constitutional means was the general election of 1918?

"At that general election, by those same constitutional means, the Irish people choose their form of government and what was the result? The parliament established by those constitutional means proclaimed illegal and the elected representatives of the people cast into prison for no other reason than they represented the people.

"The Irish people are provoked and if they had not been there would be no trouble. All we are asking from England is just what belongs to us – and nothing more. We are fighting for our country, our homes and our liberty and who the invaders are need not be questioned.

"I do not want to deny that I was in possession of explosives though I was not going to use them myself. I don't believe in the taking of lives, though the lives of Irishmen have been taken by England for hundreds of years, apart from the hundreds of thousands of Irishmen who have sacrificed their lives for England in all her wars and battles. Even in our own day, 200,000 young

LARGEST CERTIFIED NET SALE OF ANY SCOTTISH MORNING PAPER.

SUNDAY, MARCH 20, 1921.　　PRICE TWOPENCE

REVELATIONS IN BERNARD M'CABE'S LIFE

LATE SUNDAY MORNING SPECIAL.

NINE FOUND GUILTY!

HEAVY SENTENCES PASSED ON SCOTTISH SINN FEIN CONSPIRATORS.

PRISONER'S DRAMATIC OUTBURST.

Nine of the sixteen persons whose trial on a charge of complicity in a Sinn Fein conspiracy in Scotland has occupied a whole week's sitting of the High Court of Justiciary, Edinburgh, were found guilty yesterday and received sentences up to five years' penal servitude.

A dramatically defiant speech was made by Henry Coyle, one of the men found guilty, who professed his pride at being an officer in the Irish Republican Army. Sentences were also passed on Bernard M'Cabe, the well-known Glasgow produce merchant, and on the woman Jean Quinn.

M'CABE'S DUAL LIFE.

SUBTLE PRODUCE MERCHANT.

HOW HE PROFITED BY SINN FEIN.

FAMOUS GREEN CAR.

Irishmen – my fellow countrymen – went out to France and fought for England during the whole four years of the last war. They went out because they were led to believe they were fighting for the freedom of small nations, but any of them who lived to come back found their own small nation held in thrall in poverty and degradation.

"Charles McGinn, the young boy here in the dock with me, is already sentenced in another court to ten years' penal servitude for something he knew nothing about. In fact, he was in Dublin when it happened and I sent him there. The first he knew about it was when he read an account of it in the Dublin papers. So, that's a sample of British justice.

"I had the motor vehicles registered in Mr McCabe's name with his consent but neither he or Devine had any reason to believe I was going to use them for transporting war material. Devine may have been under the impression he was in McCabe's employment but he was in my employment and I paid him. Of Miss Quinn and Gillespie, Fagan and O'Donnell, I know nothing, and I know nothing of the others in the dock.

"I feel very sorry for all the other defendants who were arrested in connection with my arrest and who are now here in the dock with me. Most of them were unknown to me until this trial began. I did not know them and they did not know me or about any of the activities I had been involved in.

"I am the one and only person responsible for all that has happened. I don't mind what I suffer or what punishment I undergo, for I know I am suffering for justice sake, but I don't want to see anyone else suffering for anything I have done.

"In conclusion, I wholeheartedly share the feelings of a famous Irishman who once said:

Far dearer the grave or the prison,
Illum'd by one patriot name,
Than that of the trophies of all who have risen
On liberty's ruins to fame!"

Those lines are from the Irish writer, poet and lyricist, Thomas Moore, who published his famous *Irish Melodies* in the early 1880s. I have no doubt my father learned those lines at his mother's side as a young boy growing up in Dooyork. His extraordinary speech from the dock in Edinburgh was, I believe, a wonderful testament to his parents and his teachers at Shraigh and Geesala National Schools. To think that a man with such a rudimentary education could stand before the two most powerful legal men in Scotland – the Lord Justice General and the Lord Advocate – and deliver a speech of that calibre is truly astonishing. And to do it without a written script is unbelievable altogether. Indeed, if I did not have the many newspaper reports of the trial I would struggle to believe that the unassuming, mild-mannered man I knew as my father could deliver such a powerful, defiant declaration of his Irish republican beliefs.

By March 1921, IRA volunteers and Sinn Féin representatives were being tried before secret court-martials all over Ireland, so it was unusual for somebody in my father's position to get a chance to publicly declare their political motivations, and to do it in one of the seats of British empirical rule – the Scottish capital of Edinburgh – made it all the more momentous.

I think the timing of the speech is really important. It came at the end of a week when six of his IRA comrades went to the gallows in Dublin and I have no doubt Thomas Whelan, Patrick Moran, Thomas Bryan, Patrick Doyle, Frank Flood and Bernard Ryan were on my father's mind when he rose to his feet in the High Court of Justiciary in Edinburgh. Their sufferings and ultimate sacrifice gave him the inner strength and conviction to become a passionate, articulate advocate for Irish freedom.

The greatest endorsement of my father's speech came from the most unlikely source, Lord Justice General James Avon Clyde, who made the following remarks in imposing a sentence of five years' penal servitude on him.

"I have listened very carefully to what you have had to say," he told my father. "You not only accepted your own guilt but your desire to put on your shoulders other people's crimes and responsibility did you some credit.

"But your suggestion that you did what you did in transporting arms, explosives and ammunition because they were to be used not by you but by other people does neither you nor your courage any credit.

"I am sorry for the tone of your remarks and how little you appreciate and understand the character or seriousness of your actions. You seem to think that because your lethal cargo was not to be used in Scotland in some way lessens your guilt in this deadly conspiracy. You say you don't believe in the taking of life so how did you expect your deadly cargo to be used in a war without major loss of life and limb.

Lord Justice General James Avon Clyde presided over the Sinn Féin trial at the High Court of Justiciary in Edinburgh. In imposing sentence, he complimented my father on shouldering the blame on behalf of others.

"Hopefully, in the future, as you get older, your eyes will be opened a little wider and you will have a better understanding of how wrong your actions were. You and we can all be thankful that the revolver you grabbed from your lethal cargo on the night of your arrest was unloaded.

"For now, I have no alternative but to sentence you to five years' penal servitude. I have no doubt in my mind had you not been apprehended with your lethal cargo you would have spread death and destruction in Great Britain and Ireland."

The five-year sentence was significantly less than what my father expected. His counsel had told him to prepare for a sentence of ten years, which would have been in keeping with the term imposed on Charlie Strickland in Glasgow just a few weeks earlier. But his passionate speech convinced the Lord Justice General that Henry Peter Coyle was no mercenary – as claimed by the Crown – but was instead a principled young man willing to take responsibility for his actions. Lord Justice General Clyde did not hide the fact that he believed my father was completely misguided in his pursuit of an Irish Republic, but he did give him credit – five years' credit in the opinion of Mr Mackay – for shouldering the blame on behalf of others.

2

SINN FEIN PLOT

NINE OF ACCUSED GUILTY.

HEAVY SENTENCES

COYLE'S DRAMATIC OUTBURST.

After a trial extending over a week in the High Court of Justiciary, Edinburgh, nine of the sixteen persons ...th complicity in a....

The following were the sentences imposed on my father's co-defendants: Charlie Strickland (five years), Bernard McCabe (three years), Michael Gallagher (three years), James Fagan (three years), Robert O'Donnell (three years), James Devine (18 months) and Thomas Gillespie (12 months).

In the case of Jean Quinn, the Lord Justice General had the following to say:

"Jean Quinn, I am exceedingly sorry to see anybody like you in this position. You have been found guilty on what was ample evidence. I have tried to take as lenient a view of the position as I can, but I cannot, I am afraid, make your sentence less than 12 years' imprisonment…"

There was a gasp of surprise from Jean Quinn, but then the judge, with a smile, corrected himself and said the sentence was, in fact, 12 months. A mightily relieved Jean Quinn smiled too.

"There was no suggestion of gloom in the dock," remarked the *Daily Herald*. "The prisoners took their sentences quite cheerfully, and waved greetings to their friends in court.

"Before the court was cleared, the accused who had been found not guilty were ordered to leave the dock, and as they did so, some vigorous handshaking was indulged in."

The judge ordered the forfeiture of the car, the motorcycle and sidecar, the money, explosives, guns, ammunition and other items and equipment seized during the police investigation. He then discharged the jury of any further duty for a period of six years.

As my father and the other prisoners were being led away in handcuffs to the prison vans, the police held an impromptu press conference where they told reporters they were very pleased with the outcome of the trial.

"They are satisfied that with the arrest, conviction and jailing of Henry Peter Coyle they have landed one of the most important and daring Sinn Féiners in Scotland and Ireland," wrote the *Daily Record*, "and that he is wanted in Ireland on a long series of offences and that after he serves his present jail term he will be taken back to Ireland for trial and indictment on more serious charges than the Alloa motor car incident.

"When asked what more serious charges could Coyle face in Ireland than the conspiracy and explosive charges for which he has already been convicted, all police would say is that he will face much, much more serious charges over there and furthermore they stated that if Coyle had been convicted in Ireland on the explosives and conspiracy charges he would now be facing the death penalty."

I don't believe there were any outstanding charges against my father in Ireland because he spent so little time there during the previous two years. However, there was now a threat hanging over him that he could be shipped across to Dublin to face a court-martial on some trumped-up charges, which might very well cost him his life. In such circumstances, five years' penal servitude in the notorious Peterhead Prison on Scotland's north-eastern coast seemed like a pretty good deal for a man who was well used to bracing sea winds and back-breaking work.

CHAPTER 22

The Prison of No Hope

AFTER the court hearing, my father, Charlie Strickland, Bernard McCabe and the other convicted men were placed in a prison van and taken under armed guard to Edinburgh Railway Station to begin the long journey to Peterhead Prison.

Located on a peninsula jutting out into the North Sea, Peterhead Prison was constructed between 1886 and 1888 to house convict labourers who were to build the breakwaters for the town's so-called 'Harbour of Refuge'.

Peterhead was renowned for its fishing industry and at one time boasted the largest seal and whale fishing fleet in Britain. By the time my father arrived there, the seal and whale fishing had given way to a vibrant herring industry and there were an estimated 300 boats plying their trade from Peterhead. Visitors to the seaside town were immediately struck by the pungent smell of fish as soon as they alighted from the train.

To give a sense of how remote Peterhead Prison was it might be useful to describe the journey my father and his friends made on that spring afternoon in March 1921. Firstly, there was a 125-mile train journey to Aberdeen Joint Station where they had to change trains. The prisoners were marched in chains from the south arrivals' platform to the northern end of the station where they boarded another train for the 36-mile journey further north to Peterhead. The prison was located about a mile and a half from the railway station; a cheerless granite fortress perched on a bleak windswept headland above the town's famous harbour. To reach it, the men had to pass the Harbour of Refuge, the place where they would toil each weekday for the duration of their stay at Peterhead.

In May 1912, a journalist from *The Social Gazette*, the official newspaper of the Salvation Army, made the long trip from London to Peterhead Prison.

Peterhead Prison on the edge of the North Sea in Scotland with the south breakwater of the 'Harbour of Refuge' in the background.

"The prison stands four-square," he wrote, "sombre, isolated, grim! It is exposed to either land or sea winds… great bolt-studded double gates form the entrance to the prison."

My father and the other Irish Volunteers wouldn't have garnered much sympathy from the locals or, indeed, the prison staff. Peterhead, a town with a population of about 5,000, had lost more than 350 of its sons during the Great War, as it was being called at that time. This was an area of Scotland where loyalty to King and Empire mattered, and there weren't too many Irishmen who ventured as far north as Peterhead in the preceding decades, so sympathy for these Irish rebels would have been thin on the ground.

It would be hard to find a more forbidding place in which to construct a prison than this remote headland. Before Peterhead opened its doors in August 1888, men sentenced to penal servitude by the Scottish courts were either sent to prisons in England or exiled to Australia.

Work on Peterhead's new harbour commenced in 1886 – at the same time as the prison – and the building of the harbour's two breakers became a mammoth, labour-intensive task that would go on for 70 years. Expenditure on the project eventually topped £1 million, despite the fact that the bulk of the labour came free via the nearby prison. In 1907, it was estimated that prisoners at Peterhead provided labour for the 'Harbour of Refuge' to the value of almost £10,000. The work on the harbour involved hewing granite from the nearby Stirlinghill Quarry, a laborious, pitiless task that must have broken the backs – and spirits – of many prisoners. There was even a train that ran from the harbour to the prison such was the importance of convict labour to the project, which was overseen by the British Admirality.

Prison Song

(to the air of Mountains of Mourne)

O Mary, this prison is a wonderful sight
Where the screws are on duty by day and by night.
With a guard for to watch you when you're in your cell
If you speak through the vent sure the chief he will tell

I was speaking myself when he happened to pass
I was reported and lost a month's class
Sure it makes me fell happy when I am alone
To have a short chat with my mate on the phone.

You remember my comrade, young Charles McGinn?
Well you scarcely would know him, he is getting so thin.
The food we are getting it is very bad
And the porridge at night is driving us mad.

McGinn declares that the prison he will wreck
And all the prisoners he will bring out on strike
And when he is at leisure, his time it is spent
Telling the tale to his mate through the vent.

The great Canon Thomson, we have him up here
He has been a chaplain of the prison for many's the year
The nags gather round him to pray and to sing
But the rebels refuse to pray for the King.

What beautiful sight these rebels to see
When they go for a walk down along the North Sea
With a guard for to watch you for fear you'd escape
With his little pea-shooter in under his cape.

And I'll tell you I am longing my Mary to see
When an Irish Republic established will be.

Composed by Henry Coyle
in Peterhead Prison, 1921

Originally built for 208 inmates, Peterhead had a population of 350 in 1911 and more than 400 by the time my father stepped through those bolt-studded gates. Although it was constructed on a six-acre site, the prison's living quarters were cramped and antiquated. Prisoners were confined to tiny cells, measuring five foot by seven foot, with thick iron bars across the single windows. There was no fresh air, no heating apart from the hot water pipe and the seven-foot high ceiling in each cell added to the air of claustrophobia.

Peterhead was known as Scotland's Alcatraz for a reason. It housed the most hardened criminals in the country, including several murderers, and most of its inmates were serving very lengthy terms.

Nobody had ever managed to escape in its 33-year history. How could they? On one side was the North Sea, so the only escape route was into the town and even that proved impossible. On one occasion, a prisoner managed to clamber over the prison wall but only got as far as the governor's garden.

As well as being Scotland's Alcatraz, Peterhead was named the 'Prison of No Hope', and it was indeed a hopeless place. During my research, I came across a report from 1914 of the kind of punishment meted out to prisoners who stepped out of line in Peterhead. Two prisoners had severely assaulted a couple of warders, an offence that usually resulted in a number of lashes of the infamous cat-o'-nine-tails and solitary confinement, but in this instance the governor James Stewart imposed a more severe penalty.

"The two convicts are to receive 36 lashes with the 'cat'," wrote the *Aberdeen Daily Journal*, "and three months' solitary confinement to be followed by three months' in irons.

"The flogging is generally administered in the bathroom where the prisoner is fixed up to a steel instrument called 'Three-Legged Betty'. The punishment is performed with the cat-o'-nine-tails or a birch rod [with sharp thorns], according to the medical officer's orders.

The governor of Peterhead Prison, James Stewart (third from left) is pictured with colleagues and visitors from the Salvation Army in 1912. Stewart was still in charge when my father was an inmate in the prison almost a decade later.

"Prisoners who are flogged generally lose any remission or sentence. They wear a black and yellow [outfit] for six months and are shackled with irons for a considerable period."

I was astonished to discover that these sort of Draconian punishments were being handed out at Peterhead just a few short years before my father arrived there. In fact, the governor James Stewart was still in charge in 1921 and my father, as the leader of the Irish Volunteers in the prison, would have had quite a few battles with him.

Much of what I know about my father's time in Peterhead is captured in verse. On the previous page, I have published the lyrics of a song (to the air of *Mountains of Mourne*) that my father wrote while in Peterhead and I think it brilliantly portrays the harsh environment he and the other Irish rebels were forced to endure.

There was no such thing as recreation or rehabilitation in Peterhead. The prisoners worked every weekday in Stirlinghill Quarry and were confined to their cells for the rest of their time, apart from a few brief exercise periods.

It was an awful existence. Each morning, breakfast was served in the cells, which meant it was invariably cold, and then the men set off for a day of back-breaking work in the quarry with just a brief interlude for lunch. As soon as the prisoners returned in the evening, they were locked into their cells for the

My father passed through the famous bolt-studded doors of Peterhead Prison in March 1921 after he was jailed for five years for smuggling weapons for the IRA.

night. If the weather was inclement, they didn't leave their cells at all for the entire day.

Weekends were even worse. The prisoners were locked in their cells from midday on Saturday until Monday morning with just a brief respite on Sunday for exercise and religious worship. However, my father and the other Irish prisoners refused to attend Mass because the long-serving Catholic chaplain, Canon A.F. Thomson, insisted on saying a prayer for King George V. There was no way the Irish rebels were going to pray for the king, even if meant the loss of a much-needed escape from the terrible monotony of a whole day in a 5x7 foot cell.

The Irish prisoners went on hunger strike on three occasions during my father's time in Peterhead, but I do not know how long those strikes lasted. My father engaged with prison life as best he could and worked for a period in the tailoring workshop where he learned how to make a suit, a skill that served him well later in life. He also made use of the very limit prison library and wrote several poems and songs.

Unfortunately, I don't have any of my father's correspondence from that period and the prison records are not particularly revealing. I doubt very much my father had any visitors because Peterhead was such a long distance from Glasgow, never mind Ireland. The windswept, turbulent climate on this remote peninsula in the north-east of Scotland was not unlike that of his native Erris,

Opened in 1888, Peterhead Prison was one of the most notorious places to be incarcerated in Europe.

but the fresh air wasn't much good if you were confined to a cell for extended periods, especially in winter.

The prisoners were also not allowed to converse with each other while in their cells, although they often ignored that rule and used the air vents as a form of telephone. My father references this in his song when he talks about chatting to his good friend Charlie Strickland and then being punished for it. The punishment involved the loss of a month's classes in tailoring, which was certainly preferable to a date with Three-Legged Betty!

There were a number of prisoners in Peterhead who had been involved in very high-profile criminal cases in Scotland, not least Oscar Slater, a man who was the victim of the most notorious miscarriage of justice in the country's history. By 1921, Slater had served 13 years of a life term for bludgeoning to death a wealthy Glasgow heiress named Marion Gilchrist, who was aged 83 when she was murdered in her home. But Slater, a German Jew, was entirely innocent of the brutal crime and his case became a *cause célèbre* in Scotland, attracting the attention of *Sherlock Holmes* creator Sir Arthur Conan Doyle, who campaigned extensively for his release. Slater eventually gained his freedom in the late 1920s, having spent almost 20 years in the 'Prison of No Hope'.

My father expected to serve his full five-year term, although there was the opportunity for some remission for good behaviour. I am sure he would have read in the Irish newspapers of IRA colleagues escaping from prisons back home, but he knew there were no prospects of himself and Charlie and the rest of the Irish rebels breaking out of Peterhead. Even the prison hospital, with its commanding view of the bay from its all-glass front, was heavily barred.

But as the weeks and months slipped by, I think my father would have been mightily relieved to still be in Peterhead and not on a boat back to Ireland where the death penalty surely awaited him. His poems and songs depict a man who was taking his punishment in good spirits while still refusing to compromise on his republican principles. No matter how monotonous life in his cell became, Henry Coyle would not be reciting any Sunday prayers for the King.

I had hoped to visit Peterhead during my research but successive Covid lockdowns put paid to those plans. However, I intend to make that long journey in the near future in memory of my father and all of the other Irish republican prisoners who did time with him in the Prison of No Hope. Today, the prison is a museum and thousands of people visit it every year to gain an insight into what life was like in one of the toughest jails in Europe in the early 1900s.

One man eventually managed to achieve the impossible by escaping Peterhead. His name was Johnny Ramensky, a conman and escapologist, who somehow broke out of Scotland's Alcatraz in the 1930s. By then, the prison was a more humane place with recreational and educational opportunities for its inmates.

Thankfully, my father's time in Peterhead would be less than a year, but he was not to know that in March 1921 when the heavy door of his cell slammed shut and the warder shot the bolts into place. My father's love of Ireland and his unquenchable desire for Irish independence had landed him in a dreadful place, but like many Irish patriots before him, Henry Coyle would not let a prison cell break his rebel spirit.

CHAPTER 23

The Smashing of the Van

IN delivering such a powerful speech from the dock in the High Court in Edinburgh, my father gave the Scottish press something to think about. Up to then, the IRA's arms smuggling campaign had been characterised as the work of terrorists, men who were nothing more than ruthless criminals or, at the very least, dangerous fanatics. The headlines on Sunday, March 20, painted a more nuanced picture with most of the leading newspapers quoting liberally from my father's speech. *Prisoner's Dramatic Outburst – Proud of 'Army'* was a headline in the *Sunday Mail* while the *Scotsman* on March 21 had an article entitled *Rebel Statement in the Dock.*

Public opinion, however, remained resolutely opposed to the IRA's campaign. In a lengthy editorial, the *Scotsman* said that 'if justice has failed at all, it has not been on the side of severity'.

Considering the evidence brought forward, and the heinous and formidable character of the crime, the sentences pronounced are proof that the law, which has been grossly outraged, does not proceed to conviction or punishment in any vindictive or inconsiderate spirit. The action taken by the authorities for the protection of the community and for bringing guilt home to the evildoers has been justified.

A wave of anti-Irish sentiment swept through Glasgow in the wake of the trial. Mary Brannick experienced it at first hand when she took over the running of Jean Quinn's shop on Kent Street while the latter was in prison.

"The publicity caused by the High Court trial in Edinburgh caused the shop to be practically boycotted," she recalled. "This almost ruined [Jean's] business."

The IRA tried to pick up the pieces of its Scottish network after my father's arrest but it was far from easy. Daniel Patrick (D.P.) Walshe, a native of Fethard in Co Tipperary, was dispatched from GHQ in December 1920 to see what he could do.

2   DAILY RECORD A

CROWN CASE FAILS

12 PRISONERS ACQUITTED.

PRISON VAN AMBUSH TRIAL ENDED.

CROWD CHEERS.

ONE OF THE ACCUSED REARRESTED.

Sean O'Daire.   Daniel Branniff

All the twelve men on trial in Edin-
~~~ during th~~ fortni~~

"I did not spend very long [there]; only about ten days. I was getting my bearings," he recalled. "I was sent to Scotland to clear up the dumps and procure ammunition. The principal men in Scotland at the time were nearly all in jail and what was left were doing the best they could but they were so closely watched they could not do very much and organisation had broken down a bit."

Walshe also struggled to gain the co-operation of several key operatives in Scotland because, unlike my father, he was not a member of the Irish Republican Brotherhood. However, he returned to Glasgow in January and set up a new system of arms smuggling that involved the dispatch of consignments of 'war material' to legitimate business addresses in Dublin such as Granby Row Engineering Company, the General Electric Company on Trinity Street and Price's of Moore Street. IRA volunteers intercepted the cases at the North Wall docks, thus ensuring they never reached their supposed destinations. Walshe even opened an office in Glasgow, called McLloyd & McLloyd, and persuaded 'a Communist Press' to print false labels for him.

The change in strategy was partly caused by necessity following the seizure of the motor lorry and car, which were so vital to my father's system of arms smuggling. Walshe managed to get three or four consignments to Dublin but the Tipperary man struggled to establish a consistent supply of arms, much to Michael Collins' disappointment. Volunteers in Dundee and Edinburgh were also encouraged to send 'war material' directly to Dublin, but once again the strategy met with limited success.

"To speed up the purchase and dispatch of the arms, D.P. Walshe decided to send them packed in cases addressed to firms in Dublin," recalled Joseph Booker. "The police discovered one of these cases addressed to Hammond Lane Foundry. The members of a North of Ireland family named Doherty, whose house was used as a dump for the arms, were arrested. The son had been identified as one of the men who had sent the box.

"On another occasion, arms were sent in an egg crate by Lena McDonald of Dundee, addressed to a Mr McGlinchey, who had a provision shop in Glasgow and was a member of the IRA. A railway porter, who was attempting to pilfer eggs from the crate, found the revolvers and reported it to the police. McGlinchey was arrested, but denied any knowledge of the affair. His explanation was accepted and he was released."

With motor transport no longer available, Volunteers were now taking greater chances when sending weapons to Glasgow. My father's friend, Seán O'Doherty, was one of three Volunteers arrested at Dundee railway station in late April while putting a case containing weapons on a train to Glasgow. His accomplice Lena McDonald was detained later that day after police discovered the case was packed at her shop. The loss of O'Doherty and McDonald, two of the more prolific smugglers from my father's old network, was a significant setback to GHQ, but much worse was to come.

On April 28, police raided a house at Abbortsford Place in Glasgow and arrested a man who gave his name as Frank Somers. The man was, in fact, Frank Carty, a leading IRA member from Sligo, who had escaped from Derry Jail just months earlier.

News of Carty's arrest quickly spread among the IRA in Glasgow and plans were made to rescue him while he was being transported by van from the Central Police Station to Duke Street Prison on May 4. D.P. Walshe called a meeting of Volunteers on the night before the transfer but there were mixed views about the planned operation. Liam Mellows, who had taken over as GHQ's Director of Purchasing in England and Scotland, believed the mission, even if it were successful, would lead to widespread arrests of IRA Volunteers and sympathisers, thus disrupting the efforts to smuggle weapons to Ireland. However, D.P. Walshe insisted on going ahead and devised a plan to attack the prison van outside Duke Street Prison. Joseph Booker was one of those who helped to prepare the operation.

WEEKLY RECORD, AUGUST 19, 1921.

UNRAVELLING THE DRAMA OF PRISON-VAN MURDER.

AMAZING ALLEGATIONS OF SINN FEIN PLOT

WOUNDED DETECTIVE OFFICER POINTS ACCUSING FINGER AT NINE MEN IN DOCK.

By Our Own Reporters.

Striking scenes ushered in the trial at the High Court of Justiciary, Edinburgh, of the thirteen men accused of having been concerned in the recent fatal attack on a Glasgow police van. Allegations of a remarkable Sinn Fein plot are embodied in the evidence

"Mick O'Carroll and I were detailed to notify all the men in the Glasgow area who were known to be available," he recalled. "We walked for the best part of the night calling at all the houses. The landladies, in most cases, were very indignant and demanded to know why we wanted the men at this time of night."

Although Booker did not participate in the raid, he had to 'provide the arms and a sledge for the men carrying out the attack'.

"I delivered six automatics that morning to D.P. Walshe at the Ivanhoe Hotel, Buchanan St.," he recalled. "In the newspaper report of the attack, mention was made of a man getting out of a taxi and going into the Ivanhoe Hotel with a parcel. An accurate description of me was given, even to the clothes I was wearing, but I wasn't identified."

Several other acquaintances of my father's were involved in the attempted rescue, including Eamonn and Seán Mooney, Matthew Tipping and Seán Coyne. The operation, which became known as 'The Smashing of the Van', failed in its objective of rescuing Carty, who was handcuffed in a small cell at the front of the van and guarded by six policemen. Worse still, the doomed mission resulted in the killing of a police inspector and the wounding of a detective.

Not surprisingly, there was a widespread police crackdown in Glasgow – much worse than after my father's arrest – and 37 people were taken into custody, including a priest Fr McRory, who was supportive of the republican cause. Collins, Mulcahy and the other leaders at GHQ were furious over this unsanctioned mission because they feared it would have a disastrous effect on the Scottish IRA's ability to smuggle arms across to Ireland. Their worst fears were soon realised when the back channels that Joe Vize and my father had painstakingly built up throughout 1920 were shut down, either through direct police intervention or as a result of the inevitable public backlash. Sympathetic miners, who might once have been happy to remove a few cartridges of gelignite from the collieries in Lanarkshire, no longer wanted to be associated with a violent political movement that was shooting police officers dead in broad daylight on the streets of Glasgow.

Joseph Booker fled to Edinburgh but was eventually arrested.

"[The arrest] was indirectly due to the attempted rescue of Carty," he recalled. "Two of those taking part in it, Seán Mooney and Jim Quinn, went on the run. One Saturday evening, the police, who were on the lookout for them, followed some of their relatives on the train from Glasgow to Edinburgh. The relatives called at the home of Mr Gordon, where they knew the men had once stayed. On Sunday morning, the police raided the house and picked up Seán Nelson and myself."

Nelson was another Irish Volunteer well known to my father. Frank Gordon and his wife were detained for about a week and their young daughter ended up being temporarily placed in a children's institution. The police took possession of Gordon's house for the week and arrested any Volunteers who called there, resulting in the complete disintegration of the IRA arms smuggling network in Edinburgh. By the end of May, the Scottish gun-running operation was as good as finished and Collins was so short of 'war material' he was counting bullets in GHQ. The Truce, when it came in mid-July, was desperately needed because the weaponry just wasn't there to withstand another few months of guerilla warfare.

The role of the Scottish and English gunrunners in the War of Independence has been greatly underestimated, and I hope this book will go some way towards redressing that imbalance. Of all of the leaders in GHQ, Michael Collins was the one who showed the greatest appreciation for the efforts of men like Neill Kerr, my father and the many other Volunteers in Britain. The fact that he visited several of them in English prisons during the Treaty negotiations is indicative of the respect he had for the arms smugglers. Ever the pragmatist, Collins knew there would have been no War of Independence without the weapons from Scotland and England.

Most of the 37 men arrested following the attack on the prison van were later released, but 13 men, including D.P. Walshe and Mick O'Carroll, were charged with murder and conspiracy. The 13 went on trial in Glasgow in August alongside Seán O'Doherty, Lena McDonald and two other Dundee Volunteers, James Devaney and James Kemmit, who were all charged with attempting to send firearms and ammunition to Glasgow. The charges against Lena were withdrawn but O'Doherty, Kemmit and Devaney were convicted and each received prison sentences. In the case of O'Doherty and Kemmit, three-year terms of penal servitude were imposed, which meant they would be joining my father in Peterhead. As they left the dock, an unrepentant O'Doherty shouted 'God Save Ireland'. While he would have preferred to avoid prison, I am sure he was delighted to be reunited with his old friend 'Harry' Coyle.

The 13 men charged in relation to 'The Smashing of the Van' were either acquitted or the charges deemed 'not proven'. However, D.P. Walshe was re-arrested and sent to Manchester to face charges for breaking out of Strangeways Prison with Austin Stack, Piaras Beaslaí and others in 1919.

Frank Carty was shipped back to Ireland, court-martialled and sentenced to ten years' penal servitude in Mountjoy Prison. Elected a TD in June 1921, Carty was released from prison ahead of a meeting of Dáil Éireann. The truce had come into effect on July 13 and peace talks were about to commence between Sinn Féin representatives and the British government. In the next few months, thousands of IRA and Sinn Féin members were released from jails and internment camps all over Ireland, but there was no sign of the gates of Peterhead Prison being thrown open to the Irish prisoners.

My father and his republican comrades were facing into a long and bitterly cold winter in their tiny prison cells on the edge of the North Sea.

CHAPTER 24

'Like a band of happy young men bound for a football match'

O N the rare occasions when my father spoke about his time in Peterhead, he had one word to describe this infamous Prison of No Hope: a *hellhole*. He recalled nights in his cell when it was so cold he could see his own breath.

The main part of the prison was on the north of the six-acre site and consisted of a series of large halls, the oldest being Halls A, D and B. There was also the hospital, reception, bathhouse, kitchen, laundry, barracks, recreational hall and chapel. Halls A and D formed one long structure, originally designed as a single hall, four storeys in height with a basement and attic space. Drawings from 1897 show a pitched roof with 10 rectangular ventilation stacks and 160 cell windows on the west elevation. Without a central heating system, the cells were frigid, and there was hardly enough room for a prisoner to move around to keep warm.

Internally, Hall A had a central auditorium flanked by four galleries around which the cells were arranged. The other halls were similarly designed.

The prison expanded as the years went by, and another 200 cells were added, but the conditions did not improve. If anything, they got worse because the prison population was rising but basic facilities, such as the kitchen block, remained the same. It is little wonder then that meals were cold when they reached the inmates in cells far removed from the kitchen.

There were 27 Irish republican prisoners in Peterhead by the end of 1921. They had repeatedly sought political prisoner status, which would have exempted them from hard labour in Stirlinghill Quarry and the nearby Admirality Yard, but the authorities refused to budge, even after the Truce.

The men were served a never-ending diet of cold porridge, except on Wednesdays when they received a 'treat' of eight ounces of bread and a pint

The imposing exterior of Peterhead Convict Prison where my father spent 11 long months from March 1920 to February 1921.

of tea. If they misbehaved, they were placed in the 'silent cell', a windowless structure with nothing other than a concrete bed and a chamber pot.

My father and his comrades kept up their morale by engaging in practical jokes such as etching political slogans on various utensils. They wrote 'Up de Valera' and 'Erin Go Bragh' on stainless glass mugs and aluminum haircombs, and refused to erase them. When the warders accused them of insubordination, the men said they could not be guilty of the offence because the slogans were indelible so how could they remove something that couldn't be removed?

The Irish prisoners also struck up an unlikely friendship with Oscar Slater and became convinced of his innocence. Before entering prison, Slater had a reputation as a professional gambler and dealer in precious stones, and he impressed my father and the other prisoners with his intelligence and stoicism. Sometimes, they'd walk in the prison yard together and he'd pick up various pebbles and explain to the Irishmen the origins and characteristics of each stone. Slater, an innocent man in a living hell, clearly empathised with these political prisoners and was delighted to be able to spend time in their company.

I have no doubt my father and the other Irish prisoners followed the Treaty debate in December 1921 with a very keen interest because their freedom ultimately depended on its outcome. Opposition to the Treaty was very strong in Mayo and several of the county's most prominent TDs, including IRA commandant Tom Maguire and the renowned solicitor P.J. Ruttledge, expressed grave reservations about it. Respected republicans like Liam Mellows

The silent cell at Peterhead Convict Prison was a windowless structure with nothing other than a concrete bed and a chamber pot.

and Rory O'Connor, who my father knew from his time in Liverpool, were also in the anti-Treaty camp. My father had great affection for Mellows who he first met in October 1920 when the Galway man lodged with Neil Kerr following his return from America.

On Christmas Night 1921, my father sat in his cell and wrote the lyrics of a song published in this chapter. It is a bittersweet composition that recounts Henry Coyle's exploits as an Irish freedom fighter from the early days in Erris to his arrest in Alloa. The song ends with the poignant lines:

And now I'm in a prison, behind strong prison bars
But when Ireland gets her freedom, as she had long ago
I'll return to my Irish home in flowery sweet Mayo.

A lump forms in my throat whenever I read those lines because I think of my father in a cold, damp prison cell in Peterhead on Christmas Night 1921, dreaming of better days to come in 'flowery sweet Mayo'. Little did he know the hardships and tragedy that awaited him in the Ireland that eventually emerged from the War of Independence. A vote on the Treaty had been postponed until the New Year so he still did not know what fate awaited him in 1922. If the Treaty was approved, he was a free man; but if it failed, he was destined to serve out his sentence in Peterhead.

DAIL'S NARROW MAJORITY FOR TREATY.

De Valera Defiant to Last.

TO FIGHT UNTIL "WILL OF THE PEOPLE" IS MADE KNOWN.

Dáil Éireann, voting on Saturday, expressed its approval of the Irish Agreement, the voting resulting—

For the Treaty 64

Against ....

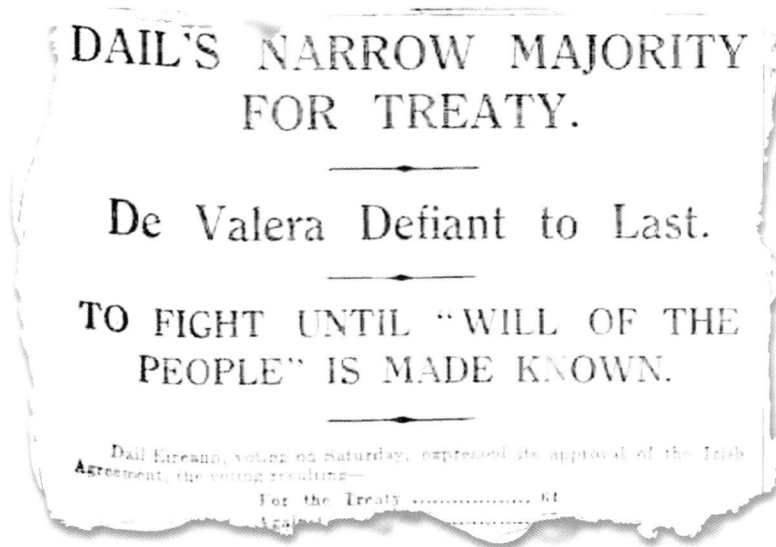

My father learned of the passing of the Anglo-Irish Treaty from this report in the *Aberdeen Daily Journal* on January 9, 1922.

My father was supportive of the Treaty but I don't think his personal situation influenced that decision. In fact, I know from later conversations with him that he would have readily gone to the gallows in order to uphold his republican principles. Any man who was willing to drive across Scotland and England with three hundred weight of explosives was not too bothered about self-preservation, so my father's support for the Treaty had more to do with his loyalty to Michael Collins than any desire for freedom. Of course he wanted to get out of Peterhead, but if Michael Collins had opposed the Treaty then Henry Coyle would have done likewise. It was that simple.

The *Aberdeen Daily Journal* was the local newspaper in Peterhead and my father read it from cover to cover during his time in prison. On Monday morning, January 9, the *Journal* carried a report from Dublin under the heading *Dáil's Narrow Majority For Treaty – De Valera Defiant to Last*. The lengthy report detailed the final debate in the Dáil on the previous Saturday, culminating in the approval of the Anglo-Irish Treaty by a narrow majority of 64 to 57.

I am sure my father's heart rejoiced at the passing of a Treaty that essentially guaranteed him and the other Irish prisoners in Peterhead their freedom, but his heart must have sank when he read of the bitter exchanges between Michael Collins and Cathal Brugha, two men who had done so much to bring England to the negotiating table. The *Journal* also contained an

My Home in Sweet Mayo

Henry Coyle is my name, the truth to you I'll tell.
I am an Irish Fenian as I'm sure you all know well.
Where I was bred and born, I mean to let you know,
I was brought up in Erris, in the county of Mayo.

I was well known in Bangor, Geesala and Kilmore,
In Ballycroy and Achill and all through Innishmore.
My parents loved me dearly and the neighbours around also,
But I was forced from my Irish home in the county of Mayo.

I laboured for my native land with comrades staunch and true,
Our firm determination was the Saxon to subdue.
The Peelers watched me night and day, they tracked me high and low,
So I bade farewell to all my friends in the county of Mayo.

When I set sail from Dublin, I hoped I soon would see,
The Saxon driven from our land and our emblem flying free.
I formed a resolution that wherever I would go,
I would never forget old Ireland and my home in sweet Mayo.

When I arrived in Glasgow and met some Fenians there,
To seek and find firearms I quickly did prepare.
And those brave lads in Scotland, their courage bold did show,
In working for old Ireland with their comrade from Mayo.

One night in dark December outside Alloa town,
Twas there I came in contact with the forces of the Crown.
They quickly apprehended me, which caused great grief and woe,
To all my friends in Dublin, in Scotland and Mayo.

They charged me with conspiracy and took my motor car
And now I'm in a prison behind strong prison bars.
But when Ireland gets her freedom, as she had long ago,
I'll return to my Irish home in flowery sweet Mayo.

**Composed in Peterhead Convict Prison, Scotland,
on Christmas Night, 1921**

A beautiful picture of 'sweet Mayo' by Henry Coyle's granddaughter, Evita Coyle.

RELEASE FROM PRISON

Sinn Feiners' Farewell to Peterhead.

" PUT MORE HEART INTO THEM."

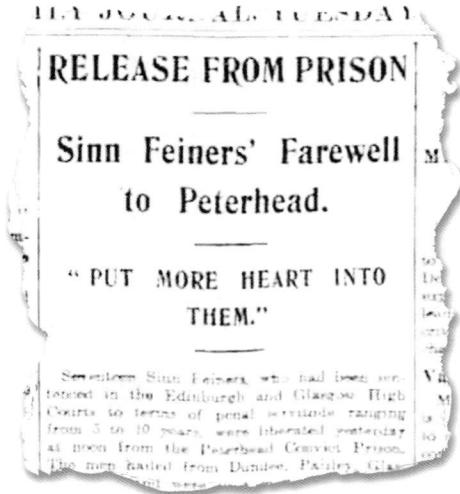

The release of the 17 Sinn Féin prisoners attracted a lot of media interest in Scotland. This headline was in the *Aberdeen Daily Journal.*

ominous report in which de Valera was quoted as saying he intended to continue the fight until the will of the people was made known. It was clear that the battle lines had already been drawn in Dublin.

But for the men in Peterhead, the passing of the Treaty was a cause for celebration. January was traditionally the toughest month in the prison, a month when the men could be confined to their icy cells for days on end if inclement weather forced a work stoppage on the Harbour of Refuge. But those dark dreary weeks of January 1922 must have flown by for my father and his friends as they counted down the days to their eventual release.

On Sunday morning, February 12, the governor of the prison, James Stewart, informed my father and 16 other republican prisoners that they were to be released the next afternoon. Such was the elation that many of the men could not eat for the rest of the day. The *Scotsman* described the moment the prisoners were released on that memorable Monday afternoon:

About noon the prison gates were flung open, and the men marched forth with beaming faces, clad in civilian clothes. They waved their hands and tossed their caps in the air to relieve their pent-up feelings, and as soon as they reached the town of Peterhead they made for tobacco shops and bought cigarettes.

They left Peterhead for their homes by the early afternoon train, and hilarious scenes were witnessed at the station. The men sang with great gusto the 'Irish Soldier's Song'.

As the train steamed out of the station, they crowded to the compartment windows and shouted derisive adieus to the grey building in which they had been incarcerated.

Their joy at release was, however, qualified by the regret that 10 comrades still remained in prison, but they expressed the opinion that they also would receive their pardon in the course of a few days.

Among the 10 left behind was Charlie Strickland who would have to wait for another two months to secure his release. My father and the rest of the freed prisoners were happy to chat to the reporters who crowded around them at Peterhead Station but one topic remained out of bounds.

"The men declined to make any statement about their life in prison," wrote the *Scotsman*. "The reason they gave for their refusal to communicate

The 17 Irish republican prisoners released from Peterhead Convict Prison in Scotland on February 13, 1922. My father is standing third from left. The other men are: Bernard McCabe (Cavan), James Fagan (Dublin), Robert O'Donnell (Donegal), Denis O'Donnell (Donegal), Eugene Canford (Cavan), Neil O'Boyle (Donegal), Michael Gallagher (Donegal), Sean O'Doherty (Laois), James Kimmet (Dundee), Patrick Kennan (Wishaw), J. Muirhead (Wishaw), Cornelius Phibbs (Wishaw), Edward O'Bryan (Limerick), Andrew Fagan (Glasgow), Richard Lennox (Glasgow), Joseph Martin (Glasgow).

anything about their prison life was because they were afraid it might have an adverse effect on those comrades who were left behind."

A reporter from the *Edinburgh Evening News* gave the following account of a conversation with my father in Peterhead Station.

The leader of the liberated men appeared to be Henry Coyle, 34 Hillfoot Street, Dennistoun, Glasgow, who served 11 months at Peterhead.

He is a young man of attractive personality and had no appearance of a criminal. Indeed, the liberated men did not seem to have suffered from their contact with hardened and habitual criminals, and they looked for the most part like a band of happy young men bound for a football match.

Coyle looked as if he had just returned from a sea trip, but despite the bronzed and healthy appearance, he said he had lost weight.

My father told the reporters he had been sentenced to five years' penal servitude for possessing explosives and firearms.

"If I had been caught in Ireland," he said, "it would have meant the gallows for me."

There was immense media interest in the release of the 17 Irish republican prisoners. Reporters were waiting for them at Aberdeen Joint Station and they were quizzed again about their time in Peterhead and about the prison's celebrity inmate.

"The Sinn Féiners struck up an acquaintance with Oscar Slater, for whom they seemed to have a deep respect," wrote the *Aberdeen Daily Journal*. "All of them expressed admiration for Slater's erudition, and many an interesting time they spent with him…"

The *Journal* published a photograph of my father and his comrades on the railway platform in Aberdeen and I am delighted to reprint it in this book. It is great to be also able to publish the names and addresses of those 17 brave men because the hardship they endured in that hellhole of a prison has never been properly acknowledged. They were fêted on the day of their release, with reception parties in Glasgow and Dundee, but that was about as good as it got. They became the forgotten men of the period and most people in Ireland would not even know that so many Irish men were incarcerated in the most northerly prison in Britain during the War of Independence.

One of the questions the men were asked as they left Peterhead Station was whether they hoped to get 'good jobs' in the new Irish government.

"They said they had no thought of any reward like that," wrote the *Scotsman*.

My father's friend, Sean O'Doherty, a native Irish speaker from Co Laois, addressed a Sinn Féin meeting in Blackness Hall in Dundee later that evening, regaling an amused audience with stories about Peterhead's porridge diet and hard labour.

"I'm a fully-qualified navvy now," he declared. "Never mind whether they are porridge and tea muscles, but I've a pair of good arms on me, and I'm ready to take a job from any of you."

My father would have had to wait until December 18, 1924, to be eligible for remission had he not been released as part of the Anglo-Irish Treaty. That was more than two and a half years away – and for a young man of 27, it must have seemed like an eternity – so no wonder he sang *Amhrán na bhFiann* with such gusto on the platform of Peterhead Railway Station. But if he knew the tragic path his life would take in the next two and a half years, I suspect Henry Coyle would have turned on his heel and marched back up the road to those bolt-studded prison gates to serve out the rest of his sentence. Nothing in life up to then – not even the notorious Prison of No Hope – could have prepared him for the nightmare to come. By December 18, 1924, Henry Coyle would be back behind bars, but this time as a common criminal in the independent Ireland he helped to create.

CHAPTER 25

A visit from Michael Collins

B Y a curious twist of fate, my father was released from Peterhead Prison on the same day the Tricolour was raised over the military barracks in Castlebar.

Mayo's county town had been one of the bastions of British rule in Connacht since the 1798 Rebellion, and the army barracks in the centre of Castlebar housed many thousands of British troops during its long history. Apart from the vast military complex, Castlebar also boasted an impressive courthouse and large county jail, making it the administrative hub of British rule in Mayo.

The raising of the Tricolour early on the morning of February 13, 1922, should have been a cause for celebration in Castlebar. This was a town that prided itself in its links to the 1798 Rebellion when, for a few glorious days, Castlebar became the capital of the new independent republic of Connacht. Now, more than a century later, Mayo's county town had its independence once again after the British Army's Border Regiment withdrew discreetly on Sunday evening, their departure described by the *Connaught Telegraph* as 'unwept, unhonoured (sic) and unsung'. The raising of the Tricolour early on Monday morning attracted a large group of locals who watched members of the West Mayo IRA Brigade parade across the famous barrack square, which for so long had been the stomping ground of British military might.

But the celebratory mood was tempered by the realisation that the IRA in Mayo was already out of step with the majority opinion in Dáil Éireann. Eight of the 13 TDs representing Mayo constituencies had voted against the Treaty, and virtually all of the county's IRA officers, including the likes of Michael Kilroy, Ned Moane, Dr John Madden and Éamon Gannon, were vehemently opposed to it. There was also strident opposition in the chamber of Mayo County Council where support for the Provisional Government was limited to about one-third of the 34-man council. Indeed, by the end of the month, the

General Richard Mulcahy presenting a Tricolour to a Free State soldier at the handover of Beggars Bush Barracks in Dublin on February 2, 1922. My father reported for duty at Beggars Bush on Monday, February 20, just one week after his release from Peterhead Prison. He was appointed to the position of Commandant in the new Free State Army.

local authority would be at loggerheads with the Provisional Government over the imposition of a controversial levy on ratepayers to support the anti-Treaty IRA in Mayo.

My father wasted no time in returning to Ireland. In his release papers, he gave his address as 34 Hillfoot Street, Dennistoun, Glasgow, which was the home of his then fiancée Margaret Maxwell Ferrie, but he departed Scotland within the week. According to his pension application, he reported for duty at Beggars Bush Barracks in Dublin on February 20, 1922, which would have been a week to the day of his release from Peterhead. His commanding officer was Major General Éamon Price, a senior figure in GHQ prior to the Truce.

Quite a number of the key men who were involved in smuggling arms from Scotland and England took the pro-Treaty side, including my father, Neill Kerr and Michael Burke, but there were a number on the anti-Treaty side too, and I think it is fair to say that the split in the IRA in Britain was about 50-50.

Not everyone took a side though. Some of the most important UK-based republicans did not take part in the Civil War at all, including the Browne sisters in Liverpool and a number of those who were on trial with my father in Edinburgh. Men like the McErlane brothers just went back to their old lives once the War of Independence ended, although they did visit Dublin in the spring of 1922 to meet Michael Collins. My father organised the meeting and told me that Collins was very appreciative of the efforts of the Scottish-born IRA members who risked so much in order to keep 'war material' flowing into Ireland when it was needed most. Having once lived in London, Collins understood better than most how difficult it was to publicly identify with the Irish independence movement in Britain and he had great sympathy for those who lost their livelihoods or were evicted because of their involvement with the IRA. Indeed, it is a sad fact that many of the people who assisted my father had to move to Ireland afterwards because they could no longer get a job in Scotland. Their scandalous neglect in the wake of Collins' death is something I will address later because I believe it is also very relevant to my father's poor treatment at the hands of the Free State government.

Westport man Joe Ring, a veteran of the West Mayo IRA Brigade, was sent to Mayo by Michael Collins to organise the new police force, the Civic Guard, while my father was sent to organise the National Army. They were both arrested by anti-Treaty forces and imprisoned in Castlebar Military Barracks.

It was inevitable Henry Coyle would be sent to Mayo to try to persuade some of the members of the county's four IRA brigades to support the Provisional Government. Only a handful of prominent IRA members in Mayo supported the Treaty and foremost among them was Joe Ring, a native of Westport and a member of the West Mayo IRA Brigade. Ring was a great friend of Michael Staines who, in turn, was one of Michael Collins' most loyal lieutenants. When Collins decided to establish a police force to replace the soon-to-be-disbanded Royal Irish Constabulary (RIC), he turned to men he could trust – and among them were Staines and Ring.

The Civic Guard was founded in the same month my father returned from Scotland. By March 1922, Joe Ring was in Mayo seeking recruits for the new police force but he got a hostile reception from his old comrades in the West Mayo IRA Brigade.

A rare photograph of the chaotic pro-Treaty rally at the Mall in Castlebar on April 2, 1922, which was attended by Michael Collins. He later visited my father and Joe Ring who were imprisoned in the local Military Barracks.

While Joe Ring tried to find recruits for the new police force, my father attempted to persuade some of his old colleagues in the Mayo Volunteers to support the Provisional Government. He had moderate success in his native Erris where Bangor Erris man John Neary helped to bring a lot of men over to the Treaty side, but he encountered strong opposition from the likes of Kilroy and Maguire, who had such an influence over the IRA in Mayo.

On St Patrick's Day, some 500 IRA men under the command of Comdt James Chambers marched through the streets of Castlebar *en route* to Mass at the Church of the Holy Rosary. The show of military strength came only weeks after impressive public ceremonies were held to mark the re-interment of the remains of two members of the West Mayo IRA Brigade who died during the War of Independence. Michael Kilroy and his flying column had rightly earned a reputation for tremendous bravery during the fight for freedom and their famous ambush at Carrowkennedy, which was one of the biggest engagements of the entire conflict, won them at a lot of respect locally and nationally. There was plenty of public support, therefore, for the anti-Treaty IRA in Mayo, which made my father's task all the more difficult.

But there were a significant minority who supported the Treaty too and they intended to have their voices heard at a rally in Castlebar on Sunday, April 2, where Michael Collins was to be the guest speaker. In the days before the rally, Kilroy's forces arrested my father and detained him in the military barracks in Castlebar. When he was being marched at gunpoint to the barracks, he told the IRA men he recognised the revolvers they were holding.

"You're arresting me with the guns I sent you from Scotland!" he said.

There was very little animosity between my father and the anti-Treaty forces, and that is reflected in an interview Michael Kilroy gave to Ernie O'Malley many years later.

"Harry Coyle [was] a Scotch helper whom we were very fond of, but we locked him up anyway," Kilroy remarked.

On the evening before the rally, Joe Ring was arrested in Westport after a standoff with anti-Treaty forces that only ended following the intervention of a local priest. Ring was quickly removed to the military barracks in Castlebar to join my father in the holding cells.

The rally went ahead at the Mall the following evening but it was a chaotic affair that ended with shots being fired by both sides. One of Collins' security personnel, Dubliner Charles Byrne, was arrested and brought to the military barracks to join my father and Joe Ring. Kilroy even sent an officer to the Imperial Hotel where Collins was staying to demand that the rest of his security men hand over their firearms. It took the intervention of Michael McHugh, Kilroy's former commanding officer in the West Mayo IRA Brigade, to defuse the tense standoff between the two sides.

Collins came to the military barracks the next morning to meet my father, Joe Ring and Charles Byrne. It is only in the last couple of years that I learned of this remarkable encounter. I use the word 'remarkable' because anyone who knows me will be aware of my long connection with Joe Ring's grandnephew, Fine Gael TD Michael Ring, who has been a party colleague and great friend for the last 20 years.

When Michael was a government minister in 2018, he and then Minister for Defence Paul Keogh helped to arrange for the Sliabh na mBan armoured car to be brought to Mayo for the Geesala Festival. The Sliabh na mBan was part of the convoy at Béal na Bláth on the day Michael Collins was killed in August 1922. Little did Michael Ring and I know that Collins visited Henry Coyle and Joe Ring in Castlebar military barracks just months before he died. Of the many amazing elements to my father's past, the connection with Joe Ring is one that just bowled me over completely. Michael Ring and I have been canvassing together in general and local elections for two decades now, and we were both aware of our respective family ties to Fine Gael going all the way back to the founding of the State, but never did we think that the paths of Joe Ring and Henry Coyle crossed all those years ago.

Deputy Michael Ring helped to bring the Sliabh na mBan to Geesala for our annual festival in 2018. Little did we realise that my father and Michael's granduncle Joe Ring were imprisoned together in the military barracks in Castlebar in April 1922, and that Michael Collins came to see them. The Sliabh na mBan was in Collins' convoy on that fateful day at Béal na Bláth in August 1922. We are pictured here with Eamonn Munnelly, a great friend and neighbour of the Coyle family.

Michael Collins was unable to secure the release of his three allies and returned to Dublin a disheartened man. My father and Joe Ring went on hunger strike to secure their release, and Joe Ring issued the following public statement addressed to his old comrade Michael Kilroy:

As Commandant of the 3rd Battalion, West Mayo Brigade, I stand loyal to the oath I took to the Republic, which is Dáil Éireann. As such I hold I have a perfect right to my opinion, and any action I have taken or may take, I am responsible to that Government and none other.

Being loyal to my oath and the Government I took it to, I hold you have no legal right to arrest or detain me, as you are no longer recognised as an officer acting for the official General Headquarters of the IRA.

My father and Charles Byrne were released later that week, but Joe Ring remained on hunger strike until Friday when he was removed to the County Infirmary where he remained for several days. He was eventually granted unconditional release and returned to a hero's welcome in Westport where he addressed a large crowd from the balcony of the Town Hall.

My father continued his efforts to recruit for the new pro-Treaty army and was taken prisoner again in Ballina later that month and detained for several days. He embarked on another hunger strike and was released soon after, according to a report in *An tOglach*, the official journal of the IRA, dated April 25, 1922. By my reckoning, the hunger strike in Ballina would have been the fifth time my father refused food in the past year – three times in Peterhead Prison and twice in Mayo. It was sad that he had to embark on this drastic form of protest against the very men for whom he risked his life and liberty during the War of Independence. It makes it all the more poignant to read an interview from Michael Kilroy in which he talks about being 'very fond' of my father. It is such a tragedy that these brave and committed republicans ended up on opposite sides in a terrible Civil War.

Before his speech was cut short in Castlebar, Michael Collins remarked: "This is not the kind of freedom all my friends and I risked our lives for."

My father would have wholeheartedly agreed with those sentiments because the cheerful optimism of that memorable day in Peterhead Railway Station was disappearing faster than anyone could have imagined.

CHAPTER 26

Married in military uniform

ON Monday, June 26, 1922, my father and Margaret Maxwell Ferrie were married at St Mary's Church in Abercromby Street in Glasgow. The ceremony made headlines on both sides of the Atlantic because it was the first time the uniform of the army of the Irish Free State had been worn outside Ireland. One of the items in this chapter is the report of the wedding that appeared on the front page of *The New York Times*. Similar reports appeared in a number of newspapers in Scotland and England, and the following was published in the *Bellshill Speaker*, which was the local newspaper in Bothwell.

Considerable interest was manifested on Monday in the marriage in Glasgow of Commandant Henry P. Coyle, IRA, and Mrs Margaret Maxwell Ferrie, daughter of Mrs Ferrie, 34 Hillfoot Street, Dennistoun.

Commandant Coyle, who belongs to County Mayo, is a prominent member of the Sinn Féin movement. He was one of the men implicated in the Alloa munitions case (when a quantity of munitions was found in a motor car) and after trial he was sentenced to five years' imprisonment, but was released in February last after serving 11 months of his term.

The wedding took place in St Mary's Church, Abercromby Street. A guard of honour from the IRA was present, the members of which, as well as the bridegroom, wore the uniform of the Army of the Irish Free State.

When the party left the church, there was cheering by a large crowd which had assembled, and Sinn Féin flags were displayed during the throwing of confetti.

A report in the *Scotsman* stated that a Free State Army commandant, a captain and seven privates accompanied my father, who is described in the marriage certificate as an IRA Staff Commandant attached to Beggars Bush Barracks in Dublin. Unfortunately, none of the newspapers named the army personnel in attendance, but the official photograph of the wedding party has survived in our family archives and I am delighted to publish it in this book. While I am unable to name most of the people in the group, there is a baby-faced Volunteer in the middle row who I am convinced is Charlie Strickland. Charlie joined the National Army shortly after his release from Peterhead Prison in late April and would have been an obvious choice as groomsman for my father.

The attendance of nine members of Ireland's National Army at St Mary's Church in Glasgow could not have happened without the authorisation of Michael Collins. Indeed, it speaks volumes for Collins' appreciation of the Scottish IRA's contribution to the fight for Irish freedom that he sanctioned such a public display by the Free State Army on foreign soil. He must have known that the attendance of nine members of Ireland's new army in full military dress would make headlines in Scotland and England, and the fact that the bridegroom was one of the few members of Sinn Féin or the IRA to have faced trial in both Scotland and England in the preceding years made the event all the more significant. Indeed, the *Liverpool Echo* was among the English newspapers to cover the wedding in a report entitled '*Man who was tried in Liverpool – Glasgow Irishman married in full military uniform*'.

"Large crowds congregated and the wedding party was given a rousing reception by their friends, accompanied by the waving of Sinn Féin flags," the *Echo* reported.

The Sinn Féin flags were, of course, the Tricolour and I am sure that many of the men and women who waved those flags are the same people whose names have featured so prominently in this book. It must have been a wonderful day of celebration for them, a day they could scarcely have imagined a year earlier when they were being hounded by the Glasgow police in the wake of the 'Smashing of the Van'.

The beautiful silver teapot, which now features in the GPO Museum, was presented to my father, the presentation being made by Sean O'Doherty on behalf of the officers and men of the Dundee Company of the IRA. It is a most impressive artifact and must have cost a considerable sum in 1922. I will return to the story of the teapot later and explain how it ended up in the GPO Museum and is no longer in the possession of the Coyle family.

On the same day my father was married in Glasgow, the funeral took place in London of Field-Marshal Sir Henry Wilson, who had been assassinated by two Irishmen on the steps of his house just days earlier. The killing of Wilson was the catalyst for Ireland's Civil War, and it wouldn't be long before my father was embroiled in the fighting, which commenced two days after his wedding with the shelling of the Four Courts in Dublin.

I doubt very much that Henry Coyle and his new bride enjoyed a honeymoon, or if they did, it was a very short one. He was needed at home to defend the Irish Free State, and once again he was not found wanting when

My father wore the uniform of the Irish Free State Army when he married Margaret Maxwell Ferrie at St Mary's Church, Abercromby Street, Glasgow, on June 26, 1922. Nine army colleagues were in attendance and the wedding made international news because it was the first time members of the Irish Free State Army were pictured outside Ireland.

Newspaper reports of my father's wedding said there were large crowds outside St Mary's Church, Abercromby Street, Glasgow, and many people were waving 'Sinn Féin flags'.

brave and loyal men were needed. He had proudly worn the uniform of the Free State Army on his wedding day, and now, just days after marrying his young bride, Henry Coyle was willing to lay down his life for that uniform. By early July, he was part of General Seán MacEoin's so-called 'Expeditionary Force' as it marched from Athlone into the West, engaging in battle with anti-Treaty forces on its journey across Connacht.

The ultimate destination of the Expeditionary Force was my father's native Mayo and, in particular, Castlebar where the anti-Treaty troops under the leadership of General Michael Kilroy were expected to make a ferocious last stand.

Tensions between the two sides had been simmering in Mayo since spring and there were several instances of shots being fired long before the Four Courts was attacked. As far back as late April, pro and anti-Treaty forces exchanged gunfire at Bangor Erris Lodge, and there were also several flashpoints in east and south Mayo. In Kiltimagh, a pro-Treaty army officer, Tommie Ruane, was shot in the hand in a row over a recruitment poster, while several National Army recruits from Ballycastle were arrested in Ballina as they boarded the morning train to Athlone.

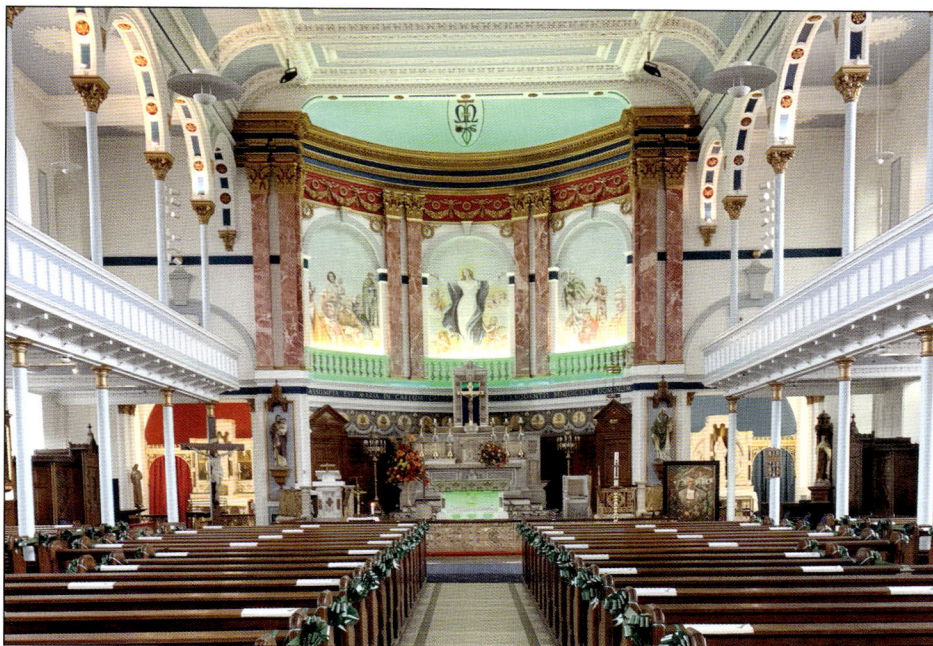

The interior of St Mary's Church, Abercromby Street, Glasgow, where my father married Margaret Maxwell Ferrie on June 26, 1922, two days before the Civil War began in Ireland.

The month of May began with a series of nationwide raids on branches of the Bank of Ireland, which was the official treasurer of the Provisional Government, and thousands of pounds were taken from branches in Westport, Ballina, Claremorris and Ballinrobe.

"The raids were carried out in daylight," recalled Dick Walsh of Balla, who had taken the anti-Treaty side. "The man in charge in each raid made a definite statement to the bank officials and demanded a definite sum. The statement, I understand, was written and signed by the divisional and brigade officers in charge of the area where each particular bank was raided. These raids were undoubtedly the first operations of what we can describe as the Civil War."

By mid-May, pro-Treaty forces were in control of the principal barracks in Galway city and Sligo town, but it was a very different story in Mayo where the anti-Treaty side, under the command of Kilroy and General Tom Maguire, were consolidating their positions in all of the key towns.

"Nearly all of the barracks in Mayo have assumed the appearance they had while in alien occupation during the reign of terror," wrote the *Western People* on May 13, "and the defensive measures, which had been removed, have

192_2_. MARRIAGES in the DISTRICT of _____ C

No.	When, Where, and How Married.	Names (in full) of Parties, with Signatures. Rank or Profession, and whether Bachelor, Spinster, Widower, Widow, or Divorced.	Age.
476	1922. on the *Twentyouxth* day of *June* at *St. Mary's Chapel, Glasgow* after Banns according to the Forms of the Roman Catholic Church.	(Name in full) *Henry Peter Coyle* (Signature) *Henry Peter Coyle, Staff Commandant. Irish Republican Army, (Bachelor.)* (Name in full) *Margaret Maxwell Ferrie.* (Signature) *Margaret Maxwell Ferrie. Typist. (Spinster.)*	26. 28.

The marriage certificate for Henry Peter Coyle and Margaret Maxwell Ferrie.

again been brought into action and are an eyesore. Barbed wire entanglements, sandbags, and steel shutters, for which we thought there was no longer any need in Ireland, are arranged as when the foreign garrison were in possession."

A day later, several officers from the National Army visited Kilmaine in the hope of starting a pro-Treaty battalion in South Mayo. They were having dinner in the home of local parish priest Fr Martin Healy when anti-Treaty troops surrounded the house and demanded that the officers surrender their weapons. A standoff ensued and only ended 24 hours later when the National Army dispatched the 'Ballinalee' armoured car and a lorry load of troops from Athlone. There were fears that the National Army would try to storm Ballinrobe barracks later in the week but they proved unfounded.

Kilroy and Maguire were in Dublin on the day the Four Courts was shelled and both men immediately rushed back to Mayo to prepare their troops for the inevitable onslaught. Kilroy was in charge in Castlebar while Maguire had control of Ballinrobe military barracks, and it was expected they would both fight fiercely to hold their respective positions.

The first shots of the Civil War were fired in Mayo on the evening of June 29 when anti-Treaty Captain Willie Moran and pro-Treaty vice-commandant Tommie Ruane were killed in an altercation outside Ruane's family pub in

ON ___ in the ___ BURGH ___ of ___ GLASGOW ___

sidence.	Name, Surname, and Rank or Profession of Father. / Name, and Maiden Surname of Mother.	If a Regular Marriage, Signature and Designation of Officiating Minister, and Signatures of Witnesses. / If an Irregular Marriage, Date of Decree of Declarator, or of Sheriff's Warrant.	When & Where Registered, and Signature of Registrar.
un. du. m.	Patrick Coyle. Farmer. Mary Coyle. m.s. Kerrigan.	(Signed) Edward Fitzgerald. Catholic Clergyman. St Mary's, Glasgow. (Signed)	1922. June 29th at Glasgow
ot r. ew.	James Ferrie. Spirit Salesman. (deceased) Mary Ann Ferrie. m.s. Murphy.	Vincent John Ferrie. 31 Hillfoot St. Glasgow. Witness. Agnes McGuire. Poncarron. Helensburgh: Witness	G.F. McFarlane. Asst. Registrar. IM.

Kiltimagh. But the county was relatively quiet during the first two weeks of July, apart from the blowing up of railway bridges and other key pieces of infrastructure in preparation for the arrival of MacEoin's forces.

It took almost three weeks for the National Army to reach Mayo but when they finally arrived on the weekend of July 22/23, they did so with devastating effect. By Monday morning, the National Army had control of Claremorris and was preparing to march on Castlebar. My father was one of hundreds of troops under the command of General Anthony Lawlor who set off for Castlebar at 10pm on Monday night. Their instructions were to advance at pace, without stopping for rest, and to remove all road blockades and construct bridges where necessary. The troops also commandeered any form of horse transport they could find, including sidecars, turf carts, drays and milk-carts. Indeed, they must have made for an unusual military cavalcade by the time they reached Mayo's county town.

While my father marched towards Castlebar, Joe Ring was leading a daring coastal invasion at Rosmoney, near his native Westport. Ring had left the Civic Guard in May and joined the National Army as a Brigadier General. He and a few hundred troops set sail from Dublin on July 21, taking a route northwards around Larne and Donegal before landing in West Mayo on the

IRISH MILITARY WEDDING.

Free State Uniforms Figure in Marriage of Officer in Glasgow.

Copyright, 1922, by The New York Times Company.
Special Cable to THE NEW YORK TIMES.

LONDON, June 26.—Ten members of the Irish Free State Army in full military uniform were present today at the marriage of Staff Commandant Henry Coyle in St. Mary's Catholic Church in Glasgow. Large crowds gathered and the wedding party received a rousing reception from their friends, accompanied by waving of Sinn Fein flags.

Coyle stood trial in Glasgow and Liverpool for alleged Sinn Fein outrages.

The New York Times
Published: June 27, 1922
Copyright © The New Y...

My father's wedding in Glasgow made the front page of *The New York Times* on June 27, 1922.

morning of July 24. Westport was taken without a shot being fired and the National Army was soon in control of Westport Quay where Ring successfully landed the Big Fella armoured car, heavy artillery, lorries and other military equipment.

Kilroy had intended to make a last stand in Castlebar, but once he realised his troops were caught in a pincer-like attack from the east and west, he decided to retreat into his old heartlands of Newport and Ballycroy where he had successfully fought a guerilla campaign during the War of Independence. By the time General Lawlor, my father and the hundreds of National Army troops arrived in Castlebar, the town was empty of anti-Treaty forces and the only evidence of their hasty retreat were the smouldering remains of the military barracks and county jail, as well as numerous roadblocks and bombed bridges.

By the end of the week, the National Army had control of all of the principal towns in Mayo, apart from Newport and Belmullet, but there was no sense of victory because the anti-Treaty forces had vowed to continue to fight to the bitter end.

Unlike many of the senior men in the National Army, my father did not have direct experience of the kind of guerilla warfare that had been the hallmark of the War of Independence. As a Volunteer in Erris in 1918-'19, he took part in several drilling exercises, but these were performed with pikes or imitation wooden guns, so it cannot have been easy for him when the first bullets of the Civil War began to fly. However, if he lacked experience it did not show, and he certainly made up for it with the sort of courage, tenacity and natural soldierly instinct that only reveals itself in the white heat of battle. In the weeks ahead, Henry Coyle would make headlines once again as he put his life on the line to protect the Provisional Government of the Irish Free State.

When he was alone in his cold prison cell in Peterhead, my father had dreamed of returning to 'flowery sweet Mayo', but he never imagined that when he got there he'd have bullets whizzing past his head, bullets fired from the very guns he and Neill Kerr and the many other Volunteers in England and Scotland sent across the Irish Sea. This was not the sort of homecoming he or the other heroes of Peterhead had envisaged.

CHAPTER 27

'The pluck of the born soldier'

BY mid-August 1922, the Civil War in Mayo had settled into a grim pattern of ambushes and counter-offensives. The National Army continued to hold all of the key towns but its forces were continuously coming under a barrage of sniper fire, especially after dark, and the anti-Treaty troops were also engaging in regular roadside attacks during the daytime.

My father was initially stationed in Claremorris, which was the command centre for the National Army in Mayo, with the troops billeted at the town's vacant workhouse and hospital, as well as Castlemacgarrett House. He later moved to Ballina and remained there for most of the Civil War, experiencing regular attacks from anti-Treaty troops who had retreated into the foothills of the Ox Mountains and joined with colleagues from Sligo.

On Monday, August 14, members of the National Army left Ballina at 2am and conducted a series of raids between Swinford and Kiltimagh, resulting in the capture of some 37 prisoners. It was a dramatic and dangerous night, and my father was lucky to make it through alive. The following report from the *Connaught Telegraph* on August 19, 1922, paints a very vivid picture of the Civil War in Mayo at that time.

The troops were all night engaged in rounding up the district between Swinford and Kiltimagh, and early in the morning came on a large party of Irregulars at Ballinamore, near Kiltimagh. Comdt-Gen Lawlor, who was in front of the troops with Comdt Coyle in a motorcar, observed an obstruction on the road and, suspecting an ambush, they immediately dismounted.

The ambushers immediately opened fire, and for a full 15 minutes, Comdt-Gen Lawlor and Comdt Coyle engaged the attackers. During this Comdt Coyle was wounded in the cheek and arm, and General Lawlor had some miraculous escapes.

Their motorcar was completely disabled, and although Comdt Coyle was badly wounded, he made his way back to the main body of troops, who were raiding some miles away.

My father was part of General Seán MacEoin's 'Expeditionary Force' that marched from Athlone to Castlebar in mid-July 1922. They arrived in Castlebar on Tuesday, July 25, to find the local military barracks a smouldering ruin after it had been set alight by the retreating anti-Treaty forces.

Picture: Wynne Collection

Comdt-Gen Lawlor speaks in terms of the highest praise of the gallantry of Comdt Coyle, who said: 'I have not long to live, and I will go back and tell the boys.' He succeeded in getting clear away and reaching the main body, who immediately dashed to the scene of the ambush. With their arrival, the resistance of the Irregulars completely gave way and firing soon died away.

The National troops captured a large number of prisoners, 37 rifles, 14 revolvers, 32 bombs, and a large quantity of ammunition. It is not known if the Irregulars suffered any casualties. The capture also included a machine for making ammunition and bombs.

Comdt-Gen Lawlor, whilst waiting the reinforcements, lay flat on the road and with rifle in hand replied to the terrific fusillade of the Irregulars.

The wounds sustained by Comdt Coyle happily proved not to be so serious as was first thought; he is progressing favourably…

It was later learned that the captures were of much greater importance than at first thought. The number of prisoners captured is by far the greatest and most important than in any other affair of its sort in Mayo.

Other newspaper reports state that the car in which my father and Comdt-Gen Lawlor were travelling was riddled with 18 bullets, one of which struck my father in the left arm while another glanced off his right neck and cheek. He clearly thought he had been struck in the neck, which was why he told Lawlor he feared he was going to die and would return to warn the rest of the troops before they marched into the ambush. The following account in the *Western People* is a chilling description of the horrors and vagaries of war

BIG ROUND-UP IN EAST MAYO.

Another dramatic blow was struck at the Irregulars in Mayo on Monday by Comdt.-Gen. Lawlor, and resulted in captures of the greatest importance.

Troops left Ballina at 2 a.m. and returned in the evening with 37 of the prisoners. The troops were all night engaged in rounding up the district between Swinford and Kiltimagh, and early in the morning came on a large party of Irregulars at Ballinamore, near Kiltimagh. Comdt.-Gen. Lawlor, who was in front of the troops with Comdt. Coyle in a motor car, observed an obstruction on the road, and, suspecting an ambush, they immediately dismounted.

The ambushers immediately opened fire, and for fully fifteen minutes Comdt.-Gen. Lawlor and Comdt. Coyle engaged the attackers. During this, Comdt. Coyle was wounded in the cheek and arm, and Gen. Lawlor had some miraculous escapes. Their motor car was completely disabled, and although Comdt. Coyle was badly wounded he made his way back to the main body of troops, who were raiding some miles away. Comdt.-Gen. Lawlor speaks in terms of the highest praise of the gallantry of Comdt. Coyle, who said:—

"I have not long to live, and I will go back and tell the boys." He succeeded in getting clear away and reaching the main ... who immediately dashed ...

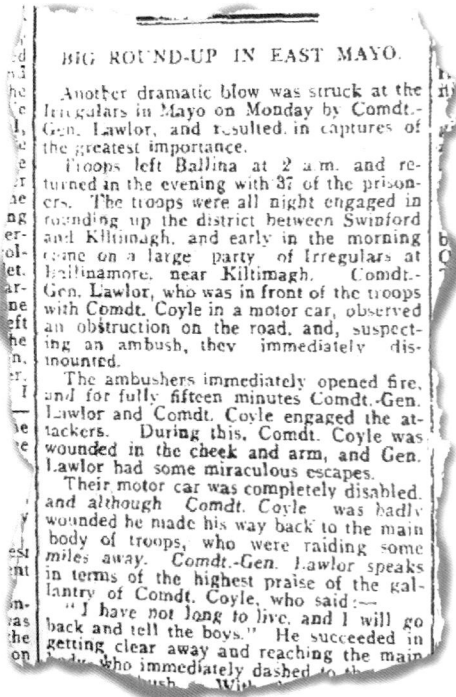

My father was shot and injured in an ambush at Ballinamore, Kiltimagh, on August 14, 1922. This report of the incident was published in the *Connaught Telegraph*.

because had that bullet gone one inch higher my father would have died on the roadside in Ballinamore.

General Lawlor, with Comdt Coyle, proceeded ahead of the main body of troops in a private motor car, and when approaching Ballinamore they observed an obstruction on the road. The car was immediately stopped, but not before the sentry of the Irregulars had observed it.

A shot rang out from the sentry, evidently intended as a signal, and in a few moments the roadside was ablaze with the flashes of rifles and other instruments of death.

The car occupied by General Lawlor and Comdt Coyle was riddled with bullets. No fewer than 18 bullets hit it during the course of the engagement. The windscreen was shattered in a thousands fragments…

While dismounting from the car, Comdt Coyle was hit – sustaining a flesh wound through the arm, the bullet ricochetting and glancing off his neck and cheek. Although he had been badly wounded through the neck, Comdt Coyle, along with General Lawlor, lay on the road and replied to the fire of the attackers with energy.

The main body of troops were a good distance behind, and Comdt Coyle volunteered to go back and notify them. This he did with the pluck of the born soldier. He crept along the ditch, now running, now taking cover, while the blood flowed freely and the bullets whistled over his head and about him.

It was not long until the 'Big Fella' [armoured car] arrived, followed by a Crossley tender and a number of motorcars with troops. The 'Big Fella' soon got into action and created consternation with the deadly stream of lead it poured on the position of the Irregulars.

The report stated that my father continued to take part in the attack despite his injuries.

Although wounded as he was, [Comdt Coyle] never for a moment flinched during the ordeal, and continued to use his rifle throughout…

The result of the operation reflects the greatest credit to the National forces engaged, and particularly on General Lawlor and Comdt Coyle, both of whose conduct in a trying situation was worthy of the highest admiration.

The front page of Cork's *Evening Echo* announcing the death of Michael Collins.

The same edition of the *Western People* carried extensive coverage of the death of the president of the Provisional Government, Arthur Griffith, which plunged the nation into mourning. But an even greater tragedy was to befall the Free State within days when General Michael Collins, the commander-in-chief of the National Army, was killed in an ambush in his native Cork on Tuesday, August 22.

"Dazed incredulity was the first sensation with which the people of Ireland heard the tragic news on Wednesday morning," wrote the *Connaught Telegraph*. "But the grim announcement in black type was not to be gainsaid, and the horror of the thing dawned on all in its full immensity. It was as if everyone, from the highest to the lowest, had lost an intimate comrade."

My father had certainly lost an 'intimate comrade' and would mourn Michael Collins' passing for the rest of his days. He regarded the death of Collins as the greatest tragedy to befall Ireland in his lifetime and never tired of telling me of the Cork man's ambitions for an independent Irish nation in the 20th century, a nation that would be an industrial innovator and a thriving exporter of agricultural produce. Henry Coyle was convinced that Collins offered the best chance of a new beginning for Ireland, the building of a

Newspaper tributes to Arthur Griffith and Michael Collins, who died within weeks of each other in August 1922. These newspapers were owned by Michael Collins' sister Kitty (pictured), who was a schoolteacher at Carragowan NS, Bohola, and was married to Joseph Sheridan, a brother of the famous Olympian Martin Sheridan.

prosperous nation where the shackles of the past would be cast off and the sons of the small landholders would finally be afforded equal opportunity.

Michael Collins was my father's idol and he was heartbroken when the sad news of the commander-in-chief's death reached Mayo. He attended the funeral in Dublin on Monday, August 28, which was exactly two weeks to the day since he nearly lost his own life at Kiltimagh.

My father also told me he was one of the pallbearers at Collins' funeral, although he could not properly carry the coffin as his arm was still in a sling. I spent many hours going through newsreel footage of the funeral during my research for this book until finally I found a clip of him with his hand on the coffin as it is carried from St Mary's Pro-Cathedral in Dublin. Indeed, the footage is used at the end of Neil Jordan's film, *Michael Collins*.

It is estimated that some 500,000 people lined the streets of Dublin on that heartbreaking day in August 1922 as the remains of Michael Collins were brought in military parade from the Pro-Cathedral to Glasnevin Cemetery. It was a fitting send-off for a truly great Irishman

My father's life changed irrevocably on the day Michael Collins died. Nobody appreciated the work of the Scottish Volunteers more than Collins and he was the greatest defender of men like my father who came from a similarly humble background to his own. Without Collins, my father would find himself vulnerable to forces in the pro-Treaty movement that did not care about the sacrifices the

Volunteers in Scotland and England had made during the War of Independence. By the mid-1920s, a somewhat dismissive view had taken hold in the upper echelons of government of the overseas Volunteers who did not see active service in Ireland from 1916-'21. That certainly wouldn't have happened had Collins survived the Civil War because he knew what men like Neill Kerr, my father and many others in England and Scotland had done for Irish freedom.

I don't think my father was ever the same after Collins' death. Like many of his generation, his loyalty to the 'Big Fella' was almost as strong as his sense of patriotism to his country. When he returned home to Dooyork from Peterhead Prison in February 1922, his brother Jack asked him what side he would be taking on the Treaty.

"I'll be on whatever side Michael Collins is on," my father replied.

After Collins' death, my father came to believe that the best way to honour the commander-in-chief's legacy was to push for a 32-county Irish Republic. I would be the first to acknowledge that Henry Coyle's political ideology would have been much closer to the anti-Treaty side than many in the National Army, but his devotion to Collins meant he was always going to support the Treaty and fight for the survival of the Provisional Government. However, he remained sympathetic to the anti-Treaty cause and strongly opposed the more drastic and Draconian policies of the Free State administration, especially when it came to the execution of republican prisoners. He was heartbroken when Liam Mellows was sentenced to death in December 1922, and often spoke in the most favourable terms of his fellow Connacht man. He certainly never regarded Mellows as an enemy combatant; he just viewed him as an old comrade who had taken a different path.

My father was one of the officers in Ballina when anti-Treaty forces briefly recaptured the town on Tuesday, September 12, after surprising the National Army troops during a month's mind mass for one of their soldiers. The officers were marched at gunpoint through the town to the workhouse where they had to instruct their men to surrender. Two innocent civilians were killed and several others wounded during 'Ballina's day of terror', as the *Western People* dubbed it. A mine was detonated near the post office. causing the windows of neighbouring premises to shatter and stopping the post office clock at the precise time of the raid, which was 11.30am. Several businesses were also raided, including three bank branches, and gunfire rang out for the best part of two hours before the National Army's troops finally surrendered.

The anti-Treaty forces withdrew at dusk and retreated in two directions, with one group under the command of Michael Kilroy setting off for Killala and the North Coast Road, and the other proceeding towards Bonniconlon

My father (extreme left) helps to carry Michael Collins' coffin from the Pro-Cathedral in Dublin on August 28, 1922. The cheek wound that he sustained in the ambush in Kiltimagh two weeks earlier is clearly visible and his left arm is in a sling. I wish to sincerely thank Darren Conroy of the Collins 22 Society (Midlands branch) for helping to source this image.

and the Ox Mountains. National Army reinforcements flooded into Ballina in the next 24 hours, and on Thursday morning, General Lawlor and Brigadier General Joe Ring led a heavily-armed battalion, supported by the Big Fella armoured car, towards Bonniconlon. The two sides clashed on the Sligo side of the border village in a fierce gunfight that cost Joe Ring his life. He was just 31 years old.

Ring's death came as another terrible blow to my father and all of the National Army troops in Mayo. The Westport man was a hugely admired figure in the county and held in the highest affection by men on both sides of the Treaty divide. Two days after Ring's death, the National Army in Mayo suffered another devastating blow when it lost six soldiers in a gun battle with Michael Kilroy's forces in the north Mayo village of Glenamoy.

I can only imagine the distress my father must have felt as the Civil War wiped out many of his old comrades in Mayo and, indeed, in other parts of the country too. Perhaps the saddest and most tragic story is that of Scottish comrade, Sean Adair, from Co Antrim, who was the quartermaster of the IRA brigade in Glasgow and would have worked closely with my father in acquiring munitions to send to Ireland.

Adair took part in the 'Smashing of the Van' and was one of the 13 men who later went on trial for that failed attempt to rescue Frank Carty. Although he was acquitted, Adair's family in Lisburn in Co Antrim were harassed as a result of the publicity surrounding the trial and they were eventually burned out of their home and had to flee as refugees to the Free State.

Adair may well have been one of the guests at my father's wedding in Glasgow on June 26. Five days later, he came across to Ireland to volunteer for the National Army, reporting to Custume Barracks in Athlone and immediately commencing active service as a member of the Midlands' Division. Like my father, Adair was made a commandant.

On July 13, 1922, Adair was one of a group of National Army troops who left Markree Castle in Sligo, where they were stationed, and travelled by the lake road towards Rockwood. The Lisburn man was in charge of the Ballinalee armoured car while the other soldiers, numbering about two dozen, travelled in Crossley tenders.

The military cavalcade was ambushed at Rockwood and Adair was killed. The leader of the anti-Treaty party was none other than Frank Carty, the man Adair tried to rescue from the prison van in Glasgow just a year earlier. The cruel irony of that incident starkly illustrates the tragedy that was Ireland's Civil War.

No wonder my father never spoke about those terrible times.

CHAPTER 28

'We shall not long have a partitioned Ireland'

IRELAND officially took its place among the nations of the world on December 6, 1922, when King George V gave Royal assent to the Constitution of a new Irish Free State.

"The formal establishment of the Free State will have a stabilising effect and is bound to bring peace to the country," predicted the *Connaught Telegraph*, "and if expectations materialise we shall not long have a partitioned Ireland."

Predictions of a swift peace were premature, however. The new state was barely 24 hours old when two members of Dáil Éireann – Seán Hales from Cork and Padraig Ó Máille from Galway – were the victims of an audacious assassination attempt as they emerged from the Ormond Hotel in Dublin on the afternoon of December 7. Hales, a hugely respected veteran of the War of Independence, died almost immediately from his injuries while Ó Máille, the deputy speaker of the Dáil, was badly injured, but survived.

The daring daylight attack on two members of the national parliament was shocking enough, but the response from the Free State government stunned the country altogether. Four prominent anti-Treaty prisoners at Mountjoy – Liam Mellows, Joe McKelvey, Robert Barrett and Rory O'Connor – were sent to face the firing squad the next morning. More executions followed in the final days of 1922, and a total of 13 anti-Treaty prisoners were put to death in December alone.

In early January, the *Western People* reported that six men from Erris, who were all on the anti-Treaty side, had 'handed in their rifles at the residence of Comdt Coyle, Geesala'. I am not aware of many other incidents during the Civil War where arms were surrendered at the home of a National Army officer, and I think the men's actions show the respect there was for Henry Coyle on the anti-Treaty side. At a time when relations between the pro and anti-Treaty sides were at their most bitter, the Erris men believed they would get a fair hearing if they surrendered to my father.

In his pension application, my father says he 'saved the lives of a number of men' during the Civil War and 'can furnish proof if required'. He wasn't asked to name names, but I know of one incident where he intervened to halt the execution of a National Army soldier who was court-martialled for deserting to the anti-Treaty side, a charge my father proved was untrue.

The Free State executions were a 'shock and awe' tactic designed to break the spirit of the anti-Treaty forces, but they had the opposite effect in Mayo where resistance against the

My father was greatly saddened by the Free State's execution of Liam Mellroy in December 1922. He knew the Galway native from their time together in England and Scotland.

National Army remained resolute in the early months of 1923. The National Army had gained control over the last anti-Treaty stronghold of Newport in mid-November, resulting in the capture of Michael Kilroy, but the guerilla war dragged on through the winter and into spring. Trains were regularly derailed, prompting the National Army to send a so-called armoured train to Mayo in March following the re-opening of the line between Claremorris and Sligo. On St Patrick's Day, shots were fired in Castlebar, resulting in the death of a National Army soldier and injuries to four others, including two civilians.

Intermittent killings continued on both sides right up to May 24 when a ceasefire was declared. By then, my father was stationed in Portobello Barracks in Dublin, having spent the early months of the year in Mayo, mainly in Ballina. In early May, he received the heartbreaking news that one of his old comrades from Peterhead Prison, Neil 'Plunkett' O'Boyle had been killed in Co Wicklow. O'Boyle was nicknamed 'Plunkett' because of his devotion to Joseph Mary Plunkett, one of the executed leaders of the 1916 Rising.

Neil had so much in common with my father. He grew up on a small farm near Burtonport in Co Donegal, spoke Irish as a youngster and emigrated to Scotland to earn money for his family following the death of his father.

Having joined the Irish Volunteers as a teenager, Neil continued to devote as much time as he could to the IRA in Scotland while also working full-time

Donegal man Neil 'Plunkett' O'Boyle was killed in controversial circumstances in Wicklow towards the end of the Civil War. My father was in Peterhead Prison with Neil and they were released on the same day.

as a miner. He was arrested in the same month as my father – December 1920 – and received a five-year term of penal servitude in Peterhead.

Released on the same day as my father, Neil took the anti-Treaty side and was arrested in Donegal at the start of the Civil War and imprisoned in Finner Camp. He immediately started to dig an escape tunnel but it was discovered by the camp authorities and Neil was transferred to Newbridge barracks in Co Kildare. Once again, he started digging a tunnel and this time it was successful. Neil and about 150 other prisoners escaped in October 1922 in one of the great prison breakouts in Irish history.

Neil saw action in the Wicklow Mountains throughout the winter and spring of 1922-'23. He was gunned down in controversial circumstances on May 8 during an engagement with National Army troops and his remains were brought back to Donegal for burial in Kinclassagh Cemetery.

I am sure my father and Neil O'Boyle spent many an hour in Peterhead plotting ways to escape from the 'Prison of No Hope'. I read somewhere that books were very hard to get in Peterhead, but Neal managed to get his hands on a Pitman Shorthand manual and taught himself shorthand.

When Neal, my father and the others sang *Amhrán na bhFiann* together in Peterhead Railway Station on that memorable February day in 1922, they would never have imagined ending up on opposing sides within a matter of months.

My father's eyes always filled with tears whenever I asked him about the Civil War and I am sure he often thought of men like Neil O'Boyle, Liam Mellows and the many other Volunteers who were struck down in their prime in 1922-'23. It is estimated that some 800 members of the National Army and about 500 anti-Treaty personnel were killed during the fighting, and the deaths continued even after the ceasefire of May 24.

In Mayo, an Ardnaree native named Joseph Healy was shot in the back while trying to flee National Army soldiers in Ballyglass, near Claremorris. At

Cumann na nGaedeal

ORGANISING FUND

In response to a general demand from our supporters all over the country, a fund has been opened for the purpose of organising the people in support of Cumann na nGaedheal, and subscriptions are now invited from all who approve of our objects and programme.

It is of vital importance to the Nation that the position already won should be made secure, and that advantage should be taken of every opportunity to strengthen our National position.

Solid foundations of Government have been laid, but there is much work yet to be done before our country is out of danger from within and without. Two great questions are still unsettled, viz., the Financial Adjustments with Great Britain and the setting up of the Boundary Commission. It will be of supreme importance that a strong Government, having the support of the best elements in the Nation shall undertake this important work.

The Irish people are now in control. The next few years will be the test of their ability to build up and strengthen the Nation.

Cumann na nGaedheal does not stand for any particular sectional interest; its policy is National; its object is to harmonise the different sections and give justice and fair play to all.

At the forthcoming elections Cumann na nGaedheal will put forward candidates pledged to its programme. It will be the duty of the organisation to ensure that the Representatives of the people shall be the best the Nation can give.

" Ireland is yours for the making."

Signed on behalf of Cumann na nGaedheal:

EOIN MacNEILL, President.
Mrs. WYSE POWER,
GEORGE NESBITT,
BATT O'CONNOR, Trustees.

Subscriptions to the Organising Fund may be sent to any of the Trustees, 5 Parnell Square, Dublin.

CUMANN NA nGAEDHEAL

OBJECTS AND PROGRAMME

To carry on the National Tradition; and

To utilise the powers of Government in the hands of the Irish people as well as other forms of public activity for the fullest development of the Nation's heritage—political, cultural and economic.

To secure the unity of Ireland and to combine the divergent elements of the nation in a common bond of citizenship, in harmony with National security.

To preserve and foster the National Language, Literature, Games, and Arts, and every element of National culture and custom which tends to give Ireland distinction as a nation.

To promote the development of agriculture, fisheries and other natural resources.

To stimulate and safeguard the development of suitable manufacturing industries by all means at our disposal.

To make the whole soil of Ireland available for the use of the people by completing land purchase and by utilising the depopulated grass-lands in accordance with a broad National plan.

To obtain the provision of adequate financial assistance for a National scheme of housing, urban and rural.

To substitute, as far as possible, for the unemployment dole, national schemes of useful work, including arterial drainage, reafforestation, improvement of roads, and waterworks.

To encourage the proper physical development of the children of Ireland.

To secure the fullest opportunities of educational advancement for every section of the community.

Subscribe Now!

This advertisement announcing the establishment of Cumann na nGaedheal appeared in the *Irish Independent* on June 16, 1923, which was the same day my father resigned his post in the National Army to become an organiser for Cumann na nGaedheal.

W.T. Cosgrave (right) and Kevin O'Higgins (left) are pictured with Arthur Griffith in early 1922. Cosgrave and O'Higgins came to Claremorris for a Cumann na nGaedheal rally on June 30, 1922 – it was the party's first meeting west of the Shannon.

an inquest into the 23-year-old's death, coroner Dr Conor Maguire said it was 'lamentable' that young men like Healy, who had fought the Black and Tans 'when men who now consider themselves great were no good', should be 'shot down like that'.

"I do not blame the army," said Dr Maguire, "but it is a pity that those on top do not put a stop to this kind of thing and call off the shooting on both sides."

My father resigned from the National Army on June 16, 1923, to take up a position as an organiser for Cumann na nGaedheal, Ireland's new political organisation.

Translated as 'Party of the Irish', Cumann na nGaedheal was founded by pro-Treaty members of Dáil Éireann in April 1923 and its leader was the president of the Free State government, W.T. Cosgrave. A general election was scheduled for September 1923 and Cumann na nGaedheal intended to put its manifesto for peace and stability before the Irish people in the hope of winning an outright majority in the Dáil.

The party was officially launched in the West on June 30 when Cosgrave, Minister for Justice Kevin O'Higgins and Minister for Defence Paddy Hogan arrived in Claremorris for a rally at the Square. Among those travelling with the ministerial deputation was Mayo native Patrick Moylett, a prominent member of Sinn Féin who had been involved in back-channel peace talks with the British government in November 1920. Moylett was a self-made businessman with several large stores in Mayo and Galway, and he had been asked to travel to Mayo to help with the launch of the new party's election campaign in the West.

As the train approached Claremorris railway station, the ministers and the members of their security team – detectives from the Free State intelligence department at Oriel House in Dublin – began loading and checking their revolvers. An astonished Moylett was having none of it:

"If you were afraid of being shot in Claremorris, you should never have left Dublin," he firmly told them. "If you show your guns, I will not leave this train and continue to Ballina."

The ministers needed Moylett more than he needed them so they told the detectives to keep their guns hidden. But the incident was instructive because it showed just how volatile the situation remained in Mayo more than a month after the ceasefire – so volatile, in fact, that men like Cosgrave and O'Higgins were worried they might not get out of Claremorris alive. They knew what had happened to Michael Collins in Castlebar before the Civil War, and although the majority of the anti-Treaty leaders were now behind bars, there were still enough of them at large to present a clear and present danger.

The rally in Claremorris passed off without any major incident but the leadership of Cumann na nGaedheal was far from confident about its prospects in Mayo in the general election. It barely had the support of one-third of councillors on Mayo County Council, and some of the most prominent TDs in the county, men like Tom Maguire and P.J. Ruttledge, were vehemently opposed to the Treaty. For the first time, Mayo was to be divided into two distinct constituencies – South (five seats) and North (four seats) – for the general election, and the majority of the outgoing TDs were in the anti-Treaty camp.

It may come as a surprise to many people to learn that Mayo had the third largest population of the 26 counties in the new Free State – only Dublin and Cork were more populous – so it was really important for Cumann na nGaedheal to achieve electoral success in a vast county that had been the bastion of anti-Treaty resistance in Connacht. I am not sure when my father was asked to become the organiser for Cumann na nGaedheal in Mayo – it may even have been before he resigned his army post – but he took up the position in early July. It was an unenviable and dangerous task, especially for a man so prominently associated with the National Army.

My father knew better than most the depth of opposition to the Treaty among the members of the IRA in Mayo. After all, they had imprisoned him twice in April 1922, and then nearly killed him the following August, so he would have been under no illusions about the task awaiting him on becoming the county organiser for Cumann na nGaedheal. But I think he hoped that by getting involved in democratic politics he could help to heal the wounds of the Civil War and eventually bring about a united Ireland, a 32-county republic where there would be no more talk of pro and anti-Treaty factions.

The Civil War left my father deeply traumatised, as it did so many of the men and women of that era. In Henry Coyle's case, he had spent long periods of solitary confinement in Peterhead, which cannot have been good for his mental health, so the impact of the Civil War must have been devastating altogether. To be honest, I have no idea how men like him came through that period and I marvel at their mental resilience in coping with everything that was thrown at them. It is easy to forget that these were very young men too. My father turned 29 in 1923, yet he had experienced more of life's highs and lows than men three times his age.

Hindsight is, of course, 20/20 vision, but there is no doubt my father made a huge mistake in getting mixed up in politics. He would later say it was Michael Collins who first suggested he should become involved in public life. Collins, no doubt, was thinking of the stirring speech my father gave in Edinburgh Courthouse, an oration worthy of any experienced politician. My father would have done anything to honour Collins' memory so I expect he didn't have to think twice when asked to go to Mayo to organise for Cumann na nGaedheal. It meant he was leaving his young wife once again to embark on a treacherous mission that could easily cost him his life, but he firmly believed it was the patriotic thing to do.

Ironically, this brave Irish soldier would soon discover that politics is not like war at all. In declaring his allegiance to Cumann na nGaedheal, my father believed his greatest opponents would be on the anti-Treaty side, but he was wrong; it was the people in his own political party who proved themselves the most dangerous enemies of all.

Henry Coyle had soldiered in 'enemy country' during the War of Independence, and then stood defiantly in the line of fire during the bitter Civil War, but the deadly 'game' of politics ultimately proved his undoing. Sadly, my father would come to bitterly regret his foray into public life.

CHAPTER 29

'I want you to stand in Mayo for Peace against Chaos'

O NE of Henry Coyle's first public appearances as an organiser for Cumann na nGaedheal was in his native Erris on July 18, 1923, when he spoke at an open-air meeting in Belmullet. The local parish priest, Canon Hegarty, chaired the event and formally introduced my father, who told the gathering that Cumann na nGaedheal was 'the organisation by which the country will be run in the future'.

"It is a national organisation and must, therefore, take in the people in general," my father said. "The organisation stands for the man back in Faulmore or out in Inniskea, who has no land, just the same as a man in any other part of the country who has a thousand acres."

Amidst loud cheers, my father then addressed the thorny issue of the Anglo-Irish Treaty, and he didn't spare Éamon de Valera!

"Now some people say that Ireland was sold when the Treaty was accepted. That is the opinion of the minority, and a very small minority at that. Ireland was not sold. If the Republic was let down, Mr de Valera was the man who did it. Instead of going over to London to negotiate with Lloyd George, why did he not get Lloyd George to come over to Dublin and negotiate with him there?

"Michael Collins and the others were sent over to London, and on hearing the terms of the Treaty these were de Valera's words – 'I never thought I would see the day when we would get such concessions from England'. His friends then came round him…"

"Mary MacSwiney," a voice shouted from the crowd.

"Yes, Mary MacSwiney and others," replied my father, "and said – 'Now Éamon, you are in the background, these [the plenipotentiaries] are the

An advertisement for Cumann na nGaedheal that appeared in the *Irish Independent* during the general election campaign in August 1923.

heroes'; and, of course, Éamon was too proud for that. Previous to that he was getting credit for work done by others.

"He then came along with Document No. 2, and his own words were that there was 'only a shadow of a difference between Document No 2 and the Treaty', or in other words, 'the value of a halfpenny stamp'. "Oh, how sad to think that the lives of hundreds of our countrymen would be sacrificed for the value of a halfpenny stamp, along with involving the country in a debt of fifty million pounds!

"This is the man whose followers will tell you that they are fighting for the love of Ireland. It is a strange way to love a country – to send it to destruction.

"You need not go further than the town we are in to see the ruins of wrecked houses – the work of the people who 'love' Ireland so much. Few of the so-called Republicans in Erris today were to be found in 1918. At that time, if the Irish Party had come along with the simple Home Rule Bill, it would gladly have been received by most of the present-day Republicans. We have now got more than the Irish Party ever asked for.

"Some of them will tell you that the British soldiers are not yet out of Ireland, that they are still in the Six Counties. Well, the men who put them out of the Twenty-Six Counties can put them out of the other six if those in opposition to the Government would only have commonsense.

"As regards the selection of candidates for the coming election, that is a matter entirely for yourselves. The day is now past when candidates were selected in London and elsewhere and sent down here to be elected by you.

"I do not wish to continue further or preach to you of the horrible past or the glorious future. The glory of the future depends upon yourselves. Within the next fortnight, a convention will be called, made up of two delegates from each affiliated Cumann, when you will have an opportunity of selecting your own candidates.

"The government of Ireland is now in the hands of the Irish people, and if they do not do what is right, they will only have themselves to blame. You will now see that it is in your own interest to have Cumanns formed immediately in your respective areas."

The *Western People* reported that 'loud and prolonged cheering' greeted my father's speech. I think that was the day when he went from Cumann na nGaedheal organiser in Mayo to being an actual candidate in the general election. The fact that the speech was published in its entirety in the *Western People* is, I think, a reflection of how it was viewed at that time. Henry Coyle had delivered an articulate, passionate endorsement of Cumann na nGaedheal's policies and his rousing oration was that of a candidate rather than a backstage organiser.

Within weeks of resigning his army post, Henry Coyle was being talked about as a potential candidate for Cumann na nGaedheal in the four-seat constituency of Mayo North. It was never his intention to run in the general election but the party was desperate to put someone with military service on the ticket in Mayo. The anti-Treaty side had nominated several heroes of the War of Independence – men like Michael Kilroy, Tom Maguire and P.J. Ruttledge – for the two Mayo constituencies but there was nobody of that stature on the pro-Treaty side. My father's trial in Scotland had made headlines in the Irish newspapers, so his name was well known in Mayo, even if he had spent most of the War of Independence overseas. But ultimately, the decision to select candidates for the upcoming election would come down to the Cumann na nGaedheal delegates who were due to hold conventions in both constituencies in mid-August ahead of polling day on Tuesday, August 27.

Four days after the meeting in Belmullet, my father organised a very successful Cumann na nGaedheal rally at Pearse Street (then King Street) in Ballina, which was attended by two pro-Treaty TDs who were running in Mayo South, Joseph MacBride and William Sears, as well as Sligo TD, Thomas O'Donnell. Prior to the speeches, my father read a letter from the Archbishop of Killala Dr James Naughton who called on the voters of Mayo North to support the Cumann na nGaedheal candidates.

"The present members of our government deserve well of our countrymen," wrote the Archbishop. "They have, indeed, proved themselves worthy of our confidence and support, and have earned our deepest gratitude for their devotion to duty in the tragic circumstances of the past 12 months.

"We have been so numbed by oppression from without and within for the past few years that it is impossible for the people to realise even in a small way the blessings of the great measure of freedom that has been secured for our country."

The Archbishop's ringing endorsement of candidates who were 'active supporters of our present government' reflected the Catholic Church's strong backing for the pro-Treaty side. There were quite a number of clergymen who chaired meetings of Cumann na nGaedheal throughout the election campaign, including in Erris where the anti-Treaty side enjoyed a lot of popular support despite the clerical interventions.

One of the big issues facing candidates in Mayo North was a proposal, dating back to the early 1900s, to build a major transatlantic port at Blacksod Bay with a rail connection to Sligo and Ballina. The British Admirality had first mooted the idea in 1907, and even sanctioned funding for the development of the railway connection, but World War I put paid to its progress and it was shelved completely once the War of Independence erupted. However, the much-talked about project became a live issue again in the 1923 election and candidates on both sides of the Treaty divide in Mayo North voiced their support for an initiative that had the potential to transform the future of the long-neglected barony of Erris.

The closing date for nominations for the general election was Saturday, August 18, and the *Connaught Telegraph* of that week said there were 22 candidates for the nine Dáil seats in Mayo. There were four men on the Cumann na nGaedheal ticket in Mayo North – Patrick O'Hara, a pro-Treaty member of Mayo County Council from Swinford; Seán T. Ruane, a rural district councillor from Kiltimagh and brother of the late National Army officer and county councillor Tommie Ruane; P.J. McAndrew, a Ballycastle-born engineer living in Dublin and a vocal supporter of the Blacksod project; and Henry Coyle, who was described as 'ex-commandant in the National Army'.

In Mayo South, a Cumann na nGaedheal convention at the courthouse in Castlebar selected five candidates – outgoing TDs Joseph MacBride and William Sears, as well as Charles Bewley, a Dublin-based barrister with ties to Mayo; Martin Nally, a pro-Treaty member of Mayo County Council; and Patrick (P.J.) O'Malley, a member of a prominent Westport business family and the owner of the Ormond Hotel in Dublin.

Joseph McGrath (left) is pictured with Michael Collins, Seán McGarry and Padraic Ó Maille. McGrath was my father's running mate in Mayo North in the general election of 1923. Dáil deputies McGarry and Ó Maille were well known to my father and Ó Maille canvassed with him in Mayo North.

The ink was barely dry on the *Connaught Telegraph's* latest edition when there were some dramatic last-minute changes to the Cumann na nGaedheal teams in both constituencies. On Wednesday, August 15, Éamon de Valera was arrested at an anti-Treaty rally in Ennis, and his position as 'President of the Irish Republic' passed to P.J. Ruttledge, who was one of the few prominent anti-Treaty Dáil deputies still at large. Mayo candidates like Michael Kilroy, Thomas Derrig and Tom Maguire were all in prison for the election campaign, although Maguire escaped from Athlone Barracks shortly before polling day.

By appointing Ruttledge as its new 'President', the anti-Treaty side had laid down the gauntlet in Mayo North where it knew Cumann na nGaedheal was weak due to the absence of candidates with military credentials, with only Ruane and my father having seen active service in the War of Independence or Civil War. Days before the deadline for nominations, W.T. Cosgrave wrote an open letter to his outgoing Minister for Industry and Commerce, Joseph McGrath, in which he appealed to the Dubliner to reconsider his decision to retire from national politics.

"I want you to stand in Mayo for Peace against Chaos," Cosgrave urged McGrath. "You have a war record to be proud of, and with this record, which

THE ELECTOR

CONTESTEI

COUNTY CONSTITUEN

PUBLIC

I, the undersigned, being the Deputy Returning Officer for the County Constituency of North M
above Constituency will be taken on the 27th day of August, 1923.

The Names of the Candidates, and other particulars of such Candidates as described in their resp

Surname.	Other Names	Abode
COYLE,	HENRY	Roy, Geesala, Co. Mayo.
CROWLEY,	JOHN	Carrowkibbick, Ballycastle.
FLYNN,	CHARLES	Tubbernavine, Lahardane, Co. Mayo,
HERON,	ARCHIE	11a Casimir Avenue, Harold's Cross,
KEAVENY,	MICHAEL	Rathrooen.
KELLY,	JOSEPH	Ballaghaderreen.
McGRATH,	JOSEPH	39 South Circular Road, Dublin.
O'CONNOR,	OLIVER J.	Claremont Hotel, Howth, Co. Dublin
O'HARA,	PATRICK	Market Street, Swinford.
O'SULLIVAN,	TIMOTHY J.	Tonroe, Killala, Co. Mayo.
RUANE,	JOHN T.	Kiltimagh, Co. Mayo.
RUTTLEDGE,	PATRICK JOSEPH	Knox Street, Ballina.

And I further give notice that the Names of such Candidates will be printed in the Ballot Paper in t
Dated this 18th day of August, 1923.

The full list of candidates for the general election in Mayo North in 1923 as published in the *Western People* on August 25.

...CT, 1923.

...ELECTION.
...OF NORTH MAYO.
...NOTICE.

...rsuance of Rule 8 in the Fifth Schedule to the Electoral Act, 1923, hereby give notice that the Poll in the

...mination Papers, and the Names of the persons who subscribed such Nomination Papers are as follows:—

...ank, Profession, or Occupation.	Names of Persons who subscribed the Nomination Paper.
...tleman and ex-Commandant National Army.	Patrick Browne, Anthony O'Malley, John Moran, Michael O Boyle, Thomas Canavan, John McHugh, Pat Cleary, John Morrow, James Hegarty, John P. Barrett.
...sician and Surgeon.	James Calleary, John Quinn, Jas. Harte, Anthony Mulloy, John Harte, Mary Cullen, Michael Diamond, Annie Diamond, John Coleman, Mary Coleman
...mer.	Rev. Wm. Heverin, C.C.; Ed. Gallagher, Jas F. Duran, Edward Dunleavy, John Hegarty, Thomas Madden, John Ruane, John Corcoran, Anthony Moran, Peter Heneghan.
...or "Voice of Labour."	Martin Bourke, Charles Gavin, John Ruane, William Calnan, Luke Ireland, Henry McGlade, John Joseph Clarke, Joseph Coutell, John Keane, John Sheridan.
...ner.	John Crowley, M.D.; Edward Bourke, John Quinn, Moses L. Farrell, Martin Hegarty, Jas. P. McGeever, Anthony Ruane, Joseph Ruane, John Griffin, Jas Jos. McNamara.
...tleman.	John Murray, Patk. Beirne, John Gaughan, Bertha James Webster, Patrick Calnan, Teresa Murray, Mary Agnes Murray, Hubert Moran, Daniel Hopkin, Sylvester Cottrill.
...ster of Industry and Commerce.	Most Rev. James Naughton, Michael Davis, Joseph McMahon, Michael O Boyle P.P., J. Mulcno, Patrick J Carroll, Michael Joseph Loftus, John Garvey, Patrick J. Gallagher, Matthew Lavin
...er.	Thomas O'Hora, Pat Duffy (Jas Domb, Anthony Fitzpatrick, Annie Henry, John Henry, Nora Casey, James O'Grady, N.T. Catherine Fitzpatrick, Maria O'Connor, Maggie Fitzpatrick.
...hant.	Right Rev. Monsignor Conington, P.P.; Bernard F Cunniffe, Edward Gallagher, John Comer, Patk. Fitzpatrick, Ed. Doherty, Richard O'Connor, Andrew Carney, Murtagh J. Egan, Thomas Dempsey
...cultural Overseer.	James Coughtry, Martin Donohue, Patrick Hannick, Peter Kelly, James Gaughan, John J. Farrell, John Bourke, John McAndrew, Robert McElroy, John Hughes.
...nal Teacher.	Rev. Martin Henry, P.P.; Frank Dorr, John M Gaughan, John Jas. Johnson, Thos. Faby, Mary Johnston, Michl. Coghlan, Patrick Gaughan, Martin S Gaughan, Patk Jones.
...tleman.	Matthew E. Farrell, Martin Hegarty, John Moran, Anthony Ruane, Michael Rooney, James Calleary, Joseph Duffy, John Rush, Path. Flannery, Hannah Corcoran

...n which they appear in this Notice.

M. J. EGAN, Deputy Returning Officer.

I would be proud to have to my credit, you must stand for Ireland in this crisis…"

McGrath had, indeed, a war record to match anyone on the anti-Treaty side. He took part in the Easter Rising and was instrumental in organising bank robberies during the War of Independence that provided badly-needed funds for the IRA. A Collins' loyalist, he was one of the Cork man's personal staff during the Treaty negotiations in London and was later put in charge of the Criminal Investigation Department of the Free State. McGrath had grave reservations about the commander-in-chief's fateful trip to Cork in August 1922 and expressed his views in a strongly-worded letter to Collins, which was written in red ink.

Joseph McGrath had connections to Mayo through his wife, Aileen Downes, from Coolcronan, Ballina, but it was his status as an outgoing government minister that made him an obvious candidate to go head-to-head in Mayo North with the stand-in 'President of the Irish Republic'. The Dubliner was duly added to the ticket in place of P.J. McAndrew, who agreed to stand down on condition that Cumann na nGaedheal publicly declare its support for the Blacksod project, which Cosgrave was more than happy to do.

But there was less harmony in Mayo South where another Cumann na nGaedheal candidate, P.J. O'Malley, was removed from the five-man ticket at the insistence of the party's central executive. O'Malley refused to stand down and instead declared as an Independent pro-Treaty candidate, having been nominated by P.J. Doris, the editor of the Westport-based *Mayo News*. Battle-lines were soon drawn between the wealthy hotelier and his four rival Cumann na nGaedheal candidates. In an open letter to the *Connaught Telegraph*, signed by Charles Bewley, Joseph MacBride, Martin Nally and William Sears, O'Malley's pro-Treaty candidature was emphatically rebuffed.

We desire through the medium of your columns to make it clear that no candidates have been sanctioned for South Mayo by the Standing Committee of Cumann na nGaedheal except the four undersigned. If the suggestion is made on behalf of any other candidate that he is sanctioned, the suggestion is incorrect. Any other candidate presenting himself for election is doing so without the sanction and against the wishes of Cumann na nGaedheal.

Days before the letter was published, Cumann na nGaedheal organiser in Mayo South, Seamus McDonagh, told a rally in Ballindine that the party executive 'would not sanction [O'Malley] because of his record in the past'.

"When that man (O'Malley) was asked by Brigadier Joe Ring for goods and cash during the fight he refused and reported the matter to the RIC," McDonagh alleged.

It was an explosive accusation that reflected the bitter fall-out from O'Malley's sudden removal from the Cumann na nGaedheal ticket in Mayo.

I was delighted to meet Darren Conroy while at Beal na Bláth for the Michael Collins' centenary commemoration in August 2022. Darren runs the National Collins22 Society (Midlands branch), which is a non-political group remembering Michael Collins. I had looked at well over 2,000 pictures in the hope of finding one of my father carrying Michael Collins' coffin and then I went to the National Collins22 Society's Facebook page and there it was. I could not believe it. My father had always told me he was at Michael Collins' funeral on August 28, 1922, but it was incredible to see it with my own eyes. Congrats to Darren on the fine work he does commemorating an Irish hero.

Of course, I have been around politics long enough to know that not everything said at political rallies is true, but what is beyond doubt is that Cumann na nGaedheal rejected P.J. O'Malley at a time when it was desperate for high-profile candidates in Mayo. Aged in his late 30s, O'Malley had been a successful sportsman in his youth, was a member of a well-connected merchant family and had plenty of money to fund a successful campaign, having purchased the Ormond Hotel earlier that year for £10,000. His cousin, Galway native Padraic Ó Máille, was also a TD for the party.

For whatever reason – whether it was the one stated by McDonagh or some other issue – the Westport native was unceremoniously scratched from the Cumann na nGaedheal ticket in Mayo South at the eleventh hour. P.J. O'Malley would continue to campaign on a 'pro-Treaty' agenda for the rest of the campaign, but his ties to Cumann na nGaedheal were well and truly severed. Or so it seemed.

CHAPTER 30

'The beginning of an era of peace and goodwill'

THE final week of the election campaign was a bruising affair as the pro and anti-Treaty sides battled for the votes that would give them a majority of the 153 seats in Dáil Éireann. Cumann na nGaedheal ran 107 candidates across the 30 constituencies while the Republicans, as they were called, had 88 contenders. There was considerable media interest in the fight for the five seats in Mayo South and the four seats in Mayo North. Labour and the Farmers' Party ran candidates in both constituencies, but they struggled to have their voices heard in an election that was really about one issue only: the Anglo-Irish Treaty.

With many of their candidates either in prison or on the run, the Republicans turned to women like Mary MacSwiney to articulate their policies to voters in Mayo. Aged in her early 50s, MacSwiney was a redoubtable woman who was well able to hold her own in the fractious atmosphere that prevailed in Mayo in August 1923. She held a rally in Castlebar on Sunday, August 12, where the 'uproar was almost continuous', according to the *Connaught Telegraph*, and she attracted partisan crowds wherever she went.

The *Telegraph* reported several 'unpleasant incidents' during the election campaign, though it did not give any specifics, but the tense mood was reflected in the frequent fighting that took place at open-air meetings. On August 15, which was the traditional fair day in Belmullet, several candidates held rallies at the Market Square, and the *Western People* was there to capture the drama.

In introducing some of the [Cumann na nGeadheal] speakers, Rev Canon Howley was assailed with a torrent of interruptions, and he was perforce compelled to call on the military to remove the disturbers. A few of these parties were at once set upon and ejected from the meeting by the military and Civic Guards, and many hand-to-hand encounters took place between the soldiers and civilians. Fortunately, however, nothing of a serious nature occurred,

CUMANN na nGAEDHEAL.

ELECTION FUND

Cumann na nGaedheal is the National Organisation, formed to carry out the policy adopted by Arthur Griffith and Michael Collins and continued by the Government of President Cosgrave.

At the coming General Election it will put forward candidates with a view to securing for that policy a great majority of seats in Dail Eireann.

The great body of public opinion recognises that, while every interest is entitled to representation, it is only a broadly National Government, based on a broadly National majority, that can be expected to take charge of the programme for which Cumann na nGaedheal stands.

All the expenses of candidature at the Election must be defrayed out of funds to be provided by individual subscription. The number of candidates will be large. We, therefore, invite every citizen, who values the work already done, to subscribe amply to the Election Fund, and thereby enable that work to be consolidated and completed.

EOIN MAC NEILL, President of Cumann na
nGaedheal.

W. T. COSGRAVE,
KEVIN O'HIGGINS,
RICHARD MULCAHY,
Treasurers.

A COLLECTION

Will take place outside the Churches at all Masses,

On SUNDAY, AUGUST 5th, 1923

Cumann na nGaedheal had a lot of support from the Catholic Church and organised a church gate collection to fund its general election campaign in 1923.

although several persons were hurt in the conflict and some innocent people were accidentally hit with missiles flung in the surging and swaying crowd.

There were several free fights, pugilistic encounters being indulged in between Free Sate sympathisers and Republicans. Matters at one time seemed very menacing but eventually order was restored. There were no further interruptions.

Joseph McGrath made his first appearance in Erris on Wednesday, August 21, when he attended a Cumann na nGaedheal rally at Carne, which was held after a horse racing event. Accompanying McGrath was Justice Denis Cohalan, a leading Irish-American who was chief advisor to New York's Tammany Hall leader Charles F. Murphy from 1906 to 1913. Cohalan was on holidays in Ireland at the time and travelled around the country with W.T. Cosgrave during the election campaign. Indeed, it was the first Irish election in which an

THE WESTERN PEOPLE AUGUST 25 1923

VOTERS OF NORTH MAYO,

IF YOU DESIRE

Peace, Employment, Progress, Freedom

then VOTE for the CUMANN NA nGAEDHEAL CANDIDATES—

McGRATH   O'HARA
COYLE   RUANE

They will protect your Markets and Fairs, save the country from Looters, Robbers, cut roads, broken bridges Wrecked Railways, Disorder, Unemployment, Famine—and keep the English Army out.

The Treaty gives you control of your own Money, Education, an Irish Army, Power to make Laws to suit the Country, to Create and Foster Industries that will enable your sons and daughters to live at home in decency and comfort— *SUPPORT THE MEN WHO SUPPORT THE TREATY.*

VOTERS! KNOW THIS:

that for the difference between THIS and THIS

I .... do solemnly swear true faith and allegiance to the Constitution of the Irish Free State as by law established, and that I will be faithful to H. M. King George V., his heirs and successors by law, in virtue of the common citizenship of Ireland with Great Britain, and her adherence to, and membership of, the group of Nations forming the British Commonwealth of Nations.
(TREATY OATH).

I ..... do swear to bear true faith and allegiance to the Constitution of Ireland and the Treaty of Association of Ireland with the British Commonwealth of Nations, AND TO RECOGNISE THE KING OF GREAT BRITAIN AS HEAD OF THE ASSOCIATED STATES.

(OATH APPROVED BY MR. DE VALERA).

Your country has been saddled with a debt of £50,000,000 by the campaign of senseless destruction waged by Mr. de Valera and his friends, and your rates and taxes are heavy accordingly.

Michael Collins and many of the best Column Leaders of the Anglo-Irish War have been slain by the roadside, together with more than six hundred other youths of the National Army. Emmet McGarry, the infant son of Deputy Sean McGarry, was burned to death, and members of his family seriously injured.

KNOW, that for the difference between the two Oaths, you are asked by Mr. de Valera and his friends

To forgo the benefits of the New Land Act and of the other beneficent measures passed by Dail Eireann

To retain the disease-ridden slums of our cities and the hovels of our countryside ;

To encourage by your votes those whom Miss MacSwiney is urging to further war ;

To encourage by your votes those who are preparing at Miss MacSwiney's behest, and with Mr. de Valera's approval, to use the horrors of Poison Gas in renewed hostilities.

VOTERS! DO NOT BE MISLED.

Give your Votes to those who will preserve the Peace and Re-construct your country to the benefit of you & your children.
VOTE for the Opponents of Irregularism—THE CANDIDATES OF CUMANN NA nGAEDHEAL.

HOW TO VOTE FOR THE CUMANN NA nGAEDHEAL CANDIDATES.—

BEFORE ELECTION DAY—Consider the Candidates carefully. Choose your favourite with especial care Make up your mind who is your second choice, your third choice, and so on.

ON ELECTION DAY VOTE AS FOLLOWS :—(a) Place the figure 1 opposite the name of your favourite. (b) Place the figure 2 opposite the name of your second choice. (c) Place the figure 3 opposite your third choice. (d) Place the figure 4 opposite your fourth choice, and so on.

(e) Go on numbering the Candidates as far as you like.

(This is most important. By marking preferences for all the Candidates of whom you approve, you make sure your vote will have the fullest possible effect)

SOME DON'TS —DON'T vote with a *X* Don't put the figure I opposite the name of more than one Candidate. DON'T think you can help your favourite by "plumping" for him or her. "Plumping" means marking a candidate with the figure "I" and marking no more figures. This does not give any advantage to the candidate you plump for, and will lead to your vote being wasted if your favourite candidate does not require it.

This advertisement for the four Cumann na nGaedheal candidates in Mayo North appeared in the *Western People* on August 25, 1923. Its content reflects the bitterness of the Civil War.

airplane was used, though I want to make it clear that Henry Coyle was not jet-setting around Erris!

Patrick O'Hara, Seán T. Ruane and my father were also on the platform in Carne as McGrath promised to develop industries in Erris 'for rich markets' overseas.

"General McGrath, Judge Cohalan and the other candidates and the parties accompanying them visited Blacksod in the evening and stayed some time at the harbour," the *Western People* reported. "They were enthusiastically received by the people. General McGrath is at present paying a visit to the lace industry centres in the barony."

The Congested Districts Board (CDB) had established more than a dozen lace schools around the barony in the late nineteenth century and several were still operating in 1923, providing valuable employment for local women. The standard of living had barely improved in Erris in the three decades since the CDB opened the lace schools. Just a year earlier, a deadly epidemic of typhus swept through the 'Mullet peninsula, resulting in several deaths, including a local relieving officer, his wife and young child. In December 1922, the Minister for Local Government Ernest Blythe told the Dáil that the disease took hold in 'a disused coastguard station in which families took up their abodes and deserted their own homes'.

"Belmullet has long been recognised as a district in which typhus may be said to be endemic," said the Minister. "The population is very poor, living in small and congested homes, with primitive habits, and the practice of housing animals in dwellings still persists. The normal disadvantages of the district have been aggravated by the unsettled conditions of the present time, and sanitary administration is being carried on in the area under the gravest disadvantages."

My father knew all about the poverty of Erris because he had lived through it, having grown up in a house in which cows slept in winter for want of an outhouse. His selection as a general election candidate represented a real triumph for the 'landless' men of Erris and it was some achievement to share a ticket with an outgoing government minister (McGrath), a shopkeeper (O'Hara) and a schoolteacher (Ruane), while his opponents included a solicitor (Ruttledge) and a doctor (John Crowley). I can only imagine how proud he must have been to stand on that platform in his native Erris alongside Justice Cohalan, one of the most famous Irish-Americans of his generation. It was a long way from picking potatoes in Scotland.

The constituency of Mayo North consisted of two distinct geographical areas with the River Moy providing a natural dividing line. West of the river was Ballina, the wider North Mayo area and Erris, while to the east were the towns of Foxford, Swinford, Kiltimagh and Charlestown.

The Republicans had two outgoing TDs in P.J. Ruttledge and Dr John Crowley, and would have had a third had Foxford-based Dr Frank Ferran not died of pneumonia in the Curragh Camp in June. Ruttledge and Crowley were both based in the west of the constituency, which made the task of securing a Dáil seat all the more difficult for my father, especially after Joseph McGrath was parachuted into the constituency. Ruttledge and McGrath were widely predicted to top the poll, which left two seats for the remaining 10 candidates. Ballycastle-based Crowley was expected to retain his seat and the battle for the fourth seat was more than likely going to be fought in the east of the constituency between the Cumann na nGaedheal duo of Patrick O'Hara (Swinford) and Seán T. Ruane (Kiltimagh), and Republican candidate IRA Comdt Joseph Kelly.

A native of Ballaghaderreen, Kelly had much in common with my father, having spent most of the War of Independence in Liverpool where he was involved in smuggling arms to Ireland. He also took part in the warehouse burnings and it is remarkable to think that two men who were involved in that incident ended up competing against each other in an Irish general election three years later.

Polling day in Mayo passed off more peacefully than many might have expected. There were soldiers standing guard at a number of the 173 polling stations in Mayo North, but there were no major flashpoints and the *Connaught Telegraph* reported that 'good humour prevailed' throughout the day. Even the islanders of Inishkea agreed to partake in a national election for the first time in their history.

"Despite the outside opinion prevailing, there was a very satisfactory poll in the island of Inishkea, where a 'free kingdom' has been in existence for 15 years, during which the islanders paid no rates to the County Council," wrote the *Connaught Telegraph*. "During the past quarter of a century, there was no disposition to pay either rent or rates, and on a famous occasion thirty years ago, a British government gunboat brought troops to the island to protect the sheriff in the work of eviction, but when the party left the island, the people returned to their houses and were not again disturbed, the CDB acquiring the land about 15 years ago."

On Sunday, August 25, the presiding officer, P.J. Monaghan, left Belmullet for the Inishkeas in a motorboat, which was towed by a Free State government gunboat, and they enjoyed a smooth passage despite some unseasonal weather. The *Connaught Telegraph* told the story of Inishkea's first general election:

The polling station was on the south island, and at the opening, the 'king' and a number of his subjects attended and voted.

The presiding officer, Mr P.J. Monaghan, rate collector, Belmullet, was received with some hostility, the islanders thinking that when he was accompanied by military he was on a rate collecting stunt, but on learning of the nature of his mission their attitude changed, and they extended every hospitality to the visitors.

At 2 o'clock, there was a blizzard rising, and though the north island is only 50 yards distant, the people of it were unable to cross to the other island to vote.

When 31 of the 60 voters on the south island had polled, the captain of the gunboat, fearing he would be wrecked in the dangerous waters around the island, decided to move off, and the poll had to be closed.

Before the election party left, the 'king', who welcomed them to the island, also gave them an enthusiastic send-off, and asked them to inform President Cosgrave that he was a supporter of the Free State government and would readily come under its laws, thus disestablishing what was possibly the most interesting monarchy in Europe, though unlike the Balkan states, it was set up without any bloodshed.

I don't know if the 'King of the Inishkeas' voted for Henry Coyle, but the people of Erris did not let down their local candidate, resulting in a much higher pro-Treaty vote than many anticipated. It had been a tough election campaign in Erris, according to the *Connaught Telegraph*:

Many of the election officers had weird experiences in Erris, owing to broken bridges and trenched roads. The voters along the north coast displayed strong Republican sympathies, while in Belmullet and Binghamstown, the pro-Treaty candidates polled strongly.

Turnout in Mayo North was lower than expected with just over 50 per cent casting their votes in the 173 polling stations to give a total poll of 27,174 out of a registered electorate of 53,719. There were an unusually high number of spoiled votes (993), which may have had something to do with the fact that this was the first general election in which proportional representation (PR) was used in Mayo North.

Not surprisingly, P.J. Ruttledge and Joseph McGrath dominated the ballot boxes and took almost 65 per cent of the vote between them, with Ruttledge topping the poll with 8,997 first preferences compared to McGrath's 8,011. With the quota set at 5,249, both men were elected comfortably in the first count and had significant surpluses to distribute.

My father came third with 2,997 votes followed by Patrick O'Hara with 2,097. Outgoing TD Dr John Crowley only managed 832 first preferences but benefitted greatly from Ruttledge's vast surplus to put him back into contention and he never really looked in danger of losing his seat, despite having to wait until the final count to be elected.

Even though my father polled much better than many expected, he still faced an uphill task because Swinford man Patrick O'Hara was well positioned to benefit from transfers, especially from Cumann na nGaedheal colleague

Seán T. Ruane, who had polled 1,082 votes. Indeed, O'Hara took slightly more of McGrath's surplus than my father to narrow the gap ahead of Ruane's elimination.

But then something unexpected happened. Six of the 12 candidates had polled less than 800 votes each but their transfers were going to make a critical difference in the tight race for the final two seats. These candidates from the Farmers' Party, Labour and Independents were mainly situated west of the River Moy, but there was no guarantee they would transfer in an election where voters had struggled with the intricacies of PR.

By the sixth count, there were 788 votes separating my father and Patrick O'Hara with over 1,500 votes still to be distributed from Ruane. The seventh count involved the distribution of the votes of Archie Heron, a prominent Dublin-based Labour activist, and my father took 174 transfers to O'Hara's 101. The same pattern continued in the eighth count when Charles Flynn, a Farmers' Party candidate from Lahardane, was eliminated, and the bulk of his votes (346) went to my father compared to 235 for O'Hara. Even in the ninth count, when Republican candidate Joseph Kelly was eliminated, my father gained 28 votes to O'Hara's 35, despite the vast geographical distance. Perhaps his connection with Kelly from their days together in Liverpool accounted for a few of those transfers.

By the time Ruane was eliminated in the tenth count, my father had stretched his lead to almost 1,000 votes, but he would need every one of those earlier transfers because O'Hara, as expected, took the lion's share of Ruane's 1,704 papers to close the gap to just 214 votes, 4,903 to 4,689. On such fine margins are political careers made and dashed.

On Friday, August 30, 1923, the new TD for Mayo North – and the first ever Teachta Dála from Erris – rose to his feet at the count centre in the National School in Ballina and began to speak:

"I am glad the election has passed off so peacefully and I hope it is the beginning of an era of peace and goodwill, and that we will all join hands in the near future and do the best we can for Ireland (applause), and by doing so we will very soon have not only 26 counties a Free State, but the whole 32 counties of Ireland a Republic (loud applause)."

My father's acceptance speech is very interesting in light of later events because his desire for a 32-county Republic of Ireland was at odds with many in Cumann na nGaedheal, including his party leader W.T. Cosgrave and the Minister for Justice Kevin O'Higgins. For them, the war was over and it was now time to work within the parameters of the Treaty, but my father took a more literal meaning of Michael Collins' famous assurance that the Treaty gave Ireland the freedom to achieve freedom, and he wanted to act sooner

Republican candidate P.J. Ruttledge (left) topped the poll in Mayo North. Although they were on opposites sides in the Treaty dispute, my father had great regard for Ruttledge and they remained good friends until the Ballina man's death in 1952.

rather than later. Henry Coyle was not the only person on the pro-Treaty side who harboured those views; many in the National Army shared his opinion and even his running mate in Mayo North, Joseph McGrath, was strongly in favour of pursuing a 32-county agenda.

I believe there were a number of factors influencing my father's desire to end partition as quickly as possible. He was, first and foremost, a republican and he would almost certainly have taken the anti-Treaty side were it not for the influence of Michael Collins.

I think it is also important to acknowledge the friendships he made in Scotland during the War of Independence. His most loyal and trusted comrade was Charlie Strickland, a young Catholic from the Falls Road in Belfast, who must have recounted many stories of sectarian discrimination and violence on those long car journeys from Glasgow to Liverpool. Many of the other men and women who assisted my father in Scotland and England were also natives of the Six Counties, including Mick Burke and Neill Kerr.

Henry Coyle was an incredibly loyal man and he would have seen it as the ultimate betrayal of his old comrades if he did not represent their views in Dáil Éireann. But his pursuit of a united Ireland would leave him at odds with the leadership of Cumann na nGeadheal and I believe it ultimately contributed to his swift downfall.

My father's victory speech in Ballina on August 30, 1923, was the beginning of one of the briefest Dáil careers in Irish political history.

CHAPTER 31

'There is practically no money in circulation'

CUMANN na nGaedheal had a good general election in 1923. The party took 63 seats compared to 44 for the Republicans, and enjoyed significant success in key constituencies, including Mayo South where it ousted sitting Republican TD Thomas Derrig to claim three of the five seats. In fact, Cumann na nGaedheal won 53 per cent of the popular vote in County Mayo compared to 37 for the Republicans and took five out of the nine seats across the two constituencies.

The party's three winning candidates in Mayo South were William Sears, Joseph MacBride, and Martin Nally, while Republicans Michael Kilroy and Tom Maguire took the other two seats. It was an election campaign to forget for the hotelier Patrick O'Malley who finished second last of the 10 candidates in Mayo South with 1,175 votes.

Although there was tension at some of the polling booths in both Mayo constituencies, with National Army troops on patrol, there were also several amusing incidents as voters struggled to grasp the complexities of the PR system. In Ardnaree, an old woman was heard to say: "I'll vote Bolshie first and I'll give all my other votes to Labour." The *Connaught Telegraph* reported that many voters accidentally spoiled their votes by marking an X beside more than one candidate, while others wrote their names on the ballot paper or statements like 'I vote Republic' or 'For Labour'.

"A correspondent, who acted as a presiding officer," reported the *Telegraph*, "says that a middle-aged man who called at his station to vote was stated to be getting the blind pension, but he refused to have his vote marked for him and did the operation himself, after carefully reading the instructions in the booth."

THE WO... ...D'S NEWS

TH...

MUCH WORK FOR THE OIREACHTAS

A FR...

DISUNIO...

A LONG SESSION ARRANGED

MARKED ACTIVITY

CABINET SITS ALL THE AFTERNOON

CORK DEPUTIES JOIN UP

The session of the Oireachtas opening to-morrow promises to be a prolonged one. Preparations have been made for a continuous sitting till December 20.

The su... ...in... of D...

Liam T. Mac Cosgair (W. T. Cosgrave)—Carlow-Kilkenny.
Enri O Comhaill (H. Coyle)—Mayo N.
Prof. Sir Jas. Craig—Dublin University.
Sean O Duinnin (Sean Dineen)—Cork E.
Seamus N. O'Dolain (S. Dolan)—Leitrim-Sligo.
Liam O Daimhin (Liam Davin)—Leix-Offaly.
P. S. Ua Dubhghaill (P. Doyle)—Dublin City S.
Osmonde Grattan-Esmonde—Wexford.
D. MacGearailt (D. Fitzgerald)—Dublin Co.
John Good—Dublin Co.
Prof. Micheal O hAodha (Prof. Hayes)—Ollscoil na h-Eireann and Dublin City S.
Micheal S. O hAoghusa (M. Hennessy)—Cork E.
Tomas MacEoin (Thos. Johnson)—Dublin Co.
Fionan O Loingsigh (Finian Lynch)—Kerry.
D. MacCarthaigh (D. MacCarthy)—Dublin City S.
...da Negla ...
Maill...

OBSTA...

The announc... han, Assi... try and C... is to be ... ing indus... conferen... concerne... ceived in...

The extrem... and sean... the I.T.... clare tha... promise o...

The gravity o... in the unempl... over 300 pe... the num... 1922...

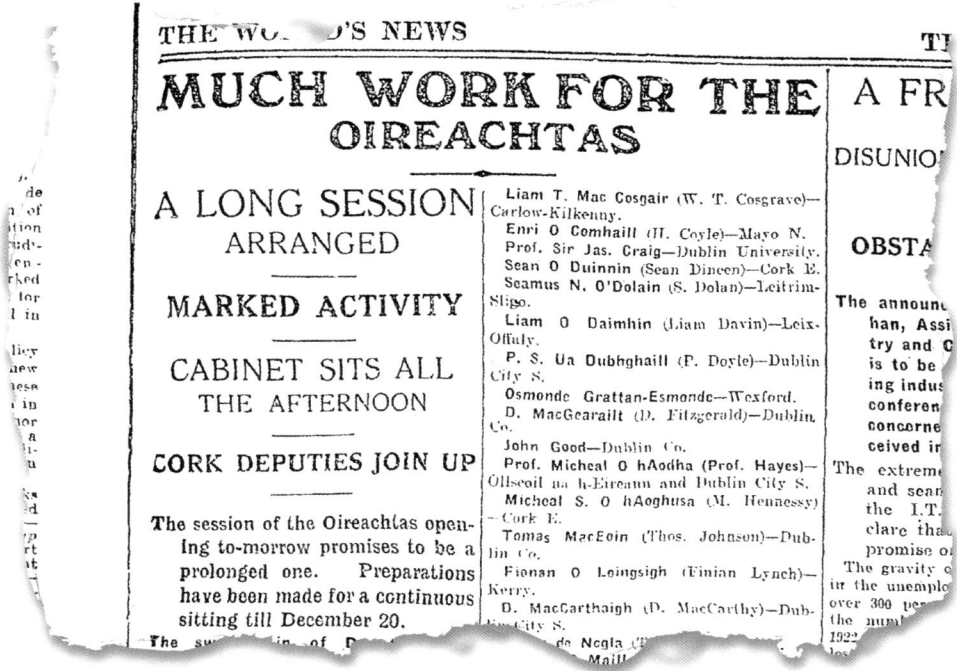

I only hope the poor man didn't lose his blind pension as a result of voting for Henry Coyle! The *Telegraph* also published short biographies of the new TDs, including the following about my father:

Mr Henry Coyle is a native of Geesala, a commandant in the Free State Army, and an organiser for Cumann na nGaedheal. He played a prominent part in the Anglo-Irish War.

While pro and anti-Treaty candidates dominated the election in Mayo, candidates from other parties had more success elsewhere and the membership of the 4th Dáil Éireann was Cumann na nGaedheal (63), Republicans (44), Independents (17), Farmers (15) and Labour (14), to give a total of 153 seats.

The first sitting of the new parliament was scheduled for Wednesday, September 19, but TDs were asked to attend Leinster House in the preceding days to be sworn in by the clerk of the Dáil. On Monday, September 17, my father took the Oath of Allegiance, as set out in the Free State constitution of 1922:

I, Henry Coyle, do solemnly swear true faith and allegiance to the Constitution of the Irish Free State as by law established, and that I will be faithful to His Majesty King George V, his heirs and successors by law, in virtue of the common citizenship of Ireland with Great Britain, and her adherence to and membership of the group of nations forming the British Commonwealth of Nations.

THE WORLD'S NEWS   THE IRISH INDEPENDENT. THURSDAY. SEPTEMBER 20, 1923.

FIRST MEETING OF THE NEW DAIL

FARMERS URGE RELEASE ANTI-TREATY DEPUTIES

LEINSTER HOUSE THRONGED

DEPUTIES CHEER PRESIDENT'S RE-ELECTION

THE ANTI-TREATYITES ABSENT

LABOUR DECISION TO ESCHEW POLITICS

CABINET NOMINATION TO-DAY

THE SPEAKER RE-ELECTED

HIS CONSPICUOUS SUCCESS

ENERGY AND VISION

MR. COSGRAVE'S GREAT ATTRIBUTES

SUPERIOR FITNESS

TWO PREMIERS MEET

ALL EYES ON PARIS

"COMMON AGREEMENT OF VIEWS"

GREAT ACTIVITY

CO-OPERATION VITAL TO

ARE WAR WEAPO LAID ASIDE?

WHAT FARMERS WANT TO KNOW

PRESIDENT'S REPLY

CHANGE OF HEART ESSENTIAL

MIDNIGHT PROPOSALS

The line about being 'faithful' to King George would not have rolled off my father's tongue too easily; this was a man who spent Sunday mornings in a cold prison cell in Peterhead rather than go to Mass to pray for the King, so I suspect he uttered that oath through gritted teeth. This was not the 32-county sovereign republic he dreamed about on those long days and nights of solitary confinement in Peterhead, but he still believed the Free State was – as Michael Collins had promised – a 'stepping stone' to full independence.

Shortly after 3.15pm on September 19, the gong sounded in Leinster House and the Clerk of the Dáil stood before the Ceann Comhairle's chair and read the proclamation convening the 4th Dáil. He then announced the names of the deputies returned in each constituency, including Enrí Ó Cumhaill for Maigh Eo Thuaidh.

The first task for deputies was the election of Professor Michael Hayes as Ceann Comhairle and W.T. Cosgrave as President. Hayes was the man whose home was raided by the British forces in November 1920, resulting in the seizure of documents that were later used against my father in the trials in Liverpool and Edinburgh.

The *Irish Independent* reported that Leinster House was 'thronged' for the first sitting of the new Dáil, with all members attending apart from the 44 anti-Treaty TDs, 11 of whom were still in prison.

There was practically a full attendance of members, and the public galleries were never so densely thronged. None of the anti-Treaty Deputies put in an appearance, but there was a demonstration outside by a number of women, who demanded the release of the prisoners. What was almost personal violence was offered to some deputies and the police were obliged to use force to move away a particularly active section.

The newspaper reported that the Strangers' Gallery, as it was called, was filled with family and friends of the newly-elected TDs. I am not sure if any members of the Coyle or Kerrigan families made the long journey from Erris, but whether they were present in person or not, it must have been an incredibly proud day for my grandparents. Their son was now a member of the national parliament of Ireland, an achievement that would have been utterly unbelievable when they were raising him in such humble circumstances in Dooyork in the early 1900s. His election as a TD was a victory for all the 'landless' people of Mayo; those smallholders who had to migrate to Scotland and England every year just to make ends meet. Indeed, by securing election to Dáil Éireann, Henry Coyle had proven that anybody could aspire to be a TD in the new, independent Ireland.

Among the famous faces milling around Leinster House that day was W.B. Yeats, who was attending the inaugural meeting of Seanad Éireann. I am not sure if my father got a chance to talk poetry with him or to show the great Nobel Laureate some of his 'Peterhead Poems'! Meanwhile, Yeats' muse Maud Gonne was outside on the street protesting at the continuing imprisonment of the Republicans, which included her 16-year-old son Seán MacBride, who was being held in Mountjoy.

Cumann na nGaedheal had a majority in the chamber due to the absence of the anti-Treaty TDs. Following his election as President of the Executive Council, W.T. Cosgrave addressed the 106 deputies in attendance.

"We have passed through a strenuous and hard time," he said, "and I think I re-echo the hope of every member when I hope that happier times await us in the future."

Cosgrave was striking an optimistic tone but there were enormous challenges facing his new administration amid declining agriculture prices and soaring unemployment. On the week before the 4th Dáil convened, the *Western People* reported that 'unemployment was never more rife in Ballina'.

Families are in a state of semi-starvation. There is practically no money in circulation. This remark applies particularly to small farmers in the neighbourhood of the town who have to pay the highest price for everything they buy, while they themselves have to sell the produce of their labour for less than it cost them to sow their crops.

The prospect for the coming winter is not at all inviting, and with the high figure at which taxation stands, with no prospect of an early reduction, there seems to be nothing but gloomy times ahead.

The weather wasn't helping the mood either. Some of the heaviest rains in living memory had wreaked havoc on farms throughout the country.

"Incessant rains have ruined the harvest and the damage can scarcely be computed," wrote the *Connaught Telegraph* on September 29. "The tragedy is that the small cultivator is the victim. Both the hay and oat crops are ruined…

"Today the crops lie rotting in the fields… Whole districts are water-logged, with the result that the potato crop, which was a fair average, is also in danger."

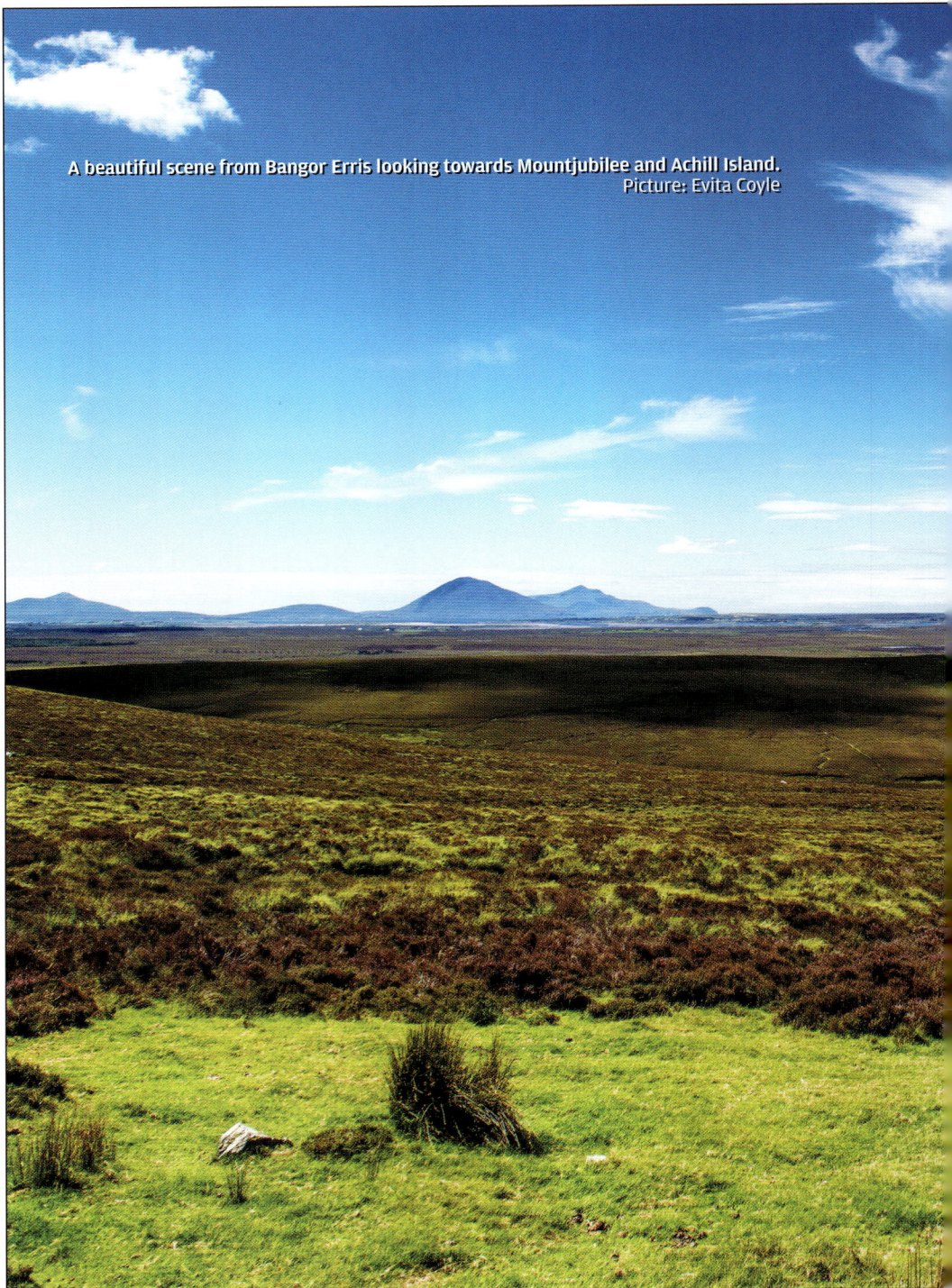

A beautiful scene from Bangor Erris looking towards Mountjubilee and Achill Island.
Picture: Evita Coyle

THE WORLD'S NEWS

NEW DAIL MEETS
TO-DAY

RES

NO CHANGE IN
THE MINISTRY

MR. DUGGAN'S POST

ANTI-TREATYITES'
ATIT UDE

OATH 'BARRIER TO UNITY

The newly-elected Dail holds its first sitting to-day.

Busy scenes were again witnessed at Leinster House yesterday, when 37 additional deputies subscribed to the oath. There w...

changes in the personnel of the Executive are stated to be without foundation, and that the same Council will be nominated by the President, namely:—Dr. MacNeill, Messrs. K. O'Higgins, E. Blythe, D. Fitzgerald, E. J. Duggan, and Jos. McGrath.

There is, however, a likelihood that Mr. O'Higgins will be Minister for Finance, and that Mr. Duggan, who was Minister without portfolio in the late Government, will be allotted the post of Minister for Home Affairs.

There is also fairly reliable authority for stating that Messrs. P. Lynch (Fisheries), J. J. Walsh (Post Office), and P. J. Hogan (Agriculture), will be nominated for their old departments.

"BARRIER TO UNITY"

MR. O RUITHLEIS AND OATH

The following was supplied last night:—
"When the final results of the recent ...ons became... ...put... for de..."

TO
ARE

That wor
stim
study
heat
opin
Sarg
tion

Bishop
dress
tion,"
clearl
dep...

Emigration, which had reduced to a trickle in recent years, was now resuming at a remorseless pace. On September 15, the *Western People* revealed that there was a 'rush to emigrate' to the United States with the American Consulate in Dublin issuing over 5,000 visas in the preceding 10 weeks.

The lace school in Bangor Erris was forced to cease operations in late September after the National Army commandeered it as living quarters. Army personnel had been camping in huts on the grounds of Bingham Lodge but the inclement weather prompted them to convert the lace school into a temporary barracks. The National Army also continued to occupy the workhouse in Belmullet.

My father spent the autumn of 1923 performing the typical tasks of a rural TD. On October 22, he addressed a constituency convention of Cumann na nGaedheal at the Town Hall in Ballina, which was attended by about 100 delegates from across north and east Mayo. The meeting passed the following resolution:

That we, the delegates of Cumann na nGaedheal for North and East Mayo, in conference assembled, wish to congratulate President Cosgrave and the Government of An Saorstat on Ireland's entry into the League of Nations, thereby taking her rightful place amongst the free and independent nations of the world.

Cumann na nGaedheal was still establishing branches across Mayo and a series of party meetings were held throughout the county in November, including one in Glencastle where 115 members attended. Among the officers elected was my granduncle John Kerrigan, and the delegates had a conciliatory message for their Civil War opponents.

"We should extend the hand of friendship to those who yet disagree with us and not regard them as enemies," said Austin Maloney, the president of the cumann. "Let bygones be bygones. The brightest days are coming."

On November 17, the *Western People* reported that production had resumed at the lace school in Bangor Erris.

Owing to the intervention of Mr Coyle, T.D., the Bangor Lace School has again been evacuated by the military and the key handed over to the teacher, who has now resumed work. The necessary repairs to the school were carried out by the Board's officials before the class was re-opened.

Four days later, my father made his maiden speech in Dáil Éireann when he participated in a debate on the future of Ireland's fishing industry. He believed fishing could lift many Erris families out of poverty.

"In the constituency that I represent, North Mayo, there are two bays which are very rich in fish, Blacksod Bay and Broadhaven Bay. The fish that is caught in Blacksod Bay must be sent to Achill Sound, that is the nearest place. The fishermen have in one day to catch the fish, and in the next day to take it to Achill Sound. They can only get into Achill Sound according to the condition of the tide.

"The railway station at Ballina, which is the nearest station to them, is 42 miles from Belmullet. In that case certainly, a motor lorry would be very convenient and very useful. The fishermen could fish every day and have their fish sent away every morning.

"With regard to the question of market for fish, if you take Athlone or Mullingar or those inland towns you will find that you can get no fish there, and at the same time the fish is going bad at Blacksod Bay and Broadhaven Bay and other places...

"Deputy [Joseph] MacBride says that we wanted fishermen and buyers. We have the fishermen; let us get the buyers. There are plenty of fishermen, and all they want is the gear. If they got proper substantial boats and proper gear, the fishermen are all right, and we can look for the buyers.

"There is a matter I would like to be made clear on. I have been informed that the territorial waters embrace the three-mile limit, and that in some places the fishing limit is nine miles. The result is that foreign boats can fish between the nine-mile limit and the three-mile limit. I would like to be made clear upon that matter, and if that is the case I do not think it is very fair to Irish fishermen.

"I hope the Minister will accept a lot of the advice that was given here. I am sure all the Deputies can be of great assistance. If they all interest themselves as much as some of those who have spoken, I am sure they can render assistance to the Minister and help very much in this important matter."

Investment in the fishing industry was certainly needed but there was little chance of it happening in the short term. Just weeks earlier, Minister for Finance Ernest Blythe delivered a grim assessment of the national finances, warning that cuts to the old age pension were inevitable. Teachers were also to be hit with a 10 per cent wage cut, a move supported by the *Connaught Telegraph*, which called for sweeping cuts in public expenditure:

The unfortunate creatures in the country, faced with a ruined harvest, high rates, and abnormal cost of food, get no bonuses or help of any kind, and it behoves the Government to look to them and not pampered pets. The country is in no mood to tamely submit to grinding taxation, and the urgent duty of the Government is to ruthlessly apply the economy axe, and a commencement should be made with the higher officials, who are wallowing in the lap of luxury, while thousands in town and country are barely able to sustain existence.

On Sunday, December 15, my father told a meeting of Cumann na nGaedheal delegates in Glencastle that 'roadworks on a large scale' would soon commence in Erris.

"I hope it will give work to everyone," he said. "The weekly wage will be £1-18s and every worker will be expected to do an honest day's work."

My father also expressed the hope that dredging work might soon commence on the channel from Pickle Point to Belmullet and reiterated his commitment to the Blacksod project.

"Anything I can do to have Blacksod made a port of call will be done," he promised.

On the face of it, my father was just like any other rural TD, doing the usual constituency work as best he could in tough times. But behind the scenes, Henry Coyle was caught up in a strange series of events that would ultimately end his political career.

All was not what it seemed in my father's life in the final weeks of 1923, and the same could be said for W.T. Cosgrave's government, which was about to be plunged into the biggest military crisis since the onset of the Civil War.

CHAPTER 32

'We all had one outlook and common aim'

WHEN Cumann na nGaedheal held its inaugural meeting in Connacht on June 30, 1923, Patrick Moylett was surprised and disappointed at some of the people joining him on the platform in Claremorris.

"I found a group that one would expect to find in such a situation ten years earlier," he wrote in his unpublished memoir. "There were a number of former supporters of the old Irish Parliamentary Party and a sprinkling of the Unionist element."

After the meeting, a skeptical Moylett asked President Cosgrave 'what he intended to base his political party on'.

"On the Unionist party and the remnant of Redmond's party," replied the President. "They supported me and I'll support them and without them there would have been no Free State."

"'You are mad," retorted the Mayo man. "England tried to rule this country through that bunch and she had more power behind her than you have and she failed."

The result of the general election proved Moylett wrong but he was far from alone in his doubts about the direction the pro-Treaty movement was taking under Cosgrave and O'Higgins. In the National Army, a cabal of senior officers – most of who had been closely aligned to Michael Collins during the War of Independence – were privately challenging the Government on a number of issues, mainly to do with the demobilisation of troops and the Free State's attitude to the Six Counties. My father shared their reservations and aligned himself with a number of TDs, including his running mate in Mayo North, Joseph McGrath, who had been members of the IRA and were supportive of the Collins' loyalists.

Confidential.

6th June 1923.

TO:
The President,
Dail Eireann.

On behalf of a number of Officers attached to G.H.Q.
and the various Commands, all of whom took part in the
Anglo-Irish war which ended in the acceptance of the
Treaty - and which Treaty was accepted by these Officers
in exactly the same spirit which we know the late Commander-
in-Chief accepted it; i.e., as we would have regarded a
successful ambush of the enemy prior to July 1921.

We, the undersigned officers, are now instructed to
ask you to arrange an interview with yourself, the
Commander-in-Chief and three or four of our officers, to
discuss the situation and place our views before you, as
Michael Collins' successor.

We feel in duty bound to make this request and we
are confident that you will accede to it in the same spirit
in which it is made.

We cannot too strongly assure you that we are not
attempting to act in an "irregular" way, but we are convinced
that a genuine effort must now be made to keep absolutely
to the forefront, the ideals and objects for which the late
Commander-in-Chief gave his life.

(Signed)

The men who became known as the 'army mutineers' outlined their demands to President W.T. Cosgrave in this letter in June 1923.

232

As early as January 29, 1923, a group of senior officers in the National Army – all veterans of the War of Independence – held a meeting to explore ways to connect with ex-IRA men across the various command areas. A second meeting was held four days later at which Major General Liam Tobin was appointed chairman.

During my research, I found a fascinating document in the Military Service Pensions Collection that outlines – in their own words – the strategy of the men who later became known as the 'army mutineers'. The following is an extract from it:

The policy decided on was to get in touch with all IRA men serving in the National Army and if they believed in our ideals to link them together in an organisation which when strong enough would demand a strong voice in Army policy with a view to securing complete independence when a suitable occasion arose. It was also decided that members of the new organisation would make every effort to get control of the vital sections of the army and oust those undesirable persons who were and are holding these positions.

The 'undesirable persons' which Tobin and his supporters were referring to were former members of the British Army who joined the National Army at the height of the Civil War. The strength of the Free State Army rose from about 7,000 to more than 50,000 in the second half of 1922, and many of the new recruits were veterans of World War I and had played no part in the War of Independence. Tobin believed these men were 'not sufficiently patriotic' and would not support a military push for a united Ireland.

A new group, the Irish Republican Army Organisation (IRAO), was established within the National Army and held a general meeting in April 1923, which was attended by five major-generals, five colonels and several commandants. My father was still in the National Army at this point, and while I don't have any record of him attending this meeting, I am satisfied from my research that he was sympathetic to the aims of the IRAO. Indeed, one of the IRAO's key men in the Western Command was Brigadier John Neary, the Bangor Erris native who my father soldiered alongside throughout the Civil War in Mayo. The IRAO was full of Collins' loyalists – men like Charles Dalton (a brother of Emmet, who was with Collins at Béal na Bláth) and Frank Thornton – so it made sense for my father to take their side.

On June 6, 1923, a number of senior members of the IRAO wrote a letter to President Cosgrave in which they called on him to honour 'the ideals and objects for which [Michael Collins] gave his life'. A few days later, IRAO representatives held a meeting with Cosgrave and Richard Mulcahy, the commander-in-chief of the National Army, at which they read a document that essentially challenged Mulcahy – 'as Michael Collins' successor' – to commit to a 32-county republic.

The following is an extract from that document, which is published in full in the Appendix I:

Previous to the negotiations with the British, which ended in the signing of the Treaty, we all had one outlook and common aim, viz., 'The setting up and maintaining of a Republican form of Government in this Country'. In this ideal, we followed the late [Commander in Chief] and accepted the Treaty in exactly the same spirit as he did. We firmly believed with him that the Treaty was only a stepping stone to a Republic. The late C. in C. (Mick Collins) told us that he had taken an oath of allegiance to the Republic and that oath he would keep, Treaty or no Treaty – this is our position exactly.

My father certainly shared some of those sentiments and I don't think it is a coincidence that he used his victory speech in Ballina to voice his support for a 32-county Irish republic. He was desperate to heal the divisions caused by the Civil War and wanted to reach out to his former colleagues on the anti-Treaty side. The best way to do that was to commit to ending Partition sooner rather than later.

In its document, the IRAO also challenged Richard Mulcahy about the membership of the National Army.

Does the C. in C. understand the temper of the old IRA who are now in the National Army? He does not! Your army is not a National Army. It is composed of 40% old IRA, 50% Ex-Britishers and 10% Ex-civilians. The majority of the civilians were and are hostile to the National Ideals…

It is time that this state of affairs ended, we intend to end it. Unless satisfactory arrangements are come to between us, our organisation will take whatever steps they consider to bring about an honest, cleaner and more genuine effort to secure the Republic.

Mulcahy walked out of the meeting without discussing the document but agreed to meet again with the IRAO leaders some weeks later following the intervention of Joseph McGrath. At that second meeting, the commander-in-chief offered to deal directly with representatives of the IRAO in an effort to address their concerns, but this was only a delaying tactic to keep the lid on the problem until after the general election. Once Cumann na nGaedheal was returned to government, Mulcahy and Cosgrave moved decisively to reduce the size of the National Army, demobilising thousands of men, including many soldiers who had been in the IRA during the War of Independence.

The policy greatly upset my father because he had encouraged many young men in Erris, including his own brother, to join the National Army at the height of the Civil War. These men put their lives on the line to protect the Free State and now they were being let go from the army with little or no financial compensation at a time when unemployment was rampant. Some of these men had families who were dependent on their army salary and the timing of their demobilisation could not have been worse as there was no

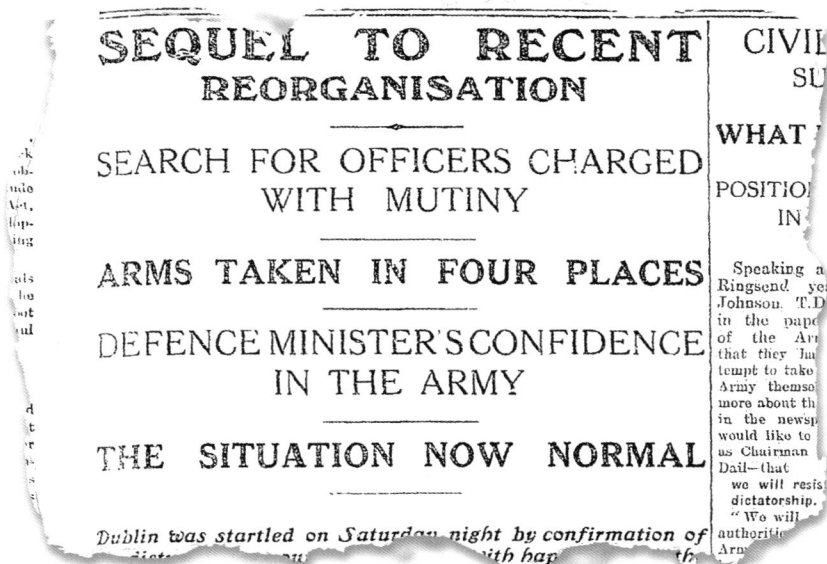

SEQUEL TO RECENT REORGANISATION

SEARCH FOR OFFICERS CHARGED WITH MUTINY

ARMS TAKEN IN FOUR PLACES

DEFENCE MINISTER'S CONFIDENCE IN THE ARMY

THE SITUATION NOW NORMAL

Dublin was startled on Saturday night by confirmation of

A headline from the *Irish Independent* on March 10, 1924, as the army mutiny began to unfold.

seasonal farmwork to be got in England or Scotland in late autumn. The lack of employment for ex-soldiers became such a huge issue that President Cosgrave was forced to issue a letter to local authorities around the country asking them to give priority to 'demobilised soldiers of the National Army on roads and other works on which you might embark'.

In November, more than 60 officers stationed at the Curragh Camp refused to accept their demobilisation papers and were discharged without pay, prompting Joseph McGrath to successfully petition the Government to establish a commitee to oversee the reorganisation of the National Army to make it more suitable for a peaceful Ireland. Of course, this was not what men like Tobin wanted to hear because they still had ambitions to move on Northern Ireland sooner rather than later. Matters came to a head in February 1924 when Tobin and most of the other members of the IRAO learned that they were about to be either demobilised or demoted.

On March 7, 1924, a representative of the IRAO called to Government Buildings and handed W.T. Cosgrave a document that re-iterated the earlier demands of the IRAO and called on the Government to remove the army council and immediately end demobilisation. Signed by Tobin and Dalton, the document amounted to an ultimatum and even included a deadline, March 12, by which the President must respond. Rumours of a military coup were

EXTREMELY GRAVE SITUATION

THREE GENERALS CALLED UPON TO RESIGN

STERN DISCIPLINE IN FUTURE

GENERAL O'DUFFY IN ABSOLUTE CONTROL NOW

GENERAL MULCAHY INDIGNANT

ACCUSES GOVERNMENT OF CONDONING MUTINY

Swift, dramatic and momentous developments yesterday, arising out of the Parnell Street raid, bring the country face to face with an extremely grave and delicate situation.

Gen. Mulcahy has resigned his officeas Minister for Defence, and three other members of the Army Council—
  GEN. SEAN MacMAHON, Chief of Staff;
  LT.-GEN. GEAROID O'SULLIVAN, Adjutant-Gen and
  LT.-GEN. SEAN O'MUIRTHUILE, Quartermaster-Gen.—
  'led upon to resign their admi'

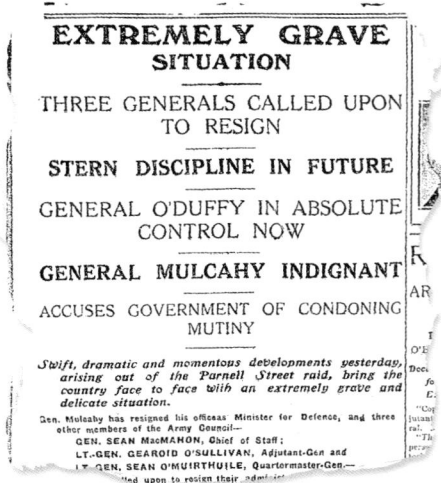

Headlines from the *Irish Independent* on March 20, 1924, as the army mutiny left W.T. Cosgrave's government in a perilous state.

soon swirling around Dublin, especially after it emerged that dozens of officers had removed weapons from a number of barracks around the country in the preceding days. More than 150 rifles, a dozen machine guns and over 50,000 rounds of ammunition were illegally removed from arms and military stores. The crisis deepened further when Joseph McGrath resigned from the Executive Council in protest over the Department of Defence's handling of the situation.

Initially, Cosgrave sought to adopt a conciliatory approach by announcing on March 12 that a Cabinet committee would inquire into the administration of the Defence Forces. A new commander-in-chief, General Eoin O'Duffy, was also appointed. Tobin and Dalton reciprocated by sending Cosgrave a new document in which they acknowledged that the army 'must be subject to the absolute control of the civil authority'. It seemed as if the crisis had been averted.

"The country is perfectly quiet," wrote the *Irish Independent* on March 13, "and there has been no recurrence of incidents anywhere."

The détente proved short-lived, however. On the night of March 18/19, the National Army, acting on the instructions of its adjutant general Gearóid O'Sullivan, raided Devlin's Pub on Parnell Street in Dublin where IRAO members had gathered. O'Sullivan believed a *coup d'etat* was being planned – and he may have been right as the men in Devlin's were all armed – but his mission did not have the authorisation of the Government. A tense stand-off developed between the National Army troops and the mutineers and it took the intervention of Joseph McGrath to calm the situation.

Cosgrave was on sick leave at the time, leaving Kevin O'Higgins as the *de facto* head of the Executive Council, and he ordered reinforcements to Devlin's to trap the mutineers in the pub. However, Tobin and Dalton escaped across the rooftops, using an old path known from the days when Devlin's was a favoured safe house for Michael Collins.

O'Higgins was determined to re-assert the authority of the Government and wasted no time in demanding the resignation of the Army Council. An infuriated Mulcahy tendered his resignation as Minister for Defence, which meant the Executive Council had lost two of its seven members within a matter of weeks. There was also widespread speculation that several TDs were about to tender their resignations too.

The crisis engulfing the Free State government worsened on Friday, March 21, when a number of IRA men, dressed in the uniform of the National Army, opened fire on a group of British soldiers at Cobh Harbour. The Anglo-Irish Treaty allowed Britain to continue to use three Free State ports at Berehaven, Spike Island (off Cobh) and Lough Swilly, so the attack on the troops had the potential to precipitate a

ATTACK BY FOUR MEN
IN MOTOR CAR

TWO MACHINE GUNS TURNED ON LEAVE PARTY

ONE DEAD AND 28 WOUNDED

TWO WOMEN IN THE CASUALTY LIST

WARSHIP ALSO FIRED UPON

NATIONAL TROOPS SEARCHING FOR PERPETRATORS

Consternation was caused by a dreadful occurrence about 7 o'clock yesterday evening at Cobh. Four men, attired as officers of the National Army, drove rapidly to the Pier in a Rolls-Royce motor car, and with two machine guns opened fire on a party of British soldiers who, with some women and children, were in the act of landing from Spike Island. Latest reports give total casualties at 29 :—

The shooting of a number of British soldiers in Cobh threatened to derail the already tense Anglo-Irish relations.

British invasion. One soldier, Private Herbert Aspinall, was killed and 18 of his colleagues were injured in the incident. Ironically, Aspinall, from Rochdale, was the son of a Mayo woman.

W.T. Cosgrave, who had returned from sick leave, described the incident as 'dastardly' and 'without parallel in its deliberation and savagery'. The anti-Treaty IRA was blamed but there were unfounded suspicions the incident might have something to do with the attempted National Army coup in Dublin. By the following Wednesday, March 26, rumours were still rife about the split at the heart of both the Army and Government, and W.T. Cosgrave was widely expected to make a statement in Dáil Éireann. It didn't happen. Instead, there was another sensational development: a TD had been arrested for alleged fraud. The following report appeared in several newspapers on March 27:

Dáil Éireann reassembled at 11 o'clock this morning, and in anticipation of a further development in the Ministerial and Army situation, there was again much demand on the part of the public for admission to the Strangers' Gallery, which, in consequence, was crowded.

Contrary to expectation, no Ministerial statement was made.

On the Speaker taking the chair, the questions on an order paper were taken up in the customary manner.

The Speaker announced that he had received a letter from Mr Lupton, chief police magistrate, stating that Henry Coyle, a Dáil member for North Mayo, had been arrested on a warrant charging him with having fraudulently induced a Dublin merchant to endorse a cheque for £450.

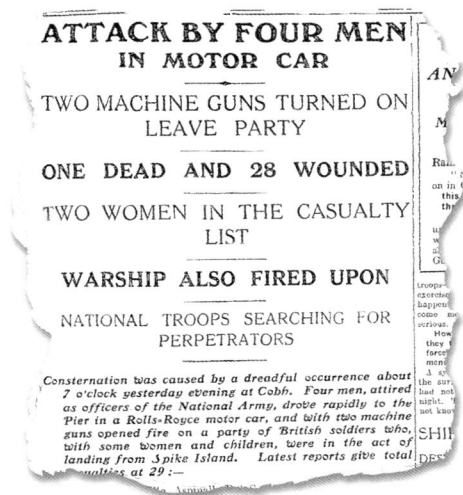

TROOPS' LONG VIGIL IN PARNELL STREET

BIG FORCES ON THE SCENE

TENSE SITUATION

LARGE ARMED PARTY BLOCKADED

MEDIATION EFFORTS

MINISTER'S VISITS TO BUILDING

A serious incident in connection with the Army troubles took place last night, when milita...

numbered eight, together with a Ford touring car, in which some staff officers had arrived, an armoured Lancia and a "whippet" armoured car.

At 12.15 Mr. Jas. Grace, part-proprietor of the establishment, was allowed out, and was promptly interviewed by an "Irish Independent" representative. The Colonel in charge of the troops had already refused politely to say anything, but Mr. Grace informed our representative of the facts described above, and said that President Cosgrave, Mr. K. O'Higgins and Mr. J. McGrath had been communicated with.

MR. McGRATH'S VIEWS.

At 12.25 Mr. Jos. McGrath, Minister for Industry and Commerce, arrived, accompanied by Mr. Paul McCarthy, the C. na N. Whip. Mr. McGrath had a short chat with Mr. Grace, and then went into the house with Mr. Grace and an officer. The officer remained on the ground floor. A few minutes passed, and then Mr. McGrath came out. He told our representative he could not say anything about the affair at present at any rate, but ... later on. ... there

The army mutiny was the biggest crisis to face the Free State government since the Civil War.

The letter added that Mr Coyle has been remanded on bail in two sureties of £500 each, but that no sureties had been forthcoming.

Mr Coyle, it is interesting to add, was one of the members whose resignation was rumoured. Mr Joseph McGrath is also a member for Mayo.

That statement in the Dáil marked the beginning of the end of my father's brief political career and the start of a personal tragedy that would change the course of his life forever. Few men in Irish public life have ever suffered a more swift or severe fall from grace, and even today he is still paying the price for the baffling events that occurred in March 1924 when the Free State teetered on the brink of a second civil war.

CHAPTER 33

'There are very strange
things in this case'

WHILE researching this book, I spent an inordinate amount of time trying to get to the bottom of the perplexing events that led to my father being prosecuted for fraud. Some of the things I discovered kept me awake at night and much of what is contained in the next two chapters is a source of great sadness to me because I firmly believe my father was – in his own words – 'very unfairly treated'.

I don't want to cause upset by pointing the finger of blame at anyone, nor do I wish to engage in idle speculation about what might or might not have occurred a century ago. In researching this book, I have tried as much as possible to use documentary evidence, such as newspaper reports, the Military Service Pensions Collection, Bureau of Military History and my father's own writings, as the basis for everything I have written, and my account of the O'Malley Cheque will be no different. Firstly, I will recount the evidence as outlined in the various court hearings in March and April of 1924, and then I will provide some interesting new material that has come to light as a result of my research. Ultimately, I will leave it to you, the reader, to make up your own mind about these matters, but I hope you will give my father a fairer and kinder hearing than the one he received a century ago.

On Saturday, March 15, 1924, Edmund Lupton, who was the chief magistrate of the Dublin Metropolitan Police Courts, issued a warrant for the arrest of Henry Coyle TD on a charge of 'fraudulently inducing Patrick James O'Malley to endorse a valuable security, to wit, a bank cheque for £450' at Upper Ormond Quay in Dublin on October 18, 1923. My father was arrested on the following Friday, March 21, and appeared before Justice Lupton the next day where he was remanded in custody on two sureties of £500. Three days later, Justice Lupton wrote to the Ceann Comhairle of the Dáil to inform

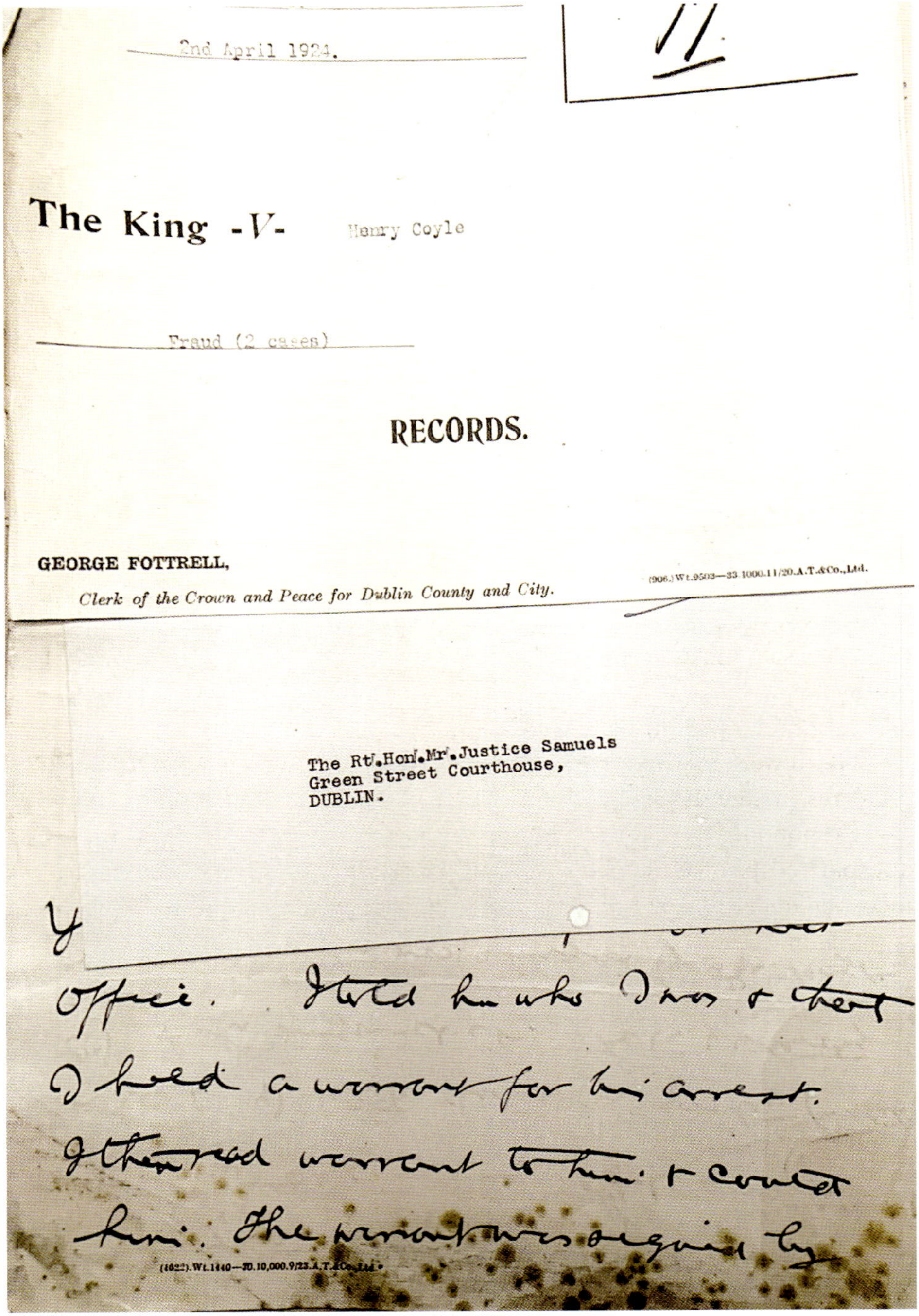

2nd April 1924.

11

The King -V- Henry Coyle

Fraud (2 cases)

RECORDS.

GEORGE FOTTRELL,

Clerk of the Crown and Peace for Dublin County and City.

(906.) Wt.9503—33 1000.11/20.A.T.&Co.,Ltd.

The Rt. Hon. Mr. Justice Samuels
Green Street Courthouse,
DUBLIN.

Y [illegible]
Office. I told him who I was & that
I held a warrant for his arrest.
I then read warrant to him & cautioned
him. The warrant was signed by

(1022).Wt.1440—30.10,000.9/23.A.T.&Co.,Ltd.

The cover on my father's case file for fraud in 1924 reads 'The King v Henry Coyle', which is somewhat ironic given that the Free State was doing the prosecution.

him of Henry Coyle's arrest and stated that the TD remained in custody because 'no sureties are yet forthcoming'.

My father was back before Justice Lupton on Thursday, March 27, where Patrick James O'Malley, the owner of the Ormond Hotel and erstwhile candidate in the general election in Mayo South, stated that he had been the victim of an alleged fraud perpetrated by Henry Coyle TD. Mr O'Malley told the hearing that my father approached him at the Ormond Hotel on October 17, 1923, and asked him to cash a cheque for £40.

"I hadn't the full change," said Mr O'Malley, "and I gave him £19."

The complainant told the court my father approached him again on Friday, October 18, and asked him to endorse a cheque for £450, explaining that he was 'unknown in town'. Mr O'Malley said he endorsed the cheque by signing the back of it, believing it was 'a good and valid cheque' from the National Bank.

On October 25, Mr O'Malley received a communication from the Bank of Ireland at Ormond Quay about paying £490, which he duly did and received a receipt for the payment, as well as the original cheques.

Cross-examined by Edward Byrne, who was representing my father, Mr O'Malley said the defendant did not tell him the cheque for £450 belonged to his uncle.

"He said it was his own cheque," witness claimed.

"Both were made payable to Henry Coyle TD," asked Mr Byrne.

"Yes," came the reply.

Responding to further questions from Mr Byrne, witness said my father approached him at his hotel in December and said he was 'sorry for the inconvenience caused'.

"Did he say he would pay the amount?" asked Mr Byrne.

"He did not, and I walked away. I said I had been to the police and that it was a most dishonourable act on his part to give me such a cheque.

"The defendant was talking the whole time but I declined to have any conversation with him. There was a reference to the police knowing about the transaction, and that he would have to deal with my solicitor about it, as the case was out of my hands. We never discussed the method of payment."

Mr O'Malley produced as evidence a number of telegrams from my father, including one sent from Crossmolina on December 15, stating: *Account sent today – Coyle.* Another telegram on December 20 stated: *Cash lodged; not sent as stated; will be advised Dublin tomorrow – Coyle,* and a third on January 21 stated: *Sorry for delays and disappointment. Full payment will be made tomorrow – Coyle.*

"Was £100 lodged to your credit in the bank?" asked Mr Byrne.

"I was told it was placed in my credit by the sub-manager, but I did not receive credit so far. I did not believe in its existence after all the disappointments. I am satisfied now that there is £100 in the bank, and that it was there since the beginning."

The court then heard from Mr Wright, a sub-manager at Bank of Ireland, who said he was at the bank sub-office at the Dublin Cattle Market on October 18 when Henry Coyle TD asked him to cash a cheque for £450. Witness said it was 'unusual to give cash for such a large amount' and he told my father if he had his cheque book with him he could 'mark the cheques as good'.

"Mr Coyle said that would not suit as he wanted the money to purchase cattle in the market. I asked him who was the drawer of the cheque and he said an uncle."

Mr Wright told the court he noted the endorsement of P.J. O'Malley on the back of the cheque and agreed to cash it because he was familiar with Mr O'Malley's signature from the Ormond Quay branch of Bank of Ireland. However, he had to ask my father to come back in half an hour because he did not have £450 in cash. The money was paid over later in the day, along with an additional £40 for the second cheque, giving a total sum of £490. Mr O'Malley later refunded the amounts of the two cheques and was credited with them.

"Did you discover £100 recently in Mr O'Malley's account and are you aware that the Royal Bank, on behalf of some person, lodged £100 to the credit of Mr O'Malley's account?" asked Mr Byrne.

"Yes," replied Mr Wright.

"The £100 was on its way to you on March 13 if not before it?"

"I think it was on that date it appeared in our books. I made inquiries and found it came from a Clydesdale bank."

The next witness was a clerk from the National Bank branch in Belmullet who told the court that Henry Coyle had no account in the bank. The cheque for £450 was sent there by Ulster Bank and later returned.

"Do you know these cheques were drawn from the Rotunda branch of your bank and that the defendant has no account there?" asked Mr Byrne.

"I don't know. I believe he had an account in the College Green branch."

Mr Byrne then explained to the court that the word 'Rotunda' was 'struck out in the cheque' and 'Belmullet' substituted in its place. This had been done 'by the bank people, possibly the manager of the Rotunda branch'.

"There are very strange things in this case," added the solicitor, "and it will be seen that the truth is funnier than can be imagined."

John McManus, a detective officer with the Dublin Metropolitan Police, told the court that he arrested Henry Coyle TD at the corner of St Stephen's

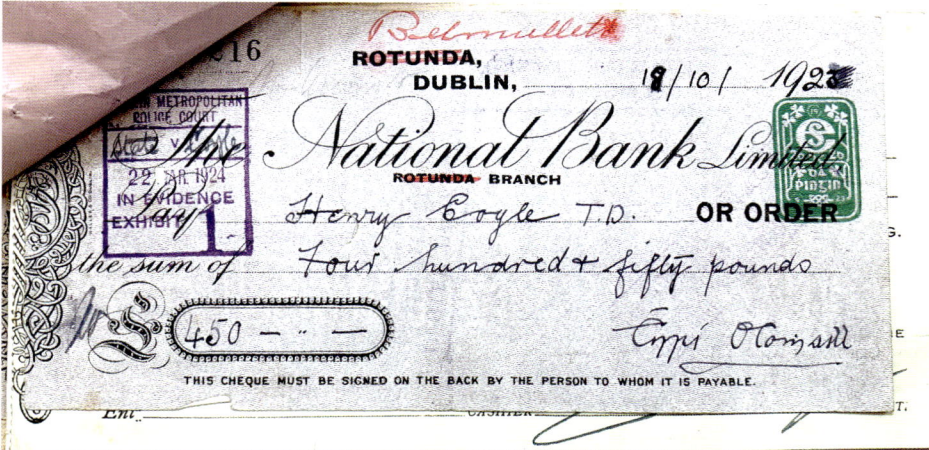

The cheque at the centre of the fraud allegation that destroyed my father's political career and led to his imprisonment.

Green and Dawson Street on Friday, March 21. When told of the charge, my father replied:

"That is very funny. On the 11th, I went with a friend of mine to a bank in Glasgow and paid in £100 to be transferred to the account of Mr O'Malley, Ormond Quay branch of the Bank of Ireland."

"Did he say where he was going?" asked Philip O'Reilly, solicitor for the prosecution.

"He said to Portobello and that it was as well he had not been entering or leaving the Dáil," replied the detective.

Mr Byrne then explained that my father had said a 'Mr Gordon' from Glasgow accompanied him to the Clydesdale Bank to transfer the £100 to Mr O'Malley's account in Dublin.

Mr O'Reilly asked to have the case forwarded for trial but Mr Byrne pleaded for the matter to be resolved through civil proceedings. The *Evening Herald*, which carried a lengthy report of the hearing, quoted Justice Lupton as stating that 'this was an important case, but he expressed no opinion on it'. The justice then returned my father for trial and kept the original bail conditions, despite a plea from Mr Byrne to have the two independent sureties of £500 reduced in recognition of the fact that £100 was already lodged in Mr O'Malley's account.

On Friday, April 4, my father appeared before Justice Samuels at Dublin City Commission where he pleaded not guilty to the charge of fraudulently inducing Patrick James O'Malley to endorse a cheque for £450. Opening for the prosecution, Mr Carrigan, instructed by the Chief State Solicitor, described the case as 'perfectly clear' and said it had 'a certain importance attached to it because of the amount involved and the position of the accused'.

In his sworn evidence, Mr O'Malley said he had known Henry Coyle for 'about two months previous to October' and recalled my father telling him that 'the cheque was issued by his uncle, who was the biggest cattle dealer in Co Mayo'. Mr O'Malley said he believed my father and consequently endorsed the cheque, only to later discover it had been 'dishonoured'.

Under cross-examination, the hotelier said he never had any previous transactions with my father and claimed the total amount now due to him was £350, having received the £100 lodged in the Clydesdale Bank.

Following Mr O'Malley's evidence, my father's solicitor Joseph O'Connor said he wished on behalf of his client to withdraw the plea of not guilty.

"And plead guilty?" asked Justice Samuels.

"Yes. There were certain negotiations between the parties – between solicitor and defendant, and I would respectfully suggest that he should be

One of the telegrams sent by my father to P.J. O'Malley in the winter of 1923-'24. It was later used as evidence against him during the trial for alleged fraud.

given an opportunity of paying this money back – the full amount. That would be done immediately."

Mr Justice Samuels: Of course, if the full amount is paid back I would take the circumstances into consideration, though it will not be a palladium.

Mr O'Connor: The money will be paid immediately.

Mr Justice Samuels: Of course, it is a palladium in a sense, but I can make no bargain. I must say Mr O'Malley behaved with considerable forbearance.

The judge then adjourned the matter to the following Monday to give my father one final opportunity to repay the money. However, when the case resumed at Green Street Courthouse on April 7, Mr O'Connor informed Justice Samuels that 'the offer of repayment could not now be carried out'. A report in the *Freeman's Journal* contains the following passage:

The prisoner said when he got Mr O'Malley to endorse the cheque, he had no intention for a moment of defrauding him. He felt very much disappointed that the case had been so pressed by the prosecution, and that his past services had not been taken into consideration – as an active organiser.

Mr Carrigan then told the court there had been 'a wire from Glasgow to the Dublin police stating that there is at present a warrant out against the accused for the fraud of £500'. On hearing this, my father responded: *When a man is down, help him down.*

In passing sentence, Justice Samuels said my father had pleaded guilty to obtaining money by false pretences, having 'occupied a most responsible position as a representative man and politician'.

"I can pass no smaller sentence than three years' penal servitude," the judge stated.

My father was then removed from the courtroom to commence his sentence, a sentence that would last a lot longer than three years.

CHAPTER 34

'When a man is down, help him down'

WHEN I commenced my research into the O'Malley Cheque, someone suggested to 'follow the money' and I'd eventually get to the bottom of this mysterious affair. But that is easier said than done because the money simply vanished into thin air. There is not a shred of evidence to suggest my father benefitted from the fraud in any way. In fact, the evidence points to him taking all of the pain and none of the gain.

One of the strange aspects of the court case is that nobody, at any stage, asked where the money went! A sum of £450 was enormous in 1924 and would have purchased a fine farm in Erris or a townhouse in Glasgow, yet my father or any member of his extended family did not come into any unexplained wealth in that period. In fact, they did not come into any wealth at all – explainable or otherwise – so, where did the money go?

The total value of the cheque was more than twice my father's annual salary as a TD. What did he do with such a sizeable sum of money and why did he insist on getting cash from the bank branch at the Dublin Cattle Market? These are questions I cannot definitely answer and I don't believe there is anybody alive today who can shed much light on this bizarre case. My father did not talk about the episode and the reason for that will become apparent in the remaining chapters. The O'Malley Cheque was the single, biggest episode in his eventful life and it effectively ruined him – personally and professionally. He got three years' penal servitude but served a life sentence.

There are so many aspects to the O'Malley Cheque that strike me as odd. Firstly, why did my father go to P.J. O'Malley to endorse such a sizeable cheque and why did O'Malley agree to do it? This is the same P.J. O'Malley who was at loggerheads with Cumann na nGaedheal's headquarters only weeks earlier,

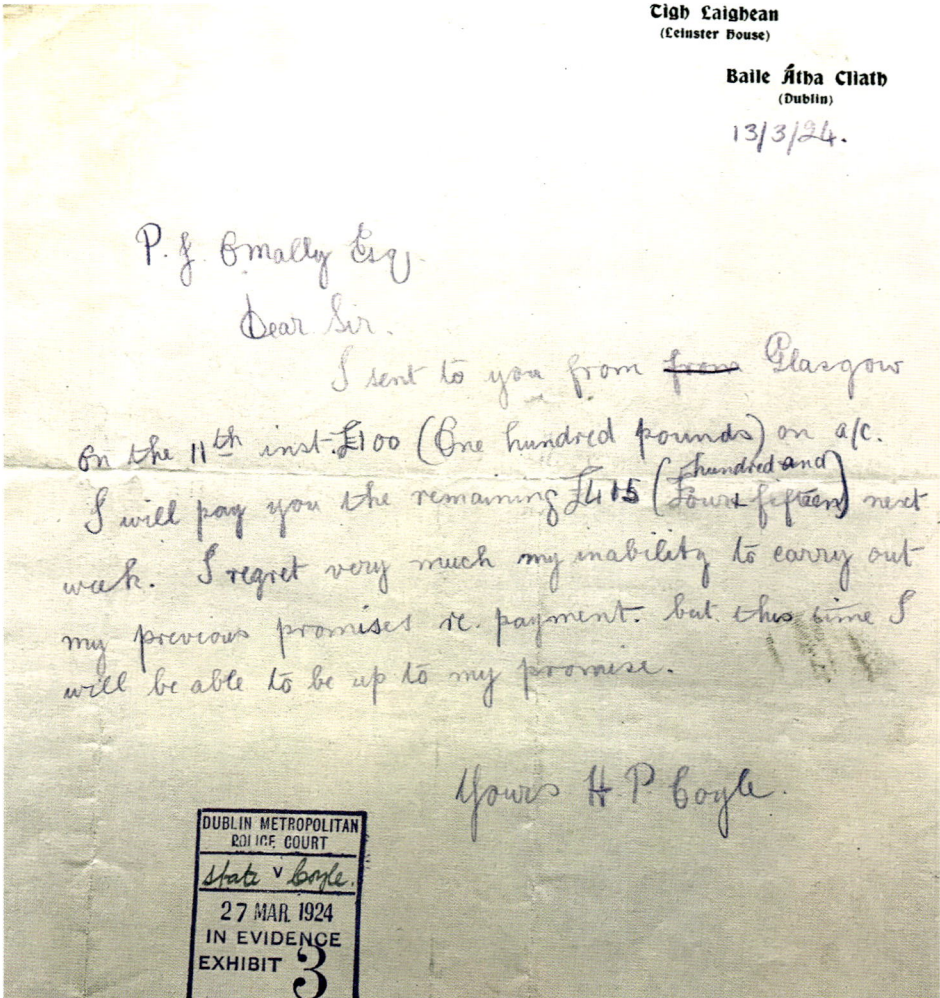

This is the letter my father wrote to P.J. O'Malley on Dáil letterhead paper in which he states he owes the hotelier £515.

yet now he is endorsing a huge cheque for one of the party's TDs. It just doesn't make sense.

Then there is the cheque itself. It is drawn on the Rotunda branch of the National Bank, but my father didn't have an account there, so how did he have a cheque for a bank where he had no account? And why was he not asked that during the court case? The cheque had even been altered when 'Rotunda' was crossed out and replaced with 'Belmullet', yet the judge saw no problem with that. Even more confusing is the convulted journey the cheque took. It was drawn on the National Bank, cashed in Bank of Ireland and ended up in the Sackville (O'Connell) Street branch of Ulster Bank before it was sent to Belmullet and altered. I was told to follow the money, but following the cheque was confusing enough.

There are also several inconsistencies in O'Malley's evidence. In his original statement to the Metropolitian Police, the hotelier said my father told him the cheque belonged to his uncle, who was 'the biggest cattle dealer in Mayo'. But during his evidence at the initial hearing on March 26, O'Malley explicitly denied that such a conversation took place. However, when he again appeared in court on April 4 he reverted to his original statement about the cheque belonging to my father's uncle, the supposed cattle dealer.

Then there is the issue of how much money my father owed P.J. O'Malley. During the various court hearings, evidence was given of two cheques – one for £450 and a second cheque for £40. O'Malley initially denied receiving a payment for £100 on March 11 but eventually conceded that the money had been lodged in his account, and said he was now owed £350.

However, in a letter my father sent to O'Malley on March 13, 1924, which I have published in this chapter, a figure of £415 is mentioned as the total amount owed once the £100 is taken into account. In other words, my father was saying that he originally owed £515 but O'Malley only gave evidence in relation to cheques valued at £490. It might seem like a minor issue but, once again, it points to a strange set of circumstances that nobody seemed willing to properly investigate at the time. Why would O'Malley tell the court he was owed £350 when, in fact, he was owed £415?

As a young man, the only mention I ever heard of the O'Malley Cheque was from John 'Mac' Barrett, a contemporary of my father, who claimed the cash was used to 'pay army men who were deserting to the anti-Treaty side'. Back then, I did not understand what he was talking about, but now with the knowledge I have acquired about the Army Mutiny in 1923-'24, the comment makes a lot more sense. Members of the National Army were being demobilised without any compensation and there was a fear some would join the anti-Treaty side – as much out of necessity as choice.

But why would P.J. O'Malley get involved? Perhaps it had something to do with his cousin, Padraic Ó Maille TD, who was closely associated with the mutineers, including men like Padraig Dunleavy and John Neary in Mayo, both former army colleagues of my father. Did the money from the O'Malley Cheque come west to pay soldiers who were being demobilised? I think there may be some credence in what John 'Mac' told me but I don't have any actual proof, only circumstantial evidence.

As I mentioned earlier, my father did not have an account in the Rotunda branch of the National Bank, but there was a secret account in that branch during the War of Independence and it was used to pay the Irish Volunteers. This is referenced in the Bureau of Military History and one of the men who had access to that account was Joseph McGrath, my father's running mate in Mayo North and another TD who supported the mutineers. Did that account still exist in 1923 and is that where the cheque came from?

At his sentencing hearing, my father said he felt 'very much disappointed that his past services had not been taken into consideration – as an *active organiser*.' What did he mean by that phrase *active organiser?* He seemed to be suggesting that the cheque had something to do with his work as an organiser, either for Cumann na nGaedheal or for some group associated with the pro-Treaty side. Was that group the Irish Republican Army Organisation?

When reflecting on the strange circumstances around the O'Malley Cheque, I keep thinking of the following headline that appeared in one of the Scottish newspapers after the trial in Edinburgh – *Coyle, in appeal to judge, shoulders all the blame*. The case in Scotland demonstrated my father's willingness to take the blame for others, even if it meant severe consequences for himself. I am convinced he took the blame for others at the trial in Dublin too, but who those others were I cannot say with any degree of certainty.

My father later said the decision to prosecute him was taken at a Cumann na nGaedheal party meeting in early March 1924. He was in Scotland at the time and claimed some TDs tried to defend him, but the party hierarchy insisted he be prosecuted.

Whether there was a direct connection between the cheque and the Army Mutiny is hard to say, but one thing I am sure about is that my father paid a very heavy price for supporting the mutineers. Had he taken the side of Cosgrave and O'Higgins in the spring of 1924, I am absolutely convinced he would never have faced criminal prosecution in relation to the cheque.

I believe it is no coincidence that just as the Army Mutiny is reaching its climax, my father inexplicably goes to Scotland and lodges £100 into the Clydesdale Bank. If my father still had the money from the cheques, why did he need to go to Scotland to lodge it? I believe he feared a prosecution was imminent and went to Scotland in a last-ditch effort to borrow some money from old friends who were willing to help him out.

One thing I am certain about is that my father didn't keep the money from the two cheques and never benefitted from them. Indeed, the subsequent chapters will show just how impoverished he was in the aftermath of his conviction and imprisonment. There was certainly no nest egg stashed away to tide him over upon his release from prison.

It was claimed at the sentencing hearing that the Glasgow police had issued a warrant for his arrest arising out of an alleged fraud of £500, yet when he was eventually released from Portlaoise Prison, the police in Glasgow said no warrant existed for Henry Coyle. What happened to the warrant and did it exist at all?

The Irish Times, in its report of the trial, quoted my father's solicitor as saying that '£300 had been made up to recoup Mr O'Malley for the loss he had suffered, but that it had now been withdrawn'. Why was this money withdrawn, especially when my father's career and liberty were at stake?

Another aspect of the case that strikes me as very odd is why P.J. O'Malley declined to pursue civil proceedings. My father was a TD on an annual salary of over £200 and would have been able to repay the money during his five-year Dáil term. There were apparently negotiations between my father and O'Malley's solicitor but then the criminal prosecution was set in motion, which effectively dashed any opportunity for O'Malley to get the £415 my father said he owed him in the letter of March 13. By taking a criminal prosecution, O'Malley was jeopardising any proposed settlement of the debt, which is precisely what happened because my father was jailed and lost his job as a TD.

But this is where the case takes another bizarre twist. On April 12, 1924, which was just four days after my father's conviction and imprisonment, P.J. O'Malley lodged a claim with the Office of Public Works for damage caused to his hotel 'during the Military occupation' from June 27 to July 6, 1922. The claim was in connection with the National Army's commandeering of the Ormond Hotel in the early days of the Civil War and O'Malley had already received £138 in compensation from the State in respect of this matter.

However, the hotelier was now lodging a new claim for the curious sum of £413-15s-2d. I say curious because the amount in question was just a pound and five shillings short of the figure referenced by my father in the letter of March 13! Again, maybe it is a coincidence but it is certainly an odd one.

O'Malley's compensation claim later increased to £439-11s-2d and included such items as furniture repairs and interior repainting, which all seemed very reasonable. However, a senior civil servant investigated the matter and discovered that the hotel hadn't been painted since the Dublin Exhibition of 1907 and was 'in urgent need of repair at the time of the military occupation'. In the end, O'Malley received £177-19s-6d in full and final settlement of his claim.

What all this means I simply do not know, but I think it shows there was more to the O'Malley Cheque than meets the eye. I am convinced my father became the fall guy and was effectively thrown to the wolves. Why do I say this? Well, the evidence is there in his prison file.

One of the things that struck me as strange when reading the reports of the court case was the failure to mention my father's previous role as a National Army commandant and as a trusted lieutenant of Michael Collins. Surely he deserved a little credit for his distinguished military past, even if he had taken the £450 to Fairyhouse Racetrack and frittered it away on some horses,

Far from getting credit for his many heroic deeds, my father was actually penalised for his role in the War of Independence. Incredible as it may sound, Henry Coyle's conviction for conspiracy in Scotland is listed as a 'criminal' offence in his prison file in Ireland.

My father made reference to this appalling misrepresentation of his past in a speech in the early 1930s, and I have to confess I initially thought there must have been some sort of misunderstanding on his part. It was only when I unearthed his prison file that I realised the full extent of the terrible injustice visited upon him in April 1924. There, in black and white, under the heading 'Record of Previous Convictions' was the following: *5 years P.S. + £500 or a further 2 years; High Court, Edinburgh; 19/3/'21; Conspiracy (two charges); Henry Peter Coyle; Peterhead Prison.*

I have reproduced the relevant sheet in this chapter because I am sure nobody would believe it without seeing the evidence with their own eyes. When I held that document for the first time in the National Archives in Dublin, my eyes filled with tears as I thought of my poor father in Mountjoy, opening that file and discovering the full extent of the betrayal perpetrated against him.

This was a man who had suffered greatly for the cause of Irish freedom. He risked life and limb transporting large quantities of explosives to Liverpool, was beaten to a pulp on the side of a Scottish road and spent long periods in solitary confinement in the most notorious prison in Britain. In March 1921, he proudly stood in the dock of Edinburgh Courthouse and proclaimed Ireland's right to self-determination and political independence, yet now his brave actions were being labelled as 'criminal' by men not worthy to lace his boots. Where were they when Michael Collins needed a brave patriot to drive a carload of gelignite across enemy country? Where were they when the bullets were flying in the Civil War and fearless men like my father stepped forward to protect the Free State? He was married in the uniform of the National Army in June 1922 and was nearly killed in that same uniform just a few weeks later, but all that was now conveniently forgotten.

It makes me very sad when I think of the treatment meted out to my father in Green Street Courthouse in April 1924. Even if he had robbed a bank with one of those Hotchkiss machine guns he sent from Liverpool, Henry Coyle deserved better than to have his proud record of patriotic duty reduced to a 'criminal' conspiracy. What a way to treat a heroic freedom fighter. A Unionist

								Fresh.	Brown.	Blue	Drop.	
On first Conviction	On Reception	In Local Prison	5	$8\frac{1}{2}$								
		In Convict Prison	5	$8\frac{1}{2}$								
	On Release		5	8¾								
After Licence revoked &c.	On Reception	In Local Prison										
		In Convict Prison										
	On Release											

DISTINCTIVE MARKS OR PECULIARITIES, NOTED ON FIRST RECEPTION OR AFTERWARDS.

Head { Right: *Bullet marks right cheek and side of neck.*
Left:

Rt. Side {

Lt. Side { *Bullet mark left upper arm.*

PHOTOGRAPHS.

On reception | On discharge

This page from my father's prison file lists the bullet marks he sustained fighting for Irish freedom – yet nobody at his trial mentioned his outstanding military record.

judge in Edinburgh begrudgingly acknowledged my father's political motives by giving him a reduced prison sentence, yet in his own native Ireland his tireless work on behalf of the IRA and Sinn Féin was used as evidence of a 'record' of law-breaking.

In voicing my criticism of the Green Street trial, I want to make one thing clear: I am not for a second suggesting that my father should have been exempted from punishment, if indeed he had committed fraud, but he certainly should not have been exempted from justice. If anybody in Ireland in 1924 was entitled to justice it was Henry Coyle, a man who literally bore the scars of his struggle for Irish independence.

In another page in my father's prison file, entitled 'Description of the Convict', there is the following passage: *Bullet marks right cheek and side of neck; bullet mark left upper arm.*

If a person were to read that file today, without knowing my father's background, they would reasonably conclude that Henry Peter Coyle was a hardened, inveterate criminal with a conviction for conspiracy in Scotland to match his conviction for fraud in Ireland, and a collection of bullet marks that would give Jesse James a run for his money. Never in their wildest imaginings would they think that this same man, Prisoner E827, was one of Ireland's finest and bravest freedom fighters.

This is a copy of the page in my father's prison file in which his conviction in Edinburgh for IRA gunrunning (conspiracy) is listed as evidence of a 'criminal' past.

The detective inspector who investigated my father's case of 'fraud' offered the following description of Prisoner E827: *He is a native of Co Mayo and originally belonged to the farming class, but for some years recently, he was engaged at business in Glasgow…*

There is no mention of Henry Coyle's membership of the National Army, and no mention of his involvement in the IRA and IRB. It was as if everything positive and noble in his past had been erased and he was now being recast as a common criminal who served jail time in Scotland for 'conspiracy' before falling back into a life of crime in Ireland. There is nothing on the file to put

	Christian Name	Surname	Prison in which undergone	Any which have been proved in Court to be marked* below
CONVICTIONS. *of date.)*				
charges)	Henry. Peter	Coyle.	Peterhead	

that conspiracy charge in its proper context or to give a fairer and more complete picture of my father's background.

"When a man is down, help him down," my father had said at his trial.

No truer words were ever spoken. The 'farming class' might have won Ireland its independence but there would be no place for them in this new elitist nation where patriots could be turned into criminals at the stroke of a pen.

CHAPTER 35

From commandant to convict

THE photograph of my father on the front cover of this book was taken within weeks of his arrest and detention for the O'Malley Cheque. I think you will agree he has the appearance of a man without a care in the world. He looks younger than his 29 years and his face betrays a hint of a smile, not what might be expected from a man facing into a professional and personal abyss.

Whenever I show the photograph to someone they immediately comment on my father's striking good looks and, in particular, his piercing eyes that stare down the camera lens. The black and white image doesn't actually do justice to his distinctive blue eyes, which were his outstanding physical feature as I remember him in his later years.

I found the photograph in my father's prison file and I was immediately struck by the apparent nonchalance in his demeanour. It left me perplexed. Did he not care about the three-year term of penal servitude just handed down to him or did he not fully appreciate the predicament he was now facing? If this book has shown anything, it is that my father was an intelligent man, well-read and capable of understanding the law and its consequences, so why did he look so unconcerned about his fate?

My own theory is that he still believed someone would step in and pay the money, and he'd be released from prison. He had a month to appeal the conviction and remained a TD in the interim, so all hope was not lost.

One of the popular misconceptions about my father is that he lost his Dáil seat because he became bankrupt. That was not the case at all.

Under the Irish Electoral Act of 1923, a person was disqualified from being a member of Dáil Éireann if they received a term of penal servitude in a Free State Court. The Ceann Comhairle told the Dáil on April 9 that Henry Coyle would be forced to forfeit his seat if his conviction and, more importantly, the three-year term of imprisonment were not successfully appealed within 30

Prisoner E827. These photographs of my father were taken in Mountjoy Prison on April 23, 1924, shortly after he was jailed in Ireland. He looked like a man without a care in the world.

days. A by-election would then have to be held to fill the vacancy in Mayo North.

My father's wife Margaret, who had been living in Dublin since the end of the Civil War, visited him in Mountjoy Prison on the day after his conviction and again on April 11. Margaret's mother, Mrs. M.A. Ferrie, accompanied her on the first visit while one of the McErlane brothers, possibly Ambrose, attended the second. That visit is described in the prison file as being about 'business matters'. Why would Ambrose McErlane travel all the way from Glasgow to visit my father? Once again, I am at a loss to explain the strange comings and goings in Henry Coyle's life at that time.

The prison file also reveals that my father wrote to Margaret on April 10 and received a letter in return with two photographs enclosed. Two days later, he signed a cheque and forwarded it to his wife, and on April 26, he signed another four blank cheques at the request of Margaret. It appears he was putting his affairs in order and paying off any outstanding bills. Perhaps at this stage he had already realised there would be nobody coming to his rescue and he was now on his own.

Dáil Eireann.

Tigh Laighean
(Leinster House)

Baile Átha Cliath
(Dublin)

8th April 1924.

Sir,

    I am directed by the Ceann Comhairle
to acknowledge receipt of your letter of
the 7th instant informing him that you have
passed a sentence of three years penal
servitude on Henry Coyle,T.D. for Mayo North.

Mise le meas,

Colm O Murchadha,

Cléireach na Dála.

The Rt.Hon.Mr.Justice Samuels
Green Street Courthouse,
DUBLIN.

This is the letter that ended Henry Coyle's brief political career. It is from the office of the Ceann Comhairle to Justice Samuels acknowledging my father's conviction and imprisonment.

On May 1, my father applied to the prison board for permission to write a 'special letter', but there is nothing on the file to suggest his request was granted. There doesn't appear to be any correspondence with his solicitor either, which suggests that an appeal was no longer being considered. There were also no further visits from Margaret who left for Glasgow on May 10, just days after the deadline for the appeal had lapsed.

The prison file reveals that my father complained of abdominal pains on May 14 and a headache on May 18, which suggests to me he was under terrible physical and mental strain. Whatever hopes he had of being rescued from this awful situation were now dashed and he was completely on his own, alone with his thoughts in a prison cell. Ironically, if he had taken the anti-Treaty side he'd have been released from Mountjoy Prison in the spring of 1924, and it must have been galling for him to watch men who had taken up arms against the Free State walk free while he faced three long years of penal servitude. It was some reward for his efforts throughout the Civil War; the commandant had become a convict, and the men who had been dubbed enemies of the Free State were being released into the bosom of family and friends.

Meanwhile, the political turbulence continued in Dáil Éireann where Cumann na nGaedheal found itself bitterly divided over the failed Army Mutiny. In April, Joseph McGrath and eight backbench TDs resigned from the party in protest at the Government's handling of the mutiny. The group included Alec MacCabe, one of Michael Collins' most loyal men west of the Shannon, and leading ex-IRA men Seán McGarry and Seán Milroy, as well as the then president of the GAA Dan McCarthy. They formed the National Party and I have no doubt Henry Coyle would have joined their ranks were he still a TD.

The nine members of the National Party resigned their Dáil seats in October 1924, triggering a spate of by-elections that were mainly won by Cumann na nGaedheal. However, the Government failed to hold my father's old seat in Mayo North, which was won by Sinn Féin's Dr John Madden, a veteran of the War of Independence.

Despite his close association with the mutineers, Padraic Ó Maille did not resign from Cumann na nGaedheal right away, but eventually left the party in 1926 amid criticism of the Irish Boundary Commission's proposals for the new border between Northern Ireland and the Free State. Ó Maille founded his own political party, Clann Éireann, in 1926, but lost his seat in the general election in 1927, and later joined Fianna Fáil.

The machinations in Leinster House mattered little to my father as he faced into three years of penal servitude. He was transferred to Portlaoise Prison (or Maryboro as it was known then) on July 4, 1924, but his health soon

SAORSTAT EIREANN.

WHEREAS, I am satisfied that convict Henry Coyle, E.827

at present confined in Portlaoighise Prison should undergo

and desires to undergo a surgical operation which cannot

properly be performed in Prison, I do hereby, pursuant to

the provisions of Section 17 (6) of the Criminal Justice

Administration Act, 1914, Order his removal to an extern

hospital for the purpose of such operation.

C. O'h. uigín

AIRE DLI AGUS CIRT.

Dated this 23ᵗᵈ day of July, 1924.

Minister for Justice Kevin O'Higgins signed a temporary prison release form for my father on July 23, 1924, so he could receive emergency medical treatment.

began to fail, and he was rushed to the prison hospital on July 20 complaining of acute abdominal pains. His medical condition must have been quite serious because the prison governor telegrammed Margaret and gave permission for a visit on compassionate grounds. Margaret, who had her own health difficulties, sent the following telegram from Glasgow on July 22: *Unable [to] travel owing [to] delicate health. My brother Vincent Ferrie crossing tonight in my stead.*

Vincent arrived the next day, just as my father was being transferred to the County Hospital in Portlaoise to undergo emergency surgery for appendicitis. The order to have him temporarily released from Portlaoise

Prison had to be signed by the Minister for Justice Kevin O'Higgins whose secretary instructed that 'steps should be taken to have this man transferred back to prison as soon as his condition will admit of this being done'. To read the letter, you would think Henry Coyle was a highly dangerous criminal instead of a man who only a year earlier had been defending the right of men like O'Higgins to govern the country.

On July 25, Margaret wrote the following letter to the governor of Portlaoise Prison:

> Dear Sir
>
> I have your letters of 21st and 22nd inst. re. my husband, Henry Coyle, and am glad to know that he is progressing favourably.
>
> Please accept my sincerest thanks for all the kindness and attention you have shown to him, also for your courtesy to my brother on his call.
>
> I am writing to Mr Coyle today and will be thankful for any further news of his condition.
>
> Yours sincerely
>
> Margaret M. Coyle

On August 5, Margaret wrote a second letter to the governor, Mr Blake:

> Dear Sir,
>
> Many thanks for your letter of 2nd. inst. re. my husband, Henry Coyle.
>
> I am glad to hear that his progress is favourable though slow as a good recovery is what is desired.
>
> I do not expect that he will be able for much solid food, but if there is any little delicacy that would be helpful to him that the doctor would allow and that you would grant him permission to have, I will gladly send it on.
>
> Trusting to again hear from you.
>
> Yours sincerely
>
> Margaret M. Coyle

I have published the two letters because I think they show Margaret's devotion to my father at a desperate time in his life. I can only imagine what she must have been thinking in the summer of 1924. Their four years of courtship and marriage had been a complete rollercoaster – from his arrest and conviction in Scotland to his unexpected release from Peterhead Prison in the spring of 1922. The joy of their wedding ceremony was quickly forgotten when she was almost widowed within a matter of weeks and she must have spent most of her first year of marriage waiting for a telegram announcing that her beloved Henry had been killed in action. His election to Dáil Éireann was surely a source of great pride for Margaret, and I expect she was in the visitors' gallery on the day he took his seat. So what then must she have thought when he was arrested and imprisoned all over again just a few months later? I find it almost impossible to get my head around the highs and lows of my father's life in the early 1920s, and I can only imagine what it must have been like for his poor wife. Margaret was not blessed with good health and it cannot have been easy for her moving from Glasgow to Dublin where she knew nobody, let alone enduring the trauma of visiting her husband in prison.

My father's recovery was surprisingly slow for a man who always enjoyed robust health, even in his later years. On August 9, Governor Blake wrote to the house surgeon at Portlaoise County Hospital asking when my father would be 'fit for removal back to prison'.

"He is now out since 20th July and this is causing a great strain on the duties of the staff of the Prison," the governor remarked.

The letter is marked 'unsent' because my father was transferred back to the prison hospital on Sunday, August 10, to complete his recovery. However, his health remained troublesome and he was treated for headaches in October and abdominal pain in December, which I firmly believe were the physical manifestations of the terrible mental strain he was under during that awful time in his life.

The prison file shows that on August 29, my father sought and was granted permission for a copybook and pencil, and I believe he wrote some songs while in Portlaoise, although I don't have any copies. I only became aware of them through my late uncle Jack who used to sing some of the songs.

On November 8, my father's brother Martin applied to see him, and the visit took place two days later, but there is nothing on the file to explain the purpose of the meeting. Nor is there any evidence of correspondence between my father and his parents during that first year in prison.

One of the more intriguing references in the prison file relates to the sale of a motorcar, which I presume was owned by my father. The purchaser appears to be Patrick Moylett, who wrote to my father on July 14, 1924, 'in reference to sale of motorcar and transfer book and the registration of same'. The fact that Moylett was willing to correspond with a man who had been jailed for fraud suggests that not everyone in the pro-Treaty movement deserted my father. Moylett must have had some sympathy for my father, but there is no evidence of any further correspondence between them.

In December 1924, my father received a letter from Seán Roche, one of his old republican colleagues in Glasgow who was applying for the newly-introduced IRA pension. The Military Service Pensions Act 1924 was partly a legacy of the issues raised during the Army Mutiny when men who had given loyal service to the State were being demobilised and left to fend for themselves in a country where unemployment was rampant.

In 1923, the Army Pensions Act sought to compensate wounded former soldiers, as well as the dependents of those who had died in either the War of Independence or the Civil War. The Military Pensions Act went one step further and offered the prospect of a life-long pension to Volunteers who could prove they were on 'active service' for all or some of the period from 1914-'24.

On December 13, 1924, my father wrote the following reference for Seán Roche:

> *I hereby certify that the bearer Seán Roche was a member of 'G' company, 1st Battalion, Scottish Brigade, from August 1919 to 1st July, 1922. He rendered very valuable services in the procuring and removing of firearms, etc. Owing to his been almost continually on the list of the unemployed, most of his time was occupied with the above named work, though without remuneration of any kind.*
>
> *Signed: Henry Coyle, ex-TD North Mayo*

The Military Service Pensions Act offered a badly-needed lifeline to my father. If he could write references for other people's military service, surely he was entitled to a pension himself? His exploits in Scotland might have been reduced to a criminal conviction in his prison file but nobody – not even his opponents in Cumann na nGaedheal – could deny his record of service in the IRA and the National Army.

The prospect of an IRA pension must have given my father renewed hope because if he had any sort of steady income stream, however modest, he could rebuild his life once he emerged from prison. So, on February 19, 1925, he wrote to the Department of Defence seeking an application form.

Obtaining an IRA pension should have been a fairly routine business for a man like Henry Coyle, whose record of service was well-documented, but my father was about to discover that his pension application was far from straightforward. A Free State court had given him three years' penal servitude, but the Free State government intended to give its former TD and party organiser an even harsher sentence.

CHAPTER 36

Nobody's child

I N order to qualify for an IRA pension, men like my father had to first apply to the Minister for Defence for a 'Certificate of Military Service'. The minister established the Army Pensions Board (also referred to as the 'Military Service Pensions Board') to assess each application, and pensions were approved based on the details provided by the applicant and, more importantly, the sworn written evidence of referees, i.e. men who had been the applicant's commanding officers or who possessed an intimate knowledge of their service record.

Henry Coyle's application for an army pension should have been an open and shut case because there was no doubt about his record of military service. There was plenty of documentary evidence of his activities during the War of Independence, while his record in the National Army during the Civil War was beyond dispute.

But my father had mixed feelings about applying for a pension at such a young age. He would have much preferred to be working for a living instead of taking a payment from the Free State, especially at a time when money was scarce and old age pensioners were being forced to take a cut in their paltry incomes. He thought long and hard about applying for an IRA pension and left it to the very last minute before finally deciding to seek an application form. On February 19, 1925, he sent a letter to the Department of Defence asking for a form under the Military Service Pensions Act, 1924, and he submitted the completed document on February 26, which was just three days before the closing date of March 1.

The application form makes for sad reading. On the opening, page, under the heading marked 'Present Address', he writes *Portlaoighise Prison*. A year earlier, he had been a TD and a retired army commandant; now he was – in the eyes of the Free State government – a convicted 'fraudster'. But others did not see him that way, and one of the most heartening aspects of the pension

Undergoing 3 years' P.S. for Fraud and false Pretences with intent to defraud.

M.S.P. 1.

Military Service Pensions Act, 1924.

APPLICATION TO THE MINISTER FOR DEFENCE FOR A CERTIFICATE OF MILITARY SERVICE.

S P 9346

This form must be filled in by every person who seeks a certificate of military service, and must be signed by him, and signature witnessed, **on or before the 1st March, 1925.** In the event of an applicant being unable to write he should affix his mark, such act being witnessed.

NAME (*to be written in* ..........COYLE...................HENRY......
block capitals).   SURNAME.   CHRISTIAN NAMES.

PRESENT ADDRESS.....PORTLAOIGHISE...PRISON.....
(*to be written in
block capitals*).

NOTE.—Before answering the questions below, the applicant is requested to note that

(*a*) All statements made in this application will be carefully investigated and satisfactory evidence must be forthcoming on request to substantiate each and every statement made.

(*b*) " If any person with a view to obtaining either for himself or any other person a grant or payment of a pension under this Act makes, signs, or uses any declaration, application or other written statement knowing the same to be false, such person shall be guilty of an offence under this section and shall be liable on summary conviction thereof to a fine not exceeding £25 (twenty-five pounds) or to imprisonment for a period not exceeding six months or at the discretion of the Court to both such fine and imprisonment." (Sec. 7 (1) of the Military Service Pensions Act, 1924).

(*c*) " If any person so convicted as aforesaid is in receipt of a pension obtained by reason of such false declaration, application, or other written statement he shall forfeit such pension as from the date of such conviction." (Sec. 7 (2) of the Military Service Pensions Act, 1924).

If the applicant is unable to read, the above note should be read to him by the witness.

The first page of father's application form for an IRA pension with his place of residence listed as 'Portlaoighise Prison'. The sad journey from commandant to convict was complete.

M.S.P. 19.

BORD MEASTOIRI

(Board of Assessors),

ACHT NA BPINSEAN SEIRBHISE MILEATA, 1924

(Military Service Pensions Act, 1924).

S.P. 9346.

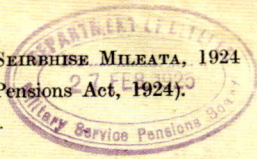

Applicants for certificates of Military Service under Military Service Pensions Act, 1924, should note that, number of applications being sufficient, sittings of the Board will be held in the undermentioned places.

Attention is directed to the fact that the onus of proof rests on the applicant and that no claim for expenses on the part of any witnesses can be entertained by the Board.

Applicants will enter on this form the centre at which they desire their claims heard, and return form without delay.

GEAROID O'SUILLEAVAIN

Runai.

LIST OF CENTRES.

Athlone	Claremorris	Kilkenny	Port Laoighse
Ballina	Clones	Letterkenny	Roscommon
Ballinasloe	Cork	Limerick	Sligo
Buncrana	Donegal	Longford	Thurles
Bantry	Dublin	Mallow	Tipperary
Caherciveen	Dundalk	Mullingar	Tralee
Carrick-on-Shannon	Dungloe	Naas	Tullamore
Carlow	Ennis	Navan	Waterford
Castlebar	Enniscorthy	Nenagh	
Cavan	Galway	Oldcastle	

Centre at which applicant desires his claim to be heard...Dublin...............

Signed...Enrí Mac Cumhaill...............

Address...Doohork,...............
(in full) ...Geesala, Co. Mayo........

(Now in Portlaoighise, Convict Prison.)

(4983).Wt. — .2.10000.2/25.A.T.&Co.,Ltd.

My father's signature on his application for an IRA pension in 1925.

application is the loyalty shown to my father by some of the men who were his commanding officers just a few years earlier.

For a man who was so good with words, my father was surprisingly reticent about his past military services and certainly did not try to embellish his case. He didn't even mention the prison term he had served while a member of the Erris Volunteers and summed up his activities during the War of Independence in one succinct sentence – *On special service in Scotland.*

When it came to the Civil War, he did not document the hunger strikes in Mayo in April 1922 or the wounds he suffered in the ambush in Kiltimagh later that year. His pension application was an exercise in understatement and I think it reflected his view, which he expressed some years later, that young men should not be in receipt of pensions. Had he not been in prison, I don't think he would have applied for a pension at all, and I believe it was his wife Margaret who persuaded him to submit the application. In my father's prison file, there is a record of him receiving a letter from Margaret on February 19, 1925, the same day he wrote to the Department for a pension application form. It seems too much of a coincidence; only Margaret, who was now living with her mother and brother in the family home in Glasgow, could have persuaded him to seek a pension.

In his application, my father says he received £4-4s per week 'while in charge of [IRA] purchases in Scotland, from [the] first week in August 1920 to 4th December, 1920'. He also notes that he 'got a grant of £100' after his release from Peterhead Prison.

"I looked on this as payment for a motor bicycle, my own private property, which was confiscated at my trial in Edinburgh, along with a motor car and a motor lorry, the property of GHQ."

In the section at the end of the form, where applicants could provide additional information, my father didn't write a single line, even though he could have wrote a book about his work on behalf of the Irish state during the past five years.

I think that pension application shows the kind of man Henry Coyle was – unassuming, honest and principled. If he was the 'fraudster' the Free State claimed him to be, he would have submitted a very different pension application and not one that actually downplayed his selflessness and bravery during the struggle for Irish freedom.

On the top of the form, someone (probably a civil servant in the department) wrote the following note: *Undergoing 3 years' P.S. for fraud and false pretences with intent to defraud.* Clearly, the officials in the department would have been happy to dismiss my father's pension application as the work of a convicted 'fraudster', but they couldn't dispute the referees who lined up to

3

(b) Continuous Service from 1st April, 1917, to 31st March, 1918.

QUERY.	REPLY.
(i.) What do you know of his connection with the Volunteers during this period?	*Lieut. in Reg. Coy. Subsequently Capt. Arrested. Sentenced in default of bail*
(ii.) To what Unit or Units was he attached?	*Erris Batt. Mayo Brigade*
(iii.) What rank did he hold?	*Lieut. Subsequently Captain*
(iv.) What was his occupation prior to and subsequent to this period, and to what extent was his ordinary living interfered with by his work as a Volunteer?	*Labourer. (Farm) Devoted almost all his time to Volunteer Work.*
(v.) What were the circumstances which enable you to testify as to his service?	*I was his (Capt) (Coy) and subsequently his Batt Comdt. for some time*

(c) Continuous Service from 1st April, 1918, to 31st March, 1919.

QUERY.	REPLY.
(i.) What do you know of his connection with the Volunteers during this period?	*Emigrated to Scotland, became Brigadier. Actively engaged securing arms & ammunition etc*
(ii.) To what Unit or Units was he attached?	*I/C Brigade Glasgow*
(iii.) What rank did he hold?	*Brigadier*
(iv.) What was his occupation prior to this period and to what extent was his ordinary living interfered with by his work as a Volunteer?	*Labourer & Subsequently insurance agent. Used the latter office only to cloak his movements & activities*
(v.) What were the circumstances which enable you to testify as to his service?	*I received arms from him. & followed his trial at Edinburgh, Blackbois he being arrested in Rotaraross, with carload of explosives for Dublin for which he was sentenced to 5 years. Released from Perthshire prison after time Subsequently Comdt. No. Army and T.D. for North Mayo*

An extract from Ned Mangan's reference in support of my father's application for an IRA pension.

give evidence on his behalf. Major General Seán MacEoin and Major General Eamon Price testified to his service in the National Army, but the most compelling evidence came from the former commanding officer of the Erris Volunteers, Ned Mangan, now a sergeant in the Civic Guard and stationed at the Phoenix Park Depot in Dublin. He and my father had been imprisoned together in Sligo in the spring of 1919 and Mangan was not about to abandon his old comrade. He wrote the following:

The applicant, in the course of his association with our Brigade (Mayo), was a trustworthy and capable officer.

The poor circumstances (financially) of his parents left him no choice but emigration in order to help them. However, while in Glasgow, he devoted his time solely to the IRA and his connection with and supply of arms to HQ are well-known facts.

I have to confess I smiled when I came across that reference because it must be the only time in the history of An Garda Síochána that a sergeant used the word 'trustworthy' to describe a man serving a prison sentence for fraud! I think Ned Mangan's sworn statement in October 1925 speaks volumes for the way my father was viewed amongst the men who served with him in the IRA. In later years, words like 'sincere', 'hardworking' and 'a good man' were all used to describe Henry Coyle – hardly the kind of language one would associate with a 'fraudster'. Ned Mangan could have wrote any other word to describe my father's record as a member of the Erris Volunteers but he chose 'trustworthy'; I don't think it was a coincidence. Ned Mangan was a great, great man for standing by an old friend who had fallen on hard times.

Another former comrade who was determined not to abandon my father was Joe Vize, now a colonel in the National Army, who gave the following reference:

During his time with me, applicant worked very hard in the Purchase Dept, getting a good amount of stuff for us… In my opinion, applicant deserves the consideration of the Board.

But the wheels of bureaucracy moved very slowly in the Department of Defence, and by the end of 1925, my father had still not received any word about his pension application. He wasn't alone. There were dozens of former colleagues from the IRA in Scotland and England who were finding it equally difficult to persuade the Army Pensions Board to approve their applications. Among them was Mick Burke, from Motherwell, who had moved back to Ireland in 1923, having lost his job as a crane driver in a Motherwell steelworks due to his IRA activities. In late 1921, Michael Collins approved a payment of £20 per month in recognition of the Armagh native's sterling service during the War of Independence, but that payment was cancelled after Collins' died. Burke moved to Dublin in 1923 to take up a position in the Marine

A great number of other names can be given if these is not sufficient to testify to my services as a Volunteer during the year 1916 and the position I held in same. I was one of the Founders of the Volunteers in Liverpool, and a member of the executive body of same, which entitled me to visit Dublin and hold conferences with Sean McDermott and others, in connexion with Volunteer work in Liverpool. In 1917 I was elected O.C of Liverpool and North of England with the Rank of Colonel, which I held up to the time I came to Dublin about the last week of June 1922 I came to Dublin by orders of Michael Collins late Com in Chief. He was to have me fixed up permently in Dublin, but was very unfortunately cut away which leaves me still unfixed and nobodys child and twelve months unemployed I trust that this statement will satisfy the Minister for Defence and the Board of Assessors. as to my claim for services during the year 1916 and up to my arrest in November 1920
— Believe me Sir
Your Obedient Servant
Neill Kerr

An extract from the letter written by Neill Kerr to the Army Pensions Board after he was denied a pension for IRA activities in 1916.

Investigation Department (MID), but with the Civil War coming to an end the MID had no work for him. By the summer of 1925, the 47-year-old was in dire circumstances. He had been forced to put his only child into the care of a woman in Motherwell after his wife died, and he was now living in lodgings off Sheriff Street in Dublin.

"I have only worked 19 weeks this last 13 months," he told the Army Pensions Board. "I am drowned over head and ears in debt. I had a letter from Motherwell yesterday informing me that the baby was taken to hospital.

"You can understand the position I am placed in. I am sorry for having to trouble you about this, but I thought this would have been settled long ago.

"I hope you will pull me through."

This is the same Mick Burke whose home in Motherwell was always open to the Irish Volunteers, who sorted and packed munitions with the assistance of his wife and elderly father-in-law and who took part in numerous raids for weapons. Now he was reduced to begging for assistance from the Free State he helped to establish. But there were even worse cases than Mick Burke.

Neill Kerr was another who had moved to Dublin following the establishment of the Free State, but by late 1924 he was also living in destitution. Incredibly, Kerr was told by the Department of Defence that he did not qualify for a full pension because he didn't have active service in 1916. This was a man who had been involved in the struggle for Irish freedom going right back to the 1890s, but now he was being told he didn't meet the 'criteria' for 'full military service' and would only receive a partial pension. On March 16, 1925, Kerr made a personal appeal to the Minister for Defence Peter Hughes:

"I came to Dublin about the last week of June 1922," he explained. "I came to Dublin by orders of Michael Collins, late Commander in Chief. He was to have me fixed up permanently in Dublin, but was unfortunately cut away, which leaves me still unfixed and nobody's child, and twelve months unemployed."

Nobody's child. It is a phrase that really resonated with me because I think my father found himself in exactly the same position after the death of Collins. Indeed, I am convinced that Henry Coyle would never have ended up in prison had Collins lived, and equally there is no way Neill Kerr, at 64 years of age, would have had to write a begging letter to the Minister for Defence. Michael Collins would have been horrified at the way men like Neill Kerr, Mick Burke and my father were treated. He urged them to return to Ireland to start new lives in the Free State, but now they were either being ignored or persecuted by the institutions of the independent Ireland for which they were willing to sacrifice their lives.

C O P Y

DEPARTMENT:- BRIGADE O.C.

L . NO. _____

8TH BRIGADE HEADQUARTERS,
PONSOMBY BARRACKS,
CURRAGH TRAINING CAMP,
17TH DECEMBER, 1925.

TO/THE SECRETARY,
BOARD OF ASSESSORS,
MILITARY SERVICE PENSIONS,
DUBLIN.

Some time ago at your own request I handed in alist of twelve (12) names of the best workers I had in Scotland, for your information. I am now receiving letters from some of them stating that their claims have been rejected, on account of not having sufficient evidence. The only two serving Officers in the Army who could verify their statements are Major J.Furlong and myself. In all fairness to the men in question, I have no hestitation in saying, that they deserve more consideration from your Board.

You have surely taken into account that they were working in the Enemy's Country, and under far more difficult circumstances than some of our men at Home. Every day they were watched, not only by the detectives and police, but by members of the Civilian Population also, and during my time in Scotland they were always on the go, purchasing, transporting, supplying information, and carrying arms and explosives all over the Country. Scotland was responsible for two-thirds of the war material received and used in this Country, and all that stuff passed through the hands of the men in question without the loss of one round of ammunition. Men of their type were very hard indeed to find in those days WHEN MEN COUNTED, at least that was my experience across channel, we had plenty of platform spouters, but when it came to going up to a Scottish Military Barracks and getting rifles, ammunition etc., across the walls in the small hours of the morning you could count the workers on your fingers.

I appeal to you in the name of justice to give them a fair show. They were not over here under the eyes of G.H.Q. they carried out their dangerous work unseen by those in authority, but they certainly carried out that work honestly, to their own credit and to my entire satisfaction, and they their services in my opinion call for some appreciation from the Government. Their names are:-

1. James Byrne, 70 Seville Place, Dublin.
2. James Fullerton, 20 Gladstone Street, Glasgow.
3. William Fullerton, 24 Villars Street, Townhead, Glasgow.
4. Michael Burke, 8 Emily Place, off Sherrif Street, Dublin.
5. Patrick O'Neill, 10 Bessborough Avenue, Strand Road, Dublin.
6. John Byrne, Creenveen, Carrick, Co. Donegal.
7. John Mills, Gortmelia, Barnatra, Ballina, Co. Mayo.
8. Hugh O'Connor, 70 Seville Place, Dublin.
9. Henry McMahon, Military Police, Collins Barracks, Dublin.
10. Pat Mills, 170 Clonliffe Road, Dublin.
11. Cpl.Charlie Strickland, Q.M.G's. Driver.
12. Eddie O'Hanlon, address unknown at the moment.

(SIGNED) JOSEPH E. VIZE COLONEL.

OFFICER COMMANDING 8TH BRIGADE.

Joe Vize's letter in support of pensions for 12 named members of the Scottish IRA Brigade.

Joe Vize took up Kerr's case and wrote a stinging letter to the secretary of the Army Pensions Board after it had asked him to complete a reference for the veteran republican.

I am returning form sent to me in connection with pension for Neill Kerr, 10 Coastguard Station, Ringsend.

After making several efforts, I came to the only possible conclusion that it would be an utter impossibility for me to attempt to put on paper Neill's pre-Truce record. I must leave that (if it is ever done) to a greater pen than mine. Certainly, no form would suffice, even if it was attempted, because, I believe, volumes could be written…

I appeal to the members of the Pensions Board on his behalf, for extra special consideration, and I have no hesitation in recommending him for the maximum grant. If that is not possible, I appeal to them to strengthen his case in another direction, namely, get his rent reduced. He is living in a house that is Government property, paying 16/- a week rent, and I got it myself from the late Commander in Chief's lips that Neill was to be set up in a little cottage and made comfortable for the rest of his days.

But how do we find him today? A physical wreck, over ten months unemployed, forbidden to live in England, his little farm in the North mortgaged, where he is also forbidden to live, the Free State solicitor sending him letters for arrears of rent, he very deep in financial difficulties; but on looking round you see people with no claim reaping the harvest of his honest toil. Comment is unnecessary.

That letter, which I have published in full in Appendix II, made me so angry when I first read it. All I could think of was the night of September 3, 1920, when Neill Kerr Jnr had been accidentally shot while serving Ireland and old Neill Kerr told my father: *Henry, he is gone, but if the three of them were gone the work must go ahead.* Now, five years later, Neill Kerr was being threatened with legal action by the independent Ireland for which one of his sons died. It's hard to believe such a thing could happen, but happen it did and the documents are there to prove it.

The similarities between my father's situation and Neill Kerr's are striking. My father was given accommodation in a State-owned flat at Wicklow Street in June 1922, but by the following year he was in dispute with the Board of Works over rent and they were threatening him with legal action. The matter was eventually resolved and the apartment handed back to the Board.

Vize's letter shamed the Army Pensions Board into recommending that Kerr be paid a pension of £135 per annum, which was later increased to £180. It was just about enough to live off for a man with two dependent children and rent of 16/- per week.

Vize remained a staunch ally of the Scottish Volunteers throughout 1925 as they continued to make their cases for IRA pensions. Several of the men, including Patrick Mills, had their applications rejected on the grounds of 'not having sufficient evidence', prompting Vize to put pen to paper once again in support of 12 named members of the Scottish Brigade. The following is an extract from a letter the Wexford man wrote to the Army Pensions Board on December 17, 1925:

Scotland was responsible for two-thirds of the war material received and used in this country, and all that stuff passed through the hands of the men in question without the loss of one round of ammunition. Men of their type were very hard indeed to find in those days WHEN MEN COUNTED, at least that was my experience across channel. We had plenty of platform spouters, but when it came to going up to a Scottish Military Barracks and getting rifles, ammunition, etc., across the walls in the small hours of the morning you could count the workers on your fingers.

I appeal to you in the name of justice to give them a fair show. They were not over here under the eyes of GHQ, they carried out their dangerous work unseen by those in authority, but they certainly carried out that work honestly, to their own credit and to my entire satisfaction, and their services in my opinion call for some appreciation from the Government.

Apart from Patrick Mills, Vize's list included Charlie Strickland, Mick Burke, and John Mills, from Gortmelia, Barnatra. My father wasn't mentioned, presumably because Vize assumed that a Volunteer who had been employed directly by GHQ would have no problem securing a pension. But he assumed wrong. By the spring of 1926, my father's application for an IRA pension was still no closer to being finalised; in fact, it had simply been ignored. Henry Coyle was, to quote Neil Kerr, *nobody's child*.

CHAPTER 37

The final betrayal of
an Irish patriot

IN August 1925, my father sent a letter to the board of Portlaoise Prison asking to have a copy of the *Glasgow Observer* sent to him each week. His request was granted. Although he was still only at the midway point of his three-year term, Henry Coyle was already preparing for a future in Scotland, and had vowed to give the prison authorities no excuse to keep him behind bars a day longer than was necessary.

He was a model prisoner for the duration of his sentence and worked as a labourer on the prison farm once he recovered from his appendicitis. His only connection to the outside world were the regular letters from Margaret and the occasional correspondence with family and friends. In his prison file, there is a reference to a letter from Seán O'Doherty, the Dundee Volunteer who presented my father with the silver teapot on his wedding day, but sadly a copy of the letter is not contained in the file. It would be interesting to find out what O'Doherty wrote because it might shed a bit more light on the O'Malley Cheque.

One of the frustrating aspects about the prison file is that there is a record of every letter sent and received by Henry Coyle, but there is only one piece of correspondence preserved and that is an extract from a letter my father wrote to Margaret on March 5, 1926. By then, he was already counting down the days to his release:

My Dear Madge,

Of course there will be only one three months of the third year. That is if I lose no remission, but I don't think I will. So far I haven't lost any, and I find that the Governor and the other officials here are pleased with my conduct, and needless to say that I am very well pleased with them, and their treatment of me. Since I came here, everybody seemed inclined to make my time as easy for me as

Licence A

SAORSTÁT ÉIREANN.

ORDER OF LICENCE UNDER THE PENAL SERVITUDE ACTS, 1853 to 1891.

Name of Convict, *E827 Henry Coyle.*

Prison, *Portlaoighise*

The Governor-General of the Irish Free State, having been so advised by the Minister for Justice, is pleased to grant to *Henry Coyle* who was convicted of *Unlawfully fraudulently did induce one Pat J. O'Malley to endorse a certain cheque for £450 by means of false pretences with intent to defraud and injure the said Pat J. O'Malley.* at the *Commission* for the *City of Dublin* on the *4th April 1924*, and was then and there sentenced to be kept in Penal Servitude for the term of *three* years, and is now confined in the *Portlaoighise* Prison, Licence to be at large from the day of his liberation under this Order during the remaining portion of his said term of Penal Servitude, unless the said *Henry Coyle*, shall, before the expiration of the said term be convicted on Indictment of some offence within Saorstát Éireann, in which case such Licence will be immediately forfeited by Law, or unless such Licence shall be sooner revoked or altered.

This Licence is given subject to the Conditions endorsed upon the same, upon the breach of any of which it will be liable to be revoked, whether such breach is followed by a Conviction or not.

And it is hereby ordered that the above-named be set at liberty within thirty days from the date of this Order.

Given under my Hand and Seal, on the 9th day of *June*, 19 26.

C. Ó h. Uigín.
MINISTER FOR JUSTICE.

No. in Convict Book. *21/19-6*
Dublin City

Note:- The sentence in this case counts from 2/4/24.

(9008).Wt.4471—155.125.1/26.A.T.&Co.,Ltd.

On June 9, 1926, Minister for Justice Kevin O'Higgins signed the order to release my father from prison on licence after he had earned the necessary remission.

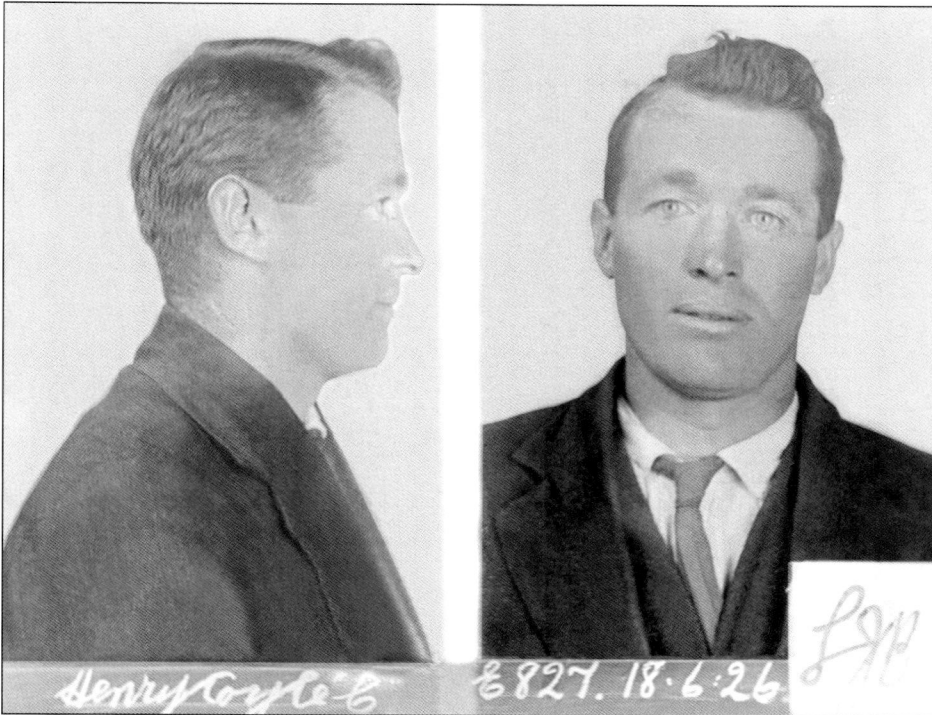

These photographs of my father were taken a few weeks before his release from Portlaoise Prison. He looks a very different man from the one who entered Mountjoy just two years earlier.

possible and I'd be very ungrateful if I didn't show my appreciation by conducting myself properly.

Sincerest love, from Henry.

I suspect that paragraph was penned for the prison governor's eyes, as much as Madge's, and not surprisingly it was retained in the file.

On June 9, 1926, Minister for Justice Kevin O'Higgins signed the licence for Henry Coyle's release from Portlaoise Prison. It was no act of mercy on O'Higgins' part; my father had earned every day of his nine months' remission and nobody could take it from him. There was, however, the small matter of that 'outstanding warrant', which the police in Glasgow had supposedly issued in 1924 for my father's arrest 'for the fraud of £500'. The warrant was mentioned at his trial in Green Street Courthouse and there was also a note about it on his prison file. Governor Blake inquired into the matter and received the following telegram on July 1, 1926, from the Superintendent of the Detective Branch in Dublin: *Henry Coyle not now wanted by Glasgow police. Thanks for attention.*

Whatever happened to the warrant, or whether it even existed, I simply do not know. It was just one of the many 'strange things' in Henry Coyle's conviction and imprisonment for fraud.

A condition of my father's early release was that he was supposed to report to the police for the remainder of his three-year term, which meant he had to stay in Ireland until the spring of 1927. He told Governor Blake he intended to go to Dublin once released but had 'no particular address' at which to live.

It was a sad, sad state of affairs. Eighteen months had passed since he applied for an IRA pension and he still hadn't heard a word from the Army Pensions Board. Instead, the Free State gave Henry Coyle a 'gratuity' of 16 shillings and sixpence on the day he left prison. Sixteen shillings and sixpence… it wasn't even a shilling for each of the 18 bullets fired into his car in Kiltimagh four years earlier when brave men were needed to defend the Free State. Joe Vize said it best in just three words: *Comment is unnecessary.*

On the previous page, I have published a photograph of my father shortly before he was released from Portlaoise. All I can say is that the man who walked out of the prison gates on July 2, 1926, was unrecognisable from the man photographed in Mountjoy in April 1924. The prison term had taken a heavy toll on him and I think that is very evident to anyone who compares the images. It is hard to believe they were taken just two years apart

My father didn't wait long in Dublin. The truth is he couldn't. He had nowhere to live and little prospect of getting work in a country where unemployment was rampant. By the end of 1926, he was back in Glasgow and living with Margaret in her old family home at 34 Hillfoot Street in Dennistoun, but the joy of being reunited with his beloved Madge was tempered by the harsh economic reality of unemployment.

It is never easy for men or women to find work after being released from prison, but my father was trying to gain employment in a city where he was well known for his IRA activities. Just six years had passed since Henry Peter Coyle was arrested with the largest quantity of illegally-held explosives ever discovered in Britain and his name had not been forgotten in the intervening period. Every morning he went out in search of work and every evening he trudged home to 34 Hillfoot Street with nothing to show for his day's efforts. It must have been soul-destroying. He was such a talented man and had an outstanding work ethic, but nobody wanted to give this Irish 'terrorist' a chance.

And who could blame them? Scotland didn't owe anything to Henry Coyle, but Ireland certainly did, and in December 1926 he decided it was about time his native country started paying its long overdue debt to him. On December 3, he wrote to the Army Pensions Board inquiring about his stalled application for an IRA pension. The board responded by asking him to

No longer a wanted man. At my father's trial in 1924, it was claimed there was a warrant out for his arrest in Glasgow, but two years later, the warrant had mysteriously disappeared, as this telegram dated July 26 reveals.

complete a sworn affidavit in front of a Commissioner of Oaths outlining once again his involvement in the War of Independence and Civil War. It was a very unnecessary request. After all, my father had already completed an application form almost two years earlier, the contents of which were corroborated by two Major-Generals, a Colonel and a Garda Sergeant, so why did the board need a sworn affidavit? It was as if they wanted to make my father jump through every hoop in order to get what was his legal entitlement.

On January 5, 1927, my father and Margaret went to a solicitor's office at Bath Street in Glasgow to complete the sworn affidavit. This time he included more details about his military service, including the prison term in Sligo, the hunger strike in Castlebar and his membership of the IRB. For me, the most revealing and poignant line in that document comes at the end when he is asked to state his present occupation. He writes just one word: *Nil*.

It is heartbreaking to think that a man who gave so much for Irish freedom had been reduced to so little. Even if he was guilty of bank robbery, did he really deserve the indignity of having to write *Nil* for present occupation? What must have been racing through his mind in those dark days in the winter of 1926-'27 when he tried as best he could to rebuild his life, only to have one door after another slammed in his face. Just six years earlier, he had stood in a courtroom in Edinburgh and declared his pride at being a soldier of the Irish Republic, but instead of lauding and rewarding him for his courage and selflessness, the newly-independent Ireland threw him into prison and then cut him adrift with sixteen shillings and sixpence in his pocket. I am sure he and Margaret could ill afford to pay a solicitor to complete the sworn affidavit but what other choice did they have? They desperately needed that pension if they were to have any prospect of building a new and brighter future together.

Under the Military Service Pensions Act, applicants were assessed on their record of military service from Easter Week 1916 up to September 30, 1923. My father had joined the Erris Volunteers in late 1917 and left the National Army in June 1923, so he should have met the criteria for almost all of the qualifying period, especially as he had provided credible references for his service record.

In April 1927, the Army Pensions Board finally issued its decision in the case of Henry Peter Coyle: he was being recommended for a pension for military service for the period from late 1919 to June 1923. In financial terms, it worked out at £100-1s per annum, which might seem like a princely sum in 1927, but it was far less than some applicants were getting, and their 'military service' wasn't nearly as impactful or dangerous as Henry Coyle's. But it was certainly better than nothing for an unemployed 31-year-old in Glasgow.

On April 2, the board sent a letter to the Department of Defence recommending that my father be issued with a certificate for military service, which he could then use to claim his pension. It should have been a formality, as it was in almost every other case, but my father's pension application took a very unexpected twist. On May 7, the Army Finance Officer sent a letter marked 'Very Confidential' to the army's intelligence division, stating:

[Henry Coyle] is an applicant for a Military Service Pension, and I am to enquire, for the information of the Minister, whether there are any circumstances within your knowledge which might influence him in refusing the Certificate in this case as, for example, internment, complicity with organisations inimical to the State, etc.

I am to request the favour of an early reply.

Three days later, a senior intelligence official sent the following reply:

I am directed to inform you for the information of the Minister that the above named was sentenced in April 1924 to three years' imprisonment for false representation. If further particulars are required the file in our records here is at your disposal.

The Army Finance Office also contacted the personnel division of the National Army for a report about my father's service record, which was a standard procedure in such cases, but the one-page document issued on May 12 was anything but standard. Under the heading 'Character and Conduct', the officer in charge of staff duties wrote: *'Clear while in Army – see covering letter'*.

4

Set out here date of joining National Army.

(5) **From the 12th day of July, 1921, to the date I joined the National Army, viz.**

Set out services here.

The Military Services rendered by me were as follows :

In Peterhead Convict prison until 11th February 1922.

In the case of an applicant who did not join the National Army he should set out here particulars of what service he rendered the National Forces, the duration and dates of same, pay received and rank held between the 1st July, 1922, and the 30th September, 1923.

(6) I joined the National Army on the *20th* day of *February 1922.*

I did not become attested until sometime in the beginning of May 1922, but it can be recalled that previous to my being attested (date of which will be on record, I had been twice arrested by the irregulars and had a weeks hunger strike in Castlebar.

I was also a member of the I.R.B.

(7) My present occupation is *Nil.*

Henry R Coyle

SWORN BEFORE ME THIS *Fifth* DAY OF

January 1927 AT *Glasgow*

AND I KNOW THE DEPONENT.

Anderson Dunn *Solicitor.*
49 Bath Street, Glasgow.
Notary Public

The above affidavit is to be sworn before a Commissioner to administer oaths in the case of an applicant residing in Saorstat Eireann, Great Britain and Northern Ireland, and in the case of an applicant residing elsewhere before a Consul or Notary Public.

M. M Ferrie
34 Hillfoot Street. Witness to above signature
Glasgow.
Typist.

The final page of the sworn affidavit sent by my father to the Army Pensions Board in January 1927. Note that under 'Present Occupation', he writes 'Nil'. It was a sad state of affairs for a man who had devoted the best part of 10 years to the fight for Irish freedom.

H. C. R. No. S.

Prison Register No. *6827*

Name *Henry Coyle*

Alias _____

[Photograph to be cut to this size and pasted here.]

to be discharged otherwise than under Sections 5, 7,

or 8 Prev. Crimes Act, on the *2nd*

day of *July* 19*26*

Date and place of birth } *1897 Doolough, Geesala Co. Mayo*	**Distinctive Marks and Peculiarities.**
Trade or Occupation *Farmer & Commission Agent*	Head { Rt. *Bullet marks rt cheek and side of neck.* Lt.
Height (without shoes) *5 ft. 8½ in*	
Complexion... *Fresh*	
Hair... *Brown*	Rt. Side
Eyes... *Blue*	Lt. Side *Bullet marks left upper arm*
Remarks _____	
Intended Address *Dublin no particular address*	

The signature of the Governor, with prison and date, will be made immediately below the entry of the
last conviction.

CONVICTIONS—(in Chronological sequence).

Sentence.	Court and Place. (State if at Ass., Qr. Sess., Petty Sess., or Police).	Date.	Offence of which prisoner was actually found guilty.	Full Christian and Surnames.
5 yrs P.S. 500 or 6 mths imp	*High Ct Edinburgh*	*19 3 21*	*Conspiracy (2 charges)*	*Henry Peter Coyle.*
3 years S.S. Dublin City Comm comg. 2.4/1924		*4 4 24*	*unlawfully fraudulently and induce one John O Malley endorse a certain cheque for £650 by means of false pretences with intent to defraud and injure the said John O Malley*	*Henry Coyle.*
				J Blake Governor
				Portlaoighise Prison. 30/5/1927

(For continuation of Convictions see overleaf.)

No. 101.

(8649).Wt.5288-90—30,560.9/20.A.T.&Co.,Ltd.

This is a copy of my father's 'criminal' record, which was used to refuse him an IRA pension. Note that the prison governor in Portlaoise has included the conviction from Edinburgh as part of a 'criminal' past.

The sting was in the last three words because 'the covering letter' contained the following:

While there is nothing recorded against this applicant during his period of service, it is understood that subsequent to the termination of his service and while a member of Dáil Éireann, he was convicted on a charge of embezzlement and sentenced to three years' penal servitude.

Armed with this latest information, the Army Finance Office then contacted the Secretary of the General Prisons Board at Dublin Castle seeking full particulars of Henry Coyle's 'criminal' past. The governor of Portlaoise Prison duly dispatched a one-page synopsis of the 'criminal record' of former prisoner E827. Once again, listed as a previous conviction, was the conspiracy case in Edinburgh in March 1921, as well as the conviction for fraud in 1924. The information was forwarded – in writing – to the Minister for Defence Peter Hughes, who issued a binding decision on June 22, 1927, which coincidentally was his final day in office. A day later, the departmental secretary wrote the following letter to my father:

A chara

With reference to your application under the Military Service Pensions Act, 1924, I am directed by the Minister for Defence to inform you that in the exercise of his discretion under subsection 2(3) of the Act, he regrets that he is unable to grant you a certificate of military service which would render you eligible for the award of a pension.

The sub-section mentioned is quoted for your information as follows:

(3) The Minister may in his absolute discretion refuse to issue a certificate of military service to any applicant who shall have prior to the making of the report by the Board of Assessors, been sentenced by a court of competent jurisdiction in Saorstat Éireann to suffer imprisonment with or without hard labour for any term exceeding three months or any term of penal servitude.

Beir Beannacht

Runaidhe

What the departmental secretary conveniently didn't include was the 'Minute Sheet', signed by the Minister on June 22, citing the reasons for refusing my father his IRA pension. Obviously, the conviction for fraud was included, but also written in the left-hand margin was the following: *Coyle was sentenced to 5 years at Edinburgh for conspiracy.* A copy of the original Minute Sheet is published on the next page because I know readers will find it hard to believe that the very thing that should have qualified my father for an IRA pension – his conviction and imprisonment in Scotland for arms smuggling – was actually cited in a ministerial order denying him one. It is simply incredible.

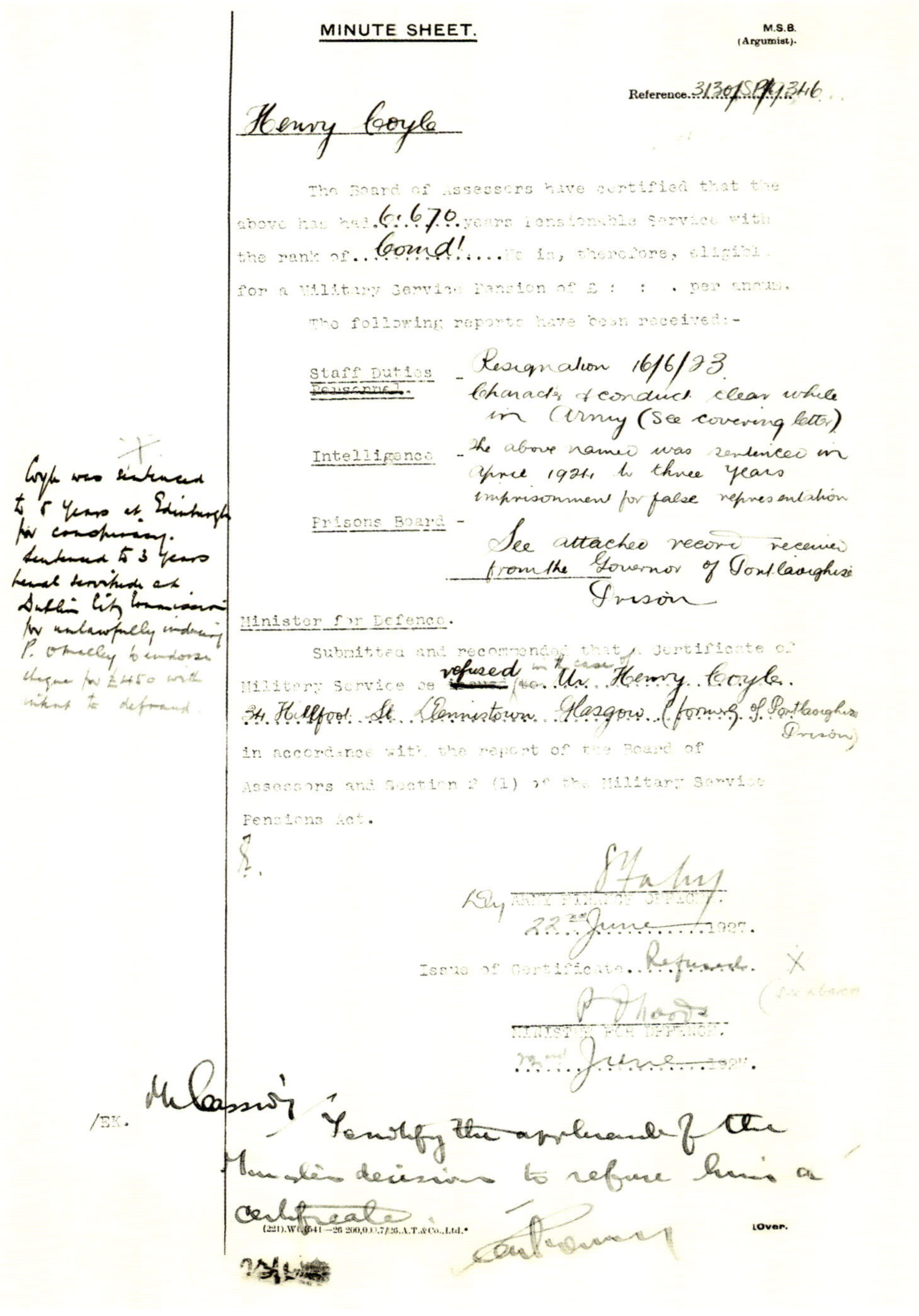

MINUTE SHEET.

M.S.B.
(Argumist).

Reference. 3130/S/9/1346

Henry Coyle

The Board of Assessors have certified that the above has had 6.670 years pensionable service with the rank of ..Comd!.. He is, therefore, eligible for a Military Service Pension of £ : : . per annum.

The following reports have been received:-

Staff Duties — Resignation 16/6/23.
Resigned. — Character & conduct clear while in Army (See covering letter)

Intelligence — The above named was sentenced in April 1924, to three years imprisonment for false representation

Prisons Board — See attached record received from the Governor of Portlaoighise Prison

Minister for Defence.

Submitted and recommended that a Certificate of Military Service be refused in the case of Mr. Henry Coyle. 34. Halfoot St. Clennistown. Glasgow. (formerly of Portlaoighise Prison)

in accordance with the report of the Board of Assessors and Section 2 (1) of the Military Service Pensions Act.

[left margin handwritten note:]
Coyle was sentenced to 5 years at Edinburgh for conspiracy. Sentenced to 3 years penal servitude at Dublin City Commission for unlawfully uttering P. O'Reilly's endorser cheque for £450 with intent to defraud

[signature]
22nd June 1927.

Issue of Certificate. Refused. X

[signature]
23rd June 1927.

/EK.

Mr Cassidy, I entirely approve of the Minister's decision to refuse him a certificate.
[signature]

(221).W.(041—26.200,000.7/26.A.T.&Co.,Ltd.*

[Over.

The original Minute Sheet from the Department of Defence refusing a pension to IRA Commandant Henry Coyle. On the left-hand column (marked with an 'X') is the notation 'Coyle was sentenced to 5 years at Edinburgh for conspiracy'. The Minister for Defence signed this document on June 22, 1927.

I can only imagine the heartbreak my poor father experienced upon reading that awful, awful letter. The sheer injustice of it hurts me today, so how must it have felt for him in June 1927 when the bullet wounds he sustained for the Free State were barely five years' old? This was the final act of betrayal, the insult heaped upon injury.

Ironically, the letter was issued on the day a new minister, Desmond FitzGerald, took office at the Department of Defence. By then, the decision had been made and FitzGerald had no involvement in it, good, bad or indifferent. But many years later, in the 1980s, I made some 'discreet inquiries into the matter' – as my father's old friend and neighbour Paddy Lindsay might have said – and I was told that Garret FitzGerald, the son of Desmond FitzGerald, believed Henry Coyle was 'badly done by'.

Badly done by he certainly was, and the people responsible were his own party colleagues who exercised their 'discretion' not to grant him what was rightfully his, and they even cited his conviction for IRA gun smuggling as one of the reasons for refusing the pension. Little did they think that the very documents they used to do down a good Irishman would fall into the hands of his youngest son almost a century later, and the injustice visited upon Henry Coyle in 1927 would finally be revealed.

CHAPTER 38

'My life has been a tragic one'

I N referring to the injustice my father suffered in the 1920s, I am acutely aware there were numerous victims of the War of Independence and Civil War, and I do not wish to diminish their terrible and traumatic experiences by focusing solely on the case of Henry Coyle. Families lost loved ones, young men and women suffered brutal assaults and many, many people bore the psychological scars of that period for the rest of their days.

The Ginnettys in Co Meath are a tragic example of the heavy price some families paid for Irish freedom. Readers will recall that Matthew Ginnetty (aka Fowler) was captured during the warehouse fires in Liverpool in November 1920 and suffered a savage beating at the hands of the police. No less a man than Neill Kerr testified to the terrible sufferings of the Meath man.

"I was in the dock with him and each time he complained of the beating he got," Kerr recalled.

Like so many young men and women who crossed the Irish Sea, Matthew never forgot his family back home and sent £1 each week from the small salary he earned as a worker in the soap factories of Port Sunlight, near Liverpool. His arrest brought financial hardship on his family in Slane who were very dependent on that weekly remittance, which always arrived without fail. There was nobody in the IRA who was going to give the Ginnettys £1 a week while their son was in prison.

Following his release under the terms of the Anglo-Irish Treaty, Matthew joined the anti-Treaty side and saw action in his native Meath before he was captured in the autumn of 1922. He spent ten months in the Tintown No 2 internment camp at the Curragh and his health gradually declined until eventually he was admitted to the prison hospital, where he died on July 23, 1923. The following is the assessment of a medical doctor, Dr O'Hanlon, who was in the Curragh with Matthew:

34 Hillfoot Street, Dennistoun, Glasgow was the home of the Ferrie family. My father and his first wife Margaret Maxwell Ferrie lived there with Margaret's mother and brother from 1926 to 1933. Today, the large four-storey house is sub-divided into flats.

"Deceased contracted a 'wasting' disease which he attributed to a beating he sustained when captured by Liverpool Police," Dr O'Hanlon wrote in 1933 in support of an application by the Ginnetty family for compensation for their dead son.

Sadly, Matthew's mother died within a year of her son – probably from a broken heart – and the family were in straitened economic circumstances by the time Fianna Fáil came to power in 1932. Matthew's father, Thomas, was eventually granted a gratuity of £112-10s for his dead son, or about two years' remittances based on what Matthew was sending home 13 years earlier. Nobody can tell me that Thomas Ginnetty got sufficient compensation for the life of his brave, precious son.

So when I use the word 'injustice' in reference to my father, I use it with the greatest of respect to the Ginnettys and the many other families who carried their own heavy crosses from that terrible period in Irish history. Those were dark, dark times and there were many casualties of Ireland's fight for freedom. But Henry Coyle didn't suffer his wounds on the battlefield; his injuries were inflicted when the fighting had ended and democracy was taking root. He survived the bullets and the bombs but could not survive the political fighting.

By the early 1930s, my father was still living at 34 Hillfoot Street in Glasgow with Margaret, but tragedy and misfortune continued to stalk them.

My father and Margaret pictured with their young daughter Margaret Mary in the winter of 1932-'33. It would be their only family photograph.

Their first-born child died in infancy and Margaret's health deteriorated to the point where she was a mere shadow of the woman she had been a decade earlier. My father eventually found work on the construction sites of Glasgow and became an accomplished stonemason, while also mastering associated skills like shuttering, plumbing, electrics and roofing.

Margaret became pregnant again in 1932 and gave birth later that year to a healthy baby girl, who they christened Margaret Mary. The proud parents visited a photographic studio a few weeks later to pose for what would be their first family portrait. Sadly, Margaret's declining health is evident from the photograph, which I have published on the opposite page; she is gaunt and looks frail. There is sadness, too, in my father's eyes and the smile seems a little forced; it is as if they both know this is the one and only time they will be pictured together as a family. Indeed, it was. Margaret passed away on February 4, 1933, leaving behind a heartbroken husband and a four-month-old baby.

Aware of her impending death, Margaret made a will in which she bequeathed her entire possessions, amounting to £118, one shilling and 11 pence, to her brother Vincent, who continued to live at 34 Hillfoot Street. Crucially, she also granted sole custody of her baby daughter to Vincent, a decision I found quite difficult to comprehend when I was a younger man. Indeed, for a long time I believed Margaret had made a terrible mistake in trying to separate my father from his new-born daughter. But as I have grown older my view has softened considerably and I can now see the situation from Margaret's perspective. She and my father were deeply in love, but in their 13 years together, there had been as much hardship as happiness, and her sole focus in those final weeks of her life was to secure the future of their infant daughter. Her brother owned the family home – a fine four-storey townhouse – so he could provide the sort of security Margaret wanted for her offspring. If I were in Margaret's shoes today, I would make exactly the same decision.

Margaret's will was read shortly after her death and my father moved out of 34 Hillfoot Street, although Vincent permitted him regular visiting hours with his daughter. Vincent was a good man who was just trying to do his best by his dead sister, and my father was attempting to be the best parent he could possibly be in awfully difficult circumstances. To be honest, I really don't know how my father did not lose his mind completely during this desperate period in his life. He had experienced so many ups and downs by 1933, but to have to bury his wife and surrender custody of his infant daughter within months of each other, well it was just too much for him to bear and so he formed a plan that made sense to his grief-stricken mind. He decided that if anybody could smuggle a child across the Irish Sea it was the man who had smuggled countless consignments of 'war material' for Michael Collins. Soon, he had a daring plan in motion.

One Saturday in the summer of 1933, my father collected Margaret as usual from 34 Hillfoot Street, but instead of going for a stroll in the park, he set off for a hotel where he had already booked a room. Later that night, he left Glasgow with his infant daughter wrapped discreetly in a coat. By the next day, he and Margaret were in Ireland and making their way to Erris.

It was an extraordinary thing to do and even as I write these words I find myself shaking my head, both in amazement and disapproval. Was it a wise decision? Of course not, but it was a decision taken for the purest and noblest of reasons: *love*. My father could not bear to be parted from his daughter, and so he decided to take her with him and start a new life together in Ireland. Initially, he placed Margaret in the care of Mamie, who had married Pat Calvey and was now living in Ballycroy, and then he set about looking for employment.

The Henry Coyle who returned to Ireland in the summer of 1933 was a man haunted by his past. He wanted to build a prosperous and secure future for his daughter but was in no frame of mind to make rational, sensible decisions. He came up with the idea of establishing a construction company and reached some sort of agreement with Ned Moane, a former IRA comrade and a Fianna Fáil TD for Mayo South, to obtain gelignite from the Louisburgh Slate Company. He then went to Dublin where he took lodgings at Shelmartin Avenue and began to search for work. The problem was that he didn't have a penny to his name and was making commitments he could not possibly honour unless he obtained work very soon. Instead, he got arrested.

On October 26, 1933, the *Evening Herald* reported that former TD Henry Coyle was in the prison hospital at Mountjoy where he was being treated for an unspecified illness. By early November, my father had been charged with possessing 'three detonators and a package of gelignite, under such circumstances as to give rise to a reasonable suspicion that he had not them for any lawful purpose'. He was further charged with attempting to obtain building materials 'under false pretences' and was remanded in custody to appear before Dublin Circuit Criminal Court early in the New Year.

On January 22, 1934, my father found himself back in Green Street Courthouse to face charges of false pretences. The prosecution's case was that he had made a series of financial commitments he could not keep by issuing three worthless cheques to the total value of about £200. My father, who defended himself, maintained that he could not be guilty of fraud because nobody had ended up out of pocket as a result of the transactions. For example, he offered to purchase slates to the value of £107-5s, but when the cheque

EX-DEPUTY'S DRAMATIC STORY

FREED ON FALSE PRETENCES CHARGE

PART IN I.R.A. ACTIVITIES IN ENGLAND: PURCHASE OF ARMS

A REMARKABLE speech was made yesterday from the dock of Green Street Courthouse, Dublin, by Henry Coyle, ex-T.D. for North Mayo, in his defence against charges of false pretences. The charges were: having obtained a motor van from J. McGuirk, 87a St. Ignatius Road, Dublin, by means of a worthless cheque for £87 10s.; having attempted to obtain slates to the value of £107 5s. from Messrs. McFerran and Gilford, Tara Street, by the pretence that he was a

when the danger was over, there were lots only too anxious to take the place of the boys from the bogs. It happened that he took personal responsibility for two cheques of £100 or £500. He did it to oblige another person. Whilst he was away in Glasgow arranging about agencies for cement and tyres, etc., there was a party meeting which he could not attend. Something cropped up there about the cheques and he was condemned in his absence, although there were a few who protested that men often had their bank accounts overdrawn. It was alleged that he had absconded to Glasgow. He was the youngest member of the Dáil at the time, being known as the " baby of the House." He sent £100 from Glasgow and returned to Dublin. Immediately he was called on to resign from the party, and when he asked for a chance to defend himself he was arrested. He was tried and, although all the money was there to be paid back, was sentenced to three years' penal servitude and he did every day of that although he had done nothing for which he should have been blamed.

His young wife's heart was broken and she went to an early grave. There he was—a boy, who, in 1919 and 1920, had been entrusted with thousands of pounds by the chiefs of the finest army ...ld—a boy wh... ...een pre... the fir...

CURIOUS ...
old Milo...

failed to clear, the slates were not delivered. Similarly, a van he purchased with an IOU was returned once it became apparent there was no money in his bank account. In fact, he didn't even have a bank account in Ireland.

The case was heard before Judge Cahir Davitt, son of Land League founder Michael Davitt, who withdrew one of the charges before putting the other three matters to the jury for decision. At this point, my father rose to his feet and addressed the members of the jury. His lengthy and extraordinary speech made headlines in all of the national newspapers the next day, including the *Irish Press*, which reported it as follows:

Addressing the jury, Coyle denied having made any false pretence. There was a lot at the back of the case which could not be mentioned by the prosecution but which he would mention. That was his 54th appearance in a dock, many of the charges being what to many would appear to be honourable.

His life had been a tragic one and he could trace much of the tragedy to the fact that at one time he had been prominently identified with Irish public life and had the misfortune to be elected to the Dáil.

He was one of a family of nine brought up on a small farm at Erris, on the shores of the Atlantic. His father was a small farmer, who used to go to England for harvesting and whom he occasionally accompanied after he reached 14.

His ancestors were some of the people who had been ordered 'to hell or to Connacht' and had elected to go to Connacht as they might have met Cromwell in the other place.

He was last harvesting in England himself in 1916 and after that got into public life. In 1919, he was sentenced by the R.M. at Belmullet at a midnight court for illegal assembly. That magistrate was afterwards shot whilst he (Coyle) was in jail.

EX-T.D. CHARGED.

Several Counts In Dublin Trial.

POLITICS & MISFORTUNE

Dublin, Monday.

Before Judge Davitt and a jury to-day in Dublin Circuit Criminal Court, Henry Coyle pleaded not guilty to a number of counts charging him—(1) With having in October last being in possession of two detonators and a stick of gelignite, in Dublin, with intent to cause serious damage to property; (2) with having at 87a, Ignatius Road, Dublin, obtained a motor James McGuirk

Mayo Man's "Speech From The Dock."

REMARKABLE STATEMENT BY EX-T.D. IN DUBLIN COURT.

"TROUBLE" RECORD REVEALED TO JURY.

54th TIME TO APPEAR IN DOCK.

A remarkable speech was made on Monday from the dock of Green Street Court-house, Dublin, by Henry Coyle, ex-T.D. for North Mayo, in his defence against charges of false pretences.

My father made headlines again in January 1934 when he was tried and acquitted on charges of false pretences. During the course of his defence, he made another remarkable speech from the dock.

On his release from Sligo in 1919, he went to Glasgow where, with associates, he started to collect arms for the IRA and IRB. At one time he was in complete charge of all purchases and had the handling of thousands of pounds. The smallest sum he ever got at a time was £1,000.

Very often he had thousands paid before he got the regular remittance as there were people who gave him hundreds of pounds, which he always devoted to the cause and repaid on getting money from Dublin. On December 4, 1920, he was arrested outside Stirling with half a ton of gelignite, three thousand detonators (sic), fuses, rifles and revolvers.

The previous Saturday night there had been a series of fires in Liverpool. That was the time the Black and Tans were burning villages in Ireland and it had been decided that the only way in which the English people could be made realise what was being done was to give them a taste of the same thing at home.

He was charged with being connected with the Liverpool burnings, of which there were some 24 (sic). Five other men and two girls – the bravest girls that ever went across – were also charged.

On March 19, 1921, he was sentenced to five years' penal servitude because he admitted he was a soldier of the Irish Republic and took the most of the blame in order to make things easier for others.

He was released from Peterhead Prison after the Treaty – on February 13, 1922. He thought at the time it was a very happy day but he had often since regretted that he had not got twenty years. But Michael Collins persuaded him to enter public life.

He was married in Glasgow in the uniform of an officer of the IRA and came to Ireland. He was in the army here as a staff officer. He was persuaded by the people of North Mayo to go forward for the Dáil and was elected in 1923. He had spent a good deal of money of his own in Glasgow for military purposes and money was due him from headquarters, including £100 for a motorcycle which was confiscated on him.

After his election to the Dáil, he found there was a class of people who had always opposed the movement for Irish independence and who considered themselves leading lights of Irish society – people who did not like to see themselves represented by the sons of small farmers from the bogs of Erris. The boys from the bogs were all right when there was any danger, but when the danger was over, there were lots only too anxious to take the place of the boys from the bogs.

It happened that he took personal responsibility for two cheques of £400 or £500. He did it to oblige another person. Whilst he was away in Glasgow arranging about agencies for cement and tyres, etc., there was a party meeting which he could not attend. Something cropped up there about the cheques and he was condemned in his absence, although there were a few who protested that men often had their bank accounts overdrawn. It was alleged that he had absconded to Glasgow. He was the youngest member of the Dáil at the time, being known as the 'Baby of the House'. He sent £100 from Glasgow and returned to Dublin. Immediately he was called on to resign from the party, and when he asked for a chance to defend himself, he was arrested. He was tried and, although all the money was there to be paid back, was sentenced to three years' penal servitude and he did every day of that although he had done nothing for which he should have been blamed.

His young wife's heart was broken and she went to an early grave. There he was – a boy, who, in 1919 and 1920, had been entrusted with thousands of pounds by the chiefs of the finest army in the world – a boy who had been prepared to face the firing squad or step on the trapdoor of the gallows for his country; a soldier of the Irish Republic, raised to the dignity of the Dáil – and yet, after all that, he was condemned on a charge connected with a mere £440.

Could they imagine it possible that, on his record, he would have been guilty of anything like what had been alleged? He had resigned from the army and sacrificed lump sum and pension, such as had been paid to others in like position. He did not think any able-bodied man should get a pension. And now, because he was convicted in 1924, he was arrested on the present charges.

He had got an opportunity of seeing his record in Mountjoy Jail and there he saw set out as part of a criminal career the five years' sentence for collecting arms to be used in the fight for national independence. Yes, 'criminal' was the word now applied to it. After his release from Portlaoighise he faded from the picture here and went into the building trade in Glasgow.

When my father finally resumed his seat, Judge Davitt said he had 'tried to stop the prisoner prejudicing his own case by going into irrelevant matters'.

"The only comment I will make is that if the prisoner had been wrongfully convicted before on a charge dealing with a cheque, one would expect him not to take any risks afterwards by issuing cheques unless he had money in the bank to meet them."

It was an entirely rational appraisal from Judge Davitt, but Henry Coyle was not a rational man in 1933. These incidents occurred only weeks after he had fled Scotland with an eight-month-old baby in his arms. He couldn't possibly have been thinking straight and his speech to the jury bore all the hallmarks of a man tortured by his tragic past. Today, he would surely be diagnosed with post-traumatic stress disorder, but in 1934 men who survived wars were expected to pick up the pieces of their old lives as if nothing had happened. Henry Coyle hadn't just survived a war; he had also served a lengthy prison sentence for fraud and endured the personal trauma of losing his wife. Indeed, my father was so irrational in January 1934 that he actually prejudiced his own case by informing a jury he had served a prison term just years earlier for a similar offence to the one now before the court. It seemed inevitable the jury would find him guilty, even though none of the alleged offences resulted in the loss of money or property.

The case had gone on all day and dusk was tightening its grip outside Green Street Courthouse when the jury returned with its verdict.

"Do you find the defendant guilty or not guilty? Judge Davitt asked the foreman.

"*Not guilty,*" came the reply.

I can only imagine the relief my father felt in the dock. He had made some unwise decisions in the summer of 1933, but a jury of his peers, of fellow Irishmen and women, had stated unequivocally that Henry Coyle was no fraudster. It was the first break he received in a long, long time.

CHAPTER 39

'I handled explosives when few could handle them'

MOST readers will assume that my father regained his freedom following his acquittal, but nothing was simple in the life of Henry Coyle in the early 1930s. Instead, he was remanded in custody to face a second trial in the Circuit Criminal Court in Dublin, this time in relation to the illegal possession of gelignite with the intent to cause damage.

This was an extraordinary charge because the court had already heard ample evidence of my father's attempts to establish a construction firm upon his arrival in Dublin. Builders in the 1930s often had gelignite in their possession – albeit under licence – and the prosecution was well aware of Henry Coyle's involvement in the building trade in Glasgow. Why then would they allege he had the explosives for some sinister purpose when it was quite obvious his only 'crime' had been to neglect to take out a licence for the single stick of gelignite and three detonators found in his possession?

If the jury had been allowed to hear the two cases together they would have acquitted him on both charges, but instead a new trial was set for February 6. By now, my father had spent 16 weeks in custody and the mental strain must have been immense, especially as he had not seen his infant daughter in all of that time. He had successfully defended himself in the first trial but now had to do it all again in front of a judge and jury, and in the full glare of the print media who reported extensively on the first trial. I simply do not know how he survived those early months of 1934.

This was a man still mourning his young wife; he had bills to pay at home in Mayo and knew a conviction in either case would result in a lengthy jail term. I cannot think of any greater mental pressure and he must have had phenomenal resilience to keep going and not buckle under the enormous strain of successive criminal prosecutions. The trial for possessing gelignite commenced two days after the first anniversary of Margaret's untimely passing, and what a terrible 12 months it had been for my father.

The second trial proved to be much ado about nothing. A number of detectives gave evidence of seizing the stick of gelignite and three detonators in the lodging house where my father resided at Shelmartin Road in Dublin in the summer of 1933. A detective officer said he ascertained from the Glasgow police that Henry Coyle was 'interested in building there'.

In his evidence, my father admitted he did not have a licence for the explosives but believed he was 'not sinning very much against society' as the gelignite was being used for 'national purposes', i.e. the building of houses. He told Judge Cahir Davitt that he obtained the gelignite from a slate quarry in Louisburgh 'on the invitation of a Mayo deputy in the Dáil', presumably Ned Moane.

My father then told the court that in 1919 and 1920 he 'handled more explosives for the IRA and IRB than any man in Ireland' and was an expert in the use of gelignite.

"I could blow up the Rock of Gibraltar, the fortifications at the Dardanelles or the Hill of Howth if I was given my own time for the job," he dramatically declared.

It was quite some statement and I can only imagine what the jury thought! But my father was far from finished.

"I handled explosives when few could handle them, and without a permit. And I can get tons of gelignite, with or without a permit."

My father then went on to tell the jury that he would have been able to establish a building and quarrying firm by now had he not spent the past 16 weeks in custody. If he had gone to the Minister for Justice P.J. Ruttledge and told him that he had the explosives for quarrying purposes, he knew the Minister would shake him by the hand and say, "I wish I had a few more like you." My father concluded his memorable evidence by telling the jury he could do more than most men to 'solve the housing problem' in Ireland if he was given half a chance.

The entire prosecution case was based on a presumption that the gelignite was to be used to blow up safes in Dublin (maybe even the safe at the Rotunda branch of the National Bank!), but there was not a scintilla of evidence produced to support these outrageous claims and the jury quickly found my father not guilty. Judge Davitt discharged him from custody but ordered the Gardaí to retain the gelignite until the appropriate licence was obtained.

I doubt there are too many people in the history of the Irish legal system who have defended themselves in two separate criminal trials and been acquitted in both. Perhaps Henry Coyle should have become a lawyer – I think he would have made a very fine one.

But both prosecutions against my father were wholly unnecessary, especially when one considers his personal circumstances in the summer of 1933. This was a man blinded by grief who had suffered enormously in the preceding months and years. What he needed was a little bit of sympathy and understanding on his return to Ireland, instead of the heavy hand of the law. Did he make mistakes at that time? Perhaps he did, but two separate juries found in his favour and I think that speaks louder than any prosecution allegations. Indeed, his life might have been very different had he sought a jury trial in 1924 in relation to the O'Malley Cheque.

The two trials in early 1934 generated plenty of headlines in the national press and it is easy to see why. My father possessed a unique and colourful turn of phrase, and his evidence was always likely to capture the attention of the court reporters. I have shown my father's remarkable speeches to several people over the last few years and they have invariably commented: 'Well, I know now where you get it from!'

There are certainly a few memorable quotes from my father that I would love to claim as my own, not least his comment about wanting to avoid Cromwell in hell, but the truth is I get very sad when I read those speeches from 1934 because I know they were delivered at a time when my father's fortunes had reached rock bottom. Everything he worked for – both in his personal and professional life – had gone up in smoke and he found himself in just about the bleakest place of all: a prison cell in Mountjoy awaiting serious criminal charges. I have some notes my father wrote, possibly in the mid-1930s, and they make for very poignant reading.

"There are two letters that separate the word 'justice' from 'injustice'," he wrote, "and I feel those two letters have been added in all of the court proceedings and charges brought against me in Ireland. Do I feel let down, confused and betrayed by a country I helped to establish? Yes, I do. I could add I was treated more fairly in the courts of the colonial power that I worked so hard to break away from.

"But I don't bear ill-will or malice towards anyone involved in what has happened to me and I will still offer them the hand of friendship. I give them forgiveness because I know that at some time in the future I will need forgiveness too, and hopefully in time I will learn to forget this very sad and troubling episode in my life. And maybe, just maybe, a day will come when the people of Ireland will remember me for the good I have done."

During the first trial, my father told the jury that his life had been 'a tragic one', and that's certainly how it must have felt for him in 1934. His acquittal

By the mid-1930s, my father was back where it all started in the family home in Dooyork. His life, which he described at that time as 'tragic', had come full circle.

afforded little cause for celebration because he now had to pick up the pieces of his life all over again. He was approaching 40, a widower with a young daughter to care for and a pension he couldn't even claim. Work had been hard to come by in Erris when he was a boy and nothing much had changed in the intervening period. Indeed, by the end of 1934, my father found himself back where he started in life, living with his parents in Dooyork and struggling to make ends meet. Mamie continued to care for Margaret at her home in Tallagh, Ballycroy and my father spent a lot of time there, doing various construction jobs and helping out in whatever way he could.

He was still mourning the loss of his wife and that is very evident from a poem he wrote for his daughter in 1935 shortly before she turned three. It was his very special way of telling little Margaret that her mother was with 'God's angels'.

I have published the poem at the end of this chapter and I think it is an incredible piece of heartfelt writing, and I have never managed to read through it without shedding a tear. In fact, I think there are bereavement counsellors who would struggle to find a gentler or more sensitive way to explain to a young child about the tragic loss of their mother. In 1969, my father wrote a letter to Margaret in which he referenced the poem:

"I wrote a lot of things in my time," he said, "but I never wrote, nor will I ever write again, anything that I'll value more."

The reason the poem makes me so emotional is because it perfectly encapsulates the Henry Coyle I knew, the kind, caring and gentle father who rarely raised his voice in anger, let alone raised his hand. I don't recognise the firebrand republican who drove across England in a car loaded with gelignite or stood up in an Edinburgh courtroom and defiantly declared his undying allegiance to an independent Ireland. That's not the man I knew at all; in fact, that man is a complete stranger to me, and if someone presented me with all of the evidence I have gathered during the course of this project, I would find it difficult to believe they were talking about Henry Coyle, my father. I'd tell them there must be some sort of mistake; that the quiet, peaceful man I knew would not be capable of such things.

Working on this book has been a revelation because it has made me realise that people can change – and change dramatically – over the course of their lifetime. My father was certainly a very different man when I knew him compared to the daring, fearless freedom fighter of his younger years. In fact, I would go so far as to say that the two characters are chalk and cheese, and I think older people in Erris who can recall my father will agree with me on that and will be just as surprised at the contents of this book as I was when I first came across the various newspaper archives and court files.

The key factor in the transformation of my father was undoubtedly Molly Ginty, my wonderful mother, who brought stability and normality into his life at a time when he needed it most. If Henry Coyle is the hero of my story, then Molly Ginty is most definitely the heroine. The day she met Henry Coyle was the beginning of a bright new chapter for a man who, up to then, believed his life would be defined by tragedy, betrayal and heartache.

The Picture On The Wall

I saw my Daddy looking at the picture on the wall
'Twas one among a number but the loveliest of
them all.
'Twas the picture of a lady, how beautiful was she,
With a pleasant smile upon her face and I thought
she smiled at me.

Then I looked into my Daddy's eyes and they
were filled with tears,
That set me wondering very much and filled my
heart with fears.
Because I love my Daddy so and, oh, how he
loves me,
The big tears flowing from his eyes I could not
bear to see.

I said 'My dear Daddy, why do you look so sad?
To know that lovely lady should only make
you glad'.
Then he took me in his arms and sat me on his
knee, saying
'That lady is your Mammy and God's own gift to
me.
It's very hard to tell you dear and disappoint you so,
But I cannot hide the truth from you, it's better
that you know.'

'But haven't I my Mammy, Daddy dear,' said I.
'And if you say she is not my Mammy, you'll only
make me cry
To have another Mammy I'm sure that cannot be
For no-one has two mammies and there is only one for me.
I know she loves me dearly and I love her so well.
And what my Mammy means to me there's no one else can tell.'

Then as if to hide from me, my Daddy stooped his head.
And said, 'My darling little pet, your Mammy dear is dead.
God's angels came and took her when you were very small.
And that's her lovely picture now, that's hanging on the wall.

'Eternal rest and happiness to her Our Lord will grant.
The one you call your Mammy now is just your only aunt.
She took you when your Mammy died and nursed you tenderly,
Just as your Mammy would have done had she been spared to thee.'

Now I'm sure you all feel sorry for a little girl like me
To know I've lost my Mammy and my age is less than three.
But I have my own dear auntie and I will give her all my love
And I know my Mammy will send down her blessings
From her bright home up above.

**- written by Henry Coyle for his
infant daughter Margaret in 1935**

CHAPTER 40

'You all certainly played a heroic part for Ireland'

IF anyone ever dared to wonder aloud why the young Molly Ginty married a man 21 years her senior, they were quickly knocked back with a witty riposte:

"'Tis better to be an old man's fancy than a young man's slave," my mother would cheerfully declare.

Molly was certainly no man's slave, young or old. She was a fiercely independent woman with a sharp intellect and a positive, can-do attitude when it came to work and life in general. Her worldly wisdom far outweighed the simple national school education she received in her native Ballycroy and I firmly believe she could have headed up some of the biggest companies in the world had she grown up in a different era. Her easygoing, hardworking and jovial manner gave us a great start in life, while her unflinching determination to overcome any obstacle contributed enormously to the person I am today.

There might have been a vast age difference between my parents but they made a great team and the big decisions always seemed to be a joint enterprise. Indeed, as children, we could not have asked for better parents. They helped their six boys and three girls in every possible way and gave us a great understanding of life by offering commonsense advice when it was needed, as well as being there in any moment of crisis.

I often tell people we were raised by degrees, not with degrees, and that is certainly true. My parents may not have had much formal education but there was no problem they couldn't solve, and every decision was rooted in pragmatism and compassion, two of the many characteristics they shared.

Although from different generations, they had a lot in common and it was obvious they were still as much in love in the mid-1960s as they had been 30 years earlier when they first set eyes on each other in Ballycroy where my father was building an extension to his sister's little shop. My mother wasn't even 21 then and I believe her parents did not approve of her marriage to a man who, in today's parlance, came with a lot of baggage. He was a widower in his early 40s with no farm or house to his name, so I can easily see why my maternal grandparents had reservations, but Molly was not to be dissuaded.

"If I don't marry him on land, I'll marry him at sea!" she told my Aunt Mamie.

It was a defiant statement worthy of Henry Coyle himself, so it is easy to see why my father fell for this feisty young Ballycroy woman. He had certainly met his match!

I won't say my father was a broken man when he met Molly – because he was too courageous and strong-willed

My mother Molly Coyle, nee Ginty, was born and raised in Dooriel, Ballycroy.

to ever be defeated by the unkind twists of fate visited upon him – but he was certainly in a dark and sad place. Molly gave him a new lease of life, a second chance in life, and he never looked back from the day he met her. The past became the past and that's where it stayed.

My parents were married in the Holy Family Church in Ballycroy on Sunday, February 7, 1937, with parish priest Fr Anthony Timlin performing the ceremony. The witnesses were John Ginty and Nora Doran. In the marriage certificate, my father gave his address as Tallagh, Ballycroy, but that was Mamie's address and I am not sure if they stayed there long.

It was a tough time for a newly-wed couple to be starting out, especially if they had neither land nor a house. Looking through the pages of the *Western People* for that first week of February 1937 is like *déjà vu*: not much had changed in the 30 years since my father was a boy growing up in Dooyork. Paid work was as hard to come by in Mayo when my father was 40 as it had been when he set off for Scotland at the age of 14.

One of the headlines in the *Western* on February 6, 1937, concerned some workers on a relief scheme in Swinford who were being paid two shillings for every ton of stone they broke. The workers went on strike in an attempt to get a wage increase but were told that if they didn't return to work immediately they'd be fired and disbarred from claiming any form of unemployment assistance. Not surprisingly, they went back to breaking stones at two shillings per ton.

There was also a flu epidemic sweeping through Mayo that had claimed several lives, while debate was raging in the Dáil about the future of the Westport to Achill railway line. When my father was a TD some 14 years earlier, all the talk had been about extending the rail service to Blacksod, but by the end of 1937, Achill had lost its rail connection as de Valera's Fianna Fáil government struggled to balance the books amid a disastrous trade war with England.

My father continued to work in construction but it cannot have been easy for him to find jobs in Erris, especially work that guaranteed a reasonable income. He was now starting out in life again and would have wanted to do the very best for his young wife, as well as the family they hoped to have together. The unclaimed pension of £100 per annum must have played on his mind constantly and he decided to do something about it in the winter of 1937.

Three years earlier, Fianna Fáil had introduced a new Military Service Pensions Act to cater for veterans of the War of Independence and Civil War

The marriage record for my parents, Molly Ginty and Henry Coyle, who were married in Ballycroy on February 7, 1937.

who had not qualified under the 1924 Act. The new act was essentially a method by which Fianna Fáil could look after its own anti-Treaty IRA members who had not applied for a pension from the Cumann na nGaedheal government.

My father's case was a curious one because he had been recommended for a pension but then turned down at ministerial level. With Civil War wounds still raw, it seemed highly unlikely that a Fianna Fáil government would grant a pension to a former National Army officer, but my father felt it was worth a shot. He had maintained good relationships with many on the anti-Treaty side, including Mayo TDs like Ned Moane, P.J. Ruttledge and Michael Kilroy, even if he still supported Cumann na nGaedheal, or Fine Gael as it became in 1933.

On December 11, 1937, my father submitted a fresh application to the Army Pensions Board, recounting once again his IRA activities from 1917 to 1923. Inevitably, he repeated many of the details contained in the earlier application, but also added some new information, including a reference to being 'badly beaten' following his arrest in Scotland on December 4, 1920, and his speech from the dock in Edinburgh. He also provided an interesting insight into his Civil War record:

Ballycroy in the Registrar's District of _Ballycroy_ in the County of _Mayo_

or Profession. (6)	Residence at the Time of Marriage (7)	Father's Name and Surname. (8)	Rank or Profession of Father (9)
lding tractor	Tallagh	Pat Coyle	Farmer
—	Dooriel	Michael Ginty	"

according to the Rites and Ceremonies of the Roman Catholic Church by me,

A. J. Timlin P.P.

in the Presence of us, John Ginty / Nora Doran

"I saved the lives of a number of men in the Republican forces while serving [in the National Army]. The names of some of these I can furnish if proof is required."

By now, my father had been denied ten years of pension payments, at a rate of £100 per annum, and he felt deeply let down by the continuing fallout from his 1924 conviction. The O'Malley Cheque, valued at £450, had cost him two years of his liberty, his career as a TD and about £1,000 in pension payments.

Unfortunately, Henry Coyle had not yet finished paying for his 'criminal' past. After a wait of over two years, his application for a pension was deemed invalid on the grounds that the Board had already recommended him for a pension under the 1924 Act and, therefore, could not now approve a new application under the 1934 Act. It was the ultimate case of Catch-22.

There is no correspondence in the file to suggest my father resisted the decision; he probably knew there was no point. Instead, he got on with living the best life he could. In 1938, he and Molly were blessed with the birth of their first child, a son whom they named Henry Joe. They may not have had much money, and the rented accommodation was no better than the cow-house my father was reared in almost half a century earlier, but Henry and Molly set about creating the most wonderful, loving home.

Times were tough, yet my father was determined to make a success of this unexpected second chance in life; and with the indomitable Molly by his side, Henry Coyle knew he could not fail.

––––––––––

My father was actually one of the more fortunate Scottish Volunteers. Many of his IRA colleagues never got a chance to rebuild their lives. Mick Burke, who had been involved in the IRB in Motherwell as far back as 1907, got a paltry annual pension of £13-12s-11d in recognition of his lifetime's devotion to Irish independence.

Having lost a good job as a crane operator in Motherwell due to his IRA activities, Burke eventually found work in Dublin as a poorly-paid boilerman in the National Gallery of Ireland, but he was never able to bring his young daughter across from Scotland. Ill health forced him to retire in 1934 at the age of 57 and he went to live with his sister in his native Keady in south Armagh.

Mick Burke died in the workhouse in Armagh City on February 27, 1940. Yes, that is correct: *he died in the workhouse.* Twenty years earlier, Mick's home had been the headquarters for the IRA in Motherwell. Joe Vize stayed there, so too did my father, Charlie Strickland, Joe Furlong and numerous other IRA

56464

M.S.P./34/1.

Military Service Pensions Act, 1934.

APPLICATION TO THE MINISTER FOR DEFENCE FOR A SERVICE CERTIFICATE.

This form must be filled in by every person who seeks a Service Certificate, and must be signed by him, and his signature witnessed. The completed form must reach the Minister for Defence on or before the 31st December, 1936. In the event of an applicant being unable to write, he should affix his mark, such act being witnessed.

NAME (to be written in block capitals). .... COYLE .... HENRY ....
SURNAME.   CHRISTIAN NAMES.

PRESENT ADDRESS ... DOOYORK. GEESALA. BALLINA. CO. MAYO ....
(to be written in block capitals).

NOTE.—Before answering the questions below, the applicant is requested to note that:

(a) This form is divided into three parts. Part I. is to be completed where the applicant had, in addition to the required pre-Truce Service, Service in the Forces in the period commencing the 1st July, 1922. Part II. is to be completed where the applicant's qualifying service in the Forces was pre-Truce only. Only one of those two parts is to be completed by any one applicant. Part III. is of general application and should be completed by all applicants.

(b) Before completing particulars as to rank the applicant should read carefully the First Schedule to the Act and also the definitions of the expressions

In December 1937, my father applied once again for an IRA pension.

arms smugglers. Mick and his wife never turned any Irish republican away from their door and many of the weapons that made it through to Ireland came via Mick. When the police in Motherwell quizzed him after the Bothwell incident and asked if he was a Sinn Féiner, Burke defiantly replied: *Yes, and one of the best.*

It is hard to believe then that one of our best republicans, a man who sacrificed so much for the cause of Irish independence should spend his dying days receiving charity from the colonial power he spent his whole adult life trying to overthrow. We should all be ashamed that this great Irishman died in a workhouse; he deserved so much better from the independent Ireland he helped to create.

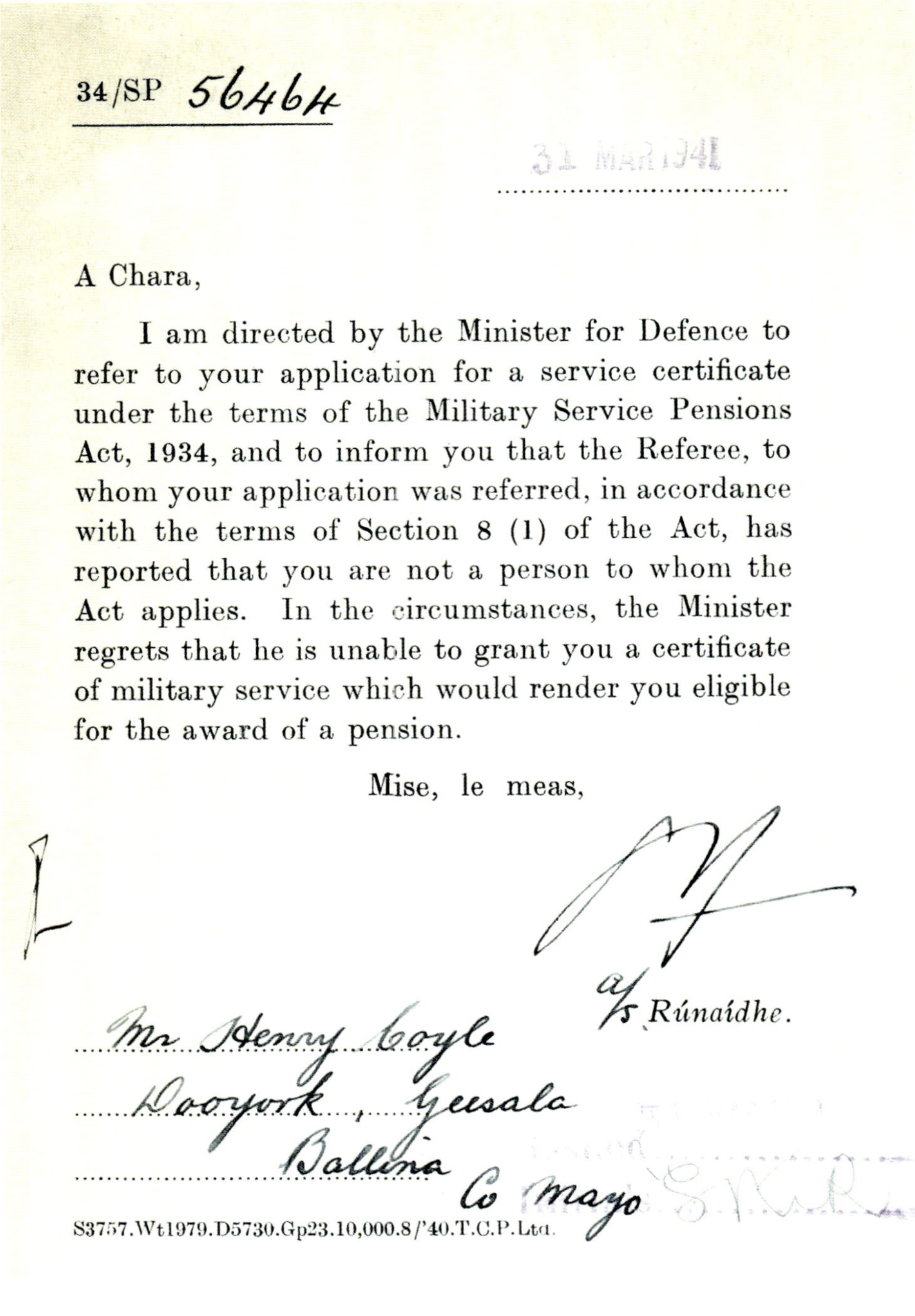

34/SP *56464*

31 MAR 1941

A Chara,

I am directed by the Minister for Defence to refer to your application for a service certificate under the terms of the Military Service Pensions Act, 1934, and to inform you that the Referee, to whom your application was referred, in accordance with the terms of Section 8 (1) of the Act, has reported that you are not a person to whom the Act applies. In the circumstances, the Minister regrets that he is unable to grant you a certificate of military service which would render you eligible for the award of a pension.

Mise, le meas,

a/s Rúnaidhe.

Mr Henry Coyle
Dooyork, Geesala
Ballina
Co Mayo

S3757.Wt1979.D5730.Gp23.10,000.8/'40.T.C.P.Ltd.

The letter from March 1941 refusing my father an IRA pension under the 1934 Act. It was the second time his application was refused despite an undisputed record of active service during the War of Independence and Civil War.

By the late 1930s, many of the Scottish Volunteers were still trying to persuade the Army Pensions Board to approve their applications. Lena McDonald, who had taken the anti-Treaty side, applied for a pension and travelled to Dublin in 1938 to be interviewed at length about her activities from 1916 to 1923. However, she was still waiting for a decision in February 1940 when the rebel priest Fr John Fahy, now serving in Ballinakill, near Loughrea, Co Galway, wrote a letter of protest to the Board.

"Pensions should be awarded, not according to the applicant's name on the waiting list but according to the applicant's record during the fight for independence," Fr Fahy stated. "Owing to Miss McDonald's work for Ireland in those days, her family lost much financially, had to close their business stores, and are still harassed and suspected by Scotland Yard. Owing to their work for Ireland, Miss McDonald and her mother are in this country today without a home or means of living. In bare justice, apart from common decency, Miss McDonald's application for a pension ought to be decided at once."

Fr Fahy allowed Lena and her mother to stay at his home until the pension application was processed, but she was still waiting for an answer in April when she made a personal appeal to An Taoiseach Éamon de Valera:

If possible would you do something about it as my mother and I have been in this country since September 1939 and find we cannot go on any longer as the money we had has gone and even with the sale of our furniture that money has gone too, and we now find ourselves without money, without a job and no home as Father Fahy could not let us remain forever.

My father's old friend, Charlie Strickland, who was now working as a bus driver, came to Lena's rescue and she and her mother stayed at his home in Inchicore during the summer of 1940. She was finally approved for a pension in January 1941, with the rate set at a mere £11-14s-9d per annum. It wasn't even a pound a month, so it is little wonder that Lena set sail for America in the mid-1940s. Ireland had shown scant appreciation for this brave woman's role in the fight for freedom.

The women activists seemed to get a particularly bad deal from the Free State. Jean Gillespie, the young woman who went on trial with my father in Edinburgh, struggled to get a pension and was eventually granted a paltry £14-14s-5d per annum. Kate Lee, who hid gelignite in her coalbunker and provided lodgings to my father in 1919-'20, returned to Sligo with her family and tried to start a new life. She applied for a pension under the 1934 Act but was told she did not qualify, prompting her to appeal the decision of the Board.

"If I could trace Henry Peter Coyle's address he could vouch for what I am stating," she wrote. "On numerous occasions I had up to hundreds of pounds [of explosives] in my possession which I held in safekeeping until it was forwarded to Dublin.

"I may also mention here that my husband and son got dismissed from their good positions [in Parkhead Forge] owing to my activities with the movement in 1921, and I held onto my home until 1922 when, owing to poor circumstances and been boycotted by my neighbours, who knew I was a Sinn Féiner, I had to leave Glasgow with my family and return to Sligo a very poor woman."

Accompanying Kate's application was the charge sheet from my father's trial in Edinburgh, and she had the following poignant message for the Board:

I would like very much that this document be returned to me as I treasure it more than any pension. Trusting again gentlemen, as a woman who did her utmost in a foreign land for the cause of freedom, you will see your way to grant me some restitution for all I did in the past.

Those lines from Kate Lee sum up the integrity and sincerity of the Scottish Volunteers. They weren't motivated by financial gain or self-interest; they did what they did for the love of Ireland, and it is terribly sad that so many of them were treated so poorly once independence had been secured. Kate Lee never got a pension, but I have reproduced in the Appendices the document she treasured so much; it is my way of paying tribute to a great Irish woman.

Neill Kerr died in June 1936 and his funeral made headlines in the Irish newspapers with Éamon de Valera and W.T. Cosgrave in attendance, along with many members of the old IRA and IRB. It was a fitting send-off for a great Irish patriot.

Shortly afterwards, Elizabeth Kerr applied for a pension under the 1934 Act because she had no proper source of income now that her husband was dead. The Kerrs were still paying rent to the State for the Coastguard cottage in Ringsend and inevitably Elizabeth fell behind in her payments and was eventually forced to take up a new position as live-in caretaker of the City Gate Lodge in the Phoenix Park. The Irish State pursued Elizabeth for the outstanding rent of £42 on the Coastguard property and docked it from her salary each week for over a year until the debt stood at £28.

When Elizabeth applied for an IRA pension, numerous veterans of the independence struggle, including Joe Vize, Charlie Strickland, Seamus Robinson, Michael O'Leary and Stephen Lanigan, came forward to corroborate her outstanding record of service from 1916 onwards. Jeremiah Hurley, who was one of the ship workers most involved in arms smuggling, had this to say about Elizabeth:

"In Neill's absence, which was often, she took complete charge of everything entrusted to her, and never a hitch in the confidence and reliance placed on her."

Incredibly, Elizabeth Kerr received a measly pension of £10 per annum (yes, ten pounds!) backdated to 1934; and to add insult to injury, the State deducted £28 for the outstanding rent on the Ringsend cottage. It's hard to comprehend how such decisions were made. Éamon de Valera enjoyed the hospitality of the Kerrs, as did so many others in the Republican movement, and I am absolutely certain that Elizabeth never got paid for all the meals she served to the many Volunteers who called to 6 Florida Street in Bootle during the War of Independence. Or the many meals she brought into Walton Prison in 1920-'21 or Knutsford Jail in 1916. Not only was that generosity not reciprocated by the Free State, she was being hounded for a few pounds in unpaid rent long after her husband had died.

Meanwhile in faraway Erris, Henry Coyle was raising a young family in abject poverty, his annual pension of £100 withheld because of a prison term dating back more than a decade.

"You all certainly played a heroic part for Ireland in those dark days," Fr John Fahy had told Jean Gillespie when she wrote to him seeking a reference for her pension application.

Indeed they had played a heroic part, but the Scottish and English Volunteers got little appreciation for their bravery and sacrifice, and in my father's case, there was no appreciation at all. By the early 1940s, Henry Coyle's family were surviving from week to week, and if it weren't for the fruits of the broad Atlantic he would have struggled to put food on the table for his growing family. Like so many of his compatriots, Comdt H.P. Coyle had been cast aside once independence was achieved.

What would Michael Collins have made of it all? I think he'd have been heartbroken to learn that the brave and loyal men and women who helped to win Ireland its freedom had been so shabbily treated by the very people who were now reaping the rewards of that same independence.

CHAPTER 41

'Up until now, I have been very unfairly treated'

MY mother was a truly extraordinary woman. I will never know how she managed to do it, but she had an amazing ability to turn a small amount of food into what seemed like a proper feast. She would go down to the strand in Doolough with a bucket in hand to pick cockles, mussels, dilsk and other seafood. There might be nothing to eat at eleven in the morning, but by lunchtime she'd be serving up the finest, healthiest meal, having walked the strand ten times over gathering cockles and mussels to ensure her children went to bed on a full stomach.

As the youngest in a family of nine, I was one of the fortunate ones and it was my older siblings who bore the brunt of the life sentence imposed on my father over the O'Malley Cheque. There was no money – *absolutely no money* – in the Coyle household in the early 1940s when my three oldest brothers, Henry Joe, Pat and Willie, were growing up.

The war years were hard for everyone in Ireland, but they were especially difficult for families who did not have land on which to grow crops and rear livestock. This was the era of the so-called Emergency, a period when people were encouraged to become self-sufficient, but how could the Coyle family be self-sufficient when all they had was a rented hovel on a tiny patch of land?

I have included some photographs in this chapter of the houses my parents and older siblings lived in during the 1940s, including a near-derelict cottage in my father's native Muingdoran that had neither running water nor well, just water from a nearby stream.

Now, I am well aware there are many, many people who had it tough growing up in Ireland in the 1940s and 1950s, and I don't wish for a second to diminish their hardship or suffering by singling out the case of my family. However, I think it is important to point out that my parents and older siblings

The little cottage at Dooyork where my older siblings were raised in the 1940s.

were living in abject poverty at a time when there was a pension withheld from my father year after year after year. In fact, 20 years after my father was jailed for the O'Malley Cheque, he was still paying a penalty – £100 per annum – for his misdeamonour. That pension would have transformed the Coyle family fortunes in the 1940s and might have even allowed my father to acquire a home or at least a fishing boat from which he could earn a steady living. Instead, he and my mother had to worry every day about keeping a roof over their heads and food on the table for their growing family.

One of the big problems facing my father was that construction work dried up in Ireland once war was declared in Europe. He even took up a position in the Reserve Defence Force and was briefly based in Co Donegal where my brother Willie was born. But it wasn't long before the Coyle family was back in Erris and struggling to make ends meet all over again. The sea was their saviour and my father got work as a fisherman, as well as taking on construction jobs whenever they became available, which wasn't very often. It was an impoverished existence from a financial perspective but my parents compensated for the shortage of money with a resourcefulness that was just incredible. Somehow they always managed to find a way to feed and clothe their children, though how they did it I simply do not know. The Miracle of the Loaves and Fishes wouldn't have held a candle to Molly and Henry Coyle's achievements in the 1940s in rearing a family on an income that, at times, was next to nothing. It is my firm belief that if their parenting skills could have been traded on the stock exchange, the great indexes of the world – the Dow Jones and the FTSE – would have closed at record highs. Molly and Henry were some team and, by God, they needed to be because they didn't have it easy in those first ten years of marriage. The greatest tribute I can pay to my parents is to quote my brother Henry Joe, who lived through the toughest of those tough years:

"We never had much," he told me, "but we always had enough."

I think it is a lovely phrase and I am sure it will resonate with other families from that era who came through similarly tough times. My parents may have had little by way of material wealth but they showered their children with love, kindness and a wonderful spirit of togetherness.

The Coyles are an incredibly close, loyal family and I have no doubt that stems from the way our parents reared us: they set the example and we followed it. Indeed, even today, we are still following Henry and Molly's inspirational example and instilling in our children and grandchildren the principles we learned all those years ago.

Henry and Molly's legacy lives on today but there must have been times in the dark days of the 1940s when even they wondered whether they'd make it through at all.

By 1949, there were over 100 pages in the pension file of Henry Peter Coyle but there was still no sign of a shilling, let alone £100. In the autumn of that year, the Dáil approved the Military Service Pensions (Amendment) Act in an attempt to finally address the anomalies in the 1924 and 1934 Acts that had left many worthy recipients without pensions or with derisory payments. One of the biggest bones of contention was the precise meaning of the term 'active service', which had been cited as the reason for denying many people a pension. These were people who might have provided vital logistical support during the War of Independence but may not have taken part in any ambushes or battles. It was hoped that by widening the scope of the definition of 'active service' the IRA veterans who were poorly rewarded or missed out entirely in 1924 and 1934 would finally get their just deserts.

Among the many voices to contribute to the Dáil debate on the matter was Michael Sheahan, an Independent TD for Cork who made the following observation:

"It is really amazing, after 25 years of native government, that some of the soldiers of the IRA who fought for the freedom of this country are still without pensions."

My father's case had nothing to do with 'active service' because nobody doubted his involvement in the IRA or the importance of the work he had undertaken from 1919-'23, so initially, the 1949 Act offered little hope of a change in his situation.

Another of the rented houses where the Coyle family lived in the 1940s and early 1950s.

The new legislation was steered through the Dáil by the Minister for Defence, Dr Thomas O'Higgins, an older brother of Kevin O'Higgins, who of course had been a key figure in Cumann na nGaedheal when my father fell out of favour in 1924. At the behest of some opposition TDs, mainly from Fianna Fáil, O'Higgins agreed to insert a clause into the 1949 Act that would allow the minister of the day to overturn refusals under the 1924 Act, in particular, refusals relating to criminal convictions. This was great news for my father because finally he could seek a review of the 1927 decision to deny him a pension.

In the spring of 1950, Henry Coyle made another plea for his pension, this time citing the 1949 legislation as grounds for a favourable review of his case. A month later, a department official sent a memo to the minister outlining the background to my father's pension application some 23 years earlier. It was only while sifting through these documents that I noticed the date on which the Army Pensions Board originally assessed my father for a pension valued at £100-1s per annum: it was April 1, 1927.

What an April Fools Joke that turned out to be because 23 years later Henry Coyle still hadn't seen a penny of that pension. By 1950, he was trying to rear a family on unemployment assistance of £1-3s per week, with an additional eight shillings for 'home assistance'. He had to pay rent, and feed and clothe a wife and five children from that paltry sum; and still the State dragged its heels on his right to an IRA pension.

When sending the memo to Minister O'Higgins, the official in the Department of Defence attached a draft order for a Certificate of Military Service made out in the name of Henry Coyle. All O'Higgins had to do was sign and date it. Instead, he ignored the order for months until eventually on

24/SP/9346.

9 Márta, 1951.

A Chara,

      With reference to your letter dated 3rd April, 1950, regarding your application under the Military Service Pensions (Amendment) Act, 1949, I am directed by the Minister for Defence to inform you that after full consideration of all the circumstances in your case it is regretted that your application for a certificate of Military Service cannot be granted.

Mise, le meas,

RÚNAÍ.

Mr. Henry P. Coyle,
Dooyork,
Geesala,
Ballina,
CO. MAYO.

My father was refused an IRA pension for the third time on March 9, 1951, some 24 years after the first refusal. By then, he had been deprived of over £2,400 in payments.

November 13, 1950, his secretary sent the file back to the official with the notation: *File no longer required by the minister.* The draft order was also returned... unsigned.

On February 15, 1951, O'Higgins finally issued his decision: he would not be granting a Certificate of Military Service to Henry Coyle under the 1949 (Amendment) Act. O'Higgins took up a new post as Minister for Industry and Commerce on March 7, but before he left the Department of Defence he instructed the secretary to issue a letter to my father, stating: *I am directed by the Minister for Defence to inform you that after full consideration of all the circumstances in your case it is regretted that your application for a certificate of Military Service cannot be granted.*

Once again, a Minister for Defence had used his final hours in office to deny Henry Coyle a pension. But my father had had enough of this gross miscarriage of justice and was not about to be deprived of his pension all over again. The whole purpose of the 1949 (Amendment) Act was to finally give justice to men like him who had been wrongfully denied an IRA pension for a quarter of a century. He was fortunate to have a very able ally in Fine Gael – his neighbour and great friend P.J. (Paddy) Lindsay, who would be elected to the Dáil in 1954, becoming the first TD from Erris since my father some 30 years earlier.

Paddy was one of the finest legal minds of his generation and he knew that what was being done to Henry Coyle was neither just nor fair. He petitioned the new Minister for Defence Seán MacEoin for an urgent review of the case. MacEoin needed no introduction to Henry Coyle because they served together in the National Army during the Civil War and my father was, as I mentioned previously, a member of MacEoin's famous Expeditionary Force that marched from Athlone to Castlebar in July 1922. In fact, MacEoin provided my father with a reference when he originally applied for the pension in 1925.

On May 3, 1951, Minister MacEoin sent a memo to the Minister for Finance Seán MacEntee seeking his agreement for the issuing of a Certificate of Military Service to Henry Coyle. He also wrote to Paddy Lindsay to say he was 'making enquiries to see if, at this stage, anything could be done to grant [Henry Coyle] a pensionable certificate of military service under the 1949 Act'. But MacEoin wasn't sure he could do anything because department officials were telling him it 'might be legally impossible' to reverse the decision of Thomas O'Higgins.

In the end, the curious case of Henry Coyle's IRA pension went all the way to the Attorney General Charles Casey who declared on May 11, 1951, that Minister MacEoin could indeed issue a Certificate of Military Service. But there was still one more twist in this never-ending saga.

I, Thomas F. O'Higgins, Minister for Defence, in exercise of the powers conferred on me by Section 7 of the Military Service Pensions (Amendment) Act, 1949, (No. 29 of 1949), hereby grant as on and from the date of this Order a Certificate of Military Service under the Military Service Pensions Act, 1924, to Mr. Henry Coyle, Dooyork, Geesala, Ballina, Co. Mayo.

Given under my Seal this _____ day of _____ 1950.

MINISTER FOR DEFENCE.

I, Oscar Traynor, Minister for Defence, in exercise of the powers conferred on my by Section 7 of the Military Service Pensions (Amendment) Act, 1949, (No. 29 of 1949), hereby grant as on and from the date of this Order a Certificate of Military Service under the Military Service Pensions Act, 1924, to Mr. Henry Coyle, Dooyork, Geesala, Ballina, Co. Mayo.

Given under my Seal this _____ *8th* _____ day of _____ *August* _____ 1951.

MINISTER FOR DEFENCE.

In a strange twist of fate, Fine Gael Minister for Defence Thomas O'Higgins refused to sign off on a pension for my father in 1950 (top), but his successor Fianna Fáil's Oscar Traynor agreed to sign the order in 1951. As a former Cumann na nGaedheal TD, my father felt very let down by some members of his old party, but he also had many great friends in Fine Gael, including his neighbour Paddy Lindsay who was instrumental in getting him an IRA pension in 1951.

Seol a fhreagra chun :—
Address any reply to :—)
AN RÚNAÍ
(The Secretary),
fén uimhir seo :—
(quoting :)

AN ROINN AIRGEADAIS
(Department of Finance),

SRÁID MHUIRBHTHEAN UACHT.,
(Upper Merrion Street),

BAILE ÁTHA CLIATH.
(Dublin.)

Roinn Co...
...
24 DEC
Clatlann na Brainre
airgeadais.

P. 20/ 65/ 51.

An Rúnaí,
An Roinn Cosanta.

Military Service Pensions Acts, 1924/49

With reference to your minute (24. SP/9346   )
of the 1st October, 1951,   intimating that a
certificate of Military Service has been granted, pursuant
to Section 2(1) of the Military Service Pensions Act, 1924, to
Mr. ex-Commandant.Henry.Coyle,............................
of...Dooyork,.Geesala,.Ballina,.Co..Mayo...............
I am directed by the Minister for Finance to convey sanction for
the grant under Section 4(1) of the Act of a pension at the rate
of £...£100..1..0..........(..One.Hundred.Pounds.and....
..One.Shilling................................) a year to
Mr. ex-Commandant.Coyle...with effect as from 8th August, 1951.

The Report of the board of assessors is returned herewith.

McCarthy
21 Nollaig, 1951.

The long-awaited certificate for a military service pension was granted to my father on Christmas Week, 1951. He had first applied for a pension in February 1925.

The resignation of Minister for Health Dr Noel Browne in April 1951 over his controversial Mother and Child Scheme plunged the First Interparty Government into crisis and Taoiseach John A. Costello was forced to declare a general election on May 4. My father's pension application was soon forgotten amid the maelstrom of a general election campaign and it still had not been approved by the time Fine Gael left office in June. Would Fianna Fáil grant a pension to an old National Army commandant and former pro-Treaty TD? It seemed unlikely… but an old friend from Ballina was about to step into the breach and see that justice was finally done.

Were it not for the intervention of P.J. Ruttledge, my father might never have got his pension. Ruttledge canvassed his Fianna Fáil ministerial colleagues and, finally, on August 8, 1951, the new Minister for Defence Oscar Traynor signed the order granting a Certificate of Military Service to Henry Coyle. It had only taken a mere 24 years and four months to get to that point, and ironically it was a Fianna Fáil minister who signed off on the pension for a former Cumann na nGaedheal TD. Long before there were 'Confidence and Supply' agreements, Henry Coyle was building bridges between the old Civil War rivals!

In October 1951, the secretary of the Department of Defence sent a letter to his counterpart in Finance informing him that Henry Coyle had been granted a pension of £100-1s per annum, effective from August 8, 1951, but nobody in the department thought to tell my father! In fact, he hadn't heard anything since Fine Gael left office six months earlier.

On the first Sunday in December 1951, my father met with P.J. Ruttledge in Bangor Erris and told him his tale of woe that went all the way back to 1924 when Ruttledge was a young anti-Treaty TD on the run. My father followed it up with a letter to Ruttledge dated December 6 that concluded with the line: *Up until now, I have been very unfairly treated.* It was the understatement of the century.

Following another intervention from Ruttledge, the Department of Finance finally signed off on my father's pension on Christmas Eve 1951 and the first payment was issued in early January 1952. Henry Joe distinctly recalls the day that first pension cheque arrived because our father immediately went into Belmullet to cash it and returned to Muingdoran with a bag of tomatoes for the kids, a rare luxury in 1950s' Ireland.

Commandant H.P. Coyle had been waiting a long, long time for those tomatoes.

CHAPTER 42

Bound for Newfoundland

A PENSION of £2 per week wasn't going to solve all of the financial problems facing the Coyle family, but it allowed my father to save a few bob, and by the summer of 1952, he was ready to buy a motorboat. On Friday, June 28, he spied an advertisement in the *Western People* offering for sale a motorboat in Galway, and set off the following Monday to inquire about purchasing it. Accompanying him was a young neighbour, Edward Mangan, from the townland of Roy Carter, and they expected to be back in Geesala with the new boat by Tuesday evening at the latest.

It is worth remembering that my father was going on 58 and many men of his age would have been preparing for retirement instead of embarking on a career as a full-time fisherman. However, Henry Coyle had six children under the age of 14, so he didn't have the luxury of retirement, and even if he had a pension of £20 per week he'd have wanted to be out working. He was never a man to be idle, nor did he ever lose his sense of adventure, as the events of early July 1952 will show.

By Tuesday evening, there was no sign of my father or Edward Mangan, nor was there a telegram from Galway explaining their delay. It was the same on Wednesday evening, and by Thursday afternoon my poor mother must have been out of her mind with worry. Finally, on Friday morning word came through that a motorboat containing my father and Ned Mangan had been found drifting in the Atlantic. When the intrepid duo eventually arrived home to Geesala later that afternoon, they had an epic seafaring story to tell. In fact, the story was so remarkable it made the pages of the *Western People* the following week under the heading *Erris Men's Adventure*. Here is the *Western's* report:

Reading an advertisement for the sale of a motorboat in Galway in last week's Western People, Henry Coyle left for the City of the Tribes, and had with him a youth named Edward Mangan, of Roy Carter, Geesala. Next day he and Henry, who had purchased the boat, launched it at Galway and set their course for Blacksod Bay.

Erris Men's Adventure

Former T.D. and a Companion Adrift in The Atlantic

Mr. Henry Coyle, of Dooyork, Geesala, on Tuesday morning of last week, had set out in a motor boat from Galway, but before reaching Blacksod, on the homeward trek, he had spent three sleepless nights, having been adrift since he left the placid waters of Galway bay.

Mr. Coyle is a man of many reminiscences. For his activities in the Old I.R.A. he had served two years in Peterhead jail, and ...

My father was back making headlines in July 1952 when his new boat ended up adrift in the Atlantic.

Of charts and maps, Henry had none. The Western People tide table was his sole textbook.

When scarcely a mile past the tranquil waters of Galway Bay, trouble set in when a leakage sprang in the petrol tank. All the fuel was lost, and the boat stood motionless in the Atlantic. Movements from that forth were only as the winds and tides directed.

This was Henry's ordeal and that of his young mate until the following Friday morning when, many miles off Achill Head, they were sighted by a British trawler, and the captain, having observed the signal of distress, steamed to their rescue and towed them to Blacksod where, following their three sleepless nights and days without food or water, they were supplied with refreshments, which restored them to their usual energy.

With repairs carried out and their boat refuelled, feeling none the worse for their plight, they sailed across the bosom of Blacksod Bay and safely arrived at Geesala, where they were met by a large crowd of waiting friends.

In addition to the engine, Mr Coyle has now the boat rigged up with sails, and with nets and lines on board has again put to sea with his dauntless companion to fish the western coastline between Valentia in Kerry and Malin Head in Donegal, and if need be are prepared to penetrate the Atlantic, they declare, as far west as Newfoundland.

I don't think my father ever reached Newfoundland on a fishing expedition but he made great use of that boat. He was a man who could turn his hand to almost anything and he built the house in which I was born from foundation to chimney, installing all of the pipe-work for the plumbing and later the electrical wiring when rural electrification came to Geesala.

The house was erected in the mid-1950s on a three-acre site provided by the Land Commission and paid for with a loan from the Department of the Gaeltacht. Obtaining that little plot of land on the shores of Doolough Strand was the biggest break my father and mother got since they married some 15 years earlier. It gave them a sense of security that had been sadly absent up to that point; they no longer had to worry about being evicted with their children from rented accommodation.

Constructed from mass concrete using the sands from the nearby strand as raw material, that little cottage was a monument to my father's ingenuity as

My mother was a great believer in the importance of a healthy diet in childhood and she reared six strapping sons! From right to left, in order of seniority: Henry Joe, Pat, Willie, John, Noel and myself. Sadly, Pat passed away in his adopted Birmingham on April 8, 2022. He was one of nature's gentlemen and I was privileged and blessed to have him as my older brother.

a multi-talented tradesman. He even used the same wood for the roof as had been used to shutter the windows, and everything was completed to the highest standard. The house was his pride and joy, and it was where he would spend some of the happiest days of his life.

Even as a youngster, I could see my father had a genius mind when it came to skilled labour of all kinds, be it construction, blacksmithing, boat-building, net-making or general carpentry. People were always coming to him with things to repair and he never failed to oblige. Sometimes they'd pay him in cash, but more often than not, payment came by way of a box of spuds or turnips or a few freshly caught salmon.

He never ceased to amaze me with the things he could do. Fishermen regularly called over to have their nets repaired or cut in half – a unique skill that few could master – and he once built a currach from scratch in the back garden. Another time he made a cart, demonstrating his blacksmithing skills by putting on the wheels, a complicated task that he also performed for several neighbours and friends who would call to the house when they needed their cartwheels repaired.

Even when he was in his seventies, he'd head off in a currach out into the Atlantic to fish for the mackerel that were such a mainstay of my childhood diet. Fishermen in Erris would say my father was an accomplished boatman who once skippered a cabin cruiser from Galway for a friend, Tony Walsh. He was an old man at that stage, and was accompanied by a young John Munnelly, who still recalls my father pointing out the various fishing grounds along the coast, all of which were etched in his memory from previous trips.

My older brother Willie (standing, extreme right) is pictured with a Dooyork football team in the 1950s. We still don't know where he got those very snazzy shorts but Willie has always been a very dapper dresser! Back row, from left: Seamus McGuire (Sonny), Tom 'Dick' Gaughan, Richard Barrett, Ben Gaughan, David Sweeney, Frank McGuire, Willie Coyle. Front row: Mickey Barrett, Joe O'Toole, Bernie Scanlon, Tommy Cullen, Seamus McGuire (Huggard), James Coyle.

Some of my earliest memories are of watching my father setting vegetables and potatoes on our little three-acre holding that he was clearly so proud to own and nurture. Each task was completed to the point of perfection. If he was making a ridge of potatoes, he'd bring the line down first and mark it out; there was no such thing as half-doing a job.

I learned so much from watching him and I learned even more from listening to him, yet there was also much about this man, my father, I did not know, and even if I had been aware of his complicated past I wouldn't have been able to properly comprehend it at such a young age. After all, my father was 63 years old when I was born.

I was the youngest of Molly and Henry's ten children, one of whom died at birth, and my parents had already bid farewell to their eldest, Henry Joe, by the time I was born. The second eldest Pat also took the emigrant ship to England in the late 1950s, and I was about six years of age before I even realised I had two older brothers. By then, Henry Joe had moved on to Chicago while a third brother Willie was now over in England, having emigrated at the tender age of 14.

But there were still six hungry, young mouths to feed, and my mother, like so many Irish women of the era, had her work cut out to make ends meet.

It helped that we were virtually self-sufficient once we got that little three-acre site. We grew our own vegetables and potatoes in the back garden, had a couple of cows for milk and butter, as well as hens, ducks and geese. My mother continued to go down to the strand to pick cockles and mussels, while my father's regular forays into the Atlantic meant there was a plentiful supply of salted mackerel.

Money might have been scarce, but there were few houses in Ireland where the children enjoyed a healthier diet. My mother was absolutely driven by a desire to provide nourishing meals for her brood because she firmly believed that good eating in childhood made for strong, healthy adults. I remember she often had us eating large goose eggs that had enough in them to keep a child fed for a week.

I realised at a young age that our family's financial resources were meagre and I often watched my mother make her few weekly grocery purchases from Dodie Shevlin, who brought his travelling shop out from Belmullet once a week. Dodie was a very decent man and was extremely kind to my mother.

No history of Henry Coyle could be written without a massive acknowledgement to Martin McIntyre's Hardware in Belmullet, which supplied all of the material used in building our house in the 1950s. Everything was supplied on credit and they never rushed my parents in the repayments. My mother often mentioned and prayed for the McIntyres in later years, and massive respect was always accorded to them in our house.

I must also mention the shopkeepers of Geesala – Gaughan's, Moran's, Munnelly's and Henry's Post Office – who were very good to the Coyle family too. We had accounts with some of them and often got goods on credit until my father's pension cheque arrived. I can recall being sent down to the village on many occasions with a note from my mother to pick up some groceries that were 'put on the book'. P.J. Moran of Moran's Shop was a life-long friend of Henry Joe, Pat and Willie. He was a lovely man.

My mother had a great respect for money and was very adept at managing the family finances. If she didn't have enough money the shopkeepers would let the bill roll over to the next week, and she somehow always managed to find enough cash in the interim because she was a woman who never let a debt go unpaid for too long.

Molly Coyle needed to be good with money because my father's income was very erratic and sometimes he'd have to wait a long time to get paid for the work he might have done because almost everyone else was in the same boat as we were.

Telephone BELMULLET   Telegrams : " McINTYRES, BELMULLET "

BELMULLET, 23/7/57 19......

M.... Henry. Coyle.

Doagh

Bought of

McINTYRES STORES LTD.

			Price			
2	13' 2×2 S Style				17	4
1	6 2½×1½ Bill Rail				4	0
1	6 2½×1½ T " do				4	0
1	10 2×4 S Bar				6	3
2	9' 1×3/4 Mops				3	9
2	12' 1×3/8 P. Bead				4	8
2	13 5×1/4 Pulley				6	0
1	7 3×3 1" cell				8	9
2	10' 4×1 Cam 3/0				11	8
2	10 4½×3/4 do				7	0
1	6' 3×1				2	0
1	6' 3×3/4				1	6
4	Pulley	1/5			5	8
					5	3 7

Amount

Tendered

0858 = 80

This is a receipt for building materials from McIntyres Stores in Belmullet, dated July 1957, when my father was constructing our family home in Doolough. The McIntyres were wonderful people and were so good to my parents.

My father received his modest farm at a time when the Land Commission was moving people from the smallholdings of Erris to the vast plains of Meath, Kildare and other Midlands' counties. The renowned Charlestown-born journalist John Healy wrote a famous book about the hardship of raising a family on 19 acres of snipe-grass in east Mayo, but try doing it on three acres of rugged coastline in west Mayo. We had a thousand acres when the tide went out… but the tide only goes out twice a day!

It's little short of a miracle my mother was able to keep all of us fed and clothed during those formative years, and it took a never-ending regime of backbreaking toil. When we got out of bed in the morning she'd be

My mother's sister, Bridget (Bridgie) McGuire, from Dooriel in Ballycroy, was incredibly kind to the Coyle family when we were struggling to make ends meet.

working away at the old range in the kitchen and she was still doing the same when we turned in for the night. Even in the depths of winter, she'd be up long before the sun rose, heating the range for our breakfast, while also preparing pots of small potatoes (or 'poreens' as we called them) for the hens and a porridge-type mixture for the calves.

The farm was her pride and joy and she looked after the animals and poultry with the same diligence she demonstrated when running the household. It was her sister, Bridgie McGuire in Ballycroy, who gave our family a big break in farming by sending over two cows, which we didn't have to pay for until their calves were sold. That was a remarkable act of generosity from a woman who herself was a widow with two young children, and Bridgie's kindness was never forgotten in the Coyle household. The two cows gave us a constant supply of fresh milk and butter while also allowing my mother to build up the family herd until eventually she was the proud owner of ten cows.

My mother worked 12 to 14 hours a day, seven days a week, but I never heard her complain about the many things she didn't have in life. Instead, she thanked God for the things she had and for the great blessing of a healthy family. She instilled a work ethic in her children, convincing us that if we worked hard enough we'd never want for anything. I struggled at times to

My older brother Willie left for England at the tender age of 14 and has spent his entire adult life there. Willie deservedly received the Erris Exile of the Year Award in 2011 for his great work on behalf of Irish emigrants in England. Willie is pictured with his wife Sonia Cronin-Coyle, son Christopher Cronin-Coyle, the extended Coyle family and friends at the presentation ceremony in the Broadhaven Bay Hotel in Belmullet where he received the award from the then President of Belmullet-Erris Lions Club Chris Tallot.   Picture: Henry Wills/*Western People*

accept the logic of that philosophy because my parents toiled day after day, week after week, just to put food on the table, and they rarely had anything left for material things. We'd kill a goose for Christmas rather than buy a turkey, we'd wear hand-me-down clothes and we'd never let any food go to waste. There were no fridges or freezers or anything like that, and there were certainly no 'Best Before' dates on the food we ate. The only best before date we knew was best to have it eaten before somebody else did!

One of my abiding childhood memories is the day I made my First Holy Communion and I was standing with my mother outside Moran's Shop, admiring all of the beautiful things in the window, items we certainly could not afford.

"If you work hard enough you can have anything you want in that window," my mother remarked, "and maybe some day you'll even have a shop of your own."

Those words came to have a special resonance for me when I opened a shop and filling station at Atticonaun in Belmullet in the early 1990s. My mother was an inspirational woman who always believed in a brighter future for her children and she continues to inspire me to this day.

CHAPTER 43

'A sleeping pill in his right glove'

THE most exciting event in my young life occurred in the summer of 1965 when Henry Joe returned from America with his wife Bridie Tierney, who was a native of Co Galway, and their new-born daughter Ann, my first niece. My eldest sibling may have been absent throughout my childhood but he was very much there in spirit because his name was revered by sports fans in Erris and beyond.

In 1959, Henry Joe became the first man from the Barony to win a national boxing title when he stunned Ireland's boxing scene with an explosive performance at the National Stadium in Dublin. A year later, he donned the Irish singlet for a trip to Germany, and there was even talk of a tilt at the 1960 Olympic Games until emigration put paid to his promising sporting career.

Boxing has been such a part of my life these past 50, and I've made friends all over the world through the sport, but there would never have been a club in Geesala were it not for the sterling efforts of a local priest Fr Joseph Harte. In the early 1950s, Fr Harte established a boxing club in Pullathomas, and when he founded another in Geesala in 1953, 14-year-old Henry Joe was among the first to join. He fell in love with the sport right away and soon started winning county and provincial titles.

In 1955, my father began building our home in Doolough and Henry Joe, who had left school at that stage, was drafted in to assist. His job was to mix the concrete in a barrow and haul bucket after bucket up to my father by way of a pulley. It was backbreaking work but it was also the best strength and conditioning programme an up-and-coming boxer could ever want. By the time the house was finished, Henry Joe was fit to take on the toughest boxers in the land, and the best part about it was nobody gave him a chance because Geesala Boxing Club was unheard of on the national scene.

In early January 1959, Henry Joe arrived at the National Stadium in Dublin as Connacht champion to fight a man named Kennedy from Munster

Fr Joseph Harte established a boxing club in Geesala in the 1950s and some of the club's first members are pictured with their collection of trophies.

in the semi-final of the National Junior Light Heavyweight division. He duly won and was drawn against Paddy Toner from Dublin in the final. Toner had received a bye because his Derry opponent McNutt was unable to travel to Dublin due to bad ice on the roads.

However, the Irish Athletic Boxing Association, in its wisdom, decided that McNutt should be given another crack at the semi-final against a boxer from Wexford, so Henry Joe's fight against the highly-fancied Toner became a semi-final instead of the final it should rightly have been. To top it all, the semi-final and final were scheduled for the same day, which was a big disadvantage for Henry Joe, who was now working in England and had to travel home to Geesala, spend a few days in training with Fr Harte before travelling to Dublin on the morning of the bouts.

Everything was stacked against Henry Joe but he wasn't about to let this golden opportunity of making a little bit of history for Erris pass him by. In the semi-final, he knocked Paddy Toner to the canvas with his opening punch – a crashing right hook – and the bout was over in 11 seconds, literally the time it took to throw the punch and count out Toner. The *Irish Independent's* boxing writer reckoned it was the fastest knockdown in the history of the National Stadium and I don't think it has ever since been beaten. How could it?

The final took slightly longer but was still over in the first round as Henry Joe, with his unorthodox southpaw style and devastating right fist, made easy work of McNutt. The members of the Dublin boxing fraternity, who up to then had never even heard of the little club from northwest Mayo, were absolutely stunned.

Henry Joe returned home to a hero's welcome and the *Western People* reported that 'bonfires blazed in the tiny seaside village of Geesala' as a huge crowd came out to greet the new national champion. The *Western* had a great description of Henry Joe's power-packed punching style, stating: *The hard-hitting southpaw showed he carried a real sleeping pill in his right glove…*

Henry Joe returned to Birmingham where he trained with another of Fr Harte's protégés, Pat McGarry, who had recently turned professional and was known as 'The Irish Tornado'. Pat and his brothers were all brilliant boxers and later became renowned in Chicago where Henry Joe also set up home.

Henry Joe is pictured in 1959 with Fr Joseph Harte after becoming Ireland's Junior Light Heavyweight Champion. It was the first national boxing title to come to Erris.

Before that, my brother had a chance to stake a claim on the Irish team for the Rome Olympics in 1960, but was working long hours in England and found it impossible to dedicate the necessary time to boxing. Henry Joe would have been very conscious of his responsibilities as the eldest in a family of nine and wanted to earn as much money as possible for his parents back home. I have no doubt he would have made the 1960 Olympics had he been able to devote himself fully to boxing. Fr Harte was actually the trainer of the Irish team and it would have been a fantastic story had Henry Joe managed to make it to Rome but, unfortunately, he surrendered his national title in March 1960.

The winner of the light heavyweight division in the 1960 Olympics was a young American boxer named Cassius Clay, which meant the odds were probably stacked against Henry Joe winning gold. But Cassius Clay never had to shunt bucket after bucket of concrete up a wall on a windy day in Doolough, so maybe Henry Joe would have given one of his famous 'sleeping pills' to the future Muhammad Ali!

The Olympic dream was not to be but a national title for a little club like Geesala was as good as an Olympic gold and Henry Joe blazed a trail for boxing in rural Ireland. He also brought great pride to our village and to the Coyle household. The 1950s had been a tough, tough decade for my parents,

Junior Boxing Finals

Powerful Punching By H. Coyle

HENRY COYLE, a comparative unknown, from Geesala, Co. Mayo, carved a special niche for himself in Irish ring history at the Stadium, Dublin, last night, on his way to taking the National Junior light-heavy title.

The first boxer from his club to compete in these, or, indeed, at any other championship of national standing, Coyle had to box twice within two hours—but his "iron" fists made light work of it.

A RECORD?

A south-paw, whose real power, strangely enough, seemed to be in his right, he knocked out Paddy Toner (Arbour Hill) in the semi-final, with the very first punch of the fight. Just as they squared up, Coyle let loose a right hook and Toner hit the canvas. The loser was on his feet

M-- Quinn To

before ten, but was groggy, and the referee rightly completed the count. It took exactly eleven seconds and must have been one of the quickest wins ever at the Stadium.

In the final Coyle battered Ulster champion, D. McNutt into submission in the first round.

A near capacity crowd was left in no doubt that this twenty-year-old will go places when he learns to conserve energy and nick his punches better.

McNutt was anything but a novice as he proved in his semi-final with Leinster champion, W. ...ley (Boulfavogue), who lasted just over half a minute.

Quick wins were the order in a thoroughly enjoyable night that had good boxing, plenty of determination and, most important of all, ..bcries. From accomplished Belfast flyweight W. Megarry, to game Longford heavy, Joe Casey, champions emerged who should be heard of in the near future.

There was no middle final. P. Plood (Corinthians) and R. McClean (B.C.S.I.), who were to box the semi-final for the right to meet D. Barber (Crumlin) the final, were both injured

GEESALA BOXER STARS

In Irish Championships

Henry Coyle Takes Title After Two Quick Wins.

Bonfires blazed in the tiny seaside village of Geesala, (Ballina), on Saturday night to welcome home a broadly-grinning 20-years-old Henry Joe Coyle, who emerged as the brightest-sparkling star in the Irish Junior Boxing firmament when he battered his way to three sensational victories in the National Championships which were "staggered" over the past four weeks at the Stadium, Dublin.

RANK OUTSIDER

Coyle, one of the first locals to join the small Mayo club when it was founded six years ago, was the first boxer from Geesala to compete ..., indeed an-- ...

My eldest brother Henry Joe made headlines in 1959 when he caused a huge upset at the National Stadium in Dublin by winning the Junior Light Heavyweight Championship.

and the night of Henry Joe's homecoming must have brought my father back to his own glory days in 1923 when bonfires blazed in Geesala after he became the first Erris man to be elected to Dáil Éireann.

The last time the family name had featured in the national press it was during a very dark period in my father's life in the spring of 1934; now, 25 years later, Henry Joe had put the Coyle name up in lights again for all the right reasons.

When I was growing up in Erris, families were reared on 'Cow & Gate': one got the cow and the rest got the gate! Emigration was as much a part of life as the salty breeze that filled our lungs every day. There wasn't a house that didn't have someone in America, England or Scotland, and often there were more members of a family living abroad than at home.

Farms were small to begin with, meaning there was little prospect of dividing them among several children. In our own case, three acres wasn't going to divide very well among nine, so my older brothers and sisters set off for foreign lands, treading the same well-worn path their uncles and aunts and granduncles and grandaunts had taken before them.

What we'd have done without emigration I simply don't know. If the youngsters had waited in a country with no real job opportunities, they'd have been a massive burden on the State; instead, they became an asset by sending

Welcome For Geesala Champ

The brilliant young Geesala boxer—Henry Coyle—who so easily w o n the Light-Heavyweight Junior Boxing Championship at the National Stadium on Friday night last is a son of Mr. Henry Coyle, Geesala, who was formerly a T.D., for North Mayo.

Henry Coyle, Junior, is one of the county's most promising young boxers and was given a heroic welcome when he reached Geesala on Saturday last. He w a s congratulated by Mr. P. P. McDonagh—well known Erris sportsman and a host of well wishers from his native district.

Although the young boxing champion has been offered a job and training facilities in England it is hoped that nothing will be left undone to retain his services for his own country.

home the money that greased the wheels of the local economy in countless rural villages like Geesala.

It is estimated that Irish emigrants living in the United Kingdom sent the equivalent of €5.7 billion back to their families in Ireland between 1940 and 1970. And that's just the United Kingdom. Huge sums were dispatched from America too, while the official statistics also omit the vast amounts of cash that arrived each month in envelopes bearing foreign stamps.

Emigration transformed the Coyle household in the 1960s. Henry Joe in America and Pat and Willie in England sent home as much money as they could and I can still recall the excitement upon seeing the postman arriving at our door with a parcel from the lads. They'd buy clothes for us for back to school, and the August parcel usually provoked a bout of fisticuffs as John, Noel and myself fought over a pair of sandals or a shirt. When people ask me today how I got into the boxing I tell them that when I was young I had to fight just to get out of the house!

There were still six of us at home, although two of the girls, Mary and Ann, worked in a hotel in Renvyle in Co Galway for the summer before eventually leaving for England along with my third sister Agnes. Our circumstances were beginning to improve even before they left and the extra few bob in the post from the older girls meant my mother and father were able to purchase things that would have been completely beyond their means just a few years earlier. I distinctly recall the day Agnes came running down the strand to where John, Noel and myself were helping our father load sand into an ass-cart for a new footpath he was laying around the house.

"The new gas cooker has arrived," she shouted.

Well, we all dropped our shovels and raced up to the house, leaving the bemused ass standing on the beach strapped to a half-full cart of sand.

The gas cooker was the greatest invention my mother had ever seen. She couldn't believe she'd now be able to instantly boil an egg or make a pot of tea instead of waiting until the fire was lit in the old range.

THE "TOP TEN"

1—CHRISTY O'CONNOR, Galway, Golf
2—WILLIE MORRIS, Galway, Athletics
3—TONY O'SULLIVAN, Galway, Rugby
4—HENRY COYLE, Mayo, Boxing
5—TOM KILCOYNE, Sligo, Athletics
6—ANDY KILFEATHER, Sligo, Athletics
7—MIKE SWEENEY, Galway, Hurling
8—FRANK EVERS, Galway, Gaelic Football
9—GERRY O'MALLEY, Roscommon, do.
10—MICK PALMER, Mayo, Cycling

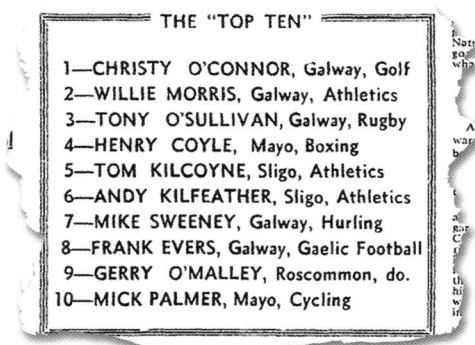

Henry Joe was in good company when the *Connacht Tribune* in Galway named him as one of the Top Ten sports stars in Connacht in 1959 and again in 1960.

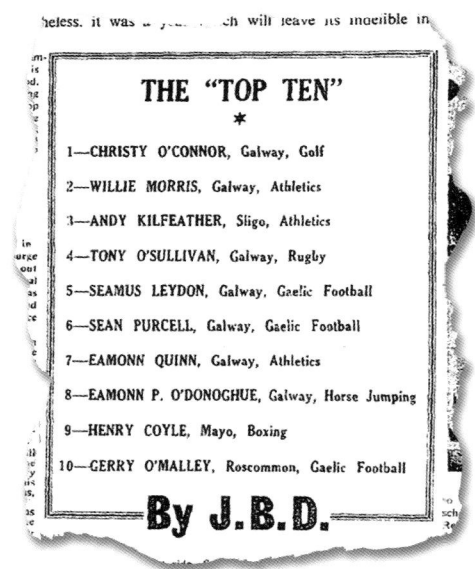

heless. it was ... ... ch will leave its indelible in

THE "TOP TEN"
*

1—CHRISTY O'CONNOR, Galway, Golf

2—WILLIE MORRIS, Galway, Athletics

3—ANDY KILFEATHER, Sligo, Athletics

4—TONY O'SULLIVAN, Galway, Rugby

5—SEAMUS LEYDON, Galway, Gaelic Football

6—SEAN PURCELL, Galway, Gaelic Football

7—EAMONN QUINN, Galway, Athletics

8—EAMONN P. O'DONOGHUE, Galway, Horse Jumping

9—HENRY COYLE, Mayo, Boxing

10—GERRY O'MALLEY, Roscommon, Gaelic Football

By J.B.D.

It's impossible today, in this era of Alexa, to understand the difference a gas cooker could make to the life of a housewife in the 1960s. Before getting that cooker, my mother was doing the housework in the same way her mother and grandmother had done it before her, so to discover she could now flick a switch and a flame miraculously appeared was as revolutionary to her as man landing on the moon. My father was equally impressed.

"That's some yoke altogether," he declared. "We'll make a pot of tea to celebrate."

The poor oul ass was forgotten about as we spent the next hour drinking tea and marvelling at this amazing contraption, the like of which we'd never seen before. Mind you, if somebody had told us that in another 50 years we'd be able to ask a lady called Alexa to turn on the gas cooker, we'd have probably told them to save their oul ráimeas for the four-legged creature waiting patiently down on the strand!

Henry Joe, Pat and Willie also chipped in to purchase an old Volkswagen Beetle for my father and it quickly became his pride and joy. Up to then, my father rarely left the village, but now he and my mother could take a trip to Belmullet or Ballina to do a little shopping or attend to business such as paying the ESB bill. My father had a troublesome hip by then, so the car gave him a new-found independence that was badly needed. It also proved a little more reliable than the Sinn Féin Motorcar!

In an era before cheap Ryanair flights into Knock Airport, it was hard for the likes of Pat and Willie to get home from England, so family reunions were rare in the 1960s, especially as Henry Joe was now married with a young family

In 1961, my father became the proud owner of a second-hand Volkswagen Beetle, purchased from Pearse Motors in Dublin. The car cost £219 and my father was able to put down a deposit of £99, thanks to the money earned in England and America by my brothers Henry Joe, Pat and Willie.

The six youngest members of the Coyle household in the early 1960s in our fine clothes from England and America! Back row, from left: Mary, Ann and Agnes. Front row: Gerry, John and Noel. This picture was originally black and white but my daughter Evita did a fantastic job colouring it.

in Chicago. As I mentioned earlier, it was sometimes confusing to know how many brothers I had because the older lads were gone before I was even out of the cot. To add to my confusion, my Aunt Mamie's girls, Margaret and Bridgie, who were both working in England, turned up at our house one summer's afternoon while we were making the hay. Margaret kept referring to my father as 'Daddy', which I, as a four-year-old, found totally perplexing. Who

My father's first-born Margaret and her husband Bernard are pictured with Aunt Mamie Calvey, who adopted Margaret when she was a toddler and raised her in Ballycroy. They were exceptionally close and Mamie was a wonderful mother to Margaret.

Margaret Coyle with her husband Bernard Donnelly and their children Margaret (Madge) and Michael.

I am pictured enjoying a light-hearted moment with Michael Donnelly on one of his many visits to Ireland.

I was very close to my wonderful older brother Pat who sadly passed away in April 2022, having spent his entire adult life in England. This photograph was taken outside our house in Doolough during Pat's last visit to his beloved Geesala. When he died, I took a sod from our parents' grave to lay on his own in Birmingham. In death, Pat was reunited with his beloved son Patrick who I am pictured with shortly before his untimely death in 2020.

was this new older sibling that had just wandered into my life and how come she didn't stay with us in Doolough when she was home?

It was only as I grew older that I learned the full story of my father's first-born. Margaret was a precious tenth member of our family up to the day she died. She married a man named Bernard Donnelly, from Co Armagh, and they had two children Margaret and Michael, who were raised in England. However, they maintained close connections with Erris and the Coyle family, and I was in regular contact with Margaret right up to her death. Indeed, if it were not for Margaret's early assistance in the research of this book, key parts of my father's story might have been lost forever, and a number of the photographs I have used, including the historic one of my father's wedding in Glasgow in 1922, came from Margaret's own personal archive. Michael Donnelly passed away suddenly on November 6, 2021, while on a visit to Geesala. We buried him in the local cemetery near his grandfather.

Six months later, I was saying another sad farewell when my brother Pat passed away in Birmingham at the age of 82. Pat was the quiet one in our house, a soft-spoken gentleman who was a wonderful son, brother, husband, father and uncle. He loved to return to Geesala for regular visits and I have included in this chapter a picture taken on his very last visit to the place he always called 'home'. I was heartbroken that Pat did not live long enough to see the publication of this book because he always had such an interest in my research and we spent hours talking about the eventful life and times of my father and how blessed we were to have had such wonderful parents. Pat was a fantastic older brother who helped me greatly when I was starting out in business and I was privileged to deliver an oration at his funeral in Birmingham. In the eulogy, I remarked that if Pat Coyle was not in Heaven then God must be there on his own. I was blessed to have Pat in my life and there isn't a day goes by that I don't think of him and say a quiet prayer for my beloved big brother.

CHAPTER 44

'I am one of the few now left...'

IN the spring of 1964, the *Western People* commissioned a series of articles about the War of Independence in Mayo. Penned by the newspaper's West Mayo correspondent, Tony Lavelle, the series provoked a huge response from readers, including several veterans of the independence struggle. Among those who decided to contribute their reminiscences of the period were Achill native Seán Mór Lynchehaun and Ballaghaderreen man John P. McPhillips, who both served with the IRA in Liverpool. Tony Lavelle published two articles about the Liverpool IRA on June 6 and 13, 1964, and they made for very interesting reading. There was, however, a man in Geesala who had lots more intriguing information about the IRA's activities in England and Scotland during the War of Independence, and he was finally ready to put pen to paper.

Up to that point, my father never spoke publicly about his involvement in the independence struggle, but the articles by Lynchehaun and McPhillips prompted him to call to the *Western People's* offices in Ballina to see if the newspaper would be interested in publishing some of his memories. Terry Reilly, then a young reporter, can still recall the day my father walked though the door of the newsroom.

"A well-dressed and softly spoken man entered the *Western People's* reporters' room in Ballina," Terry wrote in 2021. "He introduced himself as Henry Coyle from the Barony of Erris. Being into sport, I recognised him as the father of one of Mayo's great boxing legends, Henry Coyle.

"Henry Coyle Snr had some handwritten notes and it was clear he wanted to get something off his chest. He told me he had taken part in the War of Independence but did not go into any great detail. I recall he mentioned working for Michael Collins as an intelligence officer in Britain and of being involved in something big in Liverpool, and spending time in prison. I got the sense that he felt woefully wronged by subsequent events.

Three generations of the Coyle family – my late cousin Pap, his son Jackie and grandson Seán – beside the Sliabh na mBan armoured car when it visited Geesala in 2018. I wish to acknowledge the support of Pap's daughters Dr Mary Coyle (Westport) and Martina Martin and their husbands, John McNamara and John Martin, during the research for this book.

"Somewhat at a loss as to what to do, I advised him to write down details in a letter and send it to my editor, Jim McGuire.

"The former IRA commander did just that and his letter duly appeared on June 27, 1964, making almost two columns under the heading 'The Burnings in Liverpool', which related back to November 1920. Holding my breath, I read the exciting contents. Gunrunning for the IRA, arson attacks on English soil in retaliation for the Croke Park Bloody Sunday massacre and the burning of towns by the Black and Tans, imprisonment and much more."

It's incredible, really, that it was Terry who met my father all those years ago because Terry has been a great friend to me for such a long time and was very helpful in the early stages of this book when I was still trying to figure out what to do with all of the material I had gathered. I recall visiting him at his home in Ballina and showing him the various documents I had in my

My father is pictured with four of his brothers in the 1960s. Back row, from left: Martin, Pat (Sonny) and Henry. Front row: Ned and Jack.

possession. However, I was more worried about what I didn't have than what I did, and was unsure of when I should put pen to paper.

"Start now," Terry advised. "You'll never have everything, so you are better to start writing now and get everything you have down on paper."

It was the best advice I ever got. I went home that evening and started to write the chapter about the trial in Edinburgh. I used the various newspaper reports – some sourced from microfilm reels in British libraries 20 years earlier – to sketch out my father's speech from the dock. That was the beginning of this book and I have been working away since.

Terry has also been a friend of Henry Joe for over half a century, so my father was in good hands when he met that young reporter – and future editor of the *Western* – in June 1964.

I don't know how long it took my father to write his subsequent letter to the *Western*, but I have shown it to several people who are professional writers and they have marvelled at the quality of his prose and the amount of detail contained within it. My father was approaching 70 at this point, but there was certainly nothing wrong with his memory, as readers will see from the letter, which I have reprinted in its entirety.

I think it is a great testament to a man who possessed the most basic education and it shows what he could have achieved as a TD for Mayo North had he been given half a chance.

To the Editor, Western People

Dear Sir – With reference to the interesting account of the burnings of Liverpool on the 27th November, 1920, by Seán Mór Lynchehaun and John P. McPhillips, as I am one of the few now left who were most deeply implicated in what took place in England and Scotland in 1919 and '20, I feel that I cannot let the occasion pass without saying something about it. In fact, I was on trial for 16 days in Liverpool in connection with the burning of the warehouses and timber yards. As well as the 17 warehouses mentioned by Seán, there were also a number of timber yards burned. Two of the men whose photographs are in

SINN FEIN ATTACKS LIVERPOOL: FIRES

Seven Miles of Flames—Seventeen Cotton Warehouses and Timber Yards Ablaze.

YOUTH SHOT DEAD: FOUR MEN ARRESTED

Sinn Fein threats have been fulfilled. The war of assassination and destruction has been carried into this country.

> Seven miles of flames followed an attack by incendiaries on seventeen cotton warehouses and timber yards near Liverpool docks. Large quantities of petrol and paraffin and rags soaked in oil were found.
> Wreckers who were caught by the police opened fire, and a shot intended for a constable hit a youth of nineteen, named Daniel Ward, who had discovered the gang at work. He died on the way to hospital. Four men have been arrested.

Evidence is available that the men concerned in this series of crimes are agents of the Irish murder gang.

PETROL AND PARAFFIN CONVEYED BY MOTOR

Brigades' All-Night Fight— Buildings Still Burning.

> Later, one man, who refused to give his name and address, was arrested, and three others, including the man who shot the constable after the murder of Ward, are in custody.
> The incendiaries worked very fully, seemingly, clearly in accordance with a carefully laid plan.

SHOTS AT POLICE

last week's issue of the *Western People* were on trial along with me - Seamus McCaughey and Matthew Fowler, as well as five others, Neill Kerr, Sheila and Kathleen Browne, Andrew McPartlin and Michael Brennan.

Of all the fires planned, there was only one where any arrest was made or where any shooting took place.

I want to give all due credit to Seán Mór Lynchehaun and John P. McPhillips and all the others whose names they have mentioned who helped to carry the fight into the enemy's camp and whose services were most valuable and praiseworthy indeed.

John P. was quite right in saying that Neill Kerr was the guiding light in Liverpool. Neill, a native of Co Armagh, had his home in Liverpool for some years prior to 1916. He was 60 years of age at that time and was working for the cause of Irish freedom long before I was born. His three sons, Tom, Jack and Neill, came across from Liverpool and served with distinction all through Easter Week. They were among those interned in English jails and internment camps after the Rising. The youngest brother, Neill, who was 24 then, was accidentally shot in the basement of Moran's Men's Outfitters while waiting with three others, including his brother Tom, for my arrival from Scotland with a load of war material.

£1,000,000 FIRE DAMAGE.

Charges Against Sinn Feiners at Liverpool.

SENSATIONAL DISCLOSURES.

Exciting Motor Car Chase By Scottish Police.

THE Sinn Fein outrages at Liverpool, on November 27, when 12 warehouses and timber yards were set on fire, formed today the subject of remarkable disclosures, when, for the first time, the evidence against the persons arrested was fully submitted to the Liverpool Bench.

During the hearing it was stated that the damage amounted to over £1,000,000.

In the dock were eight defendants, six men and two women, all charged together in the first instance with conspiracy, and several of them with other offences, including the

THE POLICY OF TERRORISM.

(From Our Special Correspondent.)
Liverpool, Wednesday.

Opening the case for the prosecution, Mr. Simms said the charge in the first instance was one of conspiracy against all the defendants, and they were accused in that charge with having unlawfully and maliciously set fire to warehouses and other buildings on the occasion referred to. There would be added later charges of actually setting fire to the buildings and against two of the men, Matthew Fowler [...] rick McFarllin, of the wilful

murder of a civilian, and the attempted murder of a policeman, arising out of the same outrages.

Mr. Simms, of the Public Prosecutor's department, was in charge of the case for the Treasury, and Mr. Madden and Mr. Lynskey appeared for several of the defendants. The Liverpool stipendiary, Mr. Stewart Deacon, was on the bench. There were many uniformed and plain clothes officers stationed about the court, and only those having business within were allowed to enter. The public galleries were entirely closed. The hearing was adjourned till to-morrow.

Henry Peter Coyle, farmer, of co. Mayo, charged with assisting the conspiracy in various ways, and
Michael Brennan (30), dock labourer, also charged on suspicion of assisting the conspiracy.

OVER £1,000,000 DAMAGE.

Mr. Simms went on to give details of the conflagration which, he said, involved eighteen different buildings, and caused damage estimated at over a million pounds sterling.

In the warehouses afterwards were found bolt cutters and incendiary material. Evidence would be called in the case of the bolt cutters to [...] that they were [...]

John P. McPhillips has made a mistake in stating that it was his brother Jack who was shot, though I must congratulate him on how accurate he is in all the rest he has mentioned. When the accident happened, a doctor was called immediately and, of course, the police, and I was due to arrive at any minute.

The next move was to send out scouts to stop me driving right into the place. One of the scouts sent out on that occasion was a young student named Paddy Daly, now Dr Paddy Daly in some part of this country. The load I had with me was to be stored in the basement where young Kerr was shot. Then it was necessary to get another place of storage without delay and the whole load was put into a chief customs officer's private residence. This man was Stephen Lanigan from Cork. He was a chief customs officer in the British service at the time. The load consisted of 50 service rifles, a Hotchkiss machine gun, thousands of rounds of ammunition and explosives. I was a special service officer in charge of purchases. I was appointed by Michael Collins.

Liverpool was our main base for getting the stuff across. It was coming in ton loads from there under the eyes of the British authorities and they never knew. Stephen Lanigan and men of his type made the transit easy.

On the evening referred to above when young Kerr was shot, I was alone with his father in his house and we were discussing the situation as it was then. I suggested to him that it might be better to hand up the revolver to the police as by doing so it would throw off suspicion. He walked up and down the floor and didn't answer me for at least five minutes and then he turned towards me and these were his words: "Henry, if Neill lived they would never get his revolver and they'll never get it from me. He is gone, but if the three of them were gone the work must go ahead."

The spirit and determination of that man I shall never forget. It was Neill Kerr and men like him in their day who laid the foundation that the fight for freedom was afterwards built on.

I must mention here that the helpers I had in putting the load of rifles, etc., into Stephen Lanigan's house were Paddy Daly and Seamus McCaughey, assisted by Mrs Lanigan. There were only five people outside the Kerr family in Liverpool who knew me or anything about me until my arrest and trial. Those were Stephen and Mrs Lanigan, Paddy Daly, Seamus McCaughey and Mick O'Leary.

I knew Seán Lynchehaun as a member of the Volunteers

SINN FEIN SUSPECTS AT ALLOA.

DRAMATIC CAPTURE AFTER MOTOR CAR CHASE.

Big Cargo of Firearms and Explosives.

A dramatic capture of two men—said to be leading members of the Sinn Fein movement in Scotland—was effected in Alloa late on Saturday night after an exciting motor car chase.

For some time past it has been evident that the energies of the Sinn Feiners had extended to the mining areas of Fife, and that an elabor-

before I left home. I didn't meet him in Liverpool until I saw him in the Bridewell after he was arrested. I had just been brought from Scotland to stand my trial.

Seán was right in giving the date of the burnings as the 27th of November. I was arrested outside Stirling on the following Saturday night, the 4th of December.

After the burnings, that night the police and detectives raided several houses, including Kerr's. In his pocket book, they found a receipt for the price of 15 pairs of boltcutters that were used for cutting the locks of the warehouses along with another receipt which proved that I had been in Liverpool shortly before the fires.

Kathleen and Sheila Browne were sisters and natives of Cork. Kathleen was a member of the office staff in Hughes' Provision Stores, and Sheila was a teacher. They bought almost all the paraffin that was used in burning the warehouses. The evidence against them by the witnesses for the Crown broke down in cross-examination and they were acquitted. Michael Brennan, of Kiltimagh, and Andrew McPartlin, of Dublin, had nothing to do with the burnings and they were acquitted also. Kerr, McCaughey and Fowler were all sentenced to long terms of imprisonment. Though they were able to prove that I was there shortly before the fires, they couldn't prove that I was there the night of the fires.

When I was arrested in Scotland I had a full car load, including a half ton of explosives, several hundred yards of fuse and hundreds of detonators, some rifles, revolvers and ammunition. When I was arrested, I had a boy named Charlie Strickland along with me in the car. He was 19 at the time but he only looked like a boy of 12 or 13. He was very small for his age. He was the smallest assistant I had, but he was certainly the best. On several occasions, he passed unnoticed when a full-grown man would be suspected. Charlie is now a bus

Attorney General Sir Gordon Hewart led the prosecution for the Crown in the case against my father and seven others who were charged with the Liverpool warehouse burnings. By the end of 1921, Hewart was putting his name to the Anglo-Irish Treaty.

driver with CIE. He visits the West every summer with special tours. He was in Mulranny last year.

The trial in Liverpool was the first big Sinn Féin case in England, as it was then called, and the British Government sent down the Attorney General to lead the prosecution for the Crown. Sir Gordon Hewart was Attorney General at the time. He was one of the British representatives who signed the Treaty afterwards along with Lloyd George, Winston Churchill and Lord Birkenhead. It was little he thought during the course of that trial early in 1921 that he would be signing a peace treaty with the hated rebels before the end of that same year. He was Lord Chief Justice of England for a number of years afterwards. Sir Alfred Tobin was the judge and I'm sure he would be delighted in sentencing us all to death if he could.

When they failed to prove that I was there the night of the fires, our counsel demanded my acquittal. The Judge's words to the jury were: "Though I firmly believe that Coyle is a dangerous criminal I must ask the jury to return a verdict of not guilty as there is not sufficient evidence to convict him, but of course he will be handed over to the Scottish authorities to be tried in Scotland for the crime committed there."

I was handed over in court to the Scottish detectives. After a trial lasting five days, I was sentenced to five years' penal servitude in Edinburgh on the 19th March, 1921. There were 15 others on trial along with me, including my companion Charlie. Before I was sentenced, I had a lengthy speech from the dock in which I took full responsibility for my own actions and those of all the others on trial along with me. I proudly admitted being a soldier of the Irish Republic and that I didn't mind what I would suffer or what punishment I would undergo for justice, but that I didn't want to see anybody else suffer for anything I had done. I stated if I had any regrets it wasn't for what I had done, but for being deprived of the opportunity of doing more.

Seven of the others along with me on trial were acquitted and eight convicted, including Charlie. Had we been on trial in Ireland at the time we would not have recognised the courts, but if we denied the right of the British

I am pictured with my wife Geraldine outside our home when the Sliabh na mBan armoured car visited Geesala in 2018.

government to try us in our country, we didn't deny their right to try us in theirs, and furthermore, headquarters in Dublin wanted the publicity of the trials.

As well as the continued smuggling of war material from Liverpool, there were men and women smuggled from there too. President de Valera was one of these after his escape from Lincoln Gaol; Seán Milroy and Seán McGarry escaped along with him. Michael Collins planned and organised that escape. He went there personally to have it carried out. Mrs Sheehy-Skeffington was also smuggled from Liverpool to Dublin when the British government didn't want her to land in Ireland.

The work done by Irishmen across the water was no small factor in bringing the members of the British government to their senses and it proved to them that the battle wasn't going to be fought on Irish soil alone, that the people of England and Scotland would bear the brunt of it. When I mentioned the work done by Irishmen over there I should have included Irishwomen too, for they certainly done their part as well as the men.

My story, if all told, would be a long one. The foregoing are a few of the outstanding facts.

**Henry Coyle,
Geesala, Ballina.**

CHAPTER 45

Old Comrades in Arms

THERE were few houses in Ireland where Michael Collins was held in greater reverence than the Coyle homestead in Doolough. Long before he was given the Hollywood treatment, Collins was elevated to almost mythical status by my father, who remained as much in awe of 'The Big Fella' in the 1960s as he had been when they first met almost half a century earlier.

There was no portrait of Collins hanging above the fireplace, but we didn't need any physical memorial to this great Irishman because my father had that rare gift of being able to conjure evocative images with just a few short sentences. Indeed, the fireside anecdotes he occasionally recounted about 'General Collins' had a far more enduring impact on an impressionable youngster like myself than any framed photograph on a wall.

I turned eight in 1966 when Ireland celebrated the golden jubilee of the 1916 Rising, and that historic event prompted a wave of reminiscing on the fight for political freedom. Throughout the spring of 1966, I watched my father sitting at the kitchen table, newspapers spread out in front of him while he read the latest series of articles about the Easter Rising or the War of Independence, occasionally cutting out pieces and sometimes taking pen to paper to write a few notes.

In sifting through my father's papers, I came across a letter sent to him in the mid-1960s by the historian Desmond Greaves, who was then researching the life of Liam Mellows for his book *Liam Mellows and the Irish Revolution*. My father also exchanged letters with John P. McPhillips in New York in the wake of the *Western People* series of articles. This is a short extract from John's letter to my father as they reminisced about the 'olden days':

I had a letter from Steve [Lanigan] shortly before he died in the early Fifties. He was then in the Irish Customs based in Dublin. I met 'Wee' Charlie Strickland in Dublin after the Amnesty. He was a great kid. I probably met you in Liverpool seeing that we travelled much of the same ground and knew the same people. I do remember the 'Sinn Féin Motorcar', but this was after your exploits were generally known. Thank you again, Henry, for your letter in the Western.

Another piece of correspondence I came across was a letter from Michael Rooney, the then editor of the *Irish Independent*, regarding a proposed series of articles by my father. The letter was dated July 24, 1967, but unfortunately the series never happened. It's a great pity because my father had such a remarkable story to tell, and if the series had been anything like his letter to the *Western*, it would have made for compelling reading.

The most poignant letter I came across was from Charlie Strickland, written on a receipt docket from Josie Moran's grocers in Mulranny. It is undated but I presume it was sent some time in the early 1960s. The letter reads as follows:

Hello Henry

Well, here I am in Josie Moran's. The world is very small indeed.

Every time I come here I am inquiring as to how you are doing.

My thoughts go back to very sad, yet happy, days.

Some day I will make a call on you and have a good old chat. I am glad to hear you are enjoying good health.

Remember me to Mrs and family. Good night and God Bless.

Your old Comrade in Arms

Charles Strickland, alias 'McGinn'.

I think it is such a beautiful letter because it captures the enduring friendship between two men still bound together by the remarkable adventures of their youth. Four decades had rolled by since those epic voyages across Scotland and England in the Sinn Féin Motorcar, and Charlie and my father were now in the autumn of their lives, but they were still 'Comrades in Arms' and that's the way they'd remain in death and beyond.

In sourcing photographs for this book, I was determined to get an image of Charlie Strickland, especially after reading that letter. But I really struggled to obtain a photograph of sufficient quality and had resigned myself to using one in which Charlie was barely visible. The book was almost finished when I happened to come across Kate Lee's application for an IRA pension. In a letter to the Army Pensions Board she refers to seeing a photograph of Charlie Strickland in the *Irish Independent* in 1942. I immediately went searching through the editions of the *Independent* and found a wonderful image of Charlie when he was appointed a long-distance bus driver for CIE. It seems too much of a coincidence that I would come across the photograph in such an unexpected way and it convinced me the old comrades in arms are still working in mysterious ways!

JOS. MORAN
Grocer, Tea, Wine and Spirit Merchant.
MULRANNY,
Co. Mayo.

Phone : 5.

_____19_____

_____

Hello Henry

Well here I am in Josie Moran's.
The World is very small indeed.
Every Time I come here I am enquiring as to
how you are doing. My Thoughts go back
to very sad yet Happy Days. Some Day
I will make a call on you and have a
Good Old chat. I am glad to hear
you are enjoying Good Health.
    Remember me to Mrs and Family
Good night & God Bless
        Your Old Comrade in Arms
            Charles Strickland
            alias "M Gun".

**Charlie Strickland wrote to my father when he visited Mulranny as a bus driver in the early 1960s.
Inset: Charlie is pictured in 1942 when he became one of Ireland's first long-distance bus drivers.**

I don't know if Charlie ever got to visit his former commandant again. I was still too young to understand my father's pivotal role in the War of Independence; in fact, I thought every Irish child's dad had taken up arms after 1916 to help bring an end to seven centuries of British rule. It was only as I grew older that I began to fully appreciate the uniqueness of my father's story, and with that more mature perspective came a new-found realisation of the respect in which my father was held in our small, close-knit community on the Atlantic seaboard, especially among older neighbours who lived through those troubled times. People came to him to get government forms signed; they came to him when applying for Old IRA pensions; they came to him for advice and they even came to him to solve local disputes.

Years later, Eamonn Munnelly told me how my father might arrive into Munnelly's pub accompanied by two warring parties and order a pint for each of them and a ginger ale for himself because he never drank or smoked. He'd place the adversaries on either side of him and get straight to the point: "So, what's ye're difference?"

My father would listen patiently as both men aired their grievances before he'd suggest a compromise, which might be acceptable to each side.

"Don't pass this on to the next generation," he'd advise. "Let ye solve ye're differences here and get on with living."

Eamon told me the two men, who might have killed each other a few months earlier, often ended up fighting on the same side in some later dispute!

As I grew older, I became accustomed to the sight of elderly strangers turning up unannounced on our doorstep and asking to see my father. I learned that these were men he knew during the War of Independence. Sometimes, I'd catch snatches of their conversations and I'd throw in the odd question myself, and as I grew older I became increasingly fascinated by the remarkable stories these elderly men had to tell. Usually, the conversations revolved around one man – and one man only – and every time Michael Collins' name was mentioned the tears welled up in my father's eyes.

"He was born 100 years before his time," he once told me.

"How'd you make that out?" I asked.

"Well, I can remember him talking about aluminium and plastics, about planes landing on the water, about Ireland being one of the best food-producing countries in the world. He was talking about things 50 years ago that are only starting to happen in Ireland now."

My father firmly believed that Ireland would have been a very different country had Collins survived and I believe Henry Coyle's life would also have been very different. Anytime the Civil War arose in conversation, his voice trembled with emotion and he'd simply say: "We were killing each other when we should have been rebuilding our country."

He never talked about his role in the Free State Army during that dark, desperate chapter when the hundreds of guns he smuggled from Scotland to rid Ireland of imperial tyranny were used to slaughter Irishmen. The quiver in his voice said it all about the enduring heartache he carried from that period, and I think the outbreak of the Troubles in Northern Ireland in 1969 upset him greatly because he was originally a 32-county man and now the bitter harvest of Partition was being reaped. He was utterly opposed to the violence in Northern Ireland – and was horrified to see so many lives being lost in the 1970s – but he also remained steadfast in his view that Partition should never have occurred. I have fragments of a draft letter he wrote around this time in which he rails against the idea of a Unionist veto over a united Ireland.

"The six counties are part of the Irish nation and they'll never be anything else," he declared.

My father's view was very much at odds with Fine Gael, the party he supported in each election, but he was always his own man and that's the way he remained until the end. He maintained a strong friendship with Paddy Lindsay, who became Master of the High Court after his political career ended, and the two spent many an hour together during my father's later years. The Lindsays have been great friends to the Coyles for all of my life, and it is only now when I look through my father's pension application that I realise the important role played by Paddy in finally securing justice for Henry Coyle.

Paddy Lindsay's successor in Fine Gael was another neighbour, Paddy O'Toole, who served as a TD throughout the 1970s and 1980s, and was a government minister from 1982-'87. Remarkably, the three houses – Coyle's, Lindsay's and O'Toole's – were all next door to each other, and Paddy Lindsay christened our street 'Parliamentary Row'. Maybe we'll have another TD from Parliamentary Row at some stage in the future!

When I look back now, armed with the knowledge I have gathered in the course of my research, I think it is remarkable that my father never allowed the ghosts of the past to haunt the loving household into which I was so fortunate to be born and reared. Indeed, he didn't utter a word to any of his children about some of the more troublesome episodes in his earlier life. That's why I still struggle to believe that the placid, quiet gentleman I knew as my father, who sat at our kitchen table pouring over the Sunday newspapers, actually featured on the front pages of newspapers in Britain, Ireland and America at various points in his life. You'd certainly never think it to see him sitting there on a Sunday afternoon in the 1970s, still immaculately dressed in the suit and tie he always wore to Mass, as he turned the pages of the

Independent, occasionally pausing to glance contemplatively out the window towards Doolough Strand where the Atlantic tide beat out the very same gentle rhythm he first heard as a boy growing up in that little thatched hovel in neighbouring Muingdoran at the turn of the century.

On the face of it, Henry Peter Coyle hadn't travelled far from boyhood to old age – just a brisk summertime stroll across the soft sands of Doolough when the tide is out – but in truth, my father's voyage from child to pensioner had been as tempestuous as those roaring Atlantic waves on a stormy winter's night. Like all good sailors, he stayed true to his course and never gave up hope, eventually finding in my mother a truly remarkable woman who became the steady beacon that guided him into the calmer waters of his later years.

My father never expected to be widowed a second time, so it came as a terrible shock to him when my mother was struck down with terminal cancer at the young age of 63. It was a devastating blow to all of us, especially for my siblings living away from home because it happened so fast. My father was actually receiving treatment in Belmullet District Hospital when my mother was diagnosed, and I don't know what I'd have done without the support of my cousin Bridget Heston, the daughter of my aunt Bridget McGuire, who gave us the cows all those years earlier. Bridget came from Dooriel in Ballycroy and stayed with me for a number of weeks until my sisters could come home from England. She even brought her youngest son Patrick with her, leaving her husband Jim to look after the rest of the children. The kindness of the McGuire and Heston families was never forgotten in the Coyle household. I also wish to acknowledge the outstanding care given to my parents in their final months by Dr Tom Kelly, Belmullet District Hospital, and Dr John Flynn, GP Bangor Erris.

Sadly, my mother passed away within six months of being diagnosed. The late great Erris correspondent for the *Western People*, Eamon Shevlin, published an obituary that perfectly captured the wonderful woman that was Molly Coyle.

On her arrival in the Geesala area, she soon made friends and became one of the best-respected residents in the community. She was a devout Catholic and always gave first-class attention to her religious duties.

She possessed a lively personality and was the personification of goodness and her pleasant easygoing manner and her complete sincerity won for her a host of friends. Of a very quiet disposition, she was an excellent family woman and was a general favourite amongst

My cousin Bridgie Heston from Ballycroy was a fantastic help when my parents both became ill in 1978. I am forever indebted to Bridgie for everything she did at that difficult time.

the community. The late Mrs Coyle was a very helpful neighbour, kind and most likeable and seemed to have captured the magic touch in her relations with people.

My mother certainly had 'the magic touch' but she was blessed to live in the most wonderful community in Doolough where people were so good to each other. In the nearest house lived Mike and Pauline Lindsay, who were my godparents, and just a few metres further on was Ellen O'Toole, mother of the aforementioned Paddy O'Toole. In the nearest house, on the Geesala side, lived Tommy and Maggie Goonan.

All of these people made our family feel welcome in Doolough and my mother loved it when people came to visit. I remember many people from further down the Doolough road would call for tea on their way home from Mass or after collecting their shopping or pension in Geesala. Even if my mother was not home, people who were cutting and saving turf on the nearby

Former IRA Volunteer and Geesala man, Michael Cafferkey, delivered the graveside oration at my father's funeral in June 1979. Despite taking opposite sides in the Civil War, they remained the best of friends and had agreed that whoever survived the other would deliver their eulogy. Thanks to my friend Joe Carey for sourcing this picture of a great freedom fighter.

bog would come across and boil a kettle of water for the tea. My mother was a kind and generous woman who shared with others what little she had, and that generosity was always reciprocated by our fantastic neighbours and the wider community in Geesala. My mother would always mention how good, kind and generous all the neighbours were to the Coyle family when we were living in poor circumstances in Muingdoran and Dooyork. There are way too many to mention in this book but they know how grateful we are.

My mother's swift and unexpected passing left my father utterly bereft. She had been the woman who rescued him from the depths of despair in the 1930s and he couldn't countenance a life without her. She died in November 1978 and he was reunited with her within seven months.

His death in May 1979 occurred at the height of a strike at An Post and I recall the difficulties we had making contact with the Irish Army to arrange

Members of the Irish Army fire a volley of shots over my father's coffin in Geesala Cemetery in June 1979. It was a fitting send-off for a man who gave so much to the cause of Irish freedom. This photograph was taken by local woman Sadie McDonagh, a great family friend.

for a party of soldiers to come to Geesala to perform the traditional military salute at the graveside.

"This is not an emergency," the lady on the telephone exchange told me when I explained why I wanted to be connected to Renmore Barracks in Galway. An Post operated the country's telephone exchanges and were only handling emergency calls during the industrial action.

But the telephone operator wasn't going to get rid of me that easy. My father had sacrificed too much to help Ireland win its political freedom and there was no way he would be buried without appropriate recognition from the independent nation he helped to establish. I persevered and eventually made contact with the Defence Forces, who duly dispatched a party of young soldiers to give my father the military salute he so richly deserved.

In its obituary, the *Irish Independent* referred to my father as a member of 'the first Dáil Éireann under W.T. Cosgrave' and described him as 'a Chief of Staff to Michael Collins in Scotland'. The *Western People* published a very extensive obituary outlining my father's role in the War of Independence and his later involvement in the National Army and Dáil Éireann.

Mike Cafferkey, an old friend and comrade of my father's from Coolaba, Geesala, delivered the graveside oration. It was something they had agreed in advance and I think it reflects my father's willingness to cross the political divide because Mike had taken the anti-Treaty side in the Civil War and was a staunch Fianna Fáil supporter. Yet they never allowed their differing Civil War perspectives to impinge on their long-standing friendship and Henry Joe recalls nights where Mike and my father would spend hours in the kitchen chatting away about olden times.

Mr. Henry Coyle

MR. HENRY COYLE, of Geesala, Ballina, who has died, was the first Erris man to be elected to the first Dail Eireann under the leadership of W. T. Cosgrave. He was a member of the Old I.R.A. and a Commandant in the National Army. He was also Chief of Staff to Michael Collins, in Scotland, during the War of Independence. Mr. Coyle was in his eighties.

The obituary for my father that appeared in the *Irish Independent*.

I wonder was there any other veteran of the War of Independence who had a Civil War 'opponent' deliver their graveside oration? That thought crossed my mind only recently as I stood at Beal na Bláth on August 21, 2022, and watched Fianna Fáil leader Micheál Martin deliver his historic oration in memory of Michael Collins. Henry Coyle and Mike Cafferkey were certainly ahead of their time.

We buried my father in the uniform of the Irish Army and the coffin was draped in the Tricolour of his beloved Ireland. It seemed like the end of an era on that June day in the cemetery in Geesala… and it surely was. My father was 84 years old when he died and many of the men and women who soldiered with him in that eventful, historic period from 1916 to 1923 had already gone to their eternal reward. By the late 1990s, all of that remarkable generation of freedom fighters was gone, but their legacy lives on. It is impossible to overstate their achievement in winning independence for Ireland after 700 years of British rule. They were the generation who raised Ireland to the dignity of nationhood and I am so proud of my father's role in that heroic struggle.

Henry Coyle, you will be remembered
for the many brave things you done.
When you fought for dear old Ireland
with your Fenian car and Fenian gun.

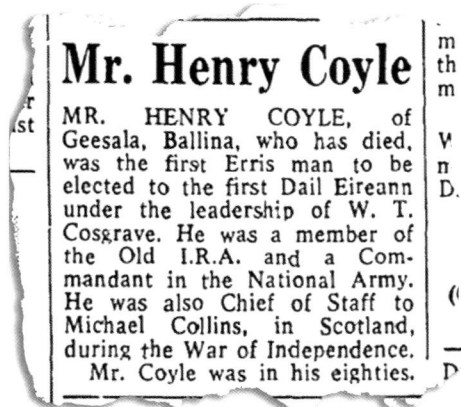

CHAPTER 46

Fighting with gloves
instead of guns

MY mother had great plans for my education and was keen to see me go the whole way to Leaving Certificate. The introduction of free education in the late 1960s meant more and more youngsters were going on to secondary school, most to Inter Cert and some to Leaving Cert.

When I finished the primary cycle at Geesala NS, my mother enrolled me in St Mary's Secondary School in Belmullet, even though I was adamant I wanted to go working like the rest of my siblings. My mother's intentions were good but I had other plans for my future.

By the age of 14, I had formed the view that the only way to get ahead in life was to start earning a bit of money. I had already developed a great interest in machinery and wanted to set up my own workshop at the house. I realised early in life that an hour with the head was better than a week with the spade.

The person who inspired me most was a local named John Harrington who worked as a fitter for Bord na Móna and was an absolute genius when it came to mechanics. He'd regularly visit my father and I particularly recall when he made a machine to pull his car trailer of turf out of the bog. I was absolutely fascinated with it, and John, Noel and I would go down to the bog in the evening when there was nobody around and start up the machine.

I was fascinated with machinery and wanted to learn how everything worked. Even when I was in secondary school, I was fixing machines at the house, so it probably came as no surprise to my parents when I decided not to go back after first year. Instead, I got a job on a fishing boat where I worked with some great people, namely Frank Cosgrove RIP, Willie Carey RIP, Martin Goonan and Joe Carey. I learned so much about life on that boat and I have very special memories of that time. It was better than any university.

Martin and Joe still live locally and we remain great friends to this day. Joe later applied his skills to traditional music and song, and he is widely known and respected throughout the country.

I eventually earned enough money to buy a tractor, which my brother Pat sourced for me in England and put on the boat at Holyhead. I travelled to Dublin with Mick McGrath, from Glenamoy, who used to run a hackney service along with his brother Paddy, bringing emigrants to the boat. I can still recall their telephone number: *Glenamoy 5.*

That first trip to the capital with Mick was an education in itself. Accompanying me was Seamus Conway, who was collecting a JCB that his brother Johnny (my brother-in-law) had sent across along with the tractor. We drove the tractor and the JCB from Dublin Port along the quays as far as Heuston Station where we put them on the train west. We later picked them up at Ballina railway station and drove out to Geesala. It was different times.

The tractor cost £180, but when I was paying Pat he gave me £20 back for good luck, and it was a lucky £20 note because I had great fortune with machinery afterwards. Pat and I had many magical days and nights travelling to auctions all over England purchasing vans and other machinery. RIP Pat.

By the age of 16, I was busy as an agricultural contractor, working from sunrise to sunset and loving every second of it. I didn't look beyond the need to earn money because I had seen my parents struggle to make ends meet for too long. I bought a second tractor and a thresher for summer work while I spent most of the winter fixing machines at the house. I started repairing tyres before graduating to scooters and tractors. I had no formal training but was absolutely fascinated with the workings of machines and I'd happily spend hours tinkering away with an engine. My father, who was confined to the house by then, often came to the window to watch as I worked. Even in his eighties, he took great interest in new technology and in seeing how things worked and he seemed pleased I was able to turn my hands to repairing machinery.

"I thought you'd never get that oul thing going again," he said to me one evening after I'd fixed a vintage tractor that must have come off the production line around the same time he was smuggling guns to Ireland.

In the spring of 1979, I married the love of my life Geraldine Lally, from neighbouring Shraigh, and she moved into the family home in Doolough where I was continuing to look after my father. My wedding to Geraldine was a great joy amidst the sadness of losing my parents within six months of each other. She was my rock then and has continued to be ever since.

Geraldine and I were unable to go on a honeymoon immediately after our wedding due to my father's illness but we made up for it later in the year when we travelled to Chicago to stay with Henry Joe and his family.

Four grandsons of Henry Coyle – all sons of my brother Noel - who achieved great success in amateur boxing, from left: Michael, Patrick, Anthony and Shane Coyle. Anthony won seven national titles, Patrick won three, while Michael and Shane were very unlucky not to win national honours too.

There was a fantastic Irish boxing scene in Chicago involving the likes of Henry Joe and the McGarry brothers, and I was quickly immersed in it.

Boxing had a big influence on all our lives in the Coyle household. Henry Joe, Pat and Willie were all members of the first club in Geesala, but it closed when Fr Harte left the parish and emigration robbed it of so many talented members, including my older brothers. However, a new club opened in Doohoma where John, Noel and I learned the skills of this wonderful sport.

Great people were in charge there – men like Laurence Howard, Sonny Sweeney and Paddy Joe Goonan. – and many good boxers came through the club. But once again emigration put paid to a promising club.

While in Chicago, Henry Joe said I should try to get the boxing club back up and running in Geesala. When I returned, I called a meeting about restarting the club, but just two people showed up – Dermot Heneghan and Patrick Barrett, who had both been involved in the old club. Dermot and his brother Willie Paul were members of the old club and Patrick Barrett had been a trainer.

Three attendees at the first meeting wasn't a very promising start but we decided to push on. We put out the word that training was to commence very soon… and the rest, as they say, is history.

Sadly, Dermot and Patrick are no longer with us, but they witnessed some great achievements and I'm sure they look down on us with pride today. The name of Geesala Boxing Club is now known around the world, but it might never have survived its early years without the generosity of a local man Peter Cosgrove. Peter emigrated to England at a young age and built up a successful construction business in London. On Christmas Night 1980, he put an envelope in my pocket while we were chatting in Munnelly's.

"That will keep the club going for next year," he said. "And I will do the same again next Christmas."

I wanted him to come to the club with it but he said he didn't want any publicity. His only request was that all of the boxers we brought to tournaments or championships should not go home hungry.

When I went home and opened the envelope, I was shocked to see that he had given £1,000, a huge sum at that time. True to his word, Peter did the same thing again the next year. In later years, he really enjoyed the success of the club, which more than likely would never have happened without his generosity. Peter later told me that when he was growing up in Erris there were so many youngsters who did not have money for any little treats or fancy beverages and that's why he wanted everyone who travelled with the boxing club to get good food and drink. What a gesture of kindness and it showed the measure of this great man. RIP Peter.

Most of Noel's sons were members and achieved great success in the amateur ranks. Shane and Michael were very unlucky not to have won national titles, while Anthony and Patrick have amassed 10 national titles – Anthony winning seven and Pat claiming three. My own three lads, Henry, Alan and Gerard, have also been members, with Henry winning two national titles before turning professional and winning the world championship on an unforgettable night in the TF Theatre in Castlebar in 2011.

Upon joining the professional ranks, Henry moved to Chicago where he was managed by my second son Alan, with the assistance of Henry Joe and John. He made his professional debut at Madison Square Garden in New York on St Patrick's Eve, 2007, with the legendary Raging Bull himself, Jake Le Motta, and Smokin' Joe Frazier among the front-row spectators. The great Andy Lee, who I trained as an amateur while manager of Ireland, was also on the ticket, while John McEnroe and Liam Neeson were in the crowd too.

A huge contingent of Henry's fans travelled from Ireland, Chicago and so many other parts of the world, and I will never forget the reception when we walked out into that famous auditorium. It was one of the great nights of my boxing life and none of it would have been possible without the support of two men with Mayo roots, Eddie and Tony McLoughlin, who were managing

My son Alan was a huge help to Henry when he turned professional and moved to Chicago, as were my brothers Henry Joe and John, who were also based in the Windy City. The 'Fab Four' are pictured in Gaelic Park in Chicago in 2018 after the Chicago MacBrides Gaelic football team won the North American club championship. They are all involved with the MacBrides.

the leading Irish fighter John Duddy at the time. Gerry Conway, a native of Inver in Erris, was another great supporter and could not do enough for us in New York in the lead-up to the fight.

We have had many magical evenings with Geesala Boxing Club over the last 43 years, not least the night in 2009 when we were named Irish Boxing Club of the Year. I'd like to mention, in particular, Johnny Carey, James Mangan, Patrick McDonagh, Micheal O Connaill and David Timlin, who were with me that night to pick up the award. They are among the many great people who have been involved with the club over the years, giving countless hours on a voluntary basis.

That award was due recognition for the countless volunteers who have devoted their time, talents and energy to Geesala Boxing Club, making it the wonderful sporting organisation it is today. When we began back in 1979, all of our members were male, but the growth of the sport amongst young girls has been phenomenal, thanks to the incredible achievements of Ireland's Olympian and world champion Katie Taylor. In recent years, Geesala BC's Ciara Ginty has won a world youth title while Aoibhe Carrabine has claimed a European youth title and won silver at the European U22 Championships.

One of the great memories from the early days of Geesala Boxing Club was the night in the mid-1980s when the 'Clones Cyclone' Barry McGuigan paid us a visit. At a personal level, it was wonderful to see my son Henry and nephews Patrick and Anthony carry on the proud family tradition by winning national titles. Henry Joe's victory in 1959 was the first of 13 national titles for the Coyle family, and hopefully there will be more to come in the next few years.

One of the few low points in boxing came in 2004 when Henry missed out on the final round of qualification for that year's Olympic Games in Athens. It took a little time to get over that disappointment, but we dusted ourselves down and made a promise that he'd get to represent his country on the international stage one way or the other. Henry was a member of the Army Reserve (FCA), and in the summer of 2005, he was given the opportunity to be part of the Irish Defences Forces team at the World Military Games in South Africa. Previous winners of this prestigious tournament included the Ukrainian-born world champion Vladimir Klitschko, so Henry was in good company.

In preparation for the tournament, Henry trained three times a day, five days a week, at the army barracks in Dundalk, and he was in the form of his life by the time he arrived in Johannesburg in July 2005. He defeated some top-quality fighters en route to the final, including a Tunisian who had earlier disposed of a former Olympian from Ukraine.

It was an incredible weekend for Geesala Boxing Club because another of our boxers, Donal Barrett, went to Canada and won the World Police championship, so we were now on course for a unique double.

In the final, Henry faced a boxer from Thailand, whose brother was crowned Olympic champion just a year earlier, so the chances of a gold medal seemed slim. But like his grandfather, after whom he was named, Henry revelled when the odds were stacked against him, and he was determined to see that Irish Tricolour hoisted in victory in South Africa. A quick flurry of punches late in the final sealed a most unexpected win for Ireland and gave Geesala Boxing Club its second world champion boxer in a matter of weeks.

The raising of the Tricolour at those finals was hugely symbolic for our family. We had, of course, hoped Henry might go to the Olympics but, in many ways, it was more fitting that he should have enjoyed victory at the World Military Games. His grandfather was, first and foremost, a military man who took pride in wearing the uniform of the Free State Army. He and his comrades sacrificed so much to bequeath us the right to raise that Tricolour in victory, and they had such great hopes when the Free State was founded. During his time in Peterhead Prison, my father dreamed of returning home to an

My daughter Evita captured this fabulous image of the annual racing on Doolough Strand.

independent Ireland, but I think even he would have struggled to believe that one day his grandson might stand proudly under the Tricolour and be crowned a champion at the World Military Games.

Almost a century after independence, a fearless, young man named Henry Coyle was still fighting for Ireland, but this time with gloves instead of guns.

My mother always harboured a healthy suspicion of politicians, and as I grew older I could see why. She had seen what politics did to her husband and she certainly would not have been keen to see any of her children embarking on a similar career. Consequently, I had no interest in getting involved in politics in my younger years; instead, I focused all of my efforts on sport and community projects.

My mother and father may have been skeptical about politics but they had a great commitment to public service, and they believed there were lots of other ways to serve the public than by becoming involved in politics. The spirit of 'meitheal' was very much alive in the Coyle household and my parents always encouraged us to assist our neighbours whenever we could. My siblings brought that spirit with them – whether it was to Manchester, Birmingham, London or Chicago – while I tried to do my bit for my native Geesala.

I didn't have to look too far for help. My oldest friend is John Munnelly and we have worked on several community projects over the years. John and I sat beside each other on our first day in Geesala National School and we have been the best of buddies ever since. Thirty years ago, we established the Geesala Festival and Doolough Races, which are held each August to coincide with the traditional homecoming holidays in Erris when emigrants returned from the UK and the USA. John is an amazing worker for his village and parish, and the Geesala Festival would not exist without his tireless efforts. He is also heavily involved in Kiltane GAA Club, having played for them in his youth and later served as an official. He is the finest, most unassuming community champion you could ever meet and I am proud to call him my friend.

In 1998, I was asked to go on Paul Claffey's Show on Midwest Radio where I spoke about some of the issues affecting Erris at that time. I spoke about the lack of opportunities for young people, the reluctance of Mayo County Council to grant planning permission for people who wanted to build homes in Erris and the shocking treatment of our emigrants who had kept the lights on at home when there was no money for the meter. I spoke from the heart and I spoke from my own life experience and that of my siblings, all of whom had been forced to take the emigrant boat in their younger years. The Celtic Tiger was beginning to roar in Ireland in 1998, but there was certainly no sign of it making an appearance beyond the bridge in Bellacorick.

The interview prompted an enormous response from listeners to Midwest and I also received a huge number of telephone calls. The local elections were due to be held in 1999 – the first elections to Mayo County Council since 1991 – and Fine Gael was seeking a candidate to replace the long-serving and legendary Bangor Erris councillor John Noel Carey. In early 1999, I was asked to put my name before the local convention with a view to running for Fine Gael later that year. I wasn't so sure about the idea. I was already heavily

The late James Coyle was a fantastic supporter in my early political career and was one of a small number of people who convinced me to put my name forward for Fine Gael in 1999.

involved in one sport – boxing – without also embracing the bloodsport that is politics; and at least boxing is governed by the Queensbury Rules! I had also expanded my business interests in the early 1990s when I purchased a shop and garage at Atticonaun in Belmullet, and I was the father of six children under the age of 18.

But there was another doubt in my mind about the wisdom of entering politics. I didn't know then much of what I know now, but I had heard enough over the years to be wary of a profession that destroyed my father in the mid-1920s. However, there is no point in giving out if you are not going to get involved. I had said my piece on Midwest Radio a year earlier and now it was time to back up that talk by trying to make a difference through democratic means. A number of people played an important role in convincing me to put my name forward. They were Phiilip Irwin, Kieran Moran, John Noel Carey (RIP), James Coyle (RIP) and his family, Michael Conmy, John Munnelly and Lily Carey.

At a Fine Gael selection convention on March 1, 1999, I was one of three Fine Gael candidates selected to run in the electoral area of Erris/Achill. I was not sure I had done the right thing but I made a commitment that however long or short my political career, I'd be very much my own man and stand up for my beliefs and principals, and I would not be dictated to or influenced by

My son Henry is pictured with his wife Regina Garrity.

Pictured, from left, are my daughter Clara with her fiancé Kyle Holmes and my daughter Evita with her husband Thomas Murphy.

party politics. Different events had shaped my thinking, mainly my mother who I witnessed crying after her nine children as they had to emigrate one by one to find work in other countries. She was one of the many Irish mothers who reared their children for export to the four corners of the world without little or no acknowledgement from successive Irish governments of the wonderful contribution they were still making to their native country by sending home money.

If I could be a voice for those emigrants and their families at home, and for other people who didn't have a voice in Irish society, then I'd be doing a good thing, and I knew my mother and father would approve, despite their understandable reservations about politics.

Some 75 years after my father lost his Dáil seat in such controversial circumstances, the Coyle name was back on an election ballot paper in Erris. The wheel of history had turned full circle.

CHAPTER 47

A good and sincere man

ONE of the first interviews I gave as a Fine Gael election candidate was to Tom Kelly of the *Connaught Telegraph* on March 10, 1999, when I remarked: "It was a very big decision, and an emotional one, for me to allow my name go forward. Politics was never that kind to my family."

I did not elaborate but Tom noted I had 'a briefcase full of press cuttings detailing much of [my] father's life and times'. My father was very much on my mind throughout that campaign and I wondered what he would have made of his youngest son's foray into politics. I approached the election with a healthy optimism but I wasn't going to be too upset if I lost either. Fianna Fáil was in the ascendancy in 1999 after two years of government and three of the four outgoing councillors in Erris/Achill (Fine Gael's Pat Kilbane, Fianna Fáil's Tim Quinn and Independent Paddy Cosgrave) were seeking re-election, so it was always going to be a tough task to take a seat at the first time of asking. The other first-time candidates were Tony Mullarkey and Michael Holmes, while my running mate in Erris was Ian McAndrew, who I have been friendly with since our youth.

The election in Erris/Achill in 1999 went down in history and the count turned out to be nearly as long as the campaign itself! I had to wait several days to be officially elected after the battle for the fourth seat came down to a fraction of one vote. Michael Holmes, who was running on an Independent ticket, and his neighbour, Frank Leneghan, from Ballycroy, endured several recounts before Frank was finally declared the winner in the sixth count, thus clearing the way for my election too. I knew Michael from our days as agricultural contractors in the 1970s and I was delighted to see him make up for the disappointment five years later when he was comfortably elected to the council. Ian McAndrew narrowly missed out too but was later elected to Údarás na Gaeltachta and I was delighted to canvass with him in that election.

Fianna Fáil had an overall majority in the council chamber when I first entered, but Fine Gael gained control in 2004 under the party leadership of

I am pictured with family members and supporters at The Mall in Castlebar on the day I was elected chairman of Mayo County Council. This photograph is all the more special because it was taken by a wonderful friend, Henry Wills, of the *Western People.*

Enda Kenny, who would go on to become Taoiseach in 2011. Enda has always taken an interest in my father's story, having first heard about Henry Coyle from his own father, the late Henry Kenny, who was TD for Mayo for over 20 years. Indeed, during my research I found a letter from Henry Kenny TD in which he was making representations on behalf of my father.

One of my proudest moments was in June 2006 when I was elected cathaoirleach (chairman) of Mayo County Council, with the support of my Fine Gael colleagues, as well as Johnny Mee of the Labour Party. Castlebar man Johnny had a long and distinguished career in politics at urban and county council level, and was a great mentor to younger councillors like myself. I would like to take this opportunity to thank the councillors who voted and supported me as cathaoirleach.

There were so many thoughts going through my mind on that June morning as I made my way from Doolough to Castlebar for the meeting. I thought, in particular, of my father and mother, and how proud they would have been to see their son elected as Mayo's first citizen. It was something they could never have imagined in those dark days in Dooyork when they barely had food to put on the table for their young family.

I was especially delighted to have Geraldine's mother Celia Lally in attendance because she represented the older generation who, like my parents, endured such tough times in Erris in the 1940s and 1950s. I spent many hours

My wife's late parents Celia and John Lally in their younger years. I interviewed Celia on many occasions about growing up in Erris and travelling to Scotland to work on the potato fields.

with Celia, recording her memories of growing up in Erris and 'tatie picking in Scotland, and it gave me a great insight into what life was like for my parents. Indeed, Celia's influence is evident in some of the issues highlighted in this book, especially around living conditions in Erris in the first half of the 20th century.

My year as chairman of the council was unforgettable and I met so many fantastic people on various trips abroad. One of the greatest experiences was an official visit to Argentina in March 2007 to coincide with the 150th anniversary of the death of Foxford-born Admiral William Brown, the founder of the Argentine Navy. The organiser of the trip was the late J.J. O'Hara, from Foxford, a wonderful community activist and staunch Fine Gael supporter, who sadly died a year later at a very young age.

I had many reservations about entering politics but I am very glad now that I took the leap of faith back in 1999. I have made so many great, life-long friends and I have been humbled to witness history in the making. I was in Dáil Éireann to see a Mayo man, Enda Kenny, elected Taoiseach in 2011 and to see a great and loyal friend, Michael Ring, appointed to Cabinet in 2017. I had the chance to shake hands with a future US President, Joe Biden, on his

I am pictured with my godmother Pauline Lindsay after I was elected cathaoirleach of Mayo County Council in 2006.

visit to Mayo in 2016, but most of all I have had the privilege to meet Mayo people at home and abroad who are doing many extraordinary things.

I wish to take this opportunity to thank all those who have supported me, personally and politically, over the years. In particular, I want to thank the officials and members of Geesala Boxing Club, the committee and members of Geesala Community Council, and the people of Erris who have voted me into Mayo County Council in six successive elections. It is something I have never taken for granted, and I am honoured to have had the opportunity to represent the people of Erris in the chamber of Mayo County Council for the last 23 years.

I also wish to pay tribute to my council colleagues, past and present. I have never seen anyone elected who did not try to do the best they could for their area and the people they represented. I also want to thank the chief executives of the council – Des Mahon, Peter Hynes and, most recently, Kevin Kelly – and all their wonderful staff who I have had the pleasure of working with since being elected 23 years ago. In particular, I wish to acknowledge the support of Padraig Brogan and the wonderful indoor and outdoor staff in the council's area office in Belmullet.

In 2006, I was proud to represent Mayo County Council as cathaoirleach at the Humbert Summer School in Ballina when the great peacemaker from Northern Ireland John Hume received the Michael Davitt Award along with former Taoiseach and another great peacemaker Albert Reynolds. Both men are now deceased. Pictured, from left: Cllr Mark Winters, chairman, Ballina Urban District Council; Tony McGarry, Humbert Summer School; Albert Reynolds, Cllr Gerry Coyle, John Hume, Fine Gael leader Enda Kenny and John Cooney, Humbert Summer School. Enda Kenny has been a great source of encouragement in writing this book and has always expressed a keen interest in my father's story.

Even on the toughest days, I have never regretted my decision to enter public life, and I hope I have repaid the faith the electors of Erris placed in me since 1999.

Some of my fondest memories of working on this book are from the early days, around the turn of the millennium, when my nephew Brendan Conway was assisting with the research. Brendan was more like a brother than a nephew to me and he was absolutely fascinated in his grandfather's involvement in the fight for Irish freedom.

Born and raised in Manchester, Brendan was one of five children born to my sister Mary and Johnny Conway, and he and his siblings were steeped in Irish history, music and culture. Indeed, I recall one occasion when the Conway children were very young and we were all seated at the kitchen table in their house.

"When are we going home?" one of the children asked their mother.

"Sure aren't you already home!" I told them.

"No," came the reply, "we mean home to Ireland, to Geesala."

John, Annie and Eamonn Munnelly are pictured with Alan and myself.

If Geesala was 'home' to Brendan and his siblings, then the Conway house in Manchester was a 'home from home' for all of the Coyles who travelled to England. We'd get the boat over to Holyhead and stop in Manchester en route to Birmingham or London. Mary would always have the finest of welcomes and her generosity was unlimited. Conway's home was open to many, many people from Erris and beyond, not just the immediate Coyle family.

Brendan was a great fan of Irish music and, in particular, Shane McGowan and the Pogues. He'd be in our house in Geesala playing all the rebel songs, and many a great night was had.

"There might be more of a rebel in you than you think," I once told him.

"What do you mean?" he replied.

I then told Brendan about his grandfather and played him some of the recordings I made with my father in the mid-1970s. He was immediately hooked and the two of us were soon visiting libraries in Liverpool and Glasgow, trying to gather as much material as we could. It was the days of microfilm, so we were limited in what we could do, but we still managed to amass quite a lot of newspaper reports relating to my father's activities as an IRA volunteer in

I am pictured with my late and much missed nephew Brendan (on right) and his brother Gerard. This photograph was taken in Wales when I was managing an Irish Amateur boxing team that included my son Henry, and there was no prouder man in the arena than Brendan.

Britain from 1919-'21. Indeed, many of the reports used in this book were sourced in the late 1990s and early 2000s, and they bear Brendan's handwriting. He often visited libraries on his own and telephoned me in Ireland when he found another fascinating nugget of information about his grandfather's past.

I have such happy memories of days in Liverpool Library with Brendan and our excitement when we came across the *Daily Mirror* front-page coverage of the warehouse fires. Brendan was astounded that his grandfather had been involved in such dramatic events.

Sadly, Brendan passed away in a freak accident in 2002 at the tender age of 32 and his death devastated everyone in the Conway and Coyle families. I could not look at this project for a long time afterwards because whenever I opened the briefcase where I kept all the files I'd be reminded of Brendan. It was just too sad and I could not imagine completing the work without him. Indeed, for several years after his death, I gave up on the project completely and concentrated instead on boxing, politics and, most importantly, my family. When Henry made his professional boxing debut at Madison Square Garden, we remembered Brendan by having the name 'Bren' embroidered in a corner of Henry's shorts.

I might never have returned to the story of Henry Peter Coyle had it not been for the publication of a book by Shane Coleman, then a political journalist for the *Sunday Tribune*. The book contained a collection of stories about Irish election campaigns and controversies of the past, including my father's imprisonment and removal from the Dáil in 1924.

Shane's article made me realise there was so much about my father the public did not know. Up to then, the only reference to Henry Coyle was in relation to that unfortunate court case in 1924, but I had all of this additional information locked away in a briefcase. Shane's article was the kickstart I needed to get back to finishing the book about my father.

I am pictured at the grave of Neill Kerr in Glasnevin Cemetery in Dublin.

A few days later, I sat down at the kitchen table and started to sift through the many newspaper clippings, notes and other material I had gathered since the 1970s. It was the first time since Brendan's untimely death I had properly looked at the contents of that briefcase and I was amazed at what we had gathered in our years working together. I decided there and then that the best way I could honour Brendan's memory – not to mention my father's – was to complete the book that had been started almost a decade earlier.

The next time I was in Dublin I called to the *Sunday Tribune* office and introduced myself to Shane as the 'son of Henry Coyle'. I think he was surprised to discover Henry Coyle had sons and daughters who were still alive and he was even more surprised when I showed him some of the articles relating to my father's trials in England and Scotland while in the IRA. In fairness to Shane, his original article was based on the information available at that time and he was not to know of Henry Coyle's involvement in the War of Independence prior to his election to Dáil Éireann. We subsequently met again on the day Enda Kenny was elected Taoiseach in March 2011 and I promised him that at sometime in the future he would read the full story of Henry Coyle.

My father's neighbour and great friend, the late Paddy Lindsay, former TD and Master of the High Court.

That was more than a decade ago, but I am glad I waited until now to finally put pen to paper because if I had published my father's story at an earlier date I'd have missed out on so many important details. The recent publication online of the Military Service Pensions Collection was a game-changer for me because I could now find out about my father's activities in Scotland through his pension file, but also by reading the pension files of those who served with him. I had already come across statements in the Bureau of Military History from people like Dr Paddy Daly and Joseph Booker – these were first published online in March 2003 – but the Military Service Pensions Collection became a goldmine for me, especially as it allowed me to tell the stories of other people, like Neill Kerr, who were such pivotal characters in my father's life during the War of Independence.

At times, the amount of material was overwhelming, and it was also very difficult to get my head around some of the more extraordinary events of my father's younger years. I needed to check and recheck many newspaper reports and documents just to make sure that this was the same man because I certainly didn't recognise the Henry Peter Coyle they were talking about.

At one stage, I called over to my old neighbour and great friend Áine Ní Chiaráin, who knew my father from her many visits to our house in the 1960s and 1970s. Like me, Áine found it hard to believe that the firebrand republican speaking from the dock in the High Court of Justiciary in Edinburgh was the same Henry Coyle who she knew as quiet, unassuming and soft-spoken neighbour.

"This can't be the Henry Coyle I knew growing up," she remarked.

A few months after our conversation, Áine's husband Séamus was in Dublin and happened to wander into the GPO Museum. While perusing the various exhibition stands, he spied an impressive silver teapot bearing the inscription: *Presented to IRA Commandant H.P. Coyle by the men of the Dundee company of the IRA on the occasion of his marriage.* He immediately took a photograph and

My father was described by one of his former comrades in the IRA in Scotland as 'a good and sincere man'. I think it is a fitting epitaph to the man I knew as a loving father 40 years later.

sent it to me. It was the first I had heard of the teapot, which was loaned to the GPO Museum by a 'private collector' after being purchased at Whyte's Auction some years ago. My father would have left the teapot behind when he fled Scotland with his infant daughter in the summer of 1933 and it was probably sold as part of an auction of the contents of the Ferrie home in Dennistoun when Vincent died many years later. I still don't know who actually owns the teapot but, hopefully, I might get to meet them at some future date and show them the photographs from the wedding of IRA Commandant H.P. Coyle.

Even as I prepare to go to print, I am gaining new insights into my father's life that is allowing me to look afresh at some of the material I gathered years ago. In recent days, the staff of the Military Service Pensions Collection unearthed the private letter sent by Paddy Lindsay to General Seán MacEoin in April 1951, seeking a review of Henry Coyle's pension application. Referring to my father's loss of his pension as a result of a criminal conviction 27 years earlier, Lindsay remarked: "Up to now, he has forfeited £2,701-7s. As well as serving his full sentence!"

I think the exclamation mark speaks volumes for Lindsay's incredulity at the injustice visited upon Henry Coyle over such a long period. But I wonder what the future Master of the High Court would have thought had he known that my father's conviction for conspiracy in Edinburgh was one of the reasons cited on a ministerial order refusing him an IRA pension in Ireland? Had he been made aware of it I am fairly sure there would have been a second letter containing a stern demand to explain how such a thing was allowed to happen.

As I said at the outset, my objective in publishing this book is not to rewrite history or to present a glorified version of my father's past.

Nor do I wish to upset anyone or point the finger of blame for things that happened a long time ago. My father always believed in extending the hand of friendship and forgiveness, and I know he would not want his legacy to be one of division or bitterness.

My sincere hope is that this book will lead to a reappraisal of the life and legacy of Henry Coyle, a forgotten freedom fighter who, up to now, has been remembered solely for an unfortunate incident that was just a single episode in an eventful and well-lived life.

While researching this book, I found so much material that made Henry Peter Coyle – my father – seem like a complete stranger to me, but then I came across the article that IRA Volunteer Seán Healy wrote in *The Corkman* newspaper in 1968. As I previously mentioned, Healy was with my father in Glasgow throughout the War of Independence and they went on several raids for arms together. Referring to Henry Coyle's appointment as IRA Director of Purchasing in 1920, Healy wrote: *He was a good and sincere man for the job.*

That statement stopped me in my tracks because I could certainly say the same thing about the man I knew four decades later: he was a good and sincere man for the 'job' of fatherhood too. So, perhaps, the Henry Coyle I knew in the 1960s was not very different at all from the daring, fearless arms smuggler of the 1920s. The circumstances of his life may have completely changed in those 40 years but his character remained unaltered: he was still the same good and sincere man he had always been.

A word of thanks

I HAVE been very lucky in my life with my family, relatives, friends, sporting and political colleagues. I can say without a shadow of a doubt that the women in my life have been a major influence on me. I was blessed with an incredible mother, I had four wonderful sisters – Margaret, Ann, Mary, and Agnes – and then luckily for me I met Geraldine. With her came her seven sisters and her wonderful mother, Celia Lally, who was a great influence on our children. Of course, I also have my own three daughters, Loretta, Evita and Clara, who always keep me on the straight and narrow.

I have been blessed too with wonderful neighbours and friends in Geesala, people like John and Mary Carolan from just down the road in Doolough who have always been so helpful to my family down the years. It has always been a pleasure to be in their company, and their advice is cherished and respected in the Coyle household. I think too of people like the late Dermot Heneghan who was involved in Geesala Boxing Club from the night we started and was always the go-to man in the village for anyone who needed help.

Dermot came to my assistance as a child when I got into a bit of trouble while ice skating on a shallow lake near our home and dropped into the water after the ice broke. He was going up the road on his bike and jumped off when he saw I was in trouble and pulled me out of the water. Dermot was of different politics to myself and we had many jokes in later years when I'd be out canvassing and I'd tell him he must be sorry now for pulling me out of the lake!

His mother Biddy was a great friend of my own mother and she'd often walk across the strand for a visit. Biddy would be joined by Julia Barrett, mother of Dermot Barrett, another great friend of the Coyle family. Dermot bought the first tractor I ever sold, and he was telling me only recently that my father, with his tailoring skills, shortened the trouser leg of the suit Dermot wore for his wedding.

Geraldine and I are pictured with our children Henry, Loretta, Alan, Evita, Clara and Gerard, and grandson Jonathan.

My family was made to feel so welcome when we established our service station and garage in Attycunnane, Belmullet, in the early 1990s. I'd especially like to thank all of the people who worked for us and with us over the years, and I must give a special mention to Jackie and Patricia Coyle and Richie and Jenny Barrett.

Writing this book was an enormous undertaking and I wish to thank all those who assisted in any way over a long number of years. Archivists, librarians and historians in Ireland, England and Scotland helped out at different points along the way and I am very grateful for their help. I also want to acknowledge the assistance of Philomena McIntyre, a local historian and researcher in Erris who was very helpful, Lisa Monaghan in Belmullet and Rory Strickland, grandson of my father's old friend Charlie.

The Coyle family has had a long association with the *Western People*, and my father's article in 1964 was one of the few times he spoke publicly about his involvement in the War of Independence. When my son Henry made his professional boxing debut at Madison Square Garden, current editor James Laffey was ringside and he was there too on those magical nights in Castlebar for the world title bouts. I first spoke to James about this book almost a decade

THE NEXT GENERATION: Geraldine and I are pictured with our daughter Loretta and her husband Pat Barrett at the christening of their son Pàid, who is joined by his very proud 'big' sister Elsie.

ago and he has advised and assisted me over the last few years. Without his help, this book – and this precious piece of forgotten Irish history – would not have been written. The first time I met James was in 1999 when he was starting out in journalism and I was embarking on my political career; little did we think we'd end up writing a book together. The extended Coyle family and I will be forever grateful to him.

Writing a book is harder than I thought and more rewarding than I could have ever imagined. None of this would have been possible without my entire family's support, but especially that of my wife Geraldine. Thank you for everything, Geraldine, your encouragement and love throughout the years, not just with this project but everything I am – and have been – involved in.

For a woman that did not like politics or boxing when she came to Geesala, she soon was ready to help in every way she could. Never once did she ever suggest not to do something.

Geraldine and I are blessed to have enjoyed some wonderful times with our own children, our siblings, wider families and friends. But some of our family and extended family have been taken far to soon, particularly in Geraldine's family with the untimely loss of her sisters Catherine and Eileen and then her only brother Pat. Our children loved them all and they are missed greatly. Pat was living locally and was always part of the many parties and celebrations in the Coyle household, and with his strong singing voice he could hold his own with some of the best ballad singers in the country.

Even when Geraldine was mourning the loss of her beloved siblings, she was always there for all of us. She has been the glue that has kept us all together; a wife and mother like no other.

I hope my father and mother would be proud of what I have tried to do. I am neither a historian nor a journalist, but I have written this book as best I can with all of the information available to me. I have put the facts down as I have uncovered them and I have tried to be fair to everyone involved and to highlight the issues that I feel are important, particularly around the poor treatment of many of the overseas freedom fighters when they applied for IRA pensions after the Free State was founded.

Readers may have more information on the topics covered and if they have I will be glad to speak to them. My email is henrypetercoyle@gmail.com and I can also be contacted via the Forgotten Freedom Fighters Facebook page.

This book commemorates the men and women, like my father, who helped to win Ireland its political independence a century ago, but I want to also acknowledge the hurt done to innocent people and families during those troubled times. I am fully aware that not everyone agreed with my father's militant republicanism in the 1920s, and I do not wish to glorify it in anyway. Like all wars, innocent people suffered terrible losses and they bore heavy burdens for decades afterwards. I offer my sincerest sympathies to the descendants of the victims of the War of Independence and Civil War – in Ireland, England and Scotland.

I mentioned earlier in the book that it was my father's wish that someday he might be remembered for the good he had done in his life. Well, Dad, you were always remembered in the Coyle family for the good you did for all of us. Sorry it took 100 years for the rest of world to know the good you did for your beloved Ireland.

Long may the memory of the freedom fighter Henry Coyle live on, and rest in peace Henry and Molly Coyle. If I can pass on to my family and to others what you both passed on to me then this world will be a better place for all of us to live in.

Gerry Coyle
September 2022

Appendix I

1   Previous to the negotiations with the British which ended in the signing of the Treaty we all had one outlook and common aim, viz., "The setting up and maintaining of a Republican form of Government in this Country". In this ideal we followed the late C. in C. and accepted the Treaty in exactly the same spirit as he did. We firmly believed with him that the Treaty was only a stepping stone to a Republic.   The late C. in C. (Mick Collins) told us that he had taken an oath of allegiance to the Republic and that oath he would keep Treaty or no Treaty - this is our position exactly.

2.   The actions of the present G.H.Q. Staff since the C. in Cs. death their open and secret hostility towards us, his Officers has convinced us that they have not the same outlook as he had. We require a definite "Yes" or "No" from the present C. in C. if this be so.

3.   Does the C. in C. understand the temper of the old I.R.A. who are now in the National Army? He does not! Your Army is not a National Army. It is composed of 40% old I.R.A. 50% Ex-Britishers and 10% Ex-civilians. The majority of the civilians were and are hostile to the National Ideals. In the Army you have men who were active British Secret Service agents, previous to the Truce and who have never yet ceased their activities.

4.   We ask that a Committee of Inquiry be set up at once to investigate the advisability of retaining or dispensing with the services of any Officer gazetted or otherwise. The findings of this Committee to be accepted and acted on by the staff. We require equal representation on this Committee.

5.   We wish to bring to your notice the following facts on which we will have we hope a full and frank discussion.

        1. The Composition of the Dublin Command
        2. The recent appointment of the D.M.P. Commissioner
        3. The staffs peace overtures to the Irregulars
        4. The setting up of an S. S. Dept.

6.   It is time that this state of affairs ended , we intend to end it . Unless satisfactory arrangements are come to between us. Our Organisation will take whatever steps they consider necessary to bring about an honest, cleaner and more genuine effort to secure the Republic.

7.   It is not our intention to cause any rupture which would give satisfaction to the enemies of Ireland. We ask the C. in C. to meet our efforts in the same spirit which he would have regarded them in 1920 and 1921.

Finis.

MILITARY ARCHIVES
CATHAL BRUGHA BARRACKS
RATHMINES,
DUBLIN, 6
TEL. 975499

This is the document the Irish Republican Army Organisation (IRAO) presented to the National Army's Commander-in-Chief Richard Mulcahy in the summer of 1923. It marked the start of a series of events that culminated in the army mutiny of March 1924.

Appendix II

PORTOBELLO BARRACKS,

5th February 1925.

------- Recd bf ------

TO:

The Secretary,
M. S. Pensions Board,
Portobello Barracks.

Sir,

    I am returning form sent to me in connection
with pension for Neill Kerr, 10, Coastguard Station,
Ringsend.

    After making several efforts, I came to the only
possible conclusion that, it would be an utter impossibility for me to attempt to put on paper Neill's
pre-Truce record, I must leave that, (if it is ever
done) to a greater pen than mine, certainly, no form
would suffice, even if it was attempted, because, I
believe volumes could be written, if one could go into
details, then the people of Ireland would have very
little time for such books as - "With the Irish in
Frongoch," "My fight for Irish Freedom" or "The Victory
of Sinn Fein."

    However, I will try to give you a brief outline of
what I know about him.

    Neill's record dates very much further back than
1916, so I will not touch on that part of it.

    He had charge of the Liverpool Brigade of Irish
Volunteers, and other Irish Ireland Organisations, and
all their activities during the Anglo-Irish Campaign,
from Easter Week, 1916, up to his imprisonment.

    He had charge of the purchasing of Arms, Ammunition,
and all war material, in Liverpool, Manchester, Birmingham, etc.

    He had charge of all war material purchased in, or
landed in England, from all over the world. He was
responsible for getting it all to Ireland, practically
every weapon used against the enemy, every round of
ammunition, every ounce of other war material, passed
through Neill's hands.

    It was always a great relief to me as D.P. to know
that the big consignments that we were often anxiously
waiting for, had got into Neill's hands, because then,
I could always count on hearing of same being smuggled
into Ireland inside 24 hours, in fact, so perfect was
Neill's organisation on the ships, that in his whole
career of handling hundreds of tons of supplies, he
only lost seven rifles, and that was through a bit of
hard luck.

    He was also in charge of the arrangements for

This is the letter Colonel Joseph Vize wrote to the Army Pensions Board in February 1925 in support of an IRA pension for the veteran republican activist Neill Kerr.

-2-

getting away safely any of our men who were badly
wanted, or whom it was impossible to keep in safety
in this country, many names of important men could
be mentioned here. He was also implicated in the
escapes from Lincoln Prison, etc.

He had charge of all the big fires, and other big
schemes in Liverpool, Manchester, Birmingham, and
many other places, and it was only when THE DAY was
practically won, was he captured.

I know I have only touched on Neill's brilliant
work, but I also know, Ireland never had a more faithful son.

Neill was THE BIG MAN'S (General Collins) idol. I
will give you an instance of Neill's sincerity; he was
one night waiting in a dump, in one of the Liverpool
basements, for a large consignment of stuff from Scotland, by road, and just five or ten minutes before the
two lorries arrived, his youngest son (Neill) was
accidentally shot dead at his feet; the two lorries
arrived at the dump, Neill gave orders for the body to
be laid aside, he set out to make arrangements in
another place for the lorries, took all the stuff that
was in the dump to safety, before reporting the accident
to the police, and then they never got the revolver that
killed him, and I believe that revolver was on its way
to Ireland, before the police thought of looking for it.

After Neill's release (he was sentenced to twelve
years penal servitude) he reported again to me, and on
instructions from the late Commander in Chief, he was
appointed on promotion to M.I.D. Officer in charge of
the East Coast of Ireland. The Ports that came under
his charge were:-

Omeath,	Annagassan,	Rush,	Greystones,
Carlingford,	Baltray,	Portrane,	Wicklow,
Greenore,	Laytown,	Malahide,	Ballinacarrig,
Whitestown Hut,	Balbriggan,	Howth,	Arklow,
Dundalk,	Skerries,	Dun Laoghaire,	Kilmichael,
Clogher Head,	Lough Shinney,	Bray,	Courtown Hb.
Cahore Point,	Blackwater,	Morris Castle,	Curracloe.
Rosslare Strand,	Wexford,	Rosslare Hb.	

I could give you a very long list of captures by the
M.I.D. from the Irregulars if I were giving an extended
report.

The East Coast was the most important, during the
Irregular Campaign, it took some management to deal with
the Cross Channel traffic, but they were trying to smuggle
on the man who taught them to smuggle.

He performed his duties in that capacity with the
same faithfulness; his conduct was at all times to his
own credit and to my entire satisfaction.

I appeal to the members of the Pensions Board on his
behalf, for extra special consideration, and I have no

-3-

hesitation in recommending him for the maximum Grant; if that is not possible, I appeal to them to strengthen his case in another direction, namely, get his rent reduced; he is living in a house that is Government property, paying 16/- a week rent, and I got it myself from the late Commander in Chief's lips, that Neill was to be set up in a little Cottage, and made comfortable for the rest of his days.

But how do we find him to-day, a physical wreck, over ten months unemployed, forbidden to live in England, his little farm in the North mortgaged, where he is also forbidden to live, the Free State Solicitor sending him letters for arrears of rent, he very deep in financial difficulties; but on looking round you see people with no claim reaping the harvest of his honest toil. Comment is unnecessary.

Surely you will agree with me, when I say that such a record should not be let go without substantial reward.

I conclude now, feeling confident that I have put his case to the best of my ability, and I am sure, without exaggeration, before a Board of Irishmen, whom, I am sure will give it the consideration it so richly deserves.

I have the honour to be,
Sir,
Your obedient Servant,

Joseph Wise COLONEL.
O/C. NO 8 BRIGADE.

Appendix III

BERNARD McCABE, HEN... PETER COYLE, CHARLES McGINN, EDM... ...AGNER, JAMES DEVINE, ROBERT McERLAN... ...NRY McERLANE, AMBROSE McERLANE, PET... QUINN, MICHAEL GALLACHER, JEAN QUINN, THOMAS GILLESPIE, PATRICK CARRIGAN, JAMES FAGAN, ROBERT O'DONNELL, and HUGH TRAYNOR, all prisoners in the prison of Glasgow, you are indicted at the instance of the Right Honourable THOMAS BR... MORISON. His Majesty's Advocate, and the char... ...nst you are that (1) in or about the year 1920 yo... ...n concert and in concert with divers other... ...Street, Glasgow unknown, in the premises at 171... occupied by or known as The Ja... ...nelly Sinn Fein Club and Sinn Fein Headquarters in Scotland, in the house occupied by you, Bernard McCabe, at 438 Cumbernauld Road, Glasgow, in the house occupied by Thomas Lee at 7 Todd Street, Parkhead, Glasgow, and in which you, Henry Peter Coyle, resided, at the motor garage at 190/200 Petershill Road, Glasgow, at Smith's motor garage, Viewpark Avenue, Dennistoun, Glasgow, in the house occupied by you, Robert McErlane, at 69 Avenue R... Springburn, Glasgow, in the house occupied by you, H... McErlane, at 63 Reid Street, Springburn, Glasgow, in the house occupied by you, Ambrose McErlane, at 14 Down St...eet, Springburn, Glasgow, in the house occupied by David McErlane at 27 Carleston Street, Springburn, Glasgow, in the house occupied by you, Peter Quinn, at 258 Garngadhill, Glasgow, in the house occupied by you, Michael Gallacher, at 33 Forge Street, Saint Rollox, Glasgow, in the shop at 47, and in the house at 49, both Kent Street, Glasgow, and bot... ...ccupied by Mary Ann Quinn, and in which house you, Jean Quinn, resided, in the house occupied by John G... ...at 16 Rhymer Street, Glasgow, and in which you, T...es Gillespie, resided, in the house occupied by you, Patrick Carrigan, at 65 Eglinton Street, Glasgow, in the shop occupied by you, Robert O'Donnell, at 44 Gairbraid Street, Maryhill, Glasgow, in the house occupied by you, Hugh Traynor, at 11 East John Street, Glasgow, and at other places in or near Glasgow or elsewhere in Scotland to the prosecutor

(Signed) P. Fleming, A.D.

This is one of the most precious documents I discovered in my many years of research into my father's IRA activities. It is the original charge sheet from his trial in the High Court of Justiciary in Edinburgh in March 1921. It was retained by Kate Lee, who submitted it to the Army Pensions Board in 1942 when she was applying for an IRA pension. It is unbelieveable to think that my father's conviction for conspiracy in Scotland was later cited on a ministerial order denying him an IRA pension in Ireland, as well as on his prison file in this country. My father once said there are only two letters separating 'justice' and 'injustice'. No truer words were ever spoken.

2

unknown, the time times and place or places being
to the prosecutor more particularly unknown in respect of
the secret character of the conspiracy hereinafter libelled, did
enter into and carry out a conspiracy to further the objects
and purposes of an organisation or association of persons
known as Sinn Fein, or of an organisation or association or
organisations or associations of persons connected or allied
therewith for the purpose of securing said objects, particulars
of certain of which objects and purposes are set forth in
Nos. 1, 13, 18, and 19 of the Productions lodged herewith, and
more particulary prosecutor unknown, by the unlawful
use of force and vio especially by means of the uses
of explosive substa firearms, ammunition, bayonets, and
other weapons to be used by you and other persons acting
in concert with you to the prosecutor unknown, for the
purpose of endangering the lives and persons and injuring
and destroying the property of the lieges in the United
Kingdom; (2) you acting in concert and being associated as
aforesaid in furtherance of the said conspiracy during said
period at the said garages at 190/200 Petershill Road,
Glasgow, and at Viewpark Avenue, Dennistoun, Glasgow,
or elsewhere in Scotland the particular time or times
and place or places being for the foresaid reason to the
prosecutor more particularly unknown, did devise and carry
into effect a scheme for the purpose of procuring and
transporting to various places in the United Kingdom to
the prosecutor unknown, explosive substances, firearms,
ammunition, bayonets, and other weapons to be used as
aforesaid, and for said last-mentioned purpose did have in
your possession and under your control at 190/200 Petershill Road aforesaid, four motor vehicles, namely, a Vulcan
motor lorry, an Austin motor car, a Fiat motor lorry, and a
motor cycle and side said motor vehicles were so
used by you—the use of said Austin motor car being more
particularly hereinafter charged in charge 4 hereof, and
the precise use of the other vehicles being to the prosecutor
more particularly unknown; (3) you, James Fagan and
Robert O'Donnell, acting in concert with you, Bernard
McCabe, Henry Peter Coyle, Charles McGinn, Edmond
Magner, James Devine, Robert McErlane, Henry McErlane,

(Signed) P. Fleming. AD

3

Ambrose McErlane, Peter Quinn, Michael Gallacher, Jean Quinn, Thomas Gillespie, Patrick Carrigan, and Hugh Traynor, and divers other persons to the prosecutor unknown, and you all, acting of common purpose and in furtherance of the said conspiracy, did, on 1st and 2nd December 1920, in the shop occupied by you, Robert O'Donnell, at 44 Gairbraid Street, Maryhill, Glasgow, instigate, incite, and attempt to induce Peter Robertson, corporal, Mechanical Transport, Royal Army Service Corps, Leith Fort, Leith, to steal a number of machine guns, 500 rifles, and a quantity of ammunition from Maryhill Barracks, Glasgow ; (4) you, Bernard McCabe, Henry Peter Coyle, Charles McGinn, Edmond Magner, James Devine, Robert McErlane, Henry McErlane, and Ambrose McErlane, in concert with you, Peter Quinn, Michael Gallacher, Jean Quinn, Thomas Gillespie, Patrick Carrigan, James Fagan, Robert O'Donnell, and Hugh Traynor, and divers other persons to the prosecutor unknown, and you all, acting of common purpose and in furtherance of the said conspiracy, did, on 4th and 5th December 1920, at Cowdenbeath, Dunfermline, and Alloa, and in the neighbourhood thereof, and particularly at Junction Place, Alloa, and in the public highway leading from Alloa to Stirling by Cambus, and in a particular part of said highway about one mile in a westerly direction from Alloa, have in your possession in said Austin motor car which was occupied by you, Henry Peter Coyle and Charles McGinn, 2980 cartridges of gelignite, 10 cartridges of samsonite, 248½ feet of fuse, and 404 detonators, 2 rifles, 3 pistols and amunition therefor and 2 bayonets ; (5) you, Peter Quinn, in concert with you, Bernard McCabe, Henry Peter Coyle, Charles McGinn, Edmond Magner, James Devine, Robert McErlane, Henry McErlane, Ambrose McErlane, Michael Gallacher, Jean Quinn, Thomas Gillespie, Patrick Carrigan, James Fagan, Robert O'Donnell, and Hugh Traynor, and divers other persons to the prosecutor unknown, and you all, acting of common purpose and in furtherance of the said conspiracy, did, on 2nd December 1920, in the house occupied by you, Peter Quinn, at 258 Garngadhill, Glasgow, have in your possession or under your control one revolver and one revolver cartridge ;

(Signed) J. P. Fleming, A.D.

389

4

(6) you, Michael Gallacher, in concert with you, Bernard McCabe, Henry Peter Coyle, Charles McGinn, Edmond Magner, James Devine, Robert McErlane, Henry McErlane, Ambrose McErlane, Peter Quinn, Jean Quinn, Thomas Gillespie, Patrick Carrigan, James Fagan, Robert O'Donnell, and Hugh Traynor, and divers other persons to the prosecutor unknown, and you, all, acting of common purpose and in furtherance of the said conspiracy, did, on 2nd December 1920, in the house occupied by you, Michael Gallacher, at 33 Forge Street, Saint Rollox, Glasgow, have in your possession or under your control 43½ cartridges of gelignite, 44 cartridges of samsonite, 2 cartridges of stomonal, 1 cartridge of compressed gunpowder, 16 detonators, 214 feet of fuse, a clip containing 3 rifle cartridges, 60 rounds of pistol ammunition, 12 sporting cartridges, 1 revolver, 3 rifle pull throughs, and an oil bottle; (7) you, Hugh Traynor, in concert with you, Bernard McCabe, Henry Peter Coyle, Charles McGinn, Edmond Magner, James Devine, Robert McErlane, Henry McErlane, Ambrose McErlane, Peter Quinn, Michael Gallacher, Jean Quinn, Thomas Gillespie, Patrick Carrigan, James Fagan, and Robert O'Donnell, and divers other persons to the prosecutor unknown, and you, all, acting of common purpose and in furtherance of the said conspiracy, did, between 15th November and 8th December 1920, in the house occupied by you, Hugh Traynor, at 11 East John Street, Glasgow, have in your possession or under your control, 2 bayonets, 4 cartridges, 5 dummy cartridges in a clip, and a military bandolier; (8) you Jean Quinn in concert with you Bernard McCabe, Henry Peter Coyle, Charles McGinn, Edmond Magner, James Devine, Robert McErlane, Henry McErlane, Ambrose McErlane, Peter Quinn, Michael Gallacher, Thomas Gillespie, Patrick Carrigan, James Fagan, Robert O'Donnell, and Hugh Traynor and divers other persons to the prosecutor unknown, and you all, acting of common purpose and in furtherance of the said conspiracy, did, between 15th November and 25th December 1920, in the shop at 47 and in the house at 49 both Kent Street, Glasgow, and both occupied by Mary Ann Quinn, in which house you Jean Quinn resided, have in your possession or under your con-

(Signed) D. P. Fleming. A.D

5

trol 11 cartridges ; (9) you Thomas Gillespie in concert with you Bernard McCabe, Henry Peter Coyle, Charles McGinn, Edmond Magner, James Devine, Robert McErlane, Henry McErlane, Ambrose McErlane, Peter Quinn, Michael Gallacher, Jean Quinn, Patrick Carrigan, James Fagan, Robert O'Donnell, and Hugh Traynor and divers other persons to the prosecutor unknown, and you all acting of common purpose and in furtherance of the said conspiracy, did between 15th November and 25th December 1920, in the house occupied by John Gillespie at 16 Rhymer Street, Glasgow, in which you Thomas Gillespie resided, have in your possession or under your control 6 cartridges ; and all said explosive substances, ammunition, firearms, bayonets, and other weapons referred to in the foregoing charges were intended to be used by all of you and other persons associated with you in said organisation or association or organisations or associations and acting in concert with you for the purpose of endangering the lives and persons and injuring and destroying the property of the lieges in the United Kingdom ; (10) *or otherwise*, and as an alternative to the fourth charge hereof, you Bernard McCabe, Henry Peter Coyle, Charles McGinn, Edmond Magner, and James Devine, while acting in concert did at the times and places libelled in said fourth charge, have in your possession or under your control explosive substances, firearms, and ammunition, namely, 2980 cartridges of gelignite, 10 cartridges of samsonite, $248\frac{1}{2}$ feet of fuse, 404 detonators, 2 rifles, and 3 pistols and ammunition therefor, with intent by means thereof to endanger life and cause serious injury to property in the United Kingdom or to enable some other person or persons to the prosecutor unknown, to endanger life or cause serious injury to property in the United Kingdom, contrary to the Explosive Substances Act 1883, Section 3, and the Firearms Act 1920, Section 7 ; (11) *or otherwise*, and as an alternative to the last-mentioned charge and as a further alternative to said fourth charge, you, Bernard McCabe, Henry Peter Coyle, Charles McGinn, Edmond Magner and James Devine, all acting in concert as aforesaid, at the times and places libelled in said fourth charge, did have in your possession or under your control explosive substances, namely, 2980 cartridges of

(Signed) D. P. Fleming, A.D.

391

gelignite, 10 cartridges of samsonite, 248½ feet of fuse, and 404 detonators under circumstances which in respect more particularly that (*a*) when required by officers of police, while acting in the execution of their duty, to stop said Austin motor car at or near Junction Place, Alloa, you refused to do so ; (*b*) you removed said explosive substances from said Austin motor car and attempted to conceal them from officers of police ; (*c*) certain documents were found on the person of you Henry Peter Coyle, namely, productions Nos. 178 to 190 inclusive of the productions lodged herewith ; (*d*) the document No. 191 of the productions lodged herewith was found on the person of you, Charles McGinn ; (*e*) you, Henry Peter Coyle, were in possession of a motor car driver's licence which had been issued to and was in name of you, Edmond Magner, being No. 178 of the productions lodged herewith ; and you, Henry Peter Coyle, were not in possession of any licence in your name ; and (*f*) the productions Nos. 167 to 177 inclusive lodged herewith were found in the house of Michael Hayes, at 49 Longwood Avenue, South Circular Road, Dublin, gave rise to a reasonable suspicion that you did not have said explosive substances in your possession or under your control for a lawful object ; contrary to the Explosive Substances Act, 1883, Section 4, Sub-section 1 ; (12) *or otherwise*, and as an alternative to the fifth charge hereof, you, Peter Quinn, at the time and place libelled in said fifth charge, did have in your possession or under your control firearms and ammunition, namely, 1 revolver and 1 revolver cartridge, with intent by means thereof to endanger life in the United Kingdom or to enable some other person or persons to the prosecutor unknown by means thereof to endanger life in the United Kingdom, contrary to the Explosive Substances Act, 1883, Section 3, and the Firearms Act, 1920, Section 7 ; (13) *or otherwise*, and as an alternative to the sixth charge hereof, you, **Michael Gallacher**, at the time and place libelled in said sixth charge, did have in your possession or under your control explosive substances, firearms and ammunition, namely 43½ cartridges of gelignite 44 cartridges samsonite, 2 cartridges of stomonal, 1 cartridge of compressed gunpowder, 16 detonators, 214 feet of fuse, a clip containing 3 rifle cartridges, 60 rounds of pistol ammunition, 12 sporting cartridges, and 1

(Signed) D. P. Fleming. A.D.

7

revolver, with intent by means thereof to endanger life or cause serious injury to property in the United Kingdom or to enable some other person or persons to the prosecutor unknown to endanger life or cause serious injury to property in the United Kingdom, contrary to the Explosive Substances Act, 1883, Section 3, and the Firearms Act, 1920, Section 7 ; (14) *or otherwise*, and as an alternative to the last-mentioned charge and as a further alternative to the sixth charge hereof, you Michael Gallacher, at the time and place libelled in said sixth charge, did have in your possession or under your control explosive substances, namely, $43\frac{1}{2}$ cartridges of gelignite, 44 cartridges of amsonite, 2 cartridges of stomonal, 1 cartridge of compressed gunpowder, 16 detonators and 214 feet of fuse, under circumstances which in respect more particularly (*a*) that the said explosive substances were stored in a place unsuitable for the storage thereof and not registered for that purpose under the Explosives Act 1875 ; (*b*) that certain documents, being Nos. 26 to 54 inclusive of the productions lodged herewith, were found in your possession, gave rise to a reasonable suspicion that you did not have said explosive substances in your possession or under your control for a lawful object, contrary to the Explosive Substances Act 1873, Section 4, Sub-section 1 ; (15) *or otherwise*, and as an alternative to the seventh charge hereof, you, Hugh Traynor, at the time and place libelled in said seventh charge, did have in your possession or under your control ammunition, namely, 4 cartridges, with intent by means thereof to endanger life in the United Kingdom or to enable some other person or persons to the prosecutor unknown by means thereof to endanger life in the United Kingdom, contrary to the Explosive Substances Act 1883, Section 3, and the Firearms Act 1920, Section 7 ; (16) *or otherwise*, and as an alternative to the eighth charge hereof, you, Jean Quinn, at the time and places libelled in said eighth charge, did have in your possession or under your control ammunition, namely, 11 cartridges, with intent by means thereof to endanger life in the United Kingdom or to enable some other person or persons to the prosecutor unknown by means thereof to endanger life in the United Kingdom, contrary to the Explosive Substances Act 1883, Section 3, and

(Signed) D. P. Fleming, A.D.

8

the Firearms Act 1920, Section 7 ; and (17) *or otherwise*, and as an alternative to the ninth charge hereof, you, Thomas Gillespie, at the time and place libelled in said ninth charge, did have in your possession or under your control ammunition, namely, 6 cartridges, with intent by means thereof to endanger life in the United Kingdom, or to enable some other person or persons to the prosecutor unknown to endanger life in the United Kingdom, contrary to the Explosive Substances Act 1883, Section 3, and the Firearms Act 1920, Section 7.

(Signed) D. P. Fleming. AD

LIST OF PRODUCTIONS.

1. Constitution of Sinn Fein.
2. Circular letter from Scottish Organiser, dated May 1920.
3/4. Two copies of *Dark Rosaleen*.
5. Rules of Scottish Comhairle Ceanntair of Sinn Fein.
6. Order of Procedure at meetings.
7. Form of Nomination of Candidates.
8/9. (8) Circular from Headquarters ; and (9) Circular from Scottish Organiser, both dated July 1920.
10. Two Agendas of Meetings of 8th May and 21st August 1920.
11. Application Form for Membership of Sinn Fein.
12. Sinn Fein Membership Card.
13. Cumman na mban Membership Card.
14. Concert ticket.
15. Handbill for Irish-Ireland Concert.
16. Form of Statistical Return.
17. Prisoners Defence Fund Subscription Sheet.
18. Irish Volunteer Membership Card.
19. Irish Citizen Army Membership Card.
20. Extract Conviction, High Court, Edinburgh, 10 years' P.S., dated 1st February 1918, applicable to Joseph Robinson.

(Signed) D. P. Fleming. AD

9

21. Extract Conviction, High Court, Glasgow, 3 years'
P.S., dated 30th April 1918, applicable to
Bernard Friel.
22. Five Extract Convictions, High Court, Edinburgh,
dated 10th September 1918, applicable to
Michael Callaghan. 3 years' P.S., Michael
Gallacher, 6 months, William Fullarton, 6
months, Charles Hilley, 3 months, and Rose
Ann Hilley, 3 months.
23. Sketch Plan with No. 7 Section's Orders.
24. Sinn Fein Membership Card in name of P. Quinn.
25. Packet of Morse Signalling Cards.
26. Sinn Fein Membership Card in name of Michael
Gallagher.
27. Irish Volunteer Membership Card in name of
Semus Hegarty.
28. Pence Card
29/30. (29) Irish Volunteer Membership Card; and (30)
Sinn Fein Membership Card, both in name of
William Fullerton.
31. Gratuity Note from Governor, Peterhead Prison, in
name of William Fullerton.
32. Sinn Fein Membership Card.
33/34. (33) Irish Volunteer Membership Card; and (34)
Sinn Fein Membership Card, both in name of
James Fullerton.
35/36. (35) Irish Volunteer Membership Card; and (36)
Sinn Fein Membership Card, both in name of
Seamus Fullerton.
37/39. Three Balance-Sheets.
40. Minute of Meeting.
41. List of Names and Addresses.
42/43. Two Subscription Sheets "G" Company, Irish
Republican Army.
44/49. Six Books.
50. Ten Targets.
51. Handbook for Irish Volunteers.
52. Pencil Note relating to explosives, etc.
53. Three copies of An Toslac.
54. Training Instructions of Irish Volunteers, dated
24/1/19.

(Signed). D. P. Fleming. A.D.

55. Instructions on the use of a rifle.
56. Sinn Fein Rebellion Handbook.
57. Rough Sketch.
58. Note Book.
59. Blank Receipt Form.
60. Three Receipts.
61. National Health Insurance Card of James Fagan.
62. Copy Current Account of Bernard McCabe with Clydesdale Bank, Limited, Dennistoun Branch.
63. Cash Book of Bernard McCabe.
64. Quotation or letter, dated 1st October 1920, by Robert McErlane to B. McCabe.
65. Order, dated 1st October 1920, by B. McCabe to McErlane.
66. Letter from B. McCabe, dated 4th October 1920.
67. Letter from Robert McErlane to B. McCabe, dated 5th October 1920.
68. Application for Motor Licence by Ross & Christie, Ltd., dated 23rd September 1920.
69. Change of Motor Ownership Application Form by Bernard McCabe, dated 5th October 1920.
70. Note of Deposit-Receipts of Bernard McCabe with Clydesdale Bank, Limited.
71. Balance-Sheet and Profit and Loss Account of Bernard McCabe.
72. Card of Authority to Coyle to attend Comhairle Ceanntair Meeting on 1st November 1919.
73/77. Five Sinn Fein Cards.
78. Handbill containing appeal for formation of Cumann.
79. Letter dated 28th March 1920, from H. Boyle to accused Coyle.
80. Letter dated 5/5/20, from Sinn Fein Headquarters to accused Coyle.
81. Irish Volunteers Membership Card in name of Hugh Traynor.
82. Pencil Note shewing election of Office-Bearers.
83. Agenda of Meeting.
84. Letter from J. O'Sheehan, dated 29/6/20.
85. Letter from M. Frieze, dated 28/7/20.

(Signed) D. P. Fleming. A.D.

11

86. Set of Instructions of Secretaries of Cumann.
87. Circular Letter from Scottish Organiser of Sinn Fein.
88. Telegram from O'Sheehan to Traynor, dated 17th August 1920.
89. Letter from Traynor to Miss Nan Behan, dated 18th August 1920.
90. Roll of Members of Language Class and Dramatic Club.
91. Constitution of Sinn Fein.
92. Scottish Reformer's Year Book and Diary.
93. Card.
94. Post Card in envelope.
95/96. Two Sinn Fein Membership Cards in name of P. Carrigan.
97. Pencilled copy Speech.
98. Letter from Patrick Carrigan to Edward Carrigan, dated 14/11/16, and relative envelope.
99. Report by John Brown.
100. Envelope containing five Sinn Fein envelopes and three sheets notepaper.
101/102. 2 Note Books.
103. Sinn Fein Ticket for Ceilidh Mhor 1918.
104. Print of aims of Sinn Fein.
105. Card of admission to Ceilidh in name of P. Carrigan.
106/110. 5 Telegrams and relative envelopes.
111/112. 2 Sinn Fein Cards in name of Jean Quinn.
113. Cumann na mban Membership Card in name of Jean Quinn.
114. Sinn Fein Membership Card in name of Nellie O'Hagan.
115. Sinn Fein Membership Card.
116/117. (116) National Council Membership Card; and (117) Sinn Fein Membership Card, both in name of Thomas Gillespie.
118. St Roch's Boys' Guild Contribution Book in name of Thomas Gillespie.
119. Columba Social and Dramatic Club Membership Card in name of Thomas Gillespie.

(Signed) D. P. Fleming, R.D.

12

120. Receipt for £29 4s. 5½d.
121. Letter signed "Jean Quinn, Lieut."
122/124. Three Subscription Sheets, "G" Company, Irish Republican Army.
125/132. 8 Collecting Cards for Sinn Fein Victory Fund.
133/137. 5 Cash Books.
138. Ledger.
139/141. 3 Note Books.
142. 5 per cent. Registered Certificate of Irish Republic for £1, in name of Jane Quinn.
143. Two sheets of paper with writing thereon.
144/148. 5 Receipts for subscriptions of Victory Fund.
149. Receipt for £4.
150. Receipt for £12.
151. Letter from George Skinnider, dated 16th February 1920.
152. Receipt by George Skinnider for £25, dated 22nd December 1919.
153. Receipt by H. Clarke to George Skinnider for £25 dated 3/2/20.
154. Receipt by Irish Volunteers, B Company, dated 30th August 1918, for £6 5s.
155. Rough Sketch.
156. Ticket for Public Meeting.
157. Quartermaster's Quarterly Report to Irish Volunteers, dated 7th April 1920.
158/160. 3 Transfer Sheets.
161. 5 Targets.
162/166. 5 letters from accused Jean Quinn to accused Gillespie.
167. Letter by Chief of Staff of Irish Republican Army, dated 12th November 1920.
168. Note signed Joseph E. Vize, shewing payments of £3600.
169. Note in handwriting of Joseph E. Vize.
170. Receipt by Vulcan Motors (Glasgow), Ltd., to Bernard McCabe for £809 7s. 6d., dated 18th September 1920.
171. Statement of Amount due by Bernard M'Cabe to Vulcan Motors (Glasgow), Ltd., dated 18th September 1920.

(Signed) D. P. Fleming. A.D.

13

172. Receipt for £4 2s. 5d. Vulcan Motors (Glasgow), Ltd., to Bernard McCabe, dated 21st September.
173. Receipt for £1 15s. 5d. from Ross & Christie, Ltd., dated 24/9/20.
174. Receipt by Ross & Christie, Ltd., to Robert McErlane for £566, dated 23rd September 1920.
175. Note shewing details of expenditure of £2000.
176. Receipt by Henry Coyle to Joe Furlong for £500, dated 27/9/20.
177. Statement showing " Cash given," etc.
178. Motor Drivers' Licence in name of Edmond Magner, and Label.
179. Letter addressed to Quartermaster, F Company, 1st Batt., Clydebank, and signed Brig. Adjutant H. P. Coyle, and Label.
180. Letter, dated 19/8/20, from H. Maloney, and Label.
181. Paper with address Miss B. Wynn, and Label.
182. Envelope with address Mrs Clark, and Label.
183. Paper with address of Patrick Connelly and Peter Grew, and Label.
184 Receipt by Pettigrew & Stephens, Ltd., Glasgow, and Label.
185. Paper with address of William Banhan, Gradice Gorvagh, and Captain Mark Reynolds, and Label.
186. Receipt for registered letter to Jack Sweeney, and Label.
187. Photograph, and Label.
188. Envelope with photograph, and Label.
189. Letter dated 29th November 1920 from " Patrick," and Label.
190. Receipt of North-Western Hotel, Liverpool, and Label.
191. Letter and relative envelope addressed to Richard Murphy or Joseph Tomoney, and Label.
192. Note-book containing notes as to the mechanism of Lewis gun, etc.
193. Register of places registered for the storage of small quantities of explosives.
194. Register of places registered for the storage of explosives.

(Signed) D. P. Fleming. A.D.

14

Label No.		1.	Sinn Fein badge.
,,	,,	2.	Flash lamp.
,,	,,	3.	Revolver.
,,	,,	4.	Revolver cartridge.
,,	,,	5.	214 feet of fuse.
,,	,,	6.	Clip containing 3 rifle cartridges.
,,	,,	7.	60 rounds of pistol ammunition.
,,	,,	8.	16 detonators in box.
,,	,,	9.	12 sporting cartridges.
,,	,,	10.	$43\frac{1}{2}$ cartridges (gelignite), 44 cartridges (samsonite), 2 cartridges (stomonal), 1 ...tridge (compressed gunpowder).
,,	,,	11.	3 rifle pull throughs and button-stick.
,,	,,	12.	Oil bottle.
,,	,,	13.	Revolver.
,,	,,	14.	Signet ring.
,,	,,	15.	Cigarette case.
,,	,,	16.	Sum of money.
,,	,, 17/18.		Two hampers.
,,	,,	19.	Two bell tents.
,,	,,	20.	Waterproof sheet.
,,	,,	21.	Roll of adhesive tape.
,,	,,	22.	Tent
,,	,,	23.	Two bed ticks.
,,	,,	24.	20 tent pegs.
,,	,,	25.	Soldier's kit bag.
,,	,, 26/27.		Two bayonets,
,,	,,	28.	Clip containing 2 live and 2 blank cartridges.
,,	,,	29.	2 Fired cases rifle ammunition.
,,	,,	30.	Clip containing 5 rounds dummy ammunition.
,,	,,	31.	Bandolier.
,,	,,	32.	Sinn Fein rosette.
,,	,,	33.	Attache case.
,,	,,	34.	Belt with sword, sling, and water bottle.
,,	,, 35/36.		Two banners.
,,	,, 37/38.		Two Sinn Fein coloured flags.
,,	,,	39.	Handbag.
,,	,,	40.	11 rifle and revolver cartridges.

(Signed) D. P. Fleming, A.D.

15

Label No.		41.	Pair of trousers and vest.
,,	,,	42.	Tunic and hat.
,,	,,	43.	Bandolier.
,,	,,	44.	Pasteboard box.
,,	,,	45.	6 cartridges and piece of paper.
,,	,,	46.	Bag containing 900 cartridges of gelignite.
,,	,,	47.	Bag containing 690 cartridges of gelignite.
,,	,,	48.	Bag containing 800 cartridges of gelignite.
,,	,,	49.	Bag containing 490 cartridges of gelignite.
,,	,,	50.	Package containing 92 cartridges of gelignite and 8 cartridges of samsonite.
,,	,,	51.	Package containing cartridges of gelignite and 2 cartridges of samsonite.
,,	,,	52.	202½ feet fuse.
,,	,,	53.	46 feet fuse.
,,	,,	54.	404 detonators.
,,	,,	55.	Rifle.
,,	,,	56.	Rifle.
,,	,,	57.	Pistol.
,,	,,	58.	Pistol in pouch with ammunition.
,,	,,	59.	Pistol in pouch.
,,	,,	60.	Bayonet.
,,	,,	61.	Bayonet.
,,	,,	62.	Austin Motor car, No. S.N. 1385.
,,	,,	63.	2 books.
,,	,,	64.	2 books.
,,	,,	65.	F.I.A.T. motor lorry.
,,	,,	66.	Motor cycle and side-car, No. H.S. 627.

(Signed) D. P. Fleming. A.D.

LIST OF WITNESSES

(all in Glasgow except Nos. 10, 17, 18, 34, 35, 38, 57, 58, 60/66, 70/74, and 77/79.

1/3. (1) Alexander Ferguson Mennie, assistant chief constable ; (2) John McGimpsey, detective lieutenant ; and (3) Andrew Nisbet Keith, detective superintendent—all Central District Police.

(Signed) D. P. Fleming. A.D.

16

4/9. (4) Patrick Thriepland MacKay, detective lieutenant; (5) Albert McKeown, detective constable; (6) William Buist, detective constable; (7) James Storrier, constable; (8) James Wilson, detective sergeant; and (9) John Wyllie, detective inspector —all Saint Rollox District Police.

10. Said Peter Robertson.

11/13. (11) William Nisbet, private, Army Service Corps; (12) Charles Learmonth, provost sergeant; and (13) Frank Kingston Sutton, lieutenant, Royal Field Artillery—all Maryhill Barracks.

14/16. (14) William ___ an, detective inspector; (15) John Finlayson, detective constable; and (16) Archibald MacPhee, lieutenant—all Maryhill District Police.

17/18. (17) Peter Paterson, 900 Yoker Road, Yoker; and (18) John Paterson, 900 Yoker Road, Yoker.

19. James William Anderson, 10 Corunna Street.

20. John Hutchison, 129 Ashfauld Road, Springburn.

21. Thomas Houston, 160 Gourlay Street, Springburn.

22. John Graham, 173 Auchentoshan Terrace, Springburn.

23/25. (23) Patrick O'Hara, (24) Joseph Munro, and (25) Robert Bruce—all constables, Saint Rollox District Police.

26. Thomas Barr Thomson, 21 Leckethill Street, Springburn.

27. Robert Wallace Rae, constable, Saint Rollox District Police.

28. Robert McFarlane, 63 Ingleby Drive, Dennistoun.

29. Mary Poane, 10 Haghill Road.

30. David Dickson, 165 Saint Vincent Street.

31. Alexander Mutch, detective sergeant, Lanarkshire Constabulary, County Buildings.

32. John George Ross, 28 Bothwell Street.

33. James McDermott, clerk, Registrar's Department, Central Police Chambers.

34. Thomas Davidson Laird, Waterside, Kirkintilloch.

35. William Martin, Kilsyth Road, Kirkintilloch.

36/37. (36) James Smith Leith, and (37) Agnes Leith, both 7 Todd Street, Parkhead.

38. Percy Walgrava Southern, lieutenant, South Lancashire Regiment, Dublin Castle, Dublin.

(Signed) D. P. Fleming. A.D.

17

39/41. (39) John Wisemen, detective constable ; (40) Donald McRitchie, detective constable ; and (41) Robert Wilson, constable—all Eastern District Police.

42/44. (42) Alexander Duncan, detective inspector ; (43) Lachlan McDonald, detective lieutenant ; and (44) Robert McBryde, detective inspector—all Southern District Police.

45. Elizabeth Carrigan, 65 Eglinton Street.

46. Andrew Carson, 2 Apsley Place, South Side.

47. John Brown, 12 Bath Street.

48. Matthew McMillan, detective constable, Northern District Police.

49/56. (49) John Montgomery, detective inspector ; (50) George Christie Stirton, detective sergeant ; (51) Louis Noble, detective inspector ; (52) James Shearer, detective sergeant ; (53) Archibald Beattie, detective sergeant ; (54) John James Ryan, detective constable ; (55) Alexander Slessor, constable ; and (56) Andrew William Park, constable—all Central District Police.

57. Owen Poole Jones, 42 Carolside Avenue, Clarkston.

58. Angus David Black, Blairpark, Eglinton Road, Ardrossan.

59. Oliver Horton, 6 Rupert Street.

60/64. (60) John Johnston, chief constable ; (61) David Kesson, constable ; (62) Alexander Duff, constable ; (63) John McCulloch, constable ; and (64) William Dow, constable—all Alloa Burgh Police.

65. John Binnie, junior, Whins Road, Alloa.

66. Thomas Marshall Cook, 221 Knowsley Road, Bootle, Liverpool.

67/69. (67) James Begg, detective sergeant ; (68) Arthur McIntosh, detective sergeant ; and (69) Angus MacRae, detective sergeant—all Central District Police.

70. George Anderson, detective constable, Lanarkshire Constabulary, Wishaw.

71. James Harris, constable and motor mechanic, Lanarkshire Constabulary, Hamilton.

(Signed) J. P. Fleming, A.D.

18

72. Robert Martin, inspector, Clackmannanshire County
Police, Alloa.
73. William Gemmell, constable, Burgh Police, Alloa.
74. James Denholm, sergeant, Burgh Police, Alloa.
75. James Henderson, lieutenant, Central District Police.
76. George Bell Smith, 1 Alexandra Park Gardens.
77. The Reverend Father Michael Harrington, St Johns
Chapel, Barrhead.
78. George Pankhurst, sergeant, South Lancashire Regiment, Wellington Barracks, Dublin.
79. Edward Ward, constable, Royal Irish Constabulary
Depot, Dublin.

(Signed) D. P. Fleming, A.L.

Charles McGuinn, Prisoner in the
Prison of Glasgow.

Take Notice, that you will have to compear before
the Sheriff of Lanarkshire within the Criminal
Court-House at Glasgow upon the FOURTH day of MARCH
1921, at ten o'clock forenoon for the first diet,
and also before the High Court of Justiciary, within
the Justiciary Court-House at Edinburgh on the
.... day of .... 1921, at ten o'clock forenoon
for the second diet, to answer to the Indictment
against you to which this Notice is attached.

Served on the Twenty-fifth day of February,
1921, by me

William Lauder, Warder
of the Prison of Glasgow

George Strong .... Witness.

Sources

Chapter 1

Western People: January 17, 1903; February 27, 1904; April 20, 1918.

Nolan, Rita, *Within The Mullet* (Mayo, 1998).

Census of Ireland, 1901 and 1911.

Chapter 2

Bureau of Military History: Michael Henry, WS1732; Richard Walsh, WS0400.

Military Service Pensions Collection: Henry Coyle, 24C282 and 24SP9346.

Connaught Telegraph: January 28, 1905; February 25, 1905.

Irish Independent: August 14, 1915.

Western People: April 22, 1905; October 2, 1954.

Gruddy, Thomas, *Independence: The Struggle for Freedom in Erris, 1919-1921* (Mayo, 2021).

Chapter 3

Bureau of Military History: Daniel Kelly, WS1004; Henry O'Hagan, WS0696.

Military Service Pensions Collection: Michael Burke, 24SP104; Denis Fitzpatrick, WMSP34REF816; James McHugh, MSP34REF56204; Eamonn Leo Mooney, MSP34REF14728; Patrick Mills, WS0777; Seamus Reader, WS0627, WS0933 and WS1767.

Coyle, Stephen, *The IRA in Scotland*, speech at The Year of Revolution seminar in Wynn's Hotel, Dublin on February 15, 1920.

Healy, Seán, *Gunrunning from Glasgow to Cork*, published in *The Corkman*, January 13, 1968.

Noonan, Gerard, *The IRA in Britain, 1919-1923* (Liverpool, 2014)

Ó Catháin, Máirtín, *Michael Collins and Scotland*

Patterson, Iain D., *The Activities of Irish Republican Physical Force Organisations in Scotland, 1919-'21* (Edinburgh, 1993)

Séamus Reader's private papers (provided by Stephen Coyle)

Chapter 4

Bureau of Military History: Joseph Booker, WS0776; Patrick Mills, WS0777.

Military Service Pensions Collection: Patrick Mills, 24SP2203; Charles Strickland (McGinn), 24SP12427.

Bray People, April 20, 2016 (Joe Vize)

Coyle, Henry, *The Burnings in Liverpool*, published in the *Western People*, June 27, 1964.

Ó Catháin, Máirtín, *Michael Collins and Scotland*

Chapter 5

Bureau of Military History: Patrick Daly, WS0814

Military Service Pensions Collection: Andrew Fagan, MSP34REF40323; Patrick McDonnell, MSP34REF21272; Eamonn Leo Mooney, MSP34REF14728; Michael Naughton, MSP34REF21271; Matthew Tipping, MSP34REF43841.

Coyle, Stephen, *The IRA in Scotland*, speech at The Year of Revolution seminar in Wynn's Hotel, Dublin on February 15, 1920.

Patterson, Iain D., *The Activities of Irish Republican Physical Force Organisations in Scotland, 1919-'21* (Edinburgh, 1993)

Chapter 6

Bureau of Military History: Patrick Daly, WS0814; Patrick Mills, WS0777.

Military Service Pensions Collection: Michael Burke, MSP24SP104; Andrew Fagan, MSP34REF40323; Jean Gillespie (Quinn), MSP34REF783; Kate Lee, MSP34REF59950; Patrick Mills, 24SP2203; Eamonn Leo Mooney, MSP34REF14728; James Rodgers, MSP34REF46580; Charles Strickland (McGinn), 24SP12427

Hart, Peter, *Mick: The Real Michael Collins* (London, 2005).

Healy, Seán, *Gunrunning from Glasgow to Cork*, published in *The Corkman*, January 13, 1968.

Noonan, Gerard, *The IRA in Britain, 1919-1923* (Liverpool, 2014)

Coyle, Stephen, *The IRA in Scotland*, speech at The Year of Revolution seminar in Wynn's Hotel, Dublin on February 15, 1920.

Patterson, Iain D., *The Activities of Irish Republican Physical Force Organisations in Scotland, 1919-'21* (Edinburgh, 1993)

Chapter 7

Bureau of Military History: Patrick Daly, WS0814.

Military Service Pensions Collection: Neill Kerr, W24SP1206; Neill Kerr Junior, DP7713; Elizabeth Kerr, WMSP34REF3967; Patrick Mills, 24SP2203.

Western People: June 6 and 13, 1964.

Coyle, Henry, *The Burnings in Liverpool*, published in the *Western People*, June 27, 1964.

Healy, Seán, *Gunrunning from Glasgow to Cork*, published in *The Corkman*, January 13, 1968.

Chapter 8

Bureau of Military History: Joseph Booker, WS0776; Henry O'Hagan, WS0696; Patrick Mills, WS0777.

Military Service Pensions Collection: Mary Brannick, MSP34REF58568; Michael Burke, MSP24SP104; Denis Fitzpatrick, WMSP34REF816; Lena McDonald, MSP34REF56964; Patrick Mills, 24SP2203; Patrick Thompson, 24SP3469.

Healy, Seán, *Gunrunning from Glasgow to Cork*, published in *The Corkman*, January 13, 1968.

Patterson, Iain D., *The Activities of Irish Republican Physical Force Organisations in Scotland, 1919-'21* (Edinburgh, 1993)

Henry Coyle's private notes.

Chapter 9

Bureau of Military History: Patrick Daly, WS0814; Patrick Mills, WS0777.

Military Service Pensions Collection: Michael Burke, MSP24SP104; Andrew Fagan, MSP34REF40323.

Healy, Seán, *Gunrunning from Glasgow to Cork*, published in *The Corkman*, January 13, 1968.

Chapter 10

Bureau of Military History: Michael Henry, WS1732; Richard Walsh, WS400; Brigade Activity Reports (Belmullet Coy and Baurhave Coy).

Military Service Pensions Collection: John Joseph Kellaghan, 1d300; Eamonn Leo Mooney, MSP34REF14728.

Price, Dominic, *The Flame and the Candle, War in Mayo, 1919-1924* (Cork, 2012).

Gruddy, Thomas, *Independence: The Struggle for Freedom in Erris, 1919-1921* (Mayo, 2021).

Chapter 11

Bureau of Military History: Hugh Early, WS1535; John Gallogly, WS0244; Patrick O'Donoghue.

Military Service Pensions Collection: Michael Burke, MSP24SP104; Eamonn Leo Mooney, MSP34REF14728.

Ryle Dwyer, T., *The Squad and the intelligence operations of Michael Collins* (Cork, 2005).

Chapter 12

Bureau of Military History: Patrick Daly, WS0814; Hugh Early, WS1535; Michael O'Leary, WS0797.

The Daily Mirror (England): November 29 and 30, 1920.

Coyle, Henry, *The Burnings in Liverpool*, published in the *Western People*, June 27, 1964.

Chapter 13

Bureau of Military History: Patrick Daly, WS0814.

Military Service Pensions Collection: Denis Fitzpatrick, WMSP34REF816; Elizabeth Kerr, WMSP34REF3967; Patrick Thompson, 24SP3469.

Freeman's Journal: November 29, 1920.

Irish Independent: November 29, 1920.

Scottish Daily Record and Mail: December 6, 1920.

The New York Times: November 29, 1920.

The Daily Mirror (England): November 30 and December 2, 1920.

Chapter 14

Bureau of Military History: Henry O'Hagan, WS0696.

Military Service Pensions Collection: Sean Coyne, MSP34REF58491; Matthew Tipping, MSP34REF43841.

Falkirk Herald: December 11, 1920.

Scottish Daily Record and Mail: December 6, 1920.

Scottish Weekly Record: December 11, 1920.

Chapter 15

Bureau of Military History: Patrick Hegarty, WS1606

Military Service Pensions Collection: Elizabeth Kerr, WMSP34REF3967;

Belfast Newsletter: December 30, 1920.

Freeman's Journal: December 10, 1920.

Irish Independent: December 10 and 17, 1920.

Lancashire Daily Post: December 29, 1920.

Nottingham Journal: December 30, 1920.

Coyle, Henry, *The Burnings in Liverpool*, published in the *Western People*, June 27, 1964.

Chapter 16

Belfast Newsletter: January 15 and February 12, 1921.

Freeman's Journal: December 30, 1920; February 2, 1921.

Taunton Courier: January 19, 1921.

The Catholic News: January 22, 1921.

The Lancashire Daily Post: February 4, 1921

The Liverpool Echo: February 11, 1921.

Coyle, Henry, *The Burnings in Liverpool*, published in the *Western People*, June 27, 1964.

Chapter 17

Military Service Pensions Collection: Sheila Browne, WMSP34REF91808; Henry Coyle, 24C282 and 24SP9346; Jean Gillespie (Quinn), MSP34REF783; Kathleen O'Sullivan, MSP34REF8425.

Aberdeen Daily Journal: February 15, 1921.

Evening Echo (Cork): February 10 and 15, 1921.

Freeman's Journal: February 8, 9 and 10, 1921.

Coyle, Henry, *The Burnings in Liverpool*, published in the *Western People*, June 27, 1964.

Chapter 18

Dundee Evening Telegraph and Post: March 14, 1921.

Evening Herald (Dublin): February 14 and 15, 1921.

Freeman's Journal: March 15, 1921.

Scottish Daily Record and Mail: March 15, 1921.

The Scotsman: March 15, 1921.

Chapter 19

Aberdeen Daily Journal: March 15, 1921.

Derry Journal: March 16, 1921.

Dundee Evening Telegraph and Post: March 15, 1921.

Evening Herald (Dublin): March 16, 1921.

Freeman's Journal: March 16, 1921.

Scottish Daily Record and Mail: March 16, 1921.
Scottish Evening Telegraph and Post: March 15 and 16, 1921.
The Scotsman: March 16, 1921.

Chapter 20

Cork Examiner: March 18, 1921.
Freeman's Journal: March 19, 1921.
Londonderry Sentinel: March 17, 1921.
Scottish Daily Record and Mail: March 18 and 19 and 21, 1921.
Scottish Evening Telegraph and Post: March 16.
The Scotsman: March 18, 1921.
Scottish Sunday Mail: March 20, 1921.

Chapter 21

Freeman's Journal: March 21, 1921.
Sheffield Daily Telegraph: March 21, 1921.
Scottish Daily Record and Mail: March 21, 1921.
Scottish Sunday Mail: March 20, 1921.
The Scotsman: March 21, 1921.
The Northern Whig and Belfast Post: March 21, 1921.
Henry Coyle's private notes and newspaper archives.

Chapter 22

Aberdeen Daily Journal: November 8, 1914; August 7, 1922.
Aberdeen Press and Journal: August 18, 1925.
Brechen Advertiser: February 10, 1931.
Buchanan Observer: June 16, 1908.
Londonderry Sentinel: August 22, 1922.
Peterhead Sentinel: June 8, 1901.
The Social Gazette: May 31, 1912.

Chapter 23

Bureau of Military History: Joseph Booker, WS0776.
Military Service Pensions Collection: Jean Gillespie (Quinn), MSP34REF783; Lena McDonald, MSP34REF56964; Daniel Patrick Walshe, MSP34REF17287.
Fermanagh Herald: August 13, 1921.
Scottish Sunday Mail: March 20, 1921.
Strabane Chronicle: August 27, 1921.
The Scotsman: March 21, 1921
The Nationalist (Tipperary): August 10, 1921.
Noonan, Gerard, *The IRA in Britain, 1919-1923* (Liverpool, 2014)
Coyle, Stephen, *The IRA in Scotland*, speech at The Year of Revolution seminar in Wynn's Hotel, Dublin on February 15, 1920.
Coyle, Stephen, *The Smashing of the Van*, published in *The Irish Voice*, April 21, 2021.
Patterson, Iain D., *The Activities of Irish Republican Physical Force Organisations in Scotland, 1919-'21* (Edinburgh, 1993)

Chapter 24

Aberdeen Daily Journal: January 9, 1922; February 14, 1922.
Dundee Evening Telegraph: February 14, 1922.
Edinburgh Evening News: February 13, 1922.
The Scotsman: February 14, 1922; December 6, 2013.
Laffey, James, *Rebels in the Courthouse: Mayo in a Time of Revolution, 1920-'25* (Mayo, 2021).
Price, Dominic, *The Flame and the Candle, War in Mayo, 1919-1924* (Cork, 2012).

Chapter 25
Military Service Pensions Collection: Henry Coyle, 24C282 and 24SP9346.
Connaught Telegraph: February 18, 1922.
An tOlgach: April 25, 1922.
Laffey, James, *Rebels in the Courthouse: Mayo in a Time of Revolution, 1920-'25* (Mayo, 2021).
O'Malley, Ernie, *The Men Will Talk To Me: The Mayo Interviews*, edited by Cormac K.H.
    O'Malley and Vincent Keane (Cork, 2014)
Peterhead Prison Archives

Chapter 26
Bureau of Military History: Richard Walsh, WS400.
Bellshill Speaker: June 27, 1922.
Liverpool Echo: June 27, 1922.
The New York Times: June 27, 1922.
The Scotsman: June 27, 1922.
Western People: May 13, 1922.
Laffey, James, *Rebels in the Courthouse: Mayo in a Time of Revolution, 1920-'25* (Mayo, 2021).
Price, Dominic, *The Flame and the Candle, War in Mayo, 1919-1924* (Cork, 2012).

Chapter 27
Military Service Pensions Collection: Sean Adair, W2DI.
Connaught Telegraph: August 19 and 26, 1922.
Freeman's Journal: August 25, 1922.
Irish Independent: August 25 and 26, 1922.
Sligo Champion: August 19, 1922.
Western People: August 19, 1922.
Laffey, James, *Rebels in the Courthouse: Mayo in a Time of Revolution, 1920-'25* (Mayo, 2021).
Price, Dominic, *The Flame and the Candle, War in Mayo, 1919-1924* (Cork, 2012).

Chapter 28
Military Service Pensions Collection: Henry Coyle, 24C282 and 24SP9346.
Connaught Telegraph: December 9, 1922.
Derry Journal: May 24, 1924
Freeman's Journal: January 13, 1923.
Irish Independent: December 8 and 9, 1922; June 16, 1923.
Western People: January 6, 1923.
Laffey, James, *Rebels in the Courthouse: Mayo in a Time of Revolution, 1920-'25* (Mayo, 2021).
Price, Dominic, *The Flame and the Candle, War in Mayo, 1919-1924* (Cork, 2012).
Article on Neil 'Plunkett' O'Boyle, Irish History 1916-1923 Facebook page.

Chapter 29
Connaught Telegraph: August 11,18 and 25, 1923
Freeman's Journal: August 25, 1923.
Irish Independent: July 23 and August 21, 1923
Western People: July 21 and 28, August 25, September 8 (all 1923).

Chapter 30
Connaught Telegraph: September 1 and 8, 1923.
The Nationalist: August 4, 1923.
Western People: August 25, September 1 and 8, 1923.
Laffey, James, *Rebels in the Courthouse: Mayo in a Time of Revolution, 1920-'25* (Mayo, 2021).

Chapter 31
Connaught Telegraph: September 8, 15, 22 and 29, November 3 and 10 (all 1923).
Irish Independent: September 18, 19 and 20, 1923.
Western People: September 15, 22 and 29, October 27, November 3, 10 and 17, December 22
    (all 1923).

Chapter 32

Military Service Pensions Collection: Patrick Dunleavy, 24SP1721; John Neary, 24SP3679; Sean O'Connell, W24SP1606.

Western People: November 3, 1923; December 15, 1923.

Dorney John, *The Army Mutiny of 1924*, published online on *The Irish Story*, December 17, 2019.

Price, Dominic, *The Flame and the Candle, War in Mayo, 1919-1924* (Cork, 2012).

Dáil Éireann records, March 1924.

Chapter 33

Connaught Telegraph: April 12, 1924.

Evening Herald: March 26 and 27, April 4, 1924.

Freeman's Journal: April 8 and 10, 1924.

Irish Independent: March 28 and April 8, 1924.

Leitrim Observer: April 12, 1924.

Mayo News: April 12, 1924.

The Kerryman: March 29 and April 5, 1924.

The Liberator: March 29, 1924.

The King v Henry Coyle: court case file held in the National Archives.

Chapter 34

The Irish Times: April 10, 1924.

The King v Henry Coyle: file held in the National Archives.

Henry Coyle (Prisoner E827, Portlaoighse): National Archives, GPB/PEN/1926/48

Patrick O'Malley, Ormond Hotel: National Archives, OPW/6/2/56.

Chapter 35

Military Service Pensions Collection: Seán Augustine Roche, W24SP8143.

Freeman's Journal: April 10, 1924.

Henry Coyle (Prisoner E827, Portlaoighse): National Archives, GPB/PEN/1926/48.

Dorney John, *The Army Mutiny of 1924*, published online on *The Irish Story*, December 17, 2019.

Chapter 36

Military Service Pensions Collection: Michael Burke, MSP24SP104; Henry Coyle, 24C282 and 24SP9346; Neill Kerr, W24SP1206; Patrick Mills, 24SP2203.

Henry Coyle (Prisoner E827, Portlaoighse): National Archives, GPB/PEN/1926/48.

Chapter 37

Military Service Pensions Collection: Henry Coyle, 24C282 and 24SP9346.

Henry Coyle (Prisoner E827, Portlaoighse): National Archives, GPB/PEN/1926/48.

Chapter 38

Military Service Pensions Collection: Henry Coyle, 24C282 and 24SP9346; Matthew Ginnetty, DP1758.

Ballina Herald: January 27, 1934.

Connaught Telegraph: January 27, 1934.

Evening Herald: October 26, 1933

Irish Examiner: January 23, 1934.

Irish Independent: November 10, 1933.

Irish Press: January 23, 1934.

Margaret Coyle (nee Ferrie) last will and testament and other private papers and photographs.

Chapter 39

Evening Herald: February 6, 1934.

Irish Press: February 7, 1934.

Henry Coyle's private notes and papers.

Chapter 40

Military Service Pensions Collection: Michael Burke, MSP24SP104; Henry Coyle, 24C282 and 24SP9346; Jean Gillespie (Quinn), MSP34REF783; Elizabeth Kerr, WMSP34REF3967; Kate Lee, MSP34REF59950; Lena McDonald, MSP34REF56964.

Western People: February 6, 1937.

Chapter 41

Military Service Pensions Collection: Henry Coyle, 24C282 and 24SP9346.

Dáil Éireann records, debate on Military Service Pensions (Amendment) Act, 1949.

Chapter 42

Western People: July 5, 1952.

Chapter 43

Ballina Herald: January 31 and September 5, 1959.

Connacht Tribune: January 9, 1960

Connaught Telegraph: March 12, 1960.

Irish Independent: January 31 and February 13, 1959.

Irish Press: March 26, 1959; January 12 and February 13, 1960.

Mayo News: February 7, 1959

Western People: February 7, 1959; March 12 and June 25, 1960; October 2, 1965.

Chapter 44

Western People: June 6, 13 and 27, 1964; June 22, 2021.

Chapter 45

Irish Independent: May 30, 1979.

Western Journal: June 22, 1979.

Western People: December 2, 1978; June 2 and 30, 1979.

Henry Coyle's private papers, notes and letters

Chapter 46

Western People: March 20 and 27, 2007.

Chapter 47

Military Service Pensions Collection: Henry Coyle, 24C282 and 24SP9346.

Connaught Telegraph: March 10, June 16 and 23, 1999.

Mayo News: June 16 and 23, 1999.

Healy, Seán, *Gunrunning from Glasgow to Cork*, published in *The Corkman*, January 13, 1968.

Coyle Family Memories

One of the last family pictures where we were all together, apart from my brother Patrick, who was in Birmingham. Back row, from left: Henry Joe, Willie, Gerry, Noel, Second row: Mary, Henry and Molly. Front row: Ann, Agnes and John.

My three sons, Henry, Alan and Gerard, are pictured with the North-American GAA Championship Cup.

Geraldine and myself are pictured with Henry after he claimed the WBF Light Middleweight Championship in 2011.

Five members of the Coyle family who are named after my father, from left: Henry Peter Coyle, Chicago; Henry Coyle, Geesala; Henry Joe Coyle, Chicago; Henry Peter Coyle, Birmingham and Henry Peter Coyle, Geesala.

Boxing promoter Brian Peters was a fantastic support when my son Henry turned professional and fought for the WBF Light Middleweight Championship in 2011. They are pictured with my son Alan who was Henry's manager during his years as a professional fighter.

My nephew Trevor Conway, from Manchester, with my son Henry after the world title fight in 2011. Trevor was a huge supporter of Henry and we couldn't have organised the two big fight nights in Castlebar without his support.

My nephew Mark Carroll and my niece and goddaughter Lisa Carey. Mark was born in Manchester, reared in Ballaghaderreen and has a keen interest in Geesala Boxing Club and Geesala Festival. He is also very passionate and knowledgeable about Irish history.

I am pictured with my sister Ann and her husband Larry Carroll after I was elected cathaoirleach of Mayo County Council.

Henry Coyle
(died 1979)

Married
Margaret Maxwell Ferrie
(died 1933)

Married
Mary (Molly) Ginty
(died 1978)

Margaret Coyle RIP
Married **Bernard Donnelly RIP**
(2 children – Michael RIP & Madge)

Henry Joe Coyle
Married **Bridie Tierney RIP**
(3 children– Ann, Henry & Mary)

Patrick Coyle (died 2022)
Married **Henrietta Hogan**
(3 children–Henry, Patrick RIP,
& David)

William Coyle
Married **Sonia Cronin**
(1 child – Christopher Cronin-Coyle)

Ann Coyle
Married **Larry Carroll**
(1 child – Mark Carroll)

Mary Coyle
Married **Johnny Conway**
(5 children– Brendan RIP, Trevor,
Aidan, Gerard & Jacinta)

Agnes Coyle
Married **P. J. Carey**
(4 children– Donna, Lisa, Brian
& Matthew)

John Coyle

Noel Coyle
Married **Vera Howard**
(6 children– Shane, Michael, Patrick,
Anthony, Henry & Deborah)

Gerard Coyle
Married **Geraldine Lally**
(6 children– Henry, Alan, Loretta,
Evita, Clara & Gerard)

**Descendants
of IRA Commandant
HENRY PETER
COYLE**